STREET ART

HOAKI

Hoaki Books, S.L.
C/ Ausiàs March, 128
08013 Barcelona, Spain
T. 0034 935 952 283
F. 0034 932 654 883
info@hoaki.com
www.hoaki.com
hoakibooks

A Street Art Anthology
An Illustrated Anthology

ISBN: 978-84-1065-022-0

First published in English by Promopress in 2016

Original title: *Anthologie du street art*
Author: Magda Danysz
Translation: Emma Sayers
Cover: VHILLS & SHEPARD FAIREY aka OBEY, *American Dreamers,* USA, 2018. Photo © Jonathan Furlong
For all artists represented by ADAGP © ADAGP, Paris, 2023

D.L.: B 2871-2025
Printed in China

STREET ART

AN ILLUSTRATED ANTHOLOGY

MAGDA DANYSZ

HOAKI

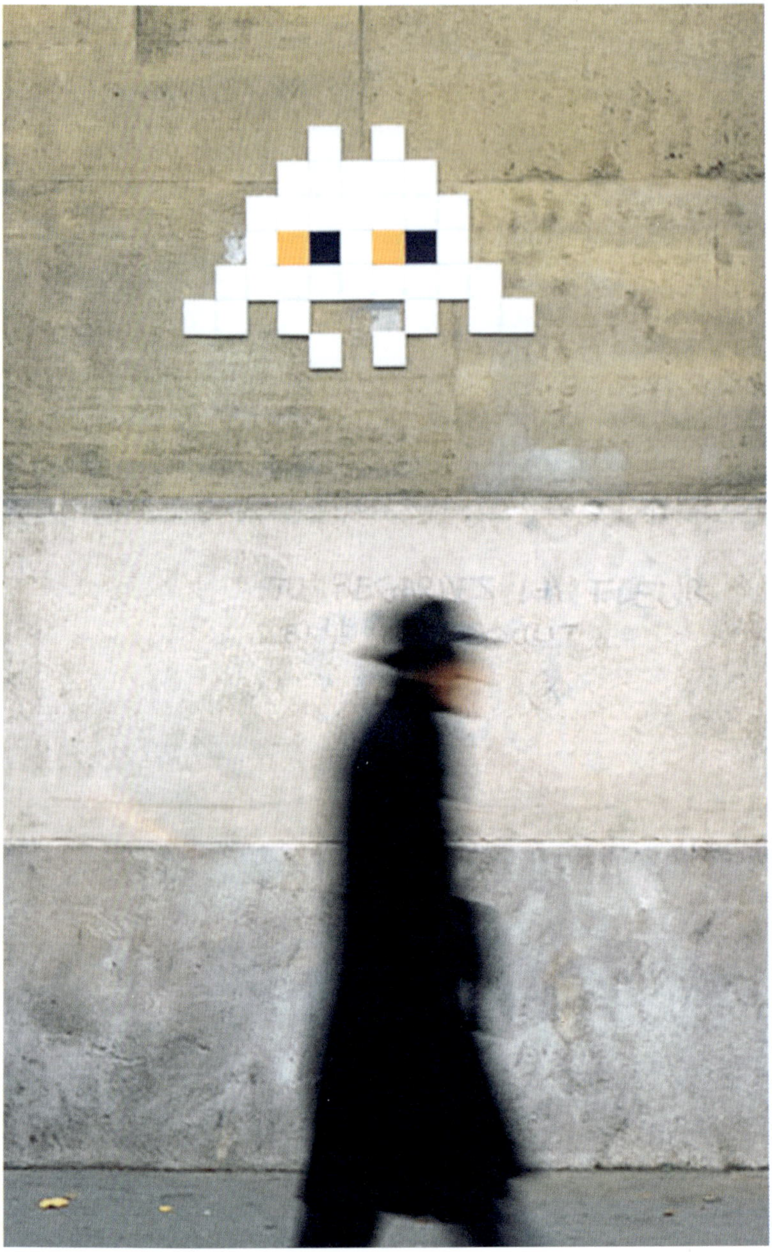

Space Invader, Paris, 2000 © A.R.R.

INTRO 6

PERCEPTIBLE AESTHETICS: THE EMERGENCE OF A WORLDWIDE MOVEMENT 8

CONTEXT 11

THE EMERGENCE OF A STYLE 17

THE ART OF LETTERING 33

THE RENEWAL AND ROOTING OF URBAN ART 74

A CONTEXT OF RETREAT AND REPRESSION 77

A WORLDWIDE OUTBREAK 83

THE ADVENT OF A CONTEXTUAL ART 126

CHANGING COURSE 129

STREET ART IS EVERYWHERE 165

STREET ART IN THE SPOTLIGHT 210

EXPOSURE AS MEANS OF LEGITIMATION 213

A PRACTICE INSCRIBED INTO THE HISTORY OF ART 229

ARTIST'S SOCIAL ENGAGEMENT AND IMPACT ON SOCIETY 247

CONCLUSION 263

APPENDICES 272

INTRO

Just about every day, new street artists appear on the world artistic scene. The need to theorize street artists' practice and make their art's intrinsic value better understood has never been stronger. There have always been many publications on the subject (certainly since the beginning of the 1980s), though it should be noted that these are normally documentary works, in which photographs take precedence over more theoretical writings. At this stage of the street art movement (which is now in its fourth decade!), it seemed important to attempt to understand its singularities and to demonstrate that street art is not simply the erratic practices of out-of-work young people or an artistic approach that should stay on the sidelines of the contemporary art world's institutional circuits. A common history is now being written, and there is also a shared system of values and an artistic corpus.

Why should we consider this movement to have a crucial importance in the history of art? At a time of unbridled globalization, in which the Internet is all powerful and communication instantaneous, what other cultural movement has been able to unite so many people from across the four corners of the planet (and do more even than that in plenty of places)? What other artistic practice has reflected our urbanized and tremendously unequal world so much? What other artworks have spoken to such a wide audience? Never in the history of art has there been such a phenomenon—either on this (global) scale or of this magnitude in terms of audience. And this is perhaps what bothers people. From a purely artistic point of view, it is irrefutable that both the techniques used (spray cans, stencils, collages, etc.) and the approaches taken (such as murals and ephemeral monumental works) by street artists redefine a particular meaning of art. We can see renewal at all levels.

Furthermore, street art clearly questions art's modes of presentation. Why confine art to museum spaces when the whole world can accommodate it? Must artworks be decontextualized and presented in the White Cube? Should we expect the museum-going public to deign to give a name to what one, as an artist, has to express? Street artists are hardly hampered by these questions. They take possession of public spaces that are visible to all, and can avail themselves of a much larger number of "visitors" than what any institutional exposure has to offer. The impact is there to see, and the art within everyone's reach.

The issue of exhibiting remains a fascinating subject. Exhibiting outdoors does not have to be incompatible with an indoor approach. One type of "exhibiting" complements the other. But street artists are no longer satisfied with the outdated opposition between inside and outside. They seek to reinvent modes of exhibiting and the ways in which they share their art. Mark Jenkins in particular uses the street as a stage for installations. He positions human-like figures that hurried passers-by could confuse with a real person. Yet neither the flesh nor pose of these amazing additions is realistic. With this very special urban hallmark, Mark Jenkins pushes us to ask ourselves about our urban environment and our own context. To see art is to see who we are.

However, it must be recognized that all too often when mentioning this type of production, art and its market merge. And today, many people are impressed by dealers' and auctions' apparent enthusiasm for this movement's works, which sometimes command exorbitant sums.
Nevertheless, we must keep things in perspective. This speculative frenzy put forward by some is relative when we know that, to date, only a figure of BANKSY's status has fetched more than one million euros at auction. Behind him, the works of SPACE INVADER or OS GÊMEOS could command more than 150,000 euros, but most of the big names—JonOne or Shepard Fairey, for example—make around fifty thousand at most. So there is no need for an outcry, especially since most works put up for sale are still very affordable in the context of the art market (from one hundred to a few thousand euros). Contrary to what people might think, the market has become organized rather than running out of control.

Moreover, the global craze is being confirmed today rather than being a new development. Young people who were thought to be infatuated with their teenage practice have turned out to be bona fide artists who have year in and year out dedicated their lives (FUTURA has just turned sixty, JONONE is fifty-two, and SHEPARD FAIREY is forty-five) to their art and built a more consistent body of work. Yet, due to a lack of knowledge, curiosity or excessive prejudice, Street Art - which is undoubtedly the most important artistic movement of the early 21st century - is still struggling to establish its credentials.

If we are to compensate for this terminology, which some consider too restrictive, shouldn't we simply talk about "Contextual Art" rather than "Street Art"? Unless another term can be coined that would give visibility to these artistic practices - which are as diverse in form as they are in content - aren't we limiting them by talking about their work as "Street Art"? Can Street Art be absorbed into Contemporary Art?

PERCEPTIBLE AESTHETICS: THE EMERGENCE OF A WORLDWIDE MOVEMENT

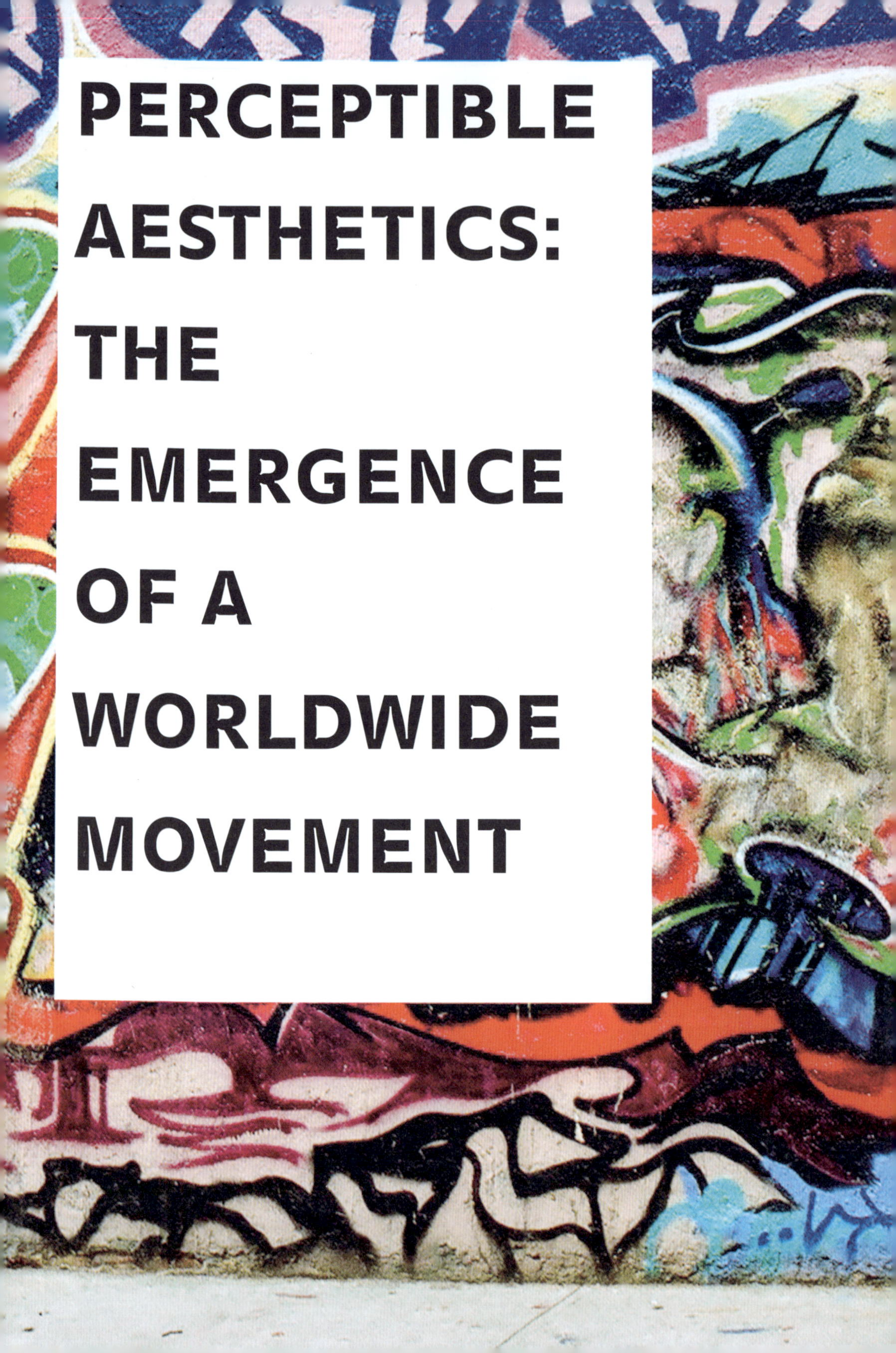

CONTEXT 11

The beginnings of graffiti 11

The scenery of the city 13

Tags and graffiti: from vandalism to art 14

THE EMERGENCE OF A STYLE 17

Arrival in New York 17

The style war 19

Expansion 28

› From trains to walls 28

› Graffiti and hip-hop 29

THE ART OF LETTERING 33

Styles, forms and subjects 33

The abstract explosion 42

The beginning of artistic recognition 52

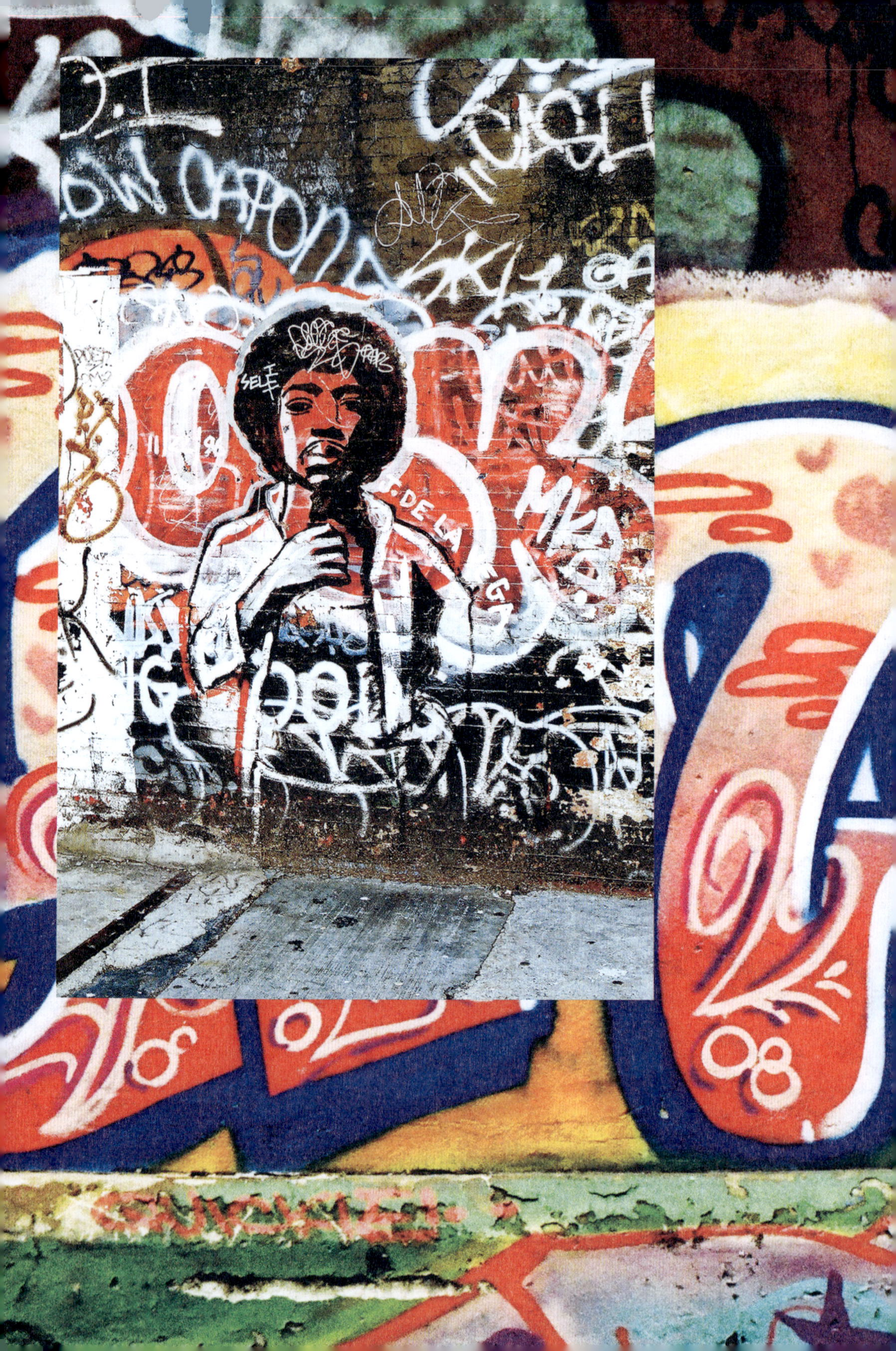

CONTEXT

The beginnings of graffiti

Pride of place goes to graffiti in the first chapter of the history of street art. This term hides an aesthetic reality and precise technique that emerged rapidly and abundantly and whose somewhat vague real beginnings have led to various versions of graffiti's origins. As HAZE, a graffiti artist who has been around since the early days, suggests, "There's no one history of graffiti. It depends on what borough you lived in, what year you were born in, and what lines you rode... The best you will ever get is a personal history of graffiti."
With time, different stories have intersected and taken hold, giving birth to legends. Modern graffiti seems to have begun around 1942, during the Second World War, when a name and a stylized written version of it were linked together. That name was KILROY. A worker in a munitions factory in Detroit (Michigan), this young man developed the habit of writing "Kilroy" *was here* on each item that passed by on his production line. The factory's bombs, which were then sent to the European front, quickly made him a celebrity. Soldiers begin to write "Kilroy was here" everywhere, and especially on walls.

But where does the term "graffiti" come from? From the Lascaux caves to Renaissance Italy, it constantly rears its head. Awareness of graffiti always seems to have been inherent to art and man's need for expression. However, in its more contemporary sense, graffiti—as well as street art as a whole—encompasses a more specific reality in the eyes of those in the know. More than an artistic style, it is a real movement and a culture that all its protagonists contribute to and share.
At first glance, it is difficult to date with precision the appearance of a practice that some reduce to markings on walls. The term "graffiti" comes from the Greek graphein, which means "write" in its most common usage, or "draw." We find this in suffix form in words such as "typography," "calligraphy," "geography," "photography" and so forth.

Graffiti in New York City. Photo © Stéphane Bisseuil

Behind: graffiti in New York City. Photo © Stéphane Bisseuil

While the Greek infinitive γράφειν—*graphein*—is translated mainly as "write," it should be recalled that the term refers more to ideographs than to words themselves. Initially, it could include nontextual elements. In ancient times, numerous types of writing—hieroglyphs, for example—had both a figurative and a semantic dimension, similar to that found in Chinese calligraphy today. From a primary *graphein*, an image and an inscription, a word and a signifier character, were born.
In its infinitive form, *graphein* also means "incise," "etch," "draw," "sketch," "write," "set out a law" and "bring legal proceedings." For its original meaning, therefore, it should be translated as "write" or "follow a design" in its most complex entirety—"I write therefore I am," in a manner of speaking.
Graffiti in the plural—graffito in the singular—or sgraffiti have an Italian semantic origin. They meaning "drawing" or the act of scribbling on a flat surface. The term originally referred to the signs found in ancient Roman architecture.
But we should not forget that "sgraffiti" is the past participle of *sgraffiare*, which means "make a work of sgraffiti," a widespread artistic technique during the Renaissance.

As a reminder:
Graffiti [graf'fito]: Italian language. *Tecnica di incisione su muro, consistente nel mettere allo scoperto, lungo la linea di incisione eseguita sull'intonaco esterno bianco, il sottostante intonaco smuro:* technique of making an incision in the painting of a wall that involves exposing along the line of incision made in the exterior white paint the undercoat colour of the wall.
Graffiare [graf'fjare]: Italian language. *Lacerare la pelle con le unghie o altro, producendo solchi più o meno profondamente:* to lacerate the skin with nails or something else to produce an indentation of a greater or lesser depth.
Graffiatùra [graffja'tura]: Italian language. *Lasciato sulla pelle da graffio non Segno; leggera ferita:* a shallow scratch left on the skin; a light wound.

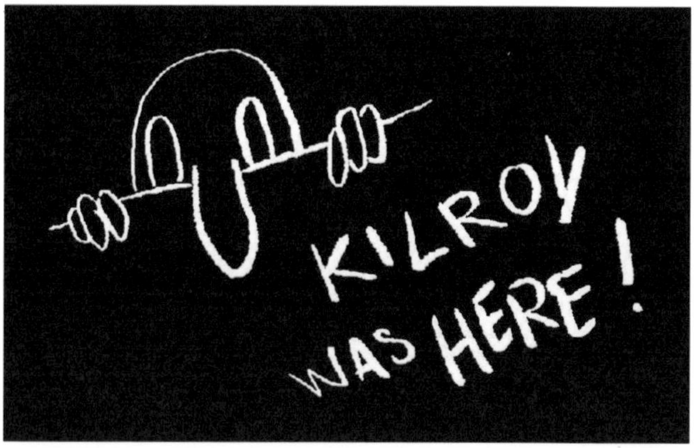

Kilroy was here, example of graffiti on the front in 1942. © A.R.R.

Sgraffito is therefore an ornamentation technique for pottery and ceramics. It is also used for wall decorations that involve making an incision in or partially removing the top layer to reveal a different undercoat colour. Sgraffito was used in Bavaria and in Germany from the thirteenth century and was commonly practised in Italy during the sixteenth century. Combined with ornamental decoration, these techniques formed an alternative to classical mural painting.

Although these practices have persisted in many countries since the Renaissance, arousing the curiosity and even the admiration of certain artists in the process (Brassaï, Gordon Matta-Clark), it is contemporary American graffiti that we are interested in here. Back in the modern era, the first chapter of street art as we understand it today more or less consciously carries with it a rich technical history. It did not by any means come about in an isolated or incidental way.

Since the advent of contemporary graffiti, its early practitioners have laid claim to an old school style. This generation, who emerged in the early 1960s, continually found new heirs to perpetuate and renew the movement.

The scenery of the city

The expansion of the street art phenomenon is, among other factors, related to recent changes in our cities, whether from an architectural, structural or social point of view. Over the centuries, the urban model has gone from a centralized kernel to a peripheral splitting, and more recently to a "network" model. However, the newer models have coexisted with rather than wholly replaced their predecessors.

In the 1970s, the stigmata of this phenomenon became the widespread construction of large social-housing projects that sprang up in suburbs across the world. At first, these new territories represented significant opportunities for housing. But they soon came to be seen for what they were: highly insipid places that were clad in bars and built in environments that marginalized their inhabitants day by day. The network model brings together people, goods, services and information in a giant system of exchanges. A dense public transport network and an incredible exchange of information have totally transformed the role of the city and its organization. The ubiquity of various signs (advertising billboards, traffic signs, leaflets, clothing and so forth) has led to a tacit but constant communication between individuals. From the beginning of all this, graffiti was the visual embodiment of a new form of urban organization that revolves around a generalized system of exchanges of signs.

Recalling his beginnings in New York, the legendary QUIK remembers his desire as a teenager to cover advertising spaces in the subway: "How were the visuals imposed by advertising any worthier of praise than the colours that we wanted to put on them? So we decided to take over these spaces. We had just as much right to them—or even more—as the advertising companies. We were doing our own advertising."
The beginnings of the movement were therefore shaped by this urban environment in which the advent of networks and advertising dominated. From the start, graffiti artists had the idea of being seen by the largest number of people as quickly as possible and of using the resources

provided by the city, and first and foremost the subway. And so the fact that graffiti exploded primarily on New York's network is not surprising.

Tags and graffiti: from vandalism to art

The tag is the most primitive manifestation of graffiti art. It comprises a pseudonym that is usually rendered using a marker or spray paint. Artistically speaking, this marking is the root of graffiti. Most often, the tag is produced in a very elaborate and singular cursive style. It is unique to each person, and like any signature it should if possible remain unchanged and attached to someone, inseparable from his or her identity. Graffiti artists must know how to write their tag before they can become accomplished artists. To become an artist, the "writer" must then find his or her style.

Since its origins, the "tag" has been distinguishable from graffiti. In English, there is a tag and a "piece"; the latter term is derived from the word "masterpiece". This semantic clarification shows that the tagger's creative intention and that of the graffiti artist are not always the same. Questioned on his beginnings, the New York graffiti artist WEST notes that "first you have to learn your ABC and then find your style." You can't be an artist just by calling yourself one.

Although graffiti as an unsolicited marking in a public space had always existed, its more artistic form is actually rooted in 1960s when CORNBREAD (real name Darryl A. McCray) and his friends KOOL EARL and TOP CAT came to the fore of the scene. From this time on, these young people's acts helped to make graffiti what it is today and help us to understand the primary motivation of all budding graffiti artists: to become famous.

Contrary to what one might expect, New York was not specifically where graffiti had its roots, but rather Philadelphia. For CORNBREAD, it all started when he wanted to attract a young woman's attention. This mission that he set himself quickly became a full-time quest. Through it, he tagged his signature with a spray can everywhere he could. The press reported on these exploits, which encouraged the young man even more. Some journalists even challenged him to tag his name in unlikely places. One of them suggested that he tag the Jackson Five jet that had landed in Philadelphia. CORNBREAD hurriedly did so while the press cheered. He added to his signature a crown above the letter B of his tag, symbolizing his grip on the city and producing at the same time the first distinguishing sign in this type of writing. Such elements would become commonplace. A new subculture swept Philadelphia like wildfire at the end of the 1960s, featuring a writing style that was adopted by other taggers and recognizable to all: long, serif letters.

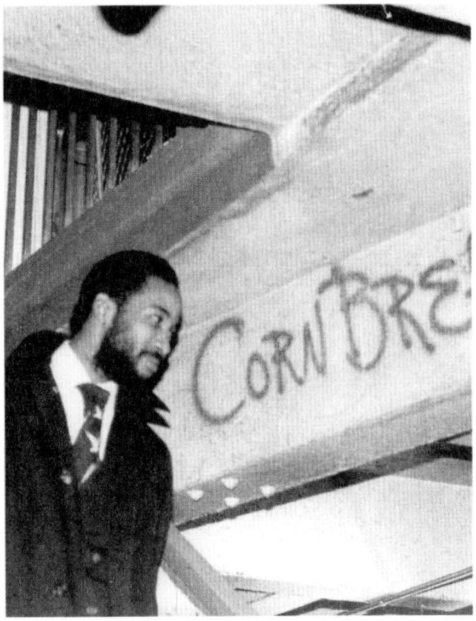

Example of the signature of CORNBREAD in Philadelphia in the 1960s. © A.R.R.

Surprisingly, a few years later, while the movement was in full swing in New York, this writing style took the name "Broadway Elegant."

The spread of the tags owed much at the time to the appearance in shops of cans of aerosol spray paint that were easy and quick to use. Although aerosol technology dates back several decades (particularly in the military sector, where sprays were used to protect soldiers from insects), its deployment in this way was new, and it lent itself to all kinds of uses. Painting becomes virtual child's play, and there was a great temptation press down on that nozzle!

Other graffiti artists then emerged in Philadelphia, such as WICKED PHILLY. This very active group soon gave its name to a style that was characterized by energetically drawn long letters, which were supposed to convey a sense of speed and haste. Lettering styles became increasingly complex, to the point where they became so distorted that they were impossible for the uninitiated to decipher. However, the embryonic state of the urban subway system acted as a brake on the spread of the phenomenon across the city, with artists limiting themselves to their own neighbourhoods.

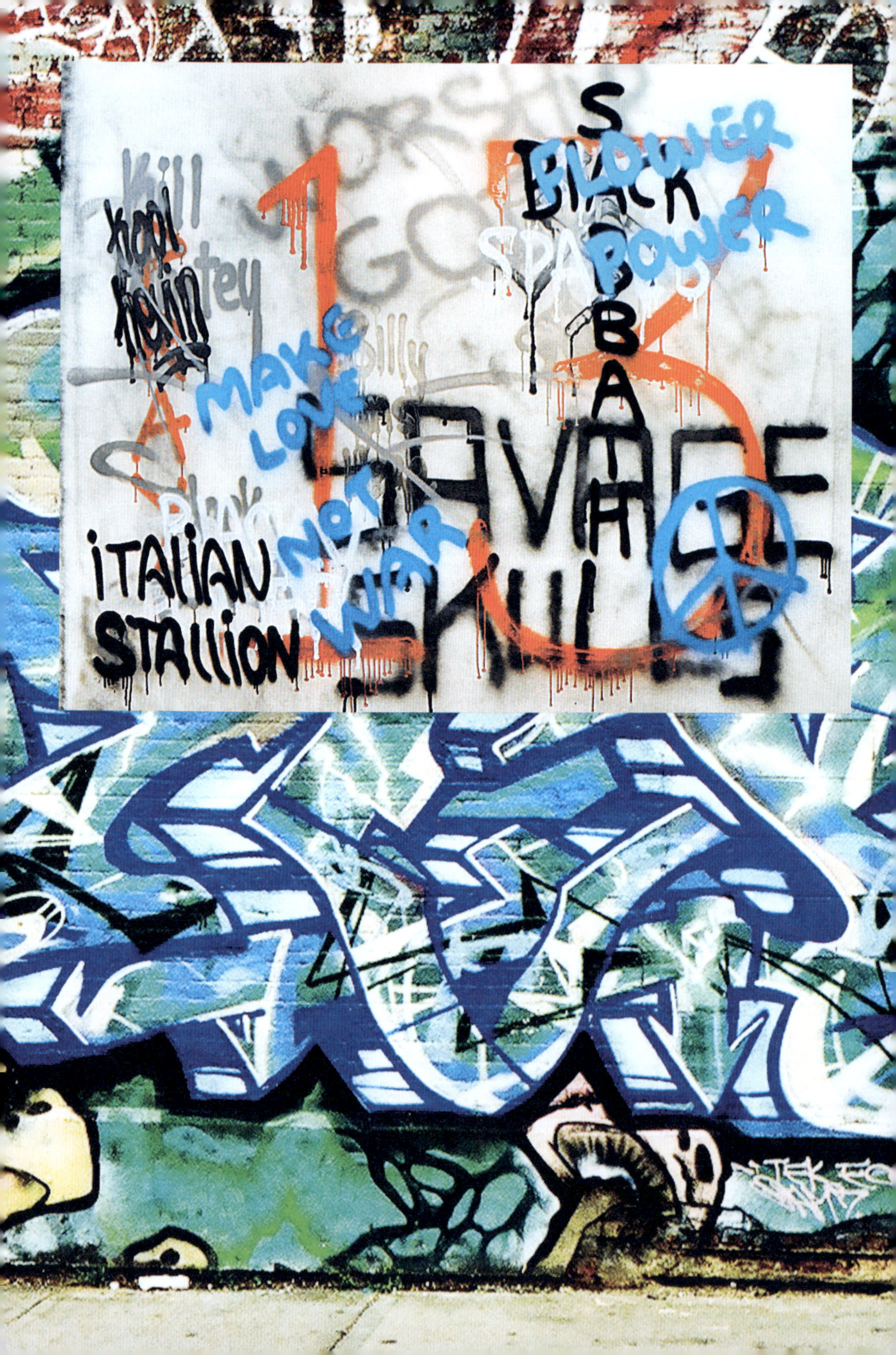
FLOWER POWER
MAKE LOVE NOT WAR
ITALIAN STALLION
BLACK

THE EMERGENCE OF A STYLE

While still teenagers, these young people, who were born between 1950 (for example, Wayne Roberts, aka STAY HIGH 149) and 1961 (for example, Richard Mirando, aka SEEN), began a true artistic movement that continued to challenge generations of practitioners to constantly reinvent their practice.

Arrival in New York

At the end of the 1960s, Philadelphia's transportation network was being built. This led in 1968 to the merger of the Pennsylvania Railroad with the New York Central Railroad, out of which the famous Penn Central Transportation Company was born. It strengthened the exchanges between these two cities in the northeastern United States.

It is undeniable that the lack of infrastructure in Philadelphia in the 1960s and then the restructuring of New York's transportation system ten years later were key factors in the evolution of the movement. No one knows exactly how or why graffiti moved from Philadelphia to New York and took off there. But the history of American rail seems to explain it for many people.

Seen, *Italian Stallion*, a tribute work to the earliest graffiti in New York City in the 1970s. © Seen Studio

Behind: graffiti in New York City. Photo © Stéphane Bisseuil

The special era that was the 1960s also saw walls invaded by political slogans that reflected the social change that the nation was undergoing. Peace signs spread across university campuses. African-American activism took off. And in most of the Hispanic *barrios*, Puerto Rican flags were painted everywhere, along with the slogan "Viva Puerto Rico libre." CORNBREAD, meanwhile, stopped tagging the walls of his city in 1972, at a time when the movement was booming in New York. In Sean McKnight's documentary entitled *Cry of the City: The Legend of Cornbread* (2006), this artist proclaims himself to have been the precursor and "king of graffiti." He sees this quest for glory as his only "ticket out of the ghetto life." The filmmaker himself confirms: "In his days, McCray was notorious. His fame is not exaggerated. And not just in Philadelphia... Cornbread is 'the first bomber,' the earliest example of a person going out on the streets with no other purpose than to write his name on everything."

While the movement was running out of steam in Philadelphia, the picture in New York was brighter. JULIO 204—a pseudonym created by connecting his name and the number of his street—began to put his tag throughout the city.

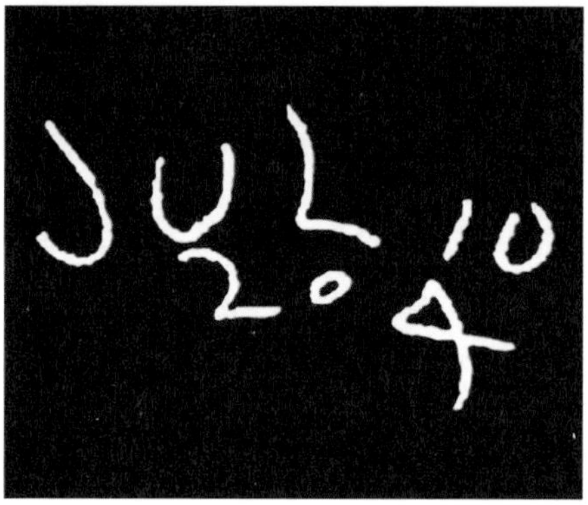

Example of graffiti by JULIO204 in the late 1960s. © A.R.R.

TOP CAT 126, a pioneer in Philadelphia, moved to New York and, alongside STAY HIGH 149, PHASE 2, FLINT 707, TRACY 168 and many others, contributed to the output of this era. Although this New York-based graffiti renaissance was disparate, it seems that it all started in the Washington Heights neighbourhood, located above Harlem in the north of Manhattan. Like TRACY 168 or TAKI 183, many of these artists juxtaposed their name and the number of their street as a sign of belonging and recognition.

And although JULIO 204 was known as the first to have added his street number to his signature, TAKI 183 was the first to become famous—as early as 1969—beyond his neighbourhood.

A young man of Greek origin named Demetrius, he paid homage to his roots by choosing TAKI as a pseudonym, a shortened form of the original version of his name: Demetraki. He decided to systematically expand his approach across the entire city. The task was made easier by his employment as a courier. Weaving through the streets throughout the day, he would place his tag on trains, mailboxes and tunnels—any visible place. Rather than being the best tagger or the one most revered by his peers, TAKI 183 was the first to be recognized by the New York media. He is also considered to be the pioneer of tagging mobile surfaces, trains and other moving vehicles. Wherever he went, he left a trace of his journey and piqued the curiosity of passers-by. In 1971, the *New York Times* interviewed him, and the resulting article, "TAKI 183 Spawns Pen Pals," reflected the growing interest of the public in this trend. Media

TAKI 183 in action in the early 1970s. © A.R.R.

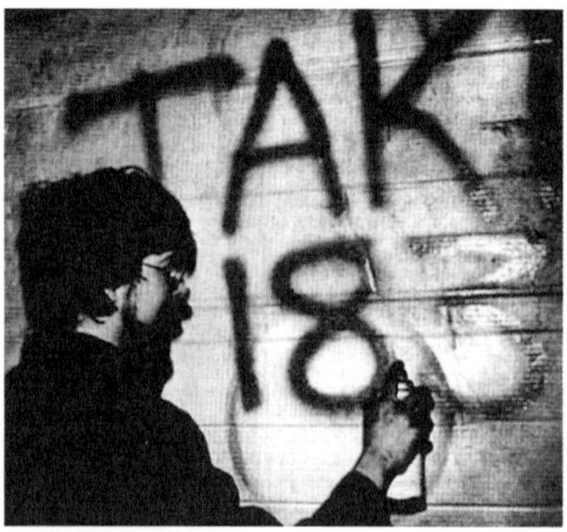

recognition of Taki led to his being emulated by hundreds of young people, who then engaged in an unbridled competition between the five main boroughs of the city: Manhattan, Brooklyn, Queens, the Bronx and, to a lesser degree, Staten Island. In spite of his unprecedented fame, TAKI 183 soon put away his spray cans.
In an interview with the *New York Daily News* dated 9 April 1989, he explained his retirement: "As soon as I got into something more productive in my life, I stopped. Eventually I got into business, got married, bought a house, had a kid. Didn't buy a station wagon, but I grew up, you could say that."

The style war

At the dawn of the 1970s, when these "writings" were flourishing everywhere, their young creators sought to distinguish themselves from one another. The first stylistic evolution was the work of LEE 163, who transformed his tag to give it the appearance of a logo. In his wake came BUG 170, CLIFF COOL 120, JOE 136, PHASE 2, SCOOTER, STAY HIGH 149 and TRACY 168, who offered their own stylized vision and signature. They all sought to be identified and to attract attention as fast as possible. Urgency and systematization became watchwords for the movement. It was no longer a question of simply putting your name here and there, but to invade the city with it. Train cars would be fully covered in one night. JOE 136 was the first to be awarded the title of King by his fellow artists for bombing the largest number of line 1 subway cars. Within a few months, the city was inundated by this mad competition, marking a definitive turning point for the movement.

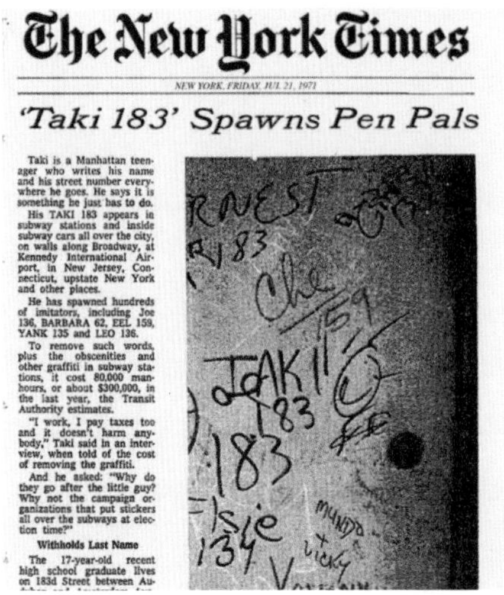
The New York Times

NEW YORK, FRIDAY, JUL 21, 1971

'Taki 183' Spawns Pen Pals

Taki is a Manhattan teenager who writes his name and his street number everywhere he goes. He says it is something he just has to do.

His TAKI 183 appears in subway stations and inside subway cars all over the city, on walls along Broadway, at Kennedy International Airport, in New Jersey, Connecticut, upstate New York and other places.

He has spawned hundreds of imitators, including Joe 136, BARBARA 62, EEL 159, YANK 135 and LEO 136.

To remove such words, plus the obscenities and other graffiti in subway stations, it cost 80,000 man-hours, or about $300,000, in the last year, the Transit Authority estimates.

"I work, I pay taxes too and it doesn't harm anybody," Taki said in an interview, when told of the cost of removing the graffiti.

And he asked: "Why do they go after the little guy? Why not the campaign organizations that put stickers all over the subways at election time?"

Withholds Last Name

The 17-year-old recent high school graduate lives on 183d Street between Au-

"'TAKI 183' Spawns Pen Pals," article in the *New York Times*, 1971 © A.R.R.

The Ingenious LEE 163 marked himself out again when he decided to systematically leave his mark on the front of all cars. Doing this ensured maximum visibility because the cars were rotated so that each one would at some point be the front car. Through their exploits, LEE 163 and his cousin PHASE 2 became masters of the Bronx. Meanwhile, in Brooklyn, FRIENDLY FREDDIE also gained great notoriety. A group of young people known as the VANDALS also appeared and they became neighbourhood icons.

The whole of the MTA (Metropolitan Transportation Authority) network was the catalyst of this fierce competition. In the early years of this decade, the scene was set for a spirit of battle between the players. A style war was ready to break out.

And major stylistic change was underway. STAY HIGH 149 added new graphical elements that marked out his individuality. The horizontal bar of the H became a marijuana joint and his signature was systematically accompanied by the silhouette of the Saint, the eponymous character of the famous TV series. And so he established for the first time a formal and visible link with the popular culture of the era.

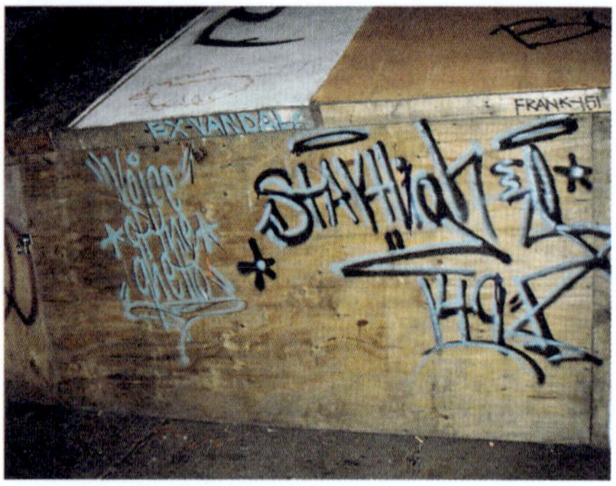

STAY HIGH 149 used multiple colours for his signature, 1969.

In 1969, STAY HIGH 149, aka the voice of the Ghetto, was 18 years old. He was already a legend. Through his stylistic advances, he contributed to the expansion of artistic graffiti. Originally from the Bronx, he was one of the first to feel the need for original expression. And he influenced many taggers who were struggling for recognition. He would add a halo or a star to his letters; simple though such ornamentation was, it constituted a real revolution in the world of taggers. He was also a pioneer due to his use of two superimposed colours: one for the bottom layer and one for the top. This lent a certain depth and relief to his lettering—something that today's graphic artists might perfectly appreciate. At the height of his fame, in 1974, he decided to leave the street and to withdraw from the graffiti scene. It would only be almost 30 years later when he would agree to briefly resurface during an exhibition at a gallery in Brooklyn.
In these years the first female taggers appeared—for example, LADY PINK. But it is clear that they would remain rare in the movement. Because of the potential dangers associated with a high-risk environment, it was a predominantly male world. The reasons for this are certainly more complex: education, social norms relating to what women should or should not do, the status of women in public spaces, the image that these illicit activities project, and so on.

What began as a neighbourhood phenomenon was to take on enormous proportions, both in terms of the surface area covered and the speed with which these teenagers would in the space of just a few weeks acquire such a high profile.
Many taggers from this period recall their lack of artistic consciousness. They all talk about an irrepressible flow and a very pure inspiration that was devoid of any intellectualization but was nevertheless prolific. The exponential number of participants in this game that had no rules and was played across the whole city made the need for distinctive signs all the more pressing. Although their original decorative purpose was to facilitate immediate recognition of one signature among many, these signs quickly came to carry special meanings. Stars, crowns, clouds and other ornaments added next to or above tags made these signatures increasingly elaborate. Slowly but surely, these would become the terms and codes of the whole movement that was forming.

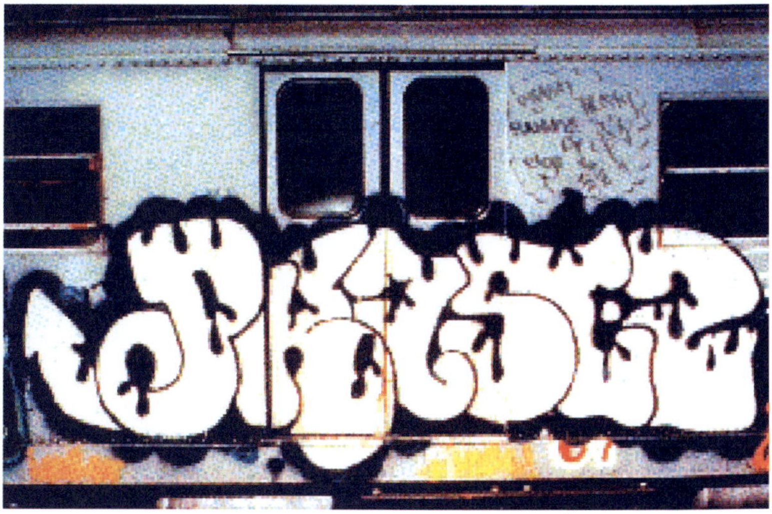

PHASE 2 thought that a good creation must begin with its outline. Each letter then takes on shape and a new dimension. © A.R.R.

PHASE 2 was one of the first to paint trains. © A.R.R.

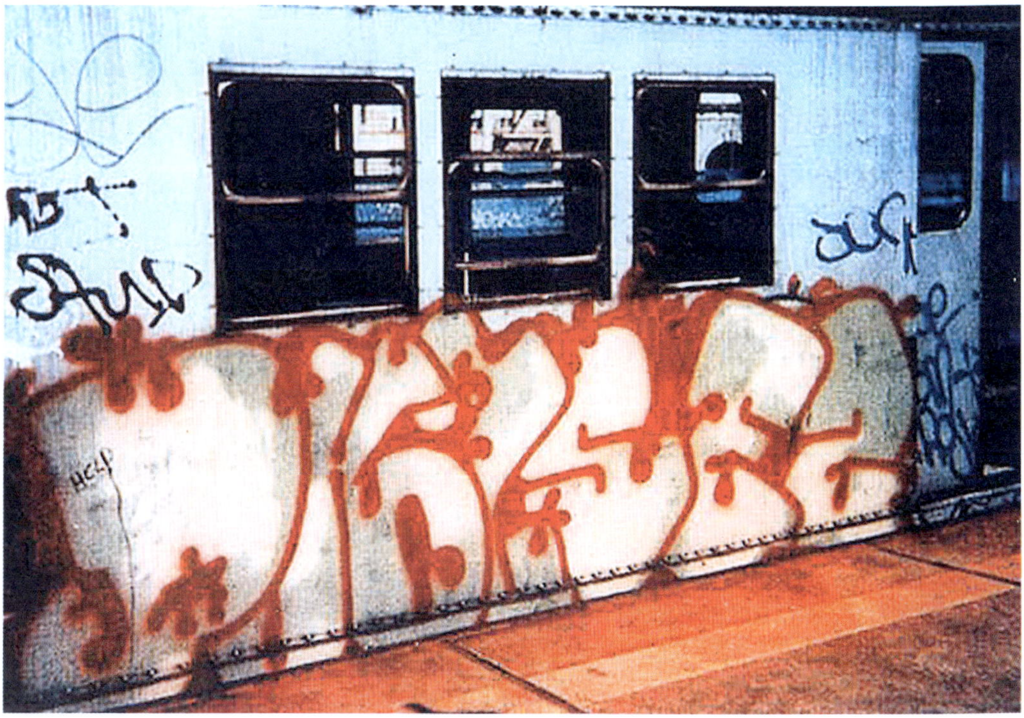

A number of artists, including PHASE 2, considered the basis for a good piece to be its outline—it became about artworks rather than tags. Far from the earlier use of simple capitals, each letter took on a form of its own and a new dimension. In the course of a night, graffiti artists could express themselves freely across the surfaces of train cars, creating what were truly frescoes as they did so. Artists like SUPER KOOL 223 produced what was then known on the scene as a *top to bottom*. Although these works were still close in their form to the original tag, the added ornamentation, the thickening of the body of the letters and the use of colour were evidence of unquestionable artistic progression. This limitless inventiveness corresponded to the creation of a specialized terminology that identified the emerging styles: "block letters," "leaning letters," "throwups," "chrome" and "blockbusters" were just some of the names given to the different types of lettering well before the concept of fonts, so widely used today, had become known to a wider audience. PHASE 2 in particular is known for having been the first to develop a distinctive style with letters in the form of bubbles, which back then became known as "softies". He is also often credited with having added an arrow to his name—something that nobody had done until that point—thereby bringing a new aesthetic rhythm to his compositions.

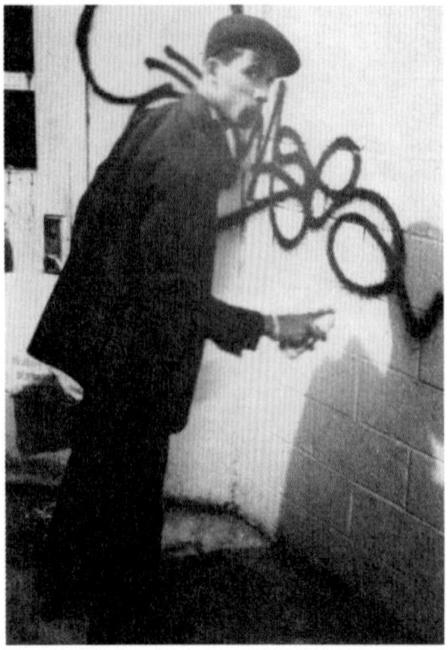

PHASE 2 in action. © A.R.R.

Lonny Wood, alias PHASE 2, was born in the Bronx in 1958. This activist from the earliest days acquired rapid recognition by inventing types of letters, which led to his being mentioned in one of the first articles on graffiti published by *Newsweek*. He additionally excelled in terms of the number of trains that he covered with his signature, and also in terms of his successive victories in his chases with the police. He even dedicated a poem to an officer who incorrectly believed that he had arrested him:

If you only knew
the real Phase 2
the super sleuth
who's still on the loose
you caught Cool T
but you didn't catch me
I got away while eating
my vanilla ice cream

PHASE 2's success was not unrelated to the early link that the graffiti artist, who was also a DJ, had with music and hip-hop scene—an intersection of rap music, break dancing, deejaying and graffiti.

Inspired by PHASE 2, more and more taggers embellished their creations with curves, twists and other variations. These were the basis of what would eventually become the iconic "wild style". With a crazy pace and amazing inventiveness, styles that were nothing alike followed one after the other. 3D made its appearance, and whereas speed and readability were initially the engine of creativity, works would come to require a great deal of preparation time and a real knowledge of lettering to decipher them.

These artists' playing field was the city and subway stations. The 149th Street station, which was close to some artists' high school (including PHASE 2), became their designated meeting place, where they converged to enjoy and comment on their latest creations. Sat on their "writers' benches", they would watch the passing trains, sketchbook in hand, and share new ideas and upcoming projects. In less than 36 months a real school had emerged. Its students had to take classes, train and tirelessly repeat their motions so that when the day arrived, they could perform quickly and perfectly.

In 1972, it was taken for granted that graffiti artists would seek to add designs to their creations. HONDO painted candy canes, a prelude to the cartoon characters and other additions that would soon emerge. One milestone was the first use by SUPER KOOL 223 of fat caps instead of regular ones to obtain a thicker and more diffuse paint spray, distinguishing his style from all the others. Size also became a distinctive element, with creations quickly taking oversized proportions. The variation in colours used to fill these elaborate letterings laid the foundations for a style that is now familiar and far removed from first tags and the restricted colour palettes that they used. It produced an incredible visual impact. The first masterpieces were, depending on the version, attributed to SUPER KOOL 223 (from the Bronx) or WAP (from Brooklyn). Some of the most famous artists came to the defence of these young people. The sculptor Claes Oldenburg, an iconic figure of pop art, stated: "You're standing there in the station, everything is grey and gloomy, and all of a sudden one of those graffiti trains slides in and brightens the place like a big bouquet from Latin America."

That same year, some graffiti artists began to earn a certain artistic credit. Hugo Martinez, a sociologist and art critic from New York University, founded United Graffiti Artists. The UGA was a collective entity through which he aimed, from the beginning, to sell graffiti. With the help of the Razor Gallery, which hosted the group, Hugo Martinez presented a first selection of graffiti considered to be artwork. COCO 144, as a graffiti artist, chaired the UGA, while Martinez focused on media coverage of the group, which he considered the elite of the genre through its association with names like PHASE 2, STAY HIGH 149, POINT 1, SNAKE 1, RIFF 170, JEC STAR, BAMA, SJK 171, CAT 87, MICO, COLT and FLINT 707.

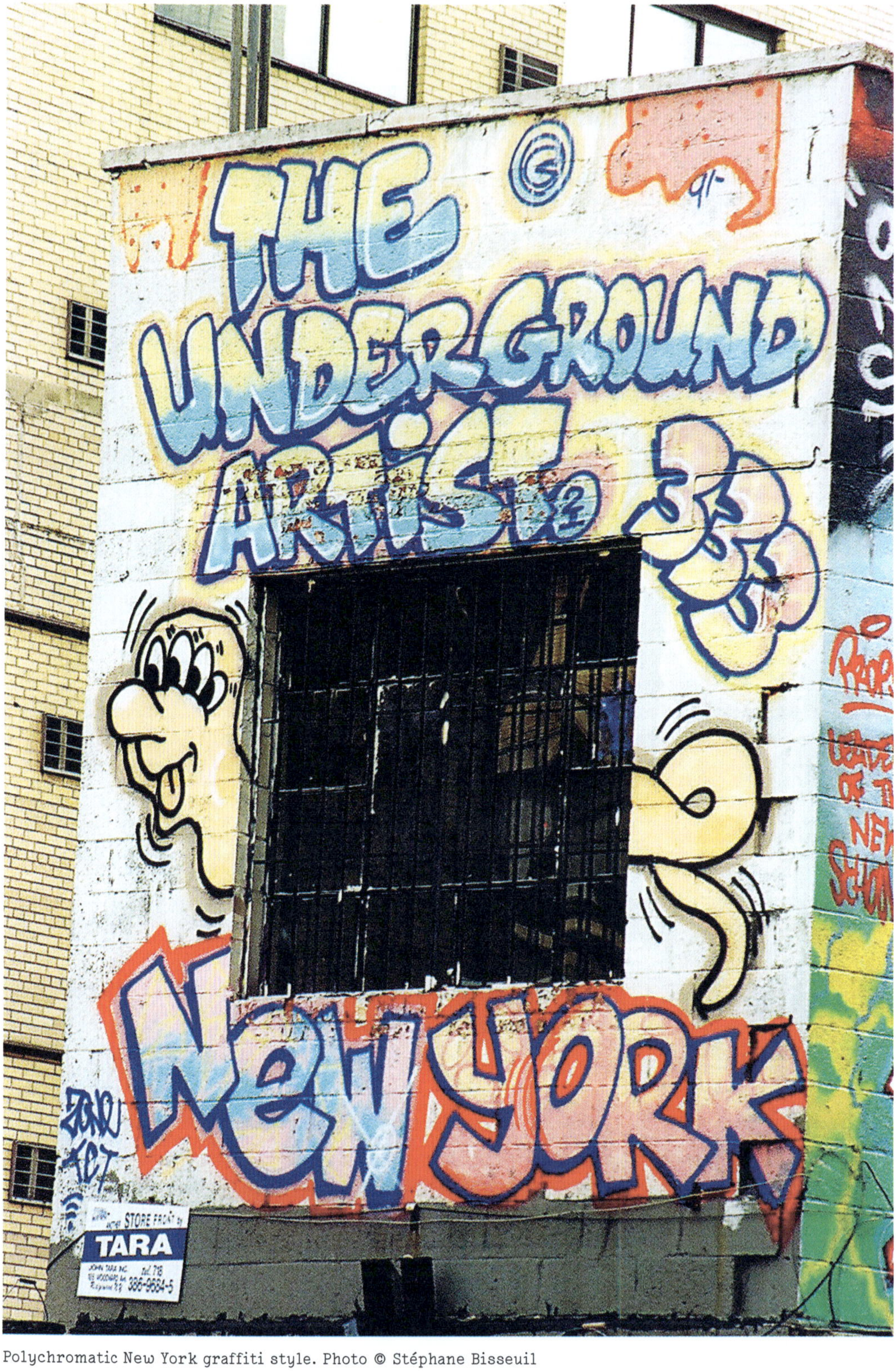

Polychromatic New York graffiti style. Photo © Stéphane Bisseuil

New York Magazine launched a graffiti competition, and journalist Richard Goldstein worked hard to bring public recognition to these artists. He wrote numerous articles on the movement and repeatedly brought up PHASE 2, NOVA, SNAKE 1 and STAY HIGH 149, providing them with increased individual recognition. In 1973, in a major article, "This Thing Has Gotten Completely Out of Control," not only did he list the most important street artists of the time, but he also firmly challenged lobbying to pass antigraffiti laws and positions taken by figures such as John Lindsey, the Mayor of New York, and the MTA. Against the general consensus that saw street artists as vandals, Richard Goldstein depicted "these kids (who) all turn out to be ordinary fourteen-to-fifteen year olds" as real artists. Because of his criticism of the widespread and lazy discourse on New York's urban crisis, Goldstein became one of the most important commentators on—and a spokesman for—hip-hop culture as a social movement.

Artist GORDON MATTA-CLARK also pays tribute to this burgeoning graffiti culture, which is rapidly transforming New York's urban landscape into a gigantic work of community art. In the summer of 1973, after a failed bid to exhibit his hand-coloured photographic prints of graffiti at the Washington Square Art Fair, he decided to organise a "happening" in protest, whereby he exhibited them right there on the street, mounted on sawhorse trestles. Before the event, he took his van to the South Bronx and invited local artists to cover it entirely in graffiti. Afterwards, he parked the van nearby and sold off pieces of it to interested parties, using a blowtorch to cut out individual sections of sheet metal.

In 1975, PHASE 2 was declared "King of style." The highly prized title "All City King" was awarded to just three street artists: TRACY 168, CLIFF 159 and KILL 3. The title was subject to numerous conditions, including both to pay tribute to the urban environment and to paint wholecars—exploits that became standard in the New York cityscape. SEEN remembers with regard to this era that "one day, I had done a wholecar and I wanted take a photo of all of it. To make sure that the work remained intact, I decided to superglue the windows shut despite the summer heat so that the passengers could not open them and alter my work."
These years were considered to have led the way in the race for innovation, and they were fundamental in the respect that this was when visual codes—still in force more than forty years later—were defined. The movement was ready to welcome a new generation of young people who were eager to learn from their masters. This new informal teaching, transmitted from generation to generation, involved several levels of learning. At the first level, the learner would choose his or her street name and work to produce it with style. At the second, students learned to make larger productions with dexterity and speed, as well as in multiple colours. They would then try to execute a true work, the only real demonstration of one's talent.

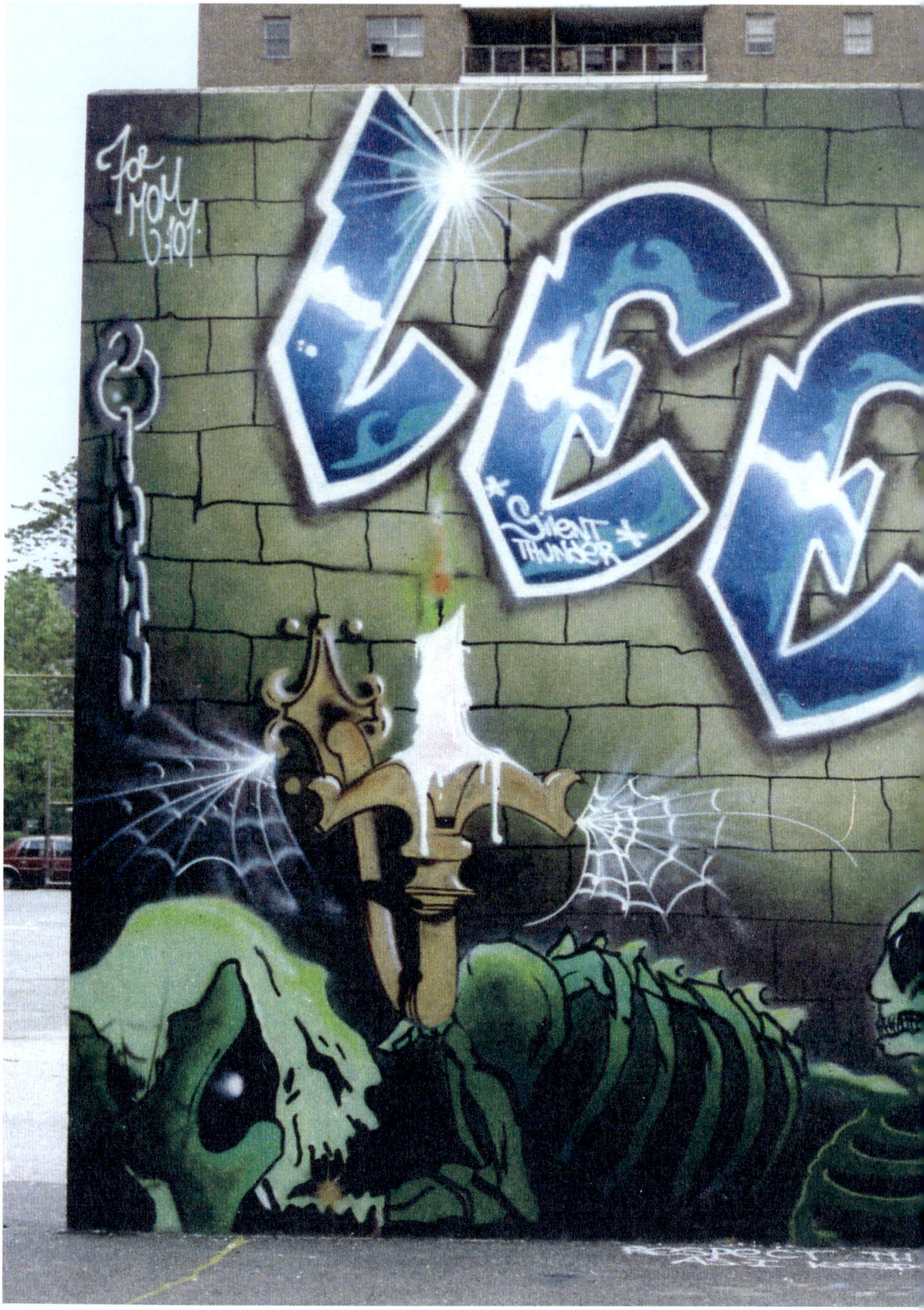

LEE QUINONES, *Lion's Den*, 1982 © Lee Quinones

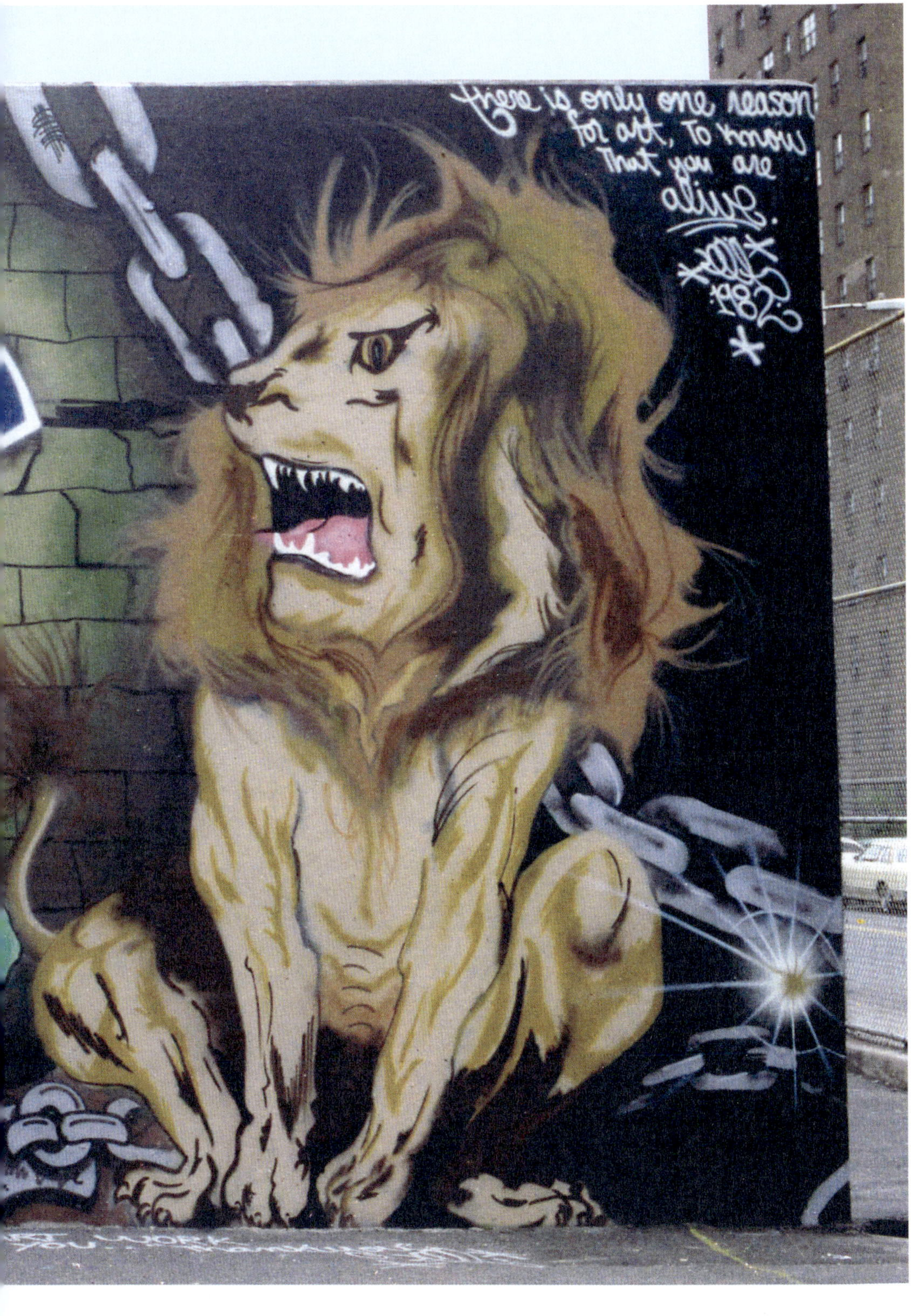
there is only one reason
for art, To know
That you are
alive
1982

During the ensuing years, the UGA became an institution in charge of promoting official events, with the support New York City. The Razor Gallery continued to host group exhibitions. A number of artists pursued art studies and acquired professional status while continuing to defy the authorities each day.

Expansion

FROM TRAINS TO WALLS

With the increasing complexity of the works created, the more difficult working conditions and some artists' growing ambitions, certain figures turned to producing authorized mural works. Yet, despite the comfort and peace of mind that this type of work brought, all agree that these achievements did not have the same impact on the environment and its inhabitants. The quest for walls that were unmissable though not necessarily authorized became crucial. A wall could not be imposed. It had to be selected by the artist because of its place in the urban landscape and its context. Whether or not a wall was legal did not play a role in choosing it. Because it was known that the only thing that would remain of the work would at best be a photograph, this contextual approach became important and would only grow over the years.

In the early 1980s, the reputation of LEE and the FABULOUS FIVE was growing, not only because they walked in the footsteps of their predecessors, but also because they complied with the code established by the old school.

In terms of style, this period saw the birth of the fundamental principles of graffiti. A very precise code was established from a technical and formal point of view, which also introduced a code of conduct.

During this period of style war, the MTA may have spent almost $150 million to clean up graffiti and install security systems to protect train depots. In 1978, the movement received a blow in the form of the introduction of a new high-pressure cleaning device called the Buff. In a few weeks, hundreds of carriages were more or less successfully cleaned. But this simply pushed more artists to turn to walls. In 1978, LEE, aka Lee Quinones, spent most of his nights at the foot of the Brooklyn Bridge, turning it into an open-air art gallery. Aware of the impact of his monumental creations, he said that "my sense of art was to create art without a reference point to art history, because this was art history in the making."

However, although LEE rejected any reference, a number of the first street artists accept that they benefited from the rich cultural context offered by New York, showing the baselessness of the prejudiced perception of artists devoid of any artistic education. CRASH remembers being strongly impressed as a child by Picasso's work exhibited at the

MoMA in 1970, 1973 and 1980[1]. "The two main museums where I would go were the MoMA (Museum of Modern Art) and the Whitney. As a child, I loved Picasso and Cubism. Discovering entire rooms of modern art was impressive. The Whitney opened my eyes to contemporary art, and entering that place to admire Calder's mobile[2] always filled me of joy."

GRAFFITI AND HIP-HOP

Graffiti is regarded as one of the four pillars of hip-hop, a cultural and artistic movement that appeared in the South Bronx in New York during the early 1970s. It was the subject of theories from very early on. It is held to be based on four components:

1 — rap (or MCing), representing lyrics;
2 — DJing, representing music;
3 — break dancing (or b-boying), representing dance and performing arts;
4 — graffiti, representing painting and visual arts.

These four methods of creative expression would sweep across the rest of the world. But with regard to first-time practitioners of graffiti, it is worth noting that this movement was still in gestation, just like their own artistic practice. The first graffiti artists did not identify themselves as part of it. The legendary SEEN remembers that the music he listened to at the time was more hard rock, a genre born in the 1960s that would have considerable popular success ten years later. "My buddies from the neighborhood were inventing rap, but this was not yet the music that you listened to on the radio," he recalls. In 1981, FUTURA participated in the world tour of world-famous punk band the Clash, which was formed in 1976. He appeared on stage alongside them and painted live during the concert.

For other street artists, the link with rap as a nascent musical current was essential. As has been mentioned, PHASE 2's success owed as much to his musical contribution to the hip-hop scene as a DJ. Beyond his fathering of several styles, he was considered one of the main instigators of the intersection between rap music, break dance, deejaying and graffiti. PHASE 2 was very active on the New York music scene and released some records.

The beginning of the 1980s, about ten years after the beginnings of the movement, was when graffiti truly became part of hip-hop and went global, as evidenced by the tour of Afrika Bambaataa, a pioneer of new trends in American music and inventor of hip-hop and Zulu culture.

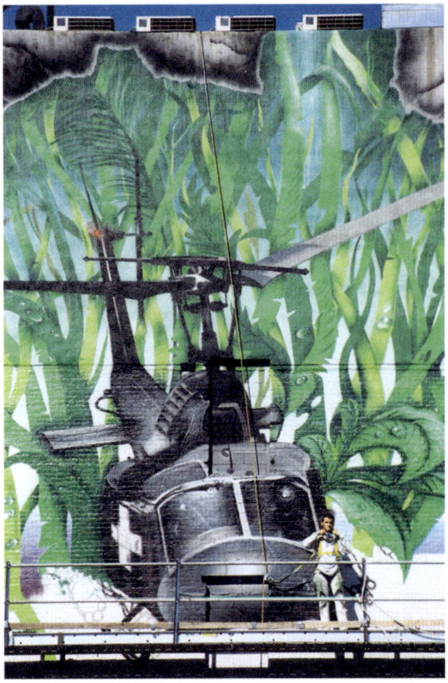

LEE QUINONES in front of one of his murals
© Lee Quinones

[1] Picasso exhibitions at the MoMA: "Picasso: Master Printmaker" [MoMA Exh. #942, October-November 1970]; "Pablo Picasso 1881-1973" [MoMA Exh. #1030, April-May 1973]; "Around Picasso" [MoMA Exh. #1289b, May-30 September 1980]; "Pablo Picasso: A Retrospective" [MoMA Exh. #1290, 16 May-September, 1980].

[2] Also exhibited at the MoMA during this period: Alexander Calder: 1898-1976 [MoMA Exh. #1153, November-December 1976].

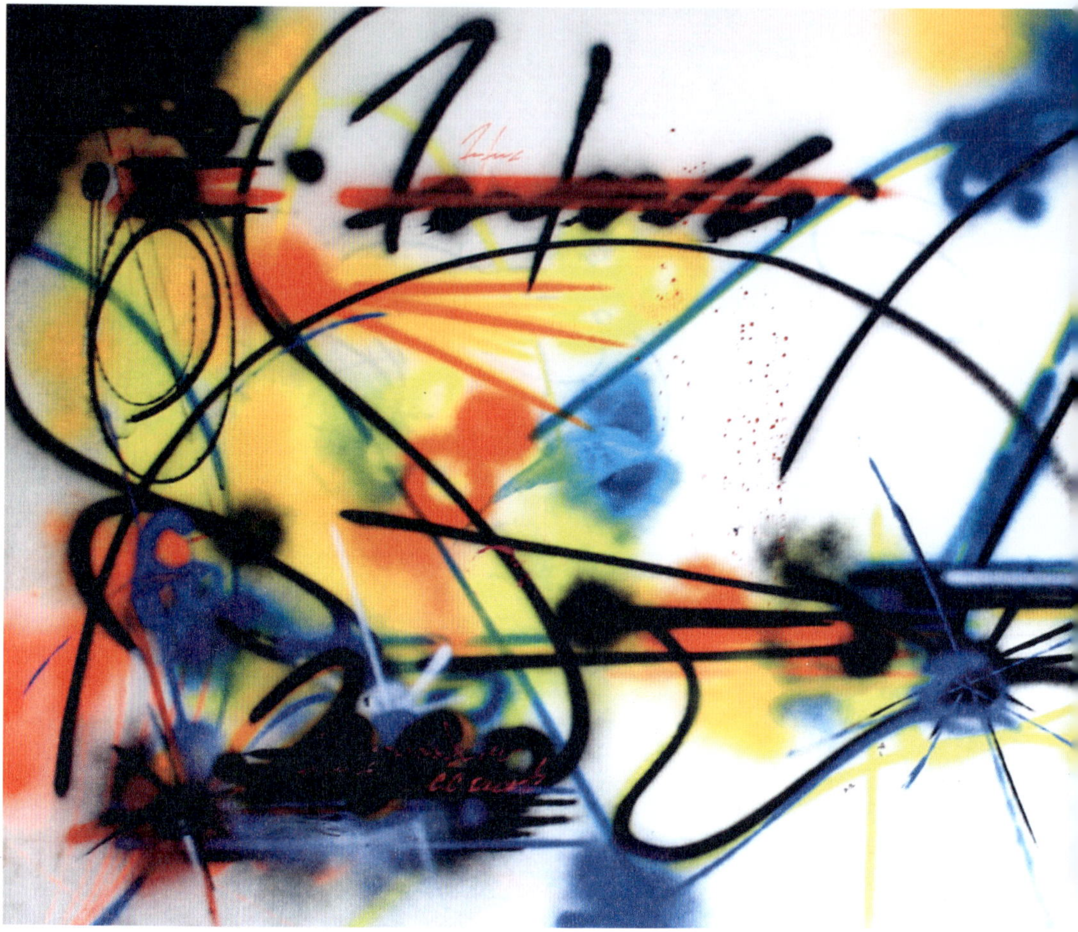

FUTURA, *Untitled*, 135 × 310 cm, 1981, The Clash concert, Théâtre Mogador, Paris
Futura went to France for the first time in 1981 with rock band The Clash, who invited him to join them on tour. Patrick Lerouge Collection.

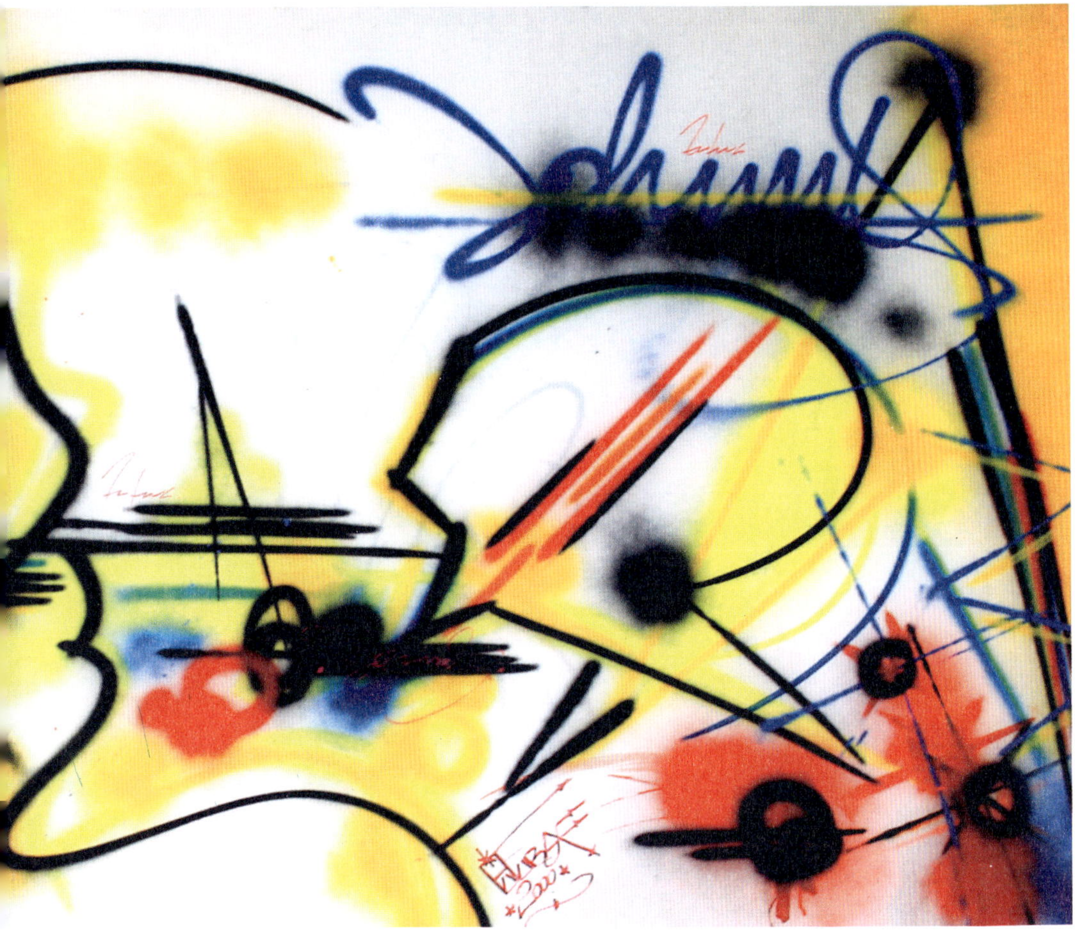

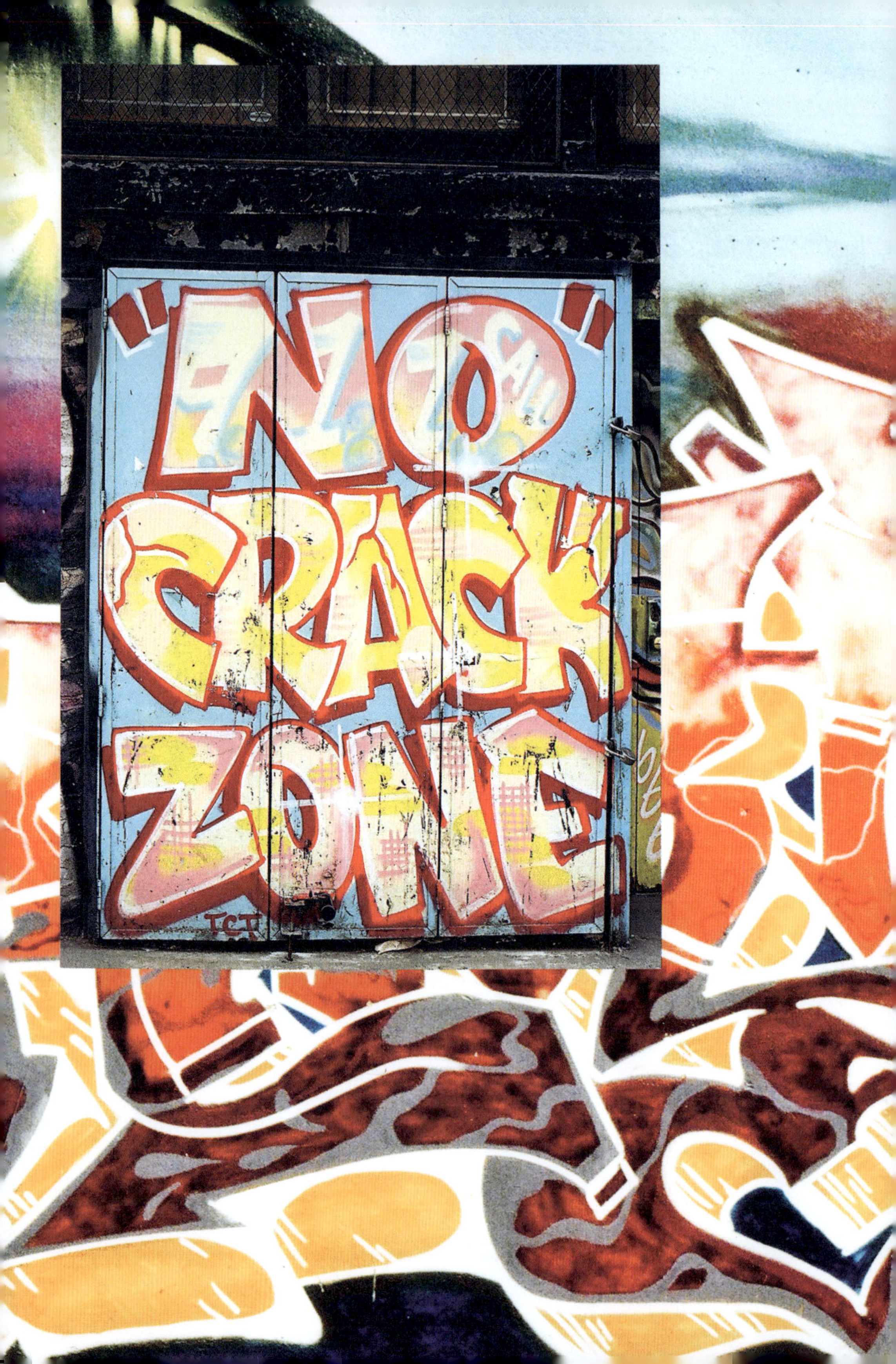
"NO"
CRACK
ZONE
TCT

THE ART OF LETTERING

Styles, forms and subjects

At the time of graffiti's explosion on the streets of New York, certain figures stand out for their artistic creativity. PHASE 2 is first and foremost one of the key examples of these graffiti artists. Lonny Wood—to use his name—is a native of the Bronx, where he was born in 1958. Thirteen years later, he made his debut in the graffiti world. He understood almost straight away that the act of merely writing his name as a tag could quickly become obsolete. Indeed, making the few recognizable but always identical letters that make up a name the main subject of the works produced could lead to going round in circles. Without abandoning this sacrosanct concept of signature, PHASE 2 constantly sought renewal not through his name, but through his style. He invented many graffiti styles and ornamentations. Well before they became part of the evolution of the movement, PHASE 2's creations were more than simple tags; they were true works of art. The journalist Jeff Chang, a specialist in hip-hop culture, describes him as being "widely recognized as defining the early genre." During this first period of the graffiti era, PHASE 2 painted thousands of trains.

But some individuals' artistic talents were not expressed on such types of support alone. For example, from 1978, SEEN also produced works on canvas while actively continuing to cover trains.

No crack zone, graffiti in New York. Photo © Stéphane Bisseuil

Behind: graffiti in New York City. Photo © Stéphane Bisseuil

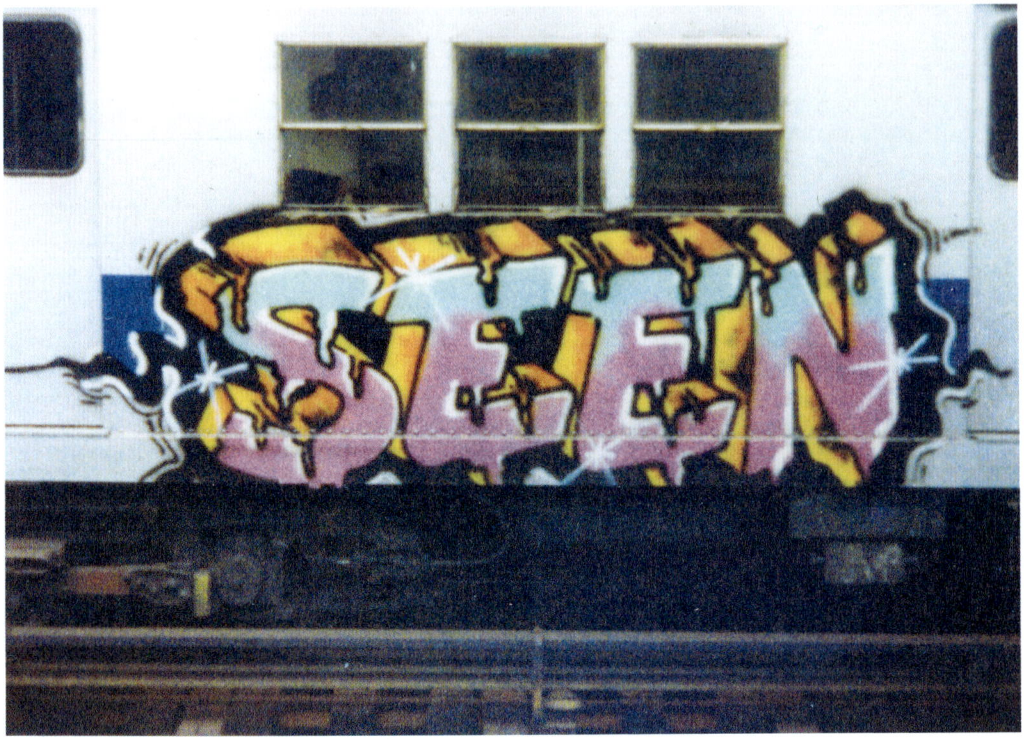

SEEN, 3D graffiti on the New York subway, 1970s-1980s. © Seen Studio

SEEN, iteration of his signature in the “flop” style, 1987. © Seen Studio

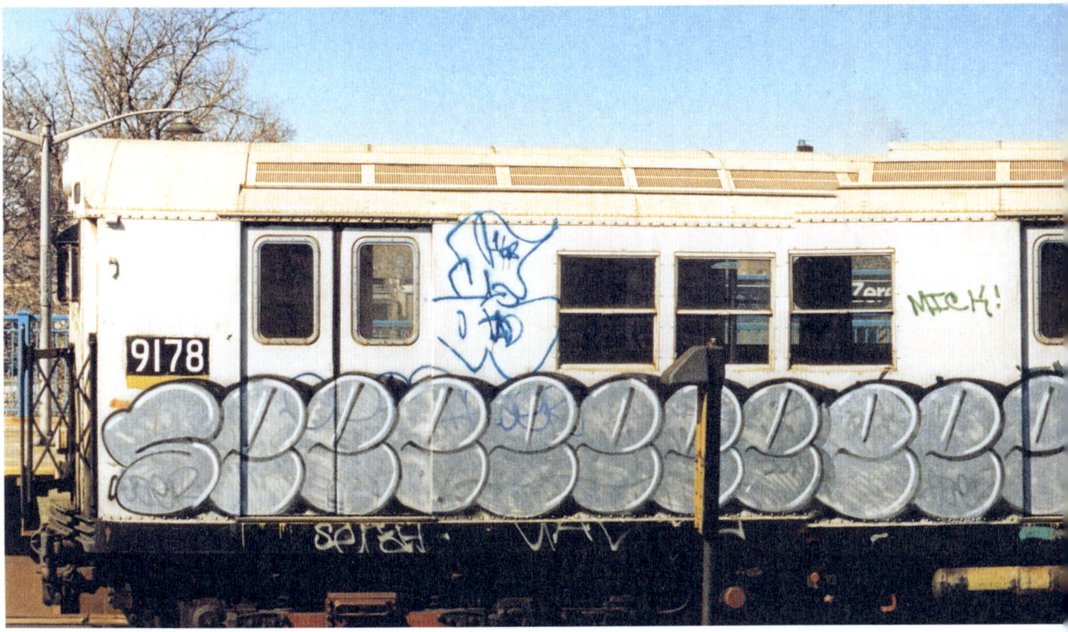

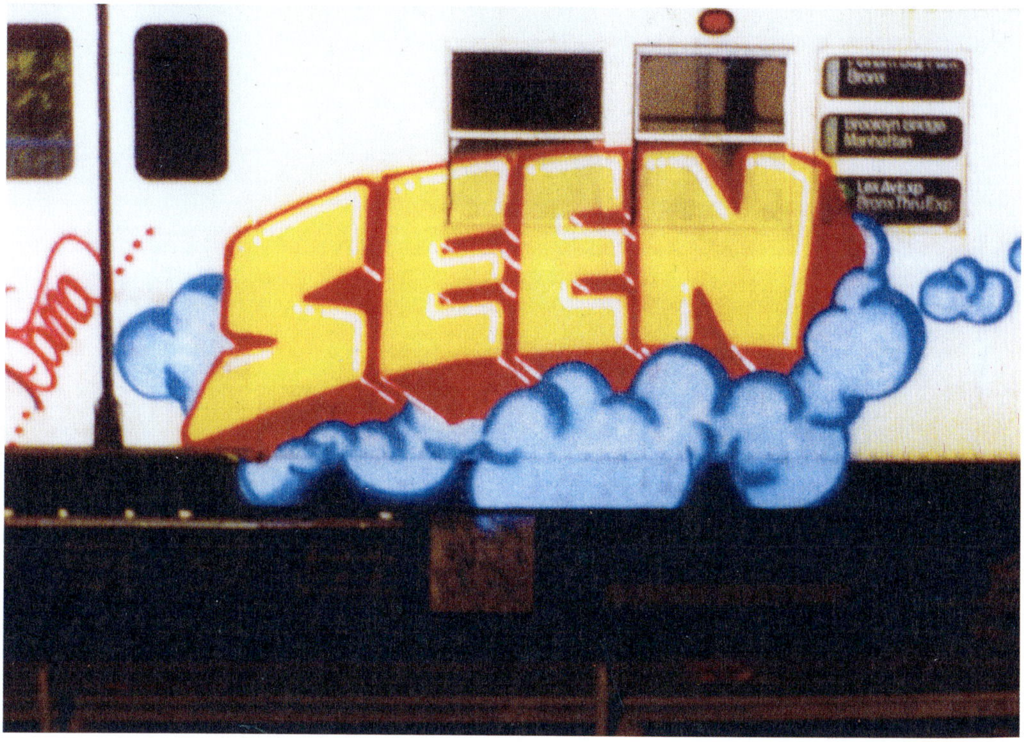

SEEN, painted lettering extending onto the windows of the train, 1970s-1980s. © Seen Studio

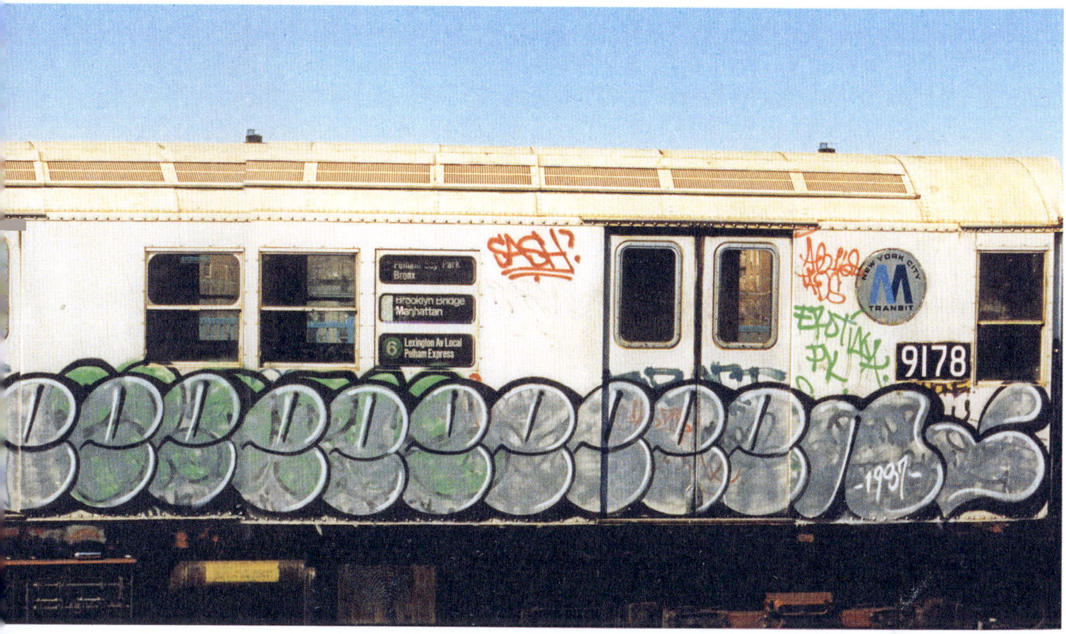

Letters in the wild style intertwine with each other and are developed to the point of becoming distorted. The ends are embellished with various symbols such as arrows, highlighting the abstraction of this very technical style.

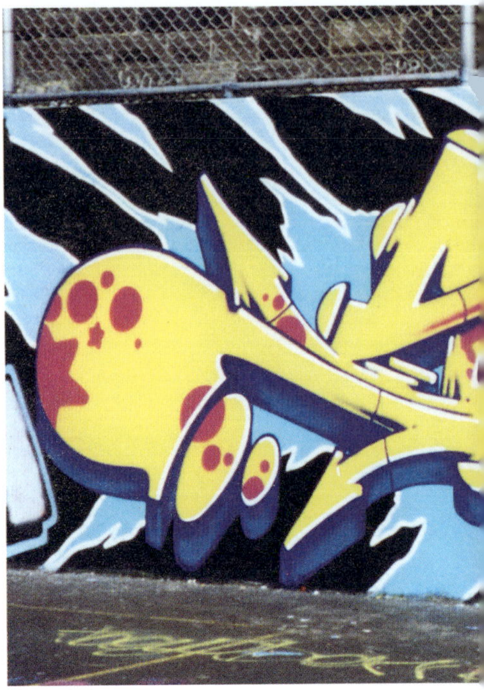

SEEN, wall on the street © Seen Studio

SEEN, example of wild style lettering © Seen Studio

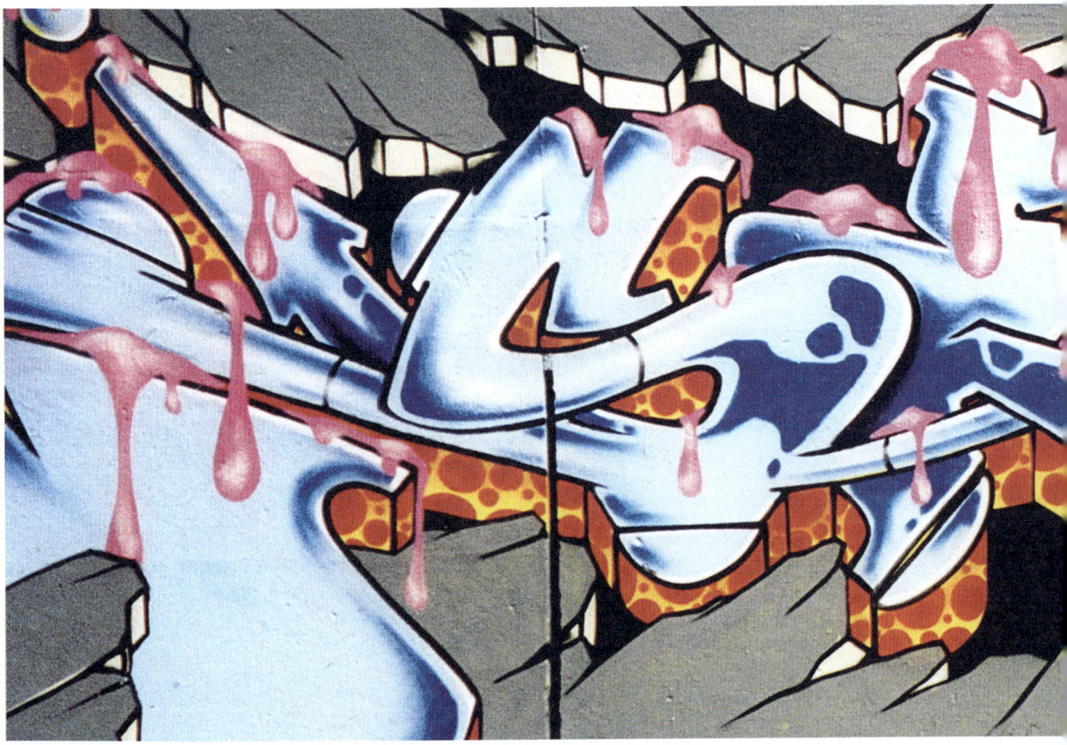

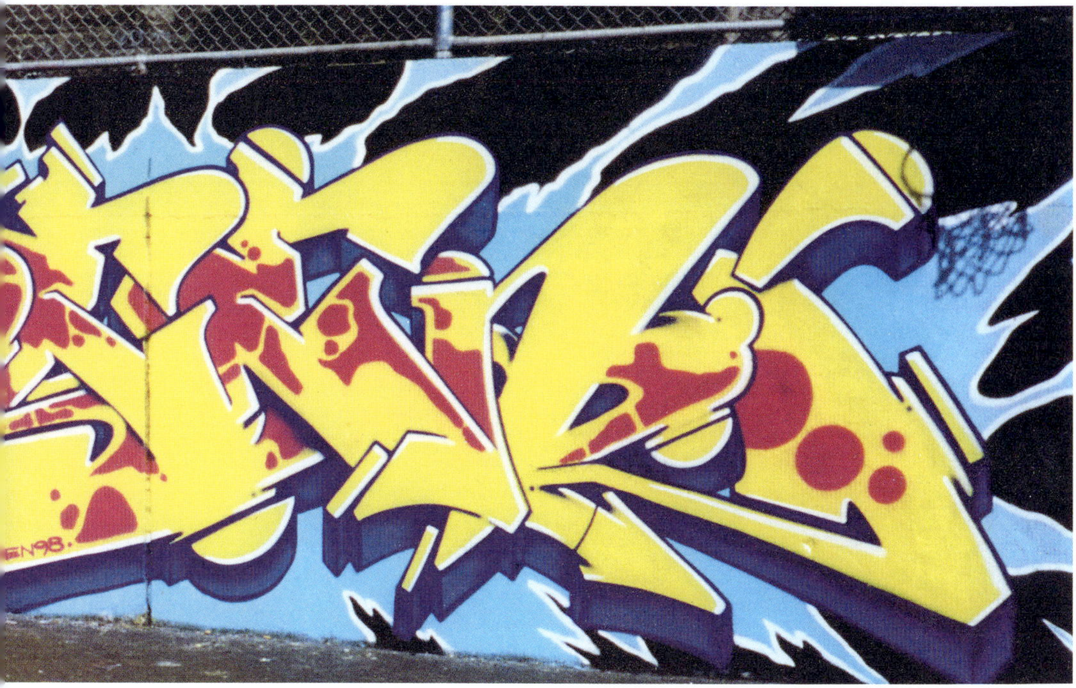

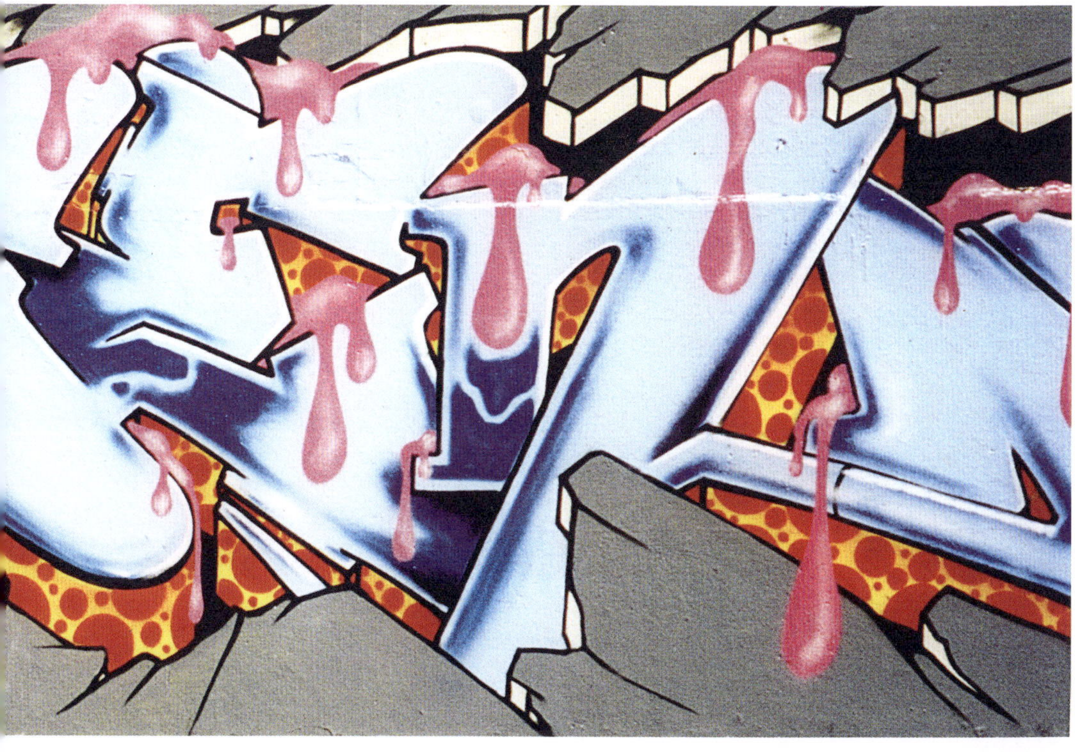

Born in 1961, Richard Mirando, aka SEEN, was known as the "Godfather of Graffiti." Having begun in 1973, he built up his reputation and earned lasting recognition for having invented and promoted a large number of styles while working with the fundamentals. He would inspire whole generations after him.
He started out early, using spray paint for the first time at the age of nine, in the garage of his uncle located just behind the train depot for line 6. He painted his first train when he was eleven. The following year, in 1973, he started painting his signature. Ceaselessly painting and with a fondness for top-to-bottom pieces, he soon gained a great deal of renown owing to both his dexterity and the impressive size of his works. Often referred to as "the man who invented modern graffiti," he prided himself on being an easily recognizable name at the same time as having a constantly evolving style. Having sworn allegiance to the graffiti movement—"graffiti was, is and always will be my life!"—his artistic work honoured different aspects of the genre. With their vivid use of colour—or at least a diverse chromatic palette—his works are a reflection of the 1980s with strong contrasts and perfectly executed large shaded areas. He expressed himself using a spray can with amazing ease. A major part of SEEN's work was his infinite executions in a multitude of styles of the four letters of his pseudonym.

Some street artists soon added new themes to letter decorations, taking inspiration from their direct environment, including comic strips and the pop art that was so ubiquitous at the time.

LEE, Born in Ponce (Puerto Rico) in 1960, grew up in New York. He is one of America's most famous street artists. He began in 1971 with his cousin PHASE 2. He is known for having been the first to go beyond the simple writing in capitals of his predecessors by connecting the letters in his tag. At the end of 1975, he created the first long train—with a length of approximately 13 metres. LEE was inspired by daily life and popular culture. He often made direct reference to music or, in a more subtle way through the rhythm of his painting, the tones and harmonies used. His colour palette—ochre and sky blue—often evoked nature, and everything was much more neutral than most of his classmates' production. His painting was at the crossroads of hip-hop culture and punk rock, and it often conveyed messages and allegories. He incorporated many characters and wild animals, and with time, human figures became increasingly significant in his work, bringing him closer to the tradition of South American muralists. LEE managed to translate the extraordinary wealth—including from a chromatic point of view—of his urban environment.

Donald Joseph White, alias DONDI WHITE, born in 1961, hailed from this same generation. He began tagging in 1975. Having been raised in Brooklyn by Italian and African American parents, he was soon painting monumental works. The best known of these, from 1978-1980, entitled *Children of the Grave Parts 1, 2 and 3*, integrated his lettering, colours

gradients and expressive characters. In an artistic impetus of self-affirmation, he was the first to break the law of anonymity that prevailed over graffiti pieces by painting DONDI on the roof of his own home. Creating innovative colour ranges, he made his lettering increasingly complex over time, including in terms of how he filled it. He effectively created works within works. A passionate and lone operator, he filled numerous sketchbooks with preparatory drawings that demonstrated his taste for experimentation in his lettering. His letters have often been defined as "acrobatic" or "aerodynamic." DONDI was a tenacious artist who could spend months on the preparation of a single work. His symbolic characters, who were usually reduced to monochrome silhouettes —shadows or icons, for example— were a nod to STAY HIGH pieces and their sketched figure of the Saint. His style was also notable for the scarcity of its outlines, which made it different to classical graffiti. He set aside the ubiquitous classic black outline to let his lettering "float." In terms of inspiration, early on DONDI also drew on religious influences from his Catholic education, as well as cultural ones through readily making references to classical painting, and especially Leonardo da Vinci. More generally, a battle against obscurantism lay at the heart of his works.
Like some other artists, he was supported by the collector Sam Esses, and he turned more towards working in the studio once his train pieces were removed by the MTA. This experience was a success, giving a new direction to his artistic career.
The style he developed over the years was characterized by a range of innovative colours. On canvas, he often used muted colours that came close to natural tones (beige, brown, ochre, green and blue). His visual writing on canvas contrasted with graffiti in bright tones executed on trains and outdoor walls.
In his works, he depicted characters in the form of monochromatic silhouettes with highly simplified outlines. The iconic aspect of these anonymous figures is reminiscent of the silhouettes of STAY HIGH 149's early works. With a stunning mastery of the spray can, he liked to include various effects in his pieces, such as blurring and gradation. He combined all his elements and colours and overlaid them to achieve a certain form of abstraction. The style developed by DONDI, who died in 1998 of AIDS, has remained crucial.

Following in his footsteps, more and more street artists gave their works an autobiographical tone or a deeper meaning.

For example, QUIK, who was born in 1958 in the Bronx, combined in his works his personal ideas and social issues that were of concern to him, such as the place of black minorities in American society. In a similar way to pop art, QUIK explored the American dream in a rather complex way. But in contrast to pop art, which in his eyes was the defender of a newly and allegedly democratized consumerist society, street artists stood in opposition to this vision. Fully committed to the fight for recognition of African-American civil rights, artists like QUIK sought to express the contradictions of the society in which they lived. As a black

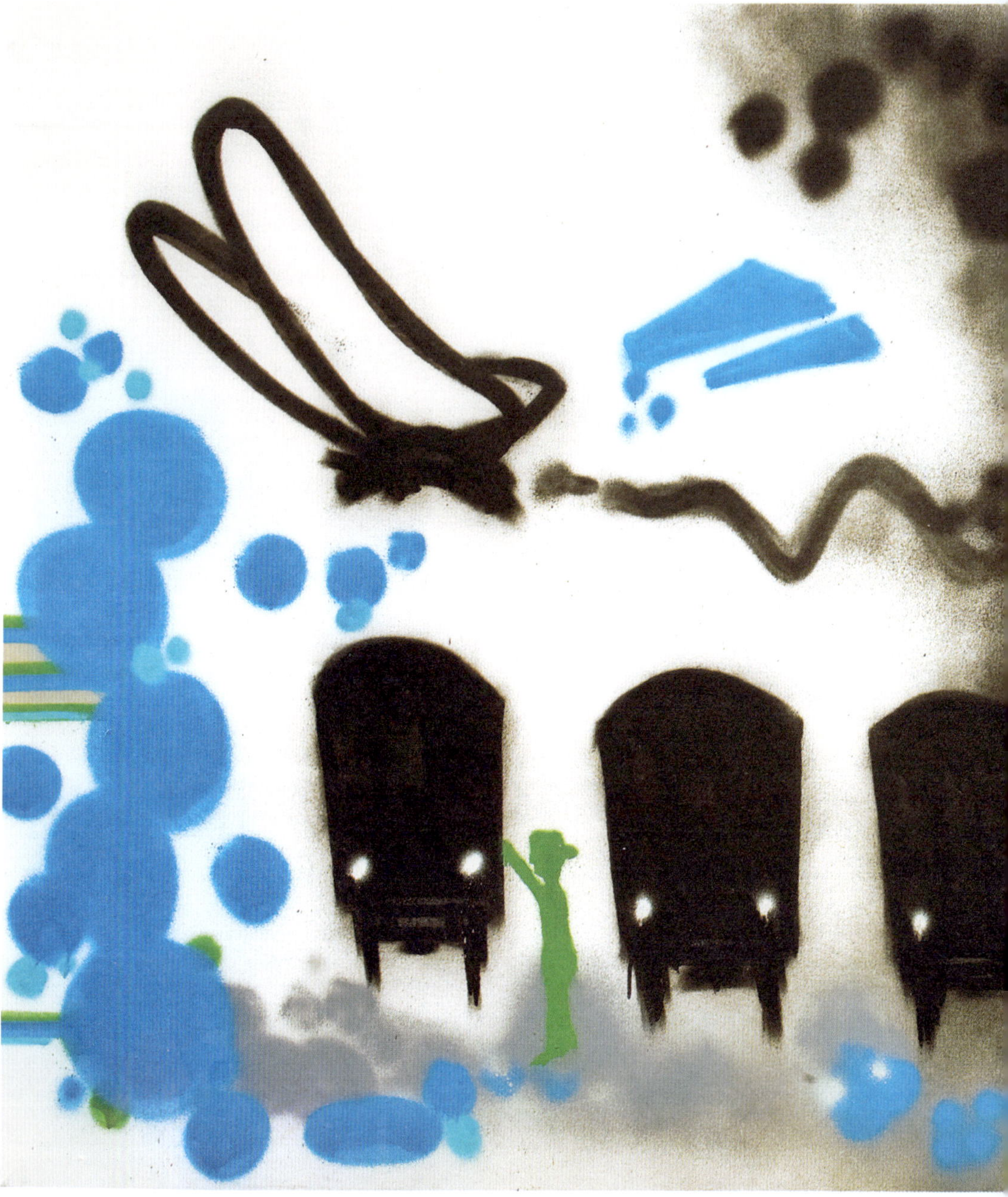

DONDI, untitled, 131×241 cm, 1984, private collection. Photo © Stéphane Bisseuil

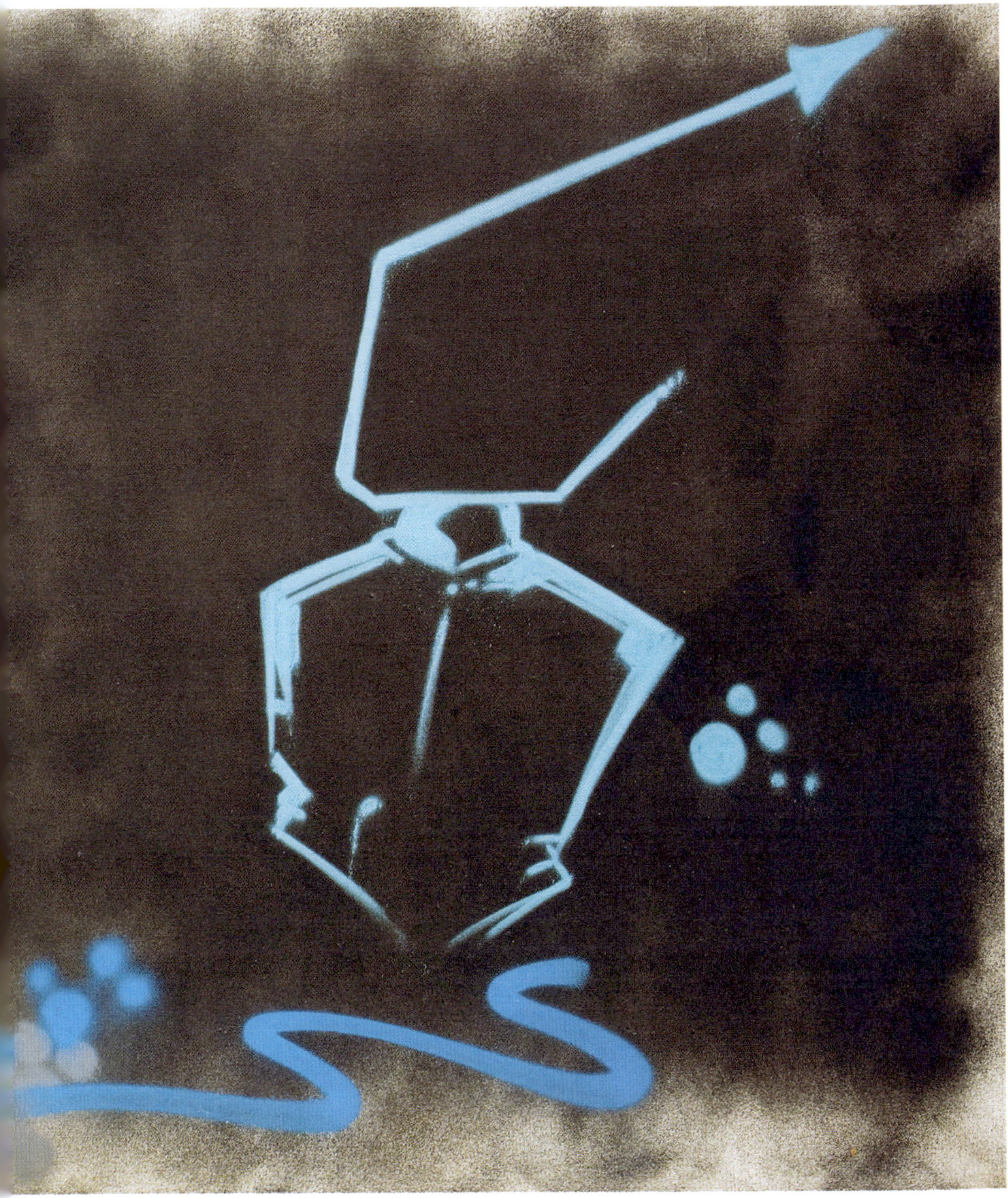

American, he incorporated this divide into his contrast-filled work, about which he offers this reflection: "I can't sing, and I can't play an instrument, so I paint the blues." Even in his simplest and most colourful works, which seem to simply be lettering, QUIK let big questions emerge. Without being political in a strict sense, his work betrayed an angst linked no doubt to a childhood spent, we should not forget, in the era of segregation. Black people were at the heart of his work, as well as the suffering faced by minorities. He was not afraid of depicting Hitler or silhouettes of members of the Ku Klux Klan on trains to give more impact to his works. He also often incorporated the American flag, both as a means to illustrate his ideas on social issues and as a homage to the Jasper Johns flag. His use of black outlines for his female figures referenced the way in which Roy Lichtenstein represented women in his works.
As is the case with many key graffiti works, the simplicity of QUIK's pieces is misleading. The initial perception is that of an obsessive artist armed with recurrent and simple pop imagery, with colourful faces and references to cartoons. But a closer examination reveals characters facing life's difficulties and bitter visions of a world where, despite everything, people need to find their place. The contrasts that some have seen as garish echo the ubiquitous advertisements and visual codes that these artists were fighting against. The idea was to shout louder. In QUIK's own words, "It's action painting, it's aggressive, energy and sweat."

The abstract explosion

In addition to working more and more on their style, street artists were also refining their technique. Despite the difficulties of executing pieces with it, spray paint offers street artists a wide range of possibilities in terms of both design and effects. Because the intensity and size of the jet of paint from the aerosol vary depending on the pressure exerted by the artist on the cap, street artists could more precisely tweak their styles. They spread colours, originally intended to fill the letters of their pseudonym, over skilful gradations. Little by little, colour was taken from the outlines of letters to fill in backgrounds or depict elements that tended toward abstraction. Some works were closer to a Pollock than to the first lettering efforts. Individualizing was about breaking codes and pushing the limits of expression. Crudely drawn clouds were transformed into much more subtle, nuanced and colourful gradients and shades.
FUTURA was one of the first artists to assert a more abstract graffiti. Born in 1955, he began, along with some other young taggers of his generation, by painting New York subway trains at the beginning of the 1970s. Speed and movement are an inherent part of graffiti, but FUTURA understood from the beginning how to convey this energy, which led to him quickly developing a strong reputation. In his artistic work, his approach was unique. He used a futuristic style (as indicated by his pseudonym) to create an abstract universe in which he mixed an explosion of colours and clean lines. The contrast between chromatic ranges, the

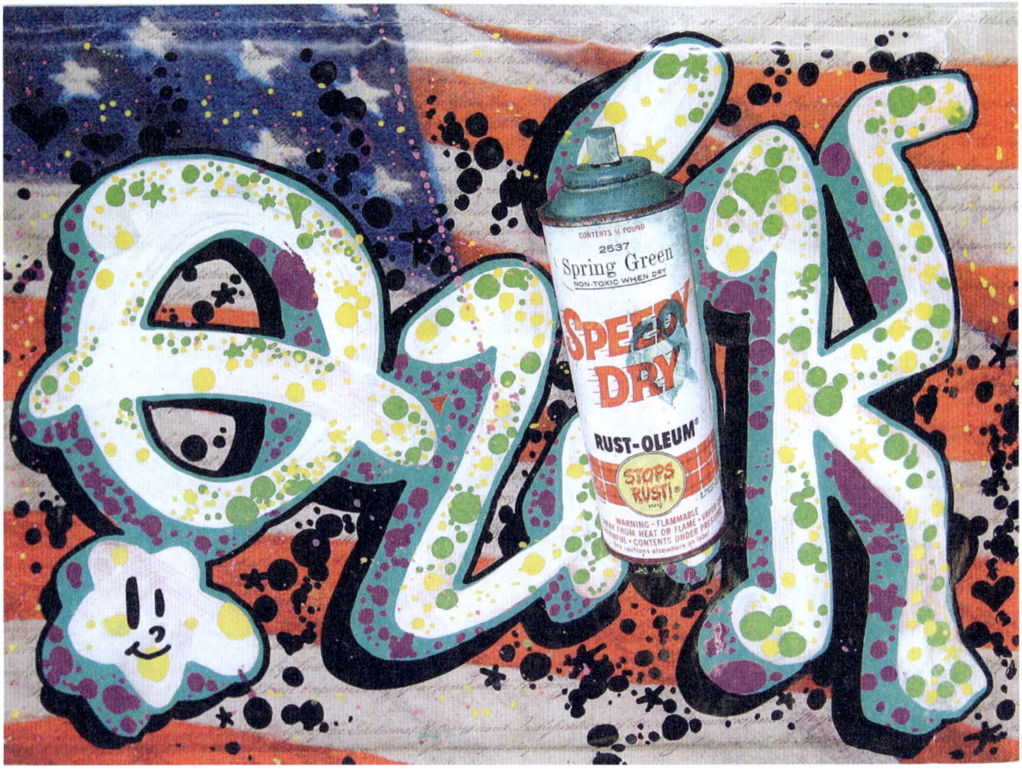

QUIK, *Speedy Day*, acrylic and spray paint on canvas © QUIK

QUIK, *Pulled Up!*, acrylic and spray paint on canvas © QUIK

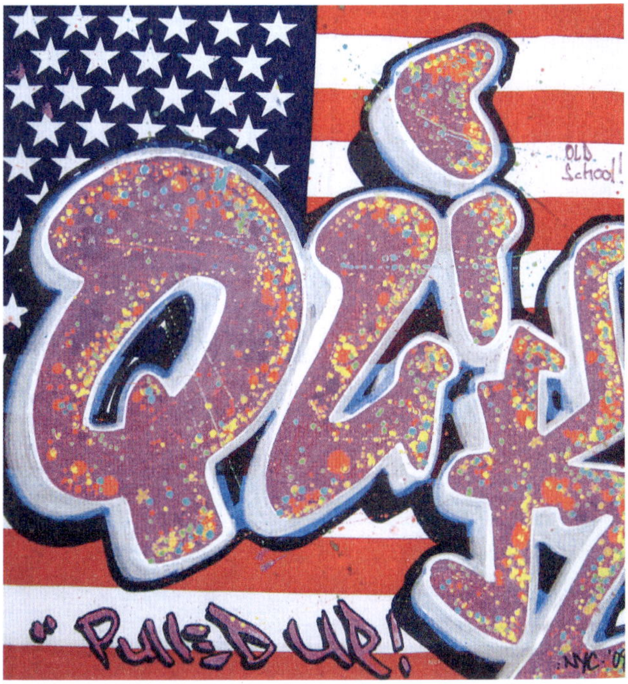

"In my work, the visual reference to the American flag refers to American graffiti, or perhaps I should say Amerikkkan graffiti, because I'm black. All my visual icons are pretty cynical deep down. It is also a way to throw them in the face of these politicos who have the power, the establishment.
For me, graffiti is a form of rebellion. That is why I desecrate the flag."

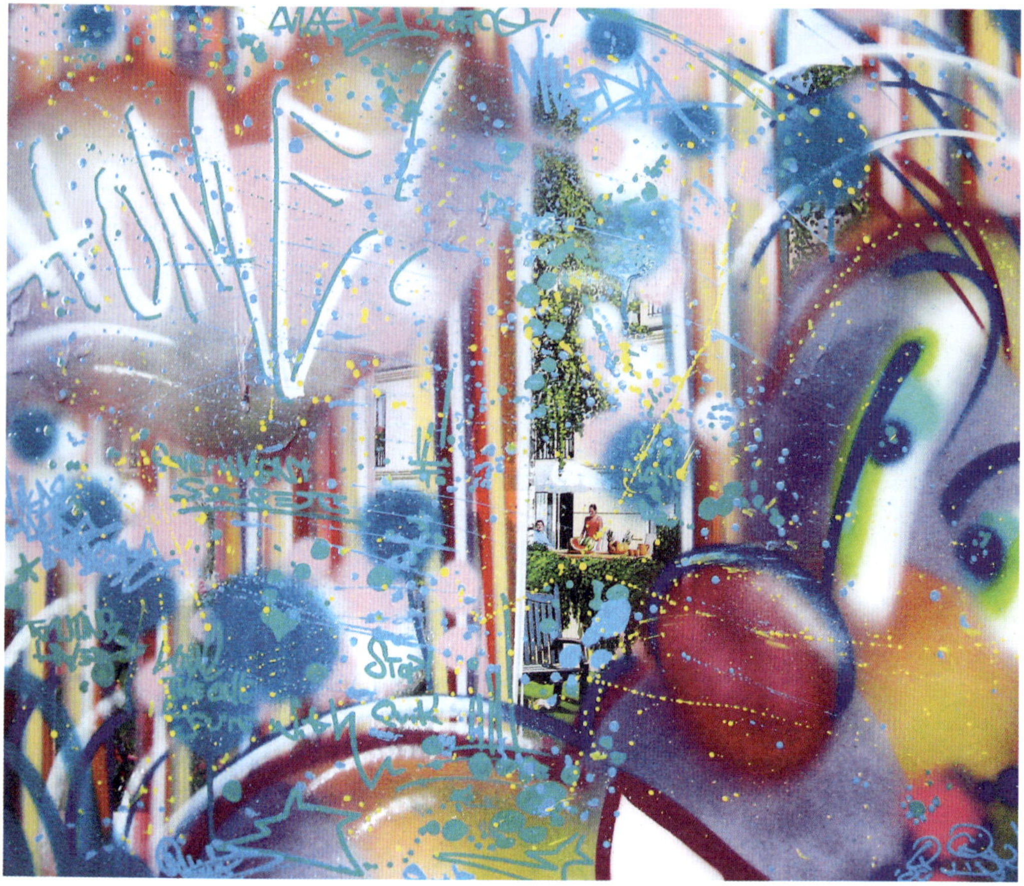

QUIK, *Home*, acrylic and spray paint on canvas © QUIK

«I often use images of women that my those who follow my work describe as 'pin-ups', as I imitate the styles of American illustrations from the 1950s and 1960s. However, an astute Dutch collector once speculated at a conference: 'These women are all Lin Felton (Quik's real name)! He uses them to hide behind in order to express his own emotions and ideas'.» QUIK

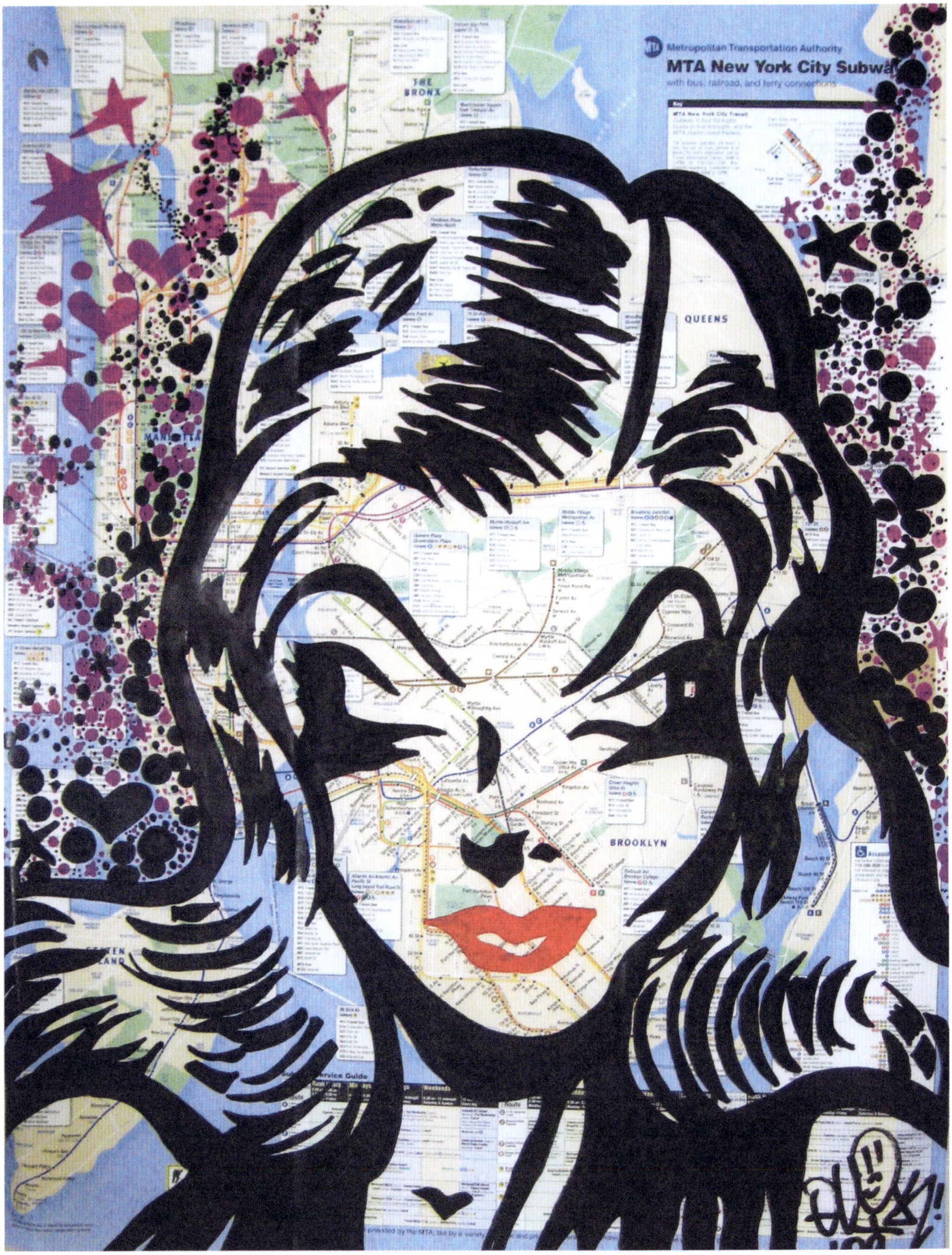

QUIK, *Jamie*, acrylic and spray paint on subway map, 73×58 cm © QUIK
QUIK paints on various media, as is the case here with this map of the New York City subway.

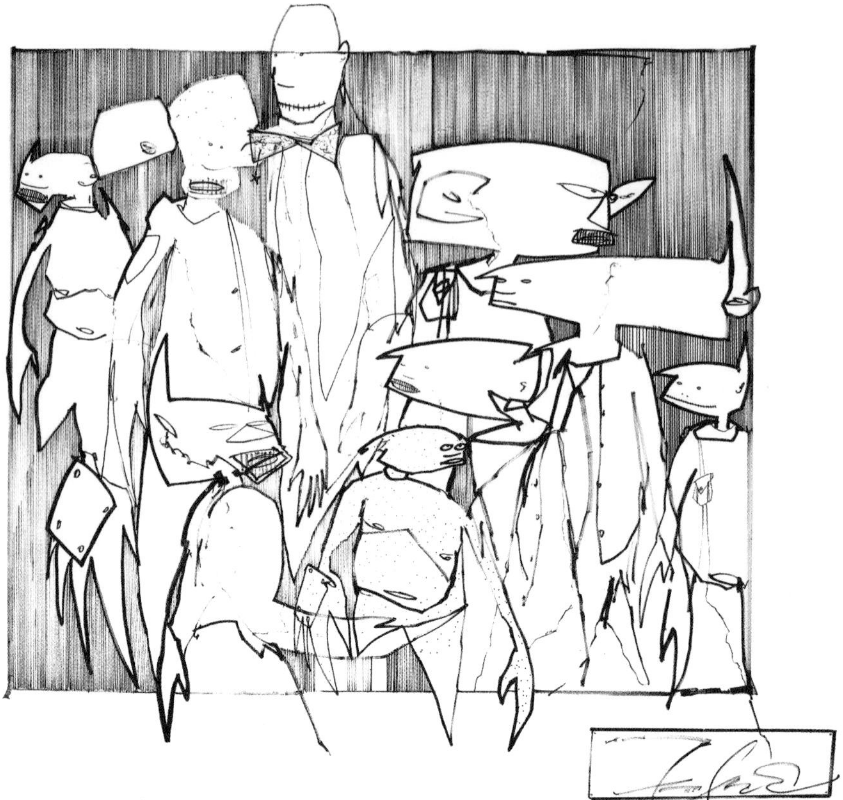

FUTURA, wall piece at the Magda Danysz gallery in the point man style.

ethereal elements and the clean lines introduced a code that is difficult to decipher and exhilarating. Spray painting allowed him to imagine subtle blends of colours and effects. Little by little, FUTURA created a true abstract language, in which each of his signs carried a specific meaning. His works were both light and evanescent. Each integrated element seems to float in a carefully applied cloud of paint. In contrast to many of his associates, FUTURA applied the rule of economy of means, seeking to give his work an ethereal quality.

RAMMELLZEE was another street artist who was a beacon of abstraction. His style is among the movement's most developed. He was born in 1960 in Queens, New York City, and began painting subway carriages around his neighbourhood in 1974. Heavily involved in the hip-hop movement, he even made a record, *Beat Bop*, whose sleeve was designed by Jean-Michel Basquiat. It would inspire generations of rappers, from the Beastie Boys to Cypress Hill. RAMMELLZEE won his peers' admiration by infiltrating difficult-to-reach areas of the metropolitan network. His passion for lettering quickly turned into an in-depth study of symbols across cultures. Alternately described as "afrofuturism" or "gothic futurism," his style in truth was his alone.

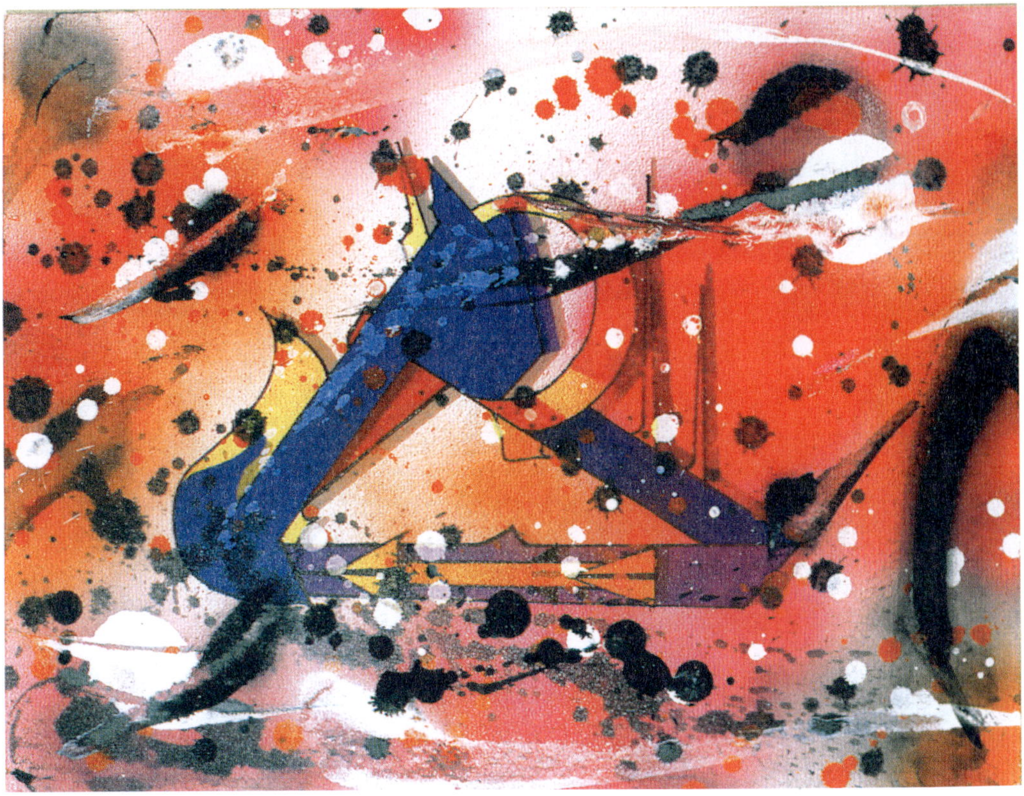

RAMMELLZEE, *Ikonoklast Panzerism - Letter S*, 50×60 cm, 1987, Henk Pijnenburg collection

He even constructed a code of symbols that went far beyond the simple Roman alphabet used by his counterparts. His passion for lettering was unique and stronger than some individuals' drive for fame. He spent part of his time in libraries doing research on ancient manuscripts, and in particular on the monastic scriptoria between the tenth and fifteenth centuries. In his opinion, these elements offered true sources of inspiration. He invented *Letter Racers* because he thought the Roman alphabet could be considered a work in progress. In 1980, even though he had often painted trains with DONDI, he decided to abandon illegal painting and to concentrate on working on canvas.

This artist's visual writing hides an illuminated side and a substantial element of mystery that he worked on extensively. All of his work featured a hallmark in the form of a more profound reflection on the meaning of things and the world's order.

His alias was also designed as a code or mathematical equation. He added an "M" for Magnitude to the initial "RAM." To this he added the sign "Sigma," the first summation operator, then an "L" for "longitude" and another for "latitude," and so on. Surprisingly, this taste for the hidden meaning that each letter of the alphabet might take has similarities with France's VILLEGLÉ, who began his sociopolitical writings in Paris in 1969.

FUTURA uses recurring symbols in his works that make him immediately identifiable.

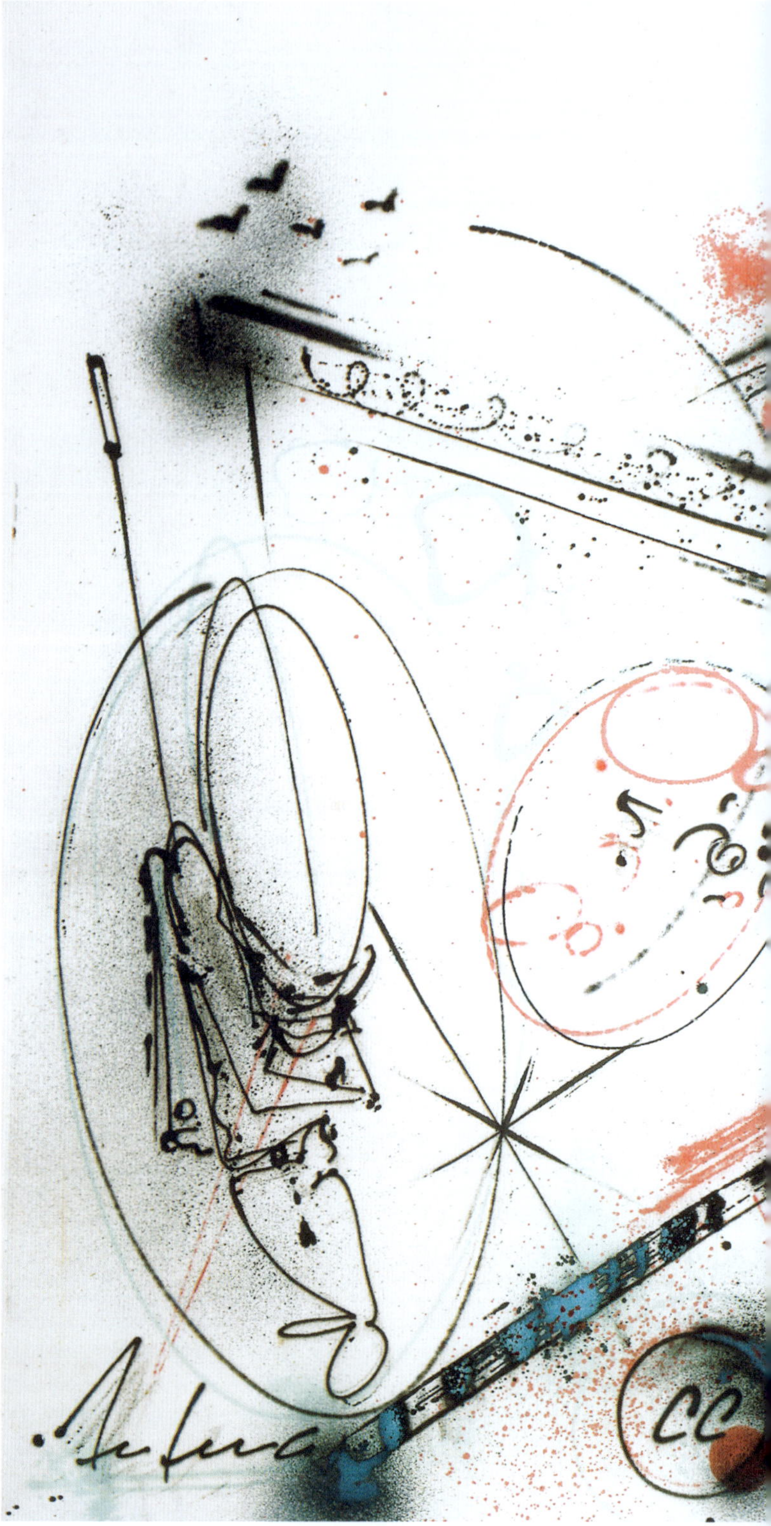

FUTURA, *Bar Code*, work on canvas, private collection

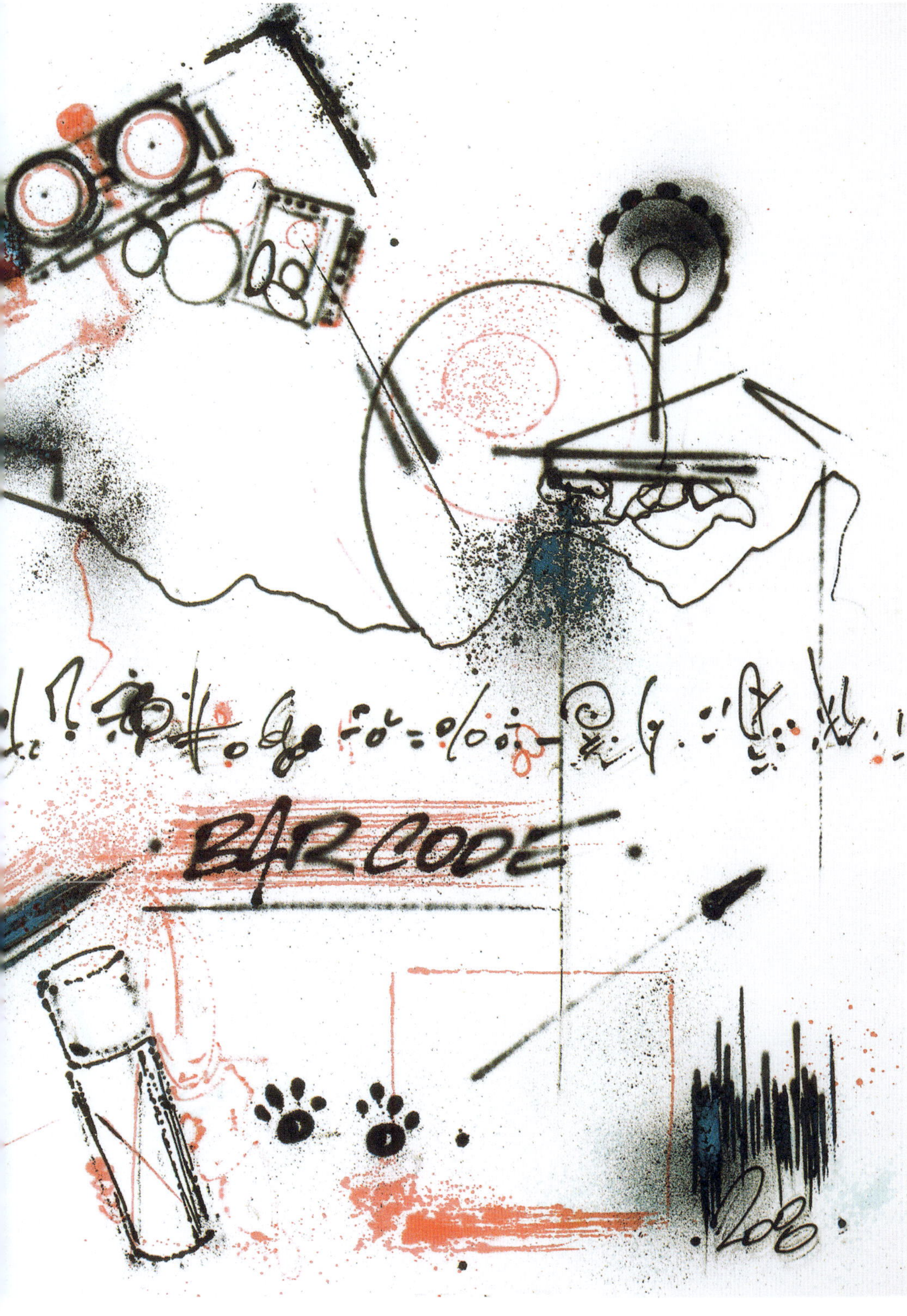
BAR CODE

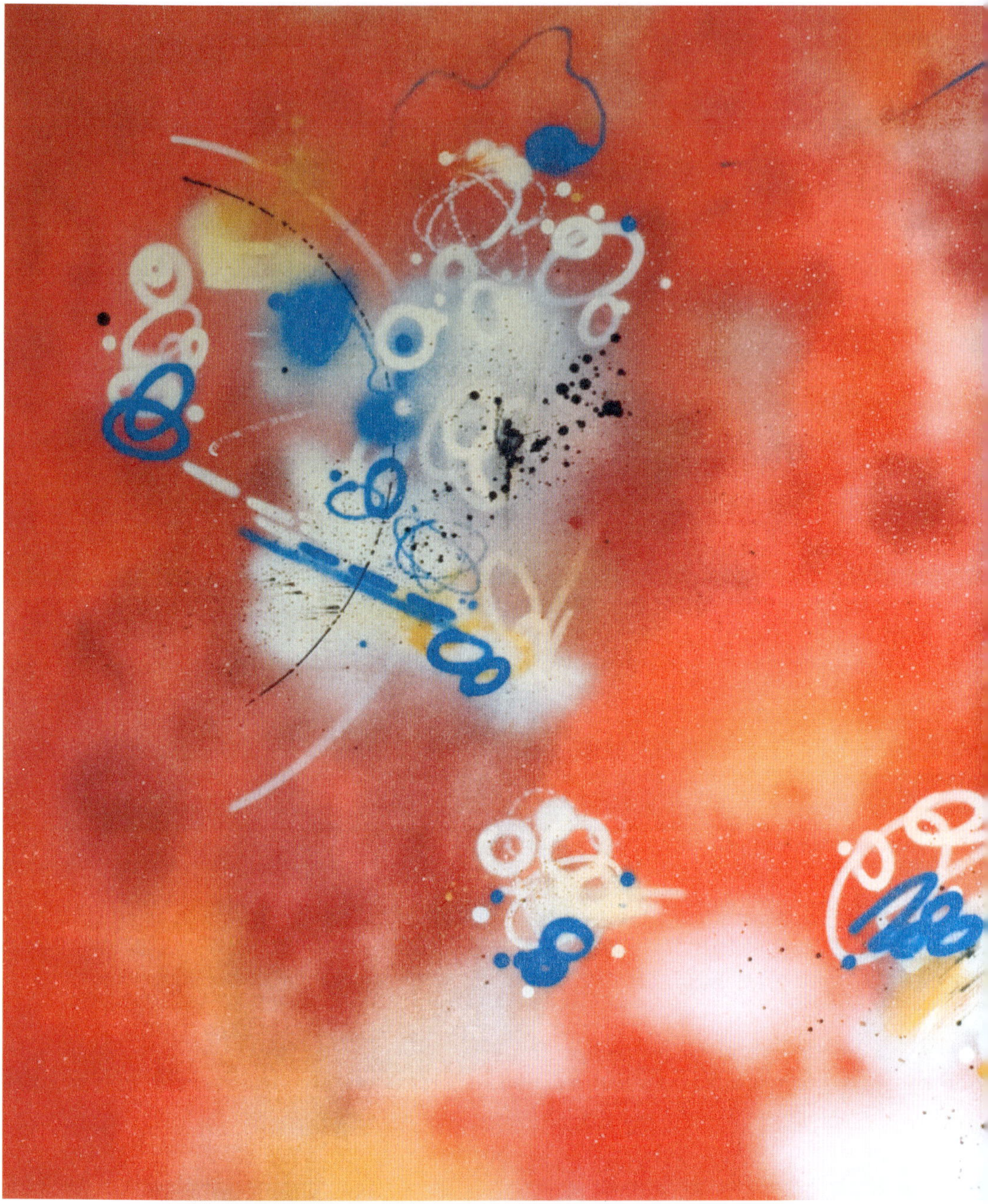

FUTURA, *Pony*, 1982, acrylic and spray paint on canvas, 120×240 cm, private collection

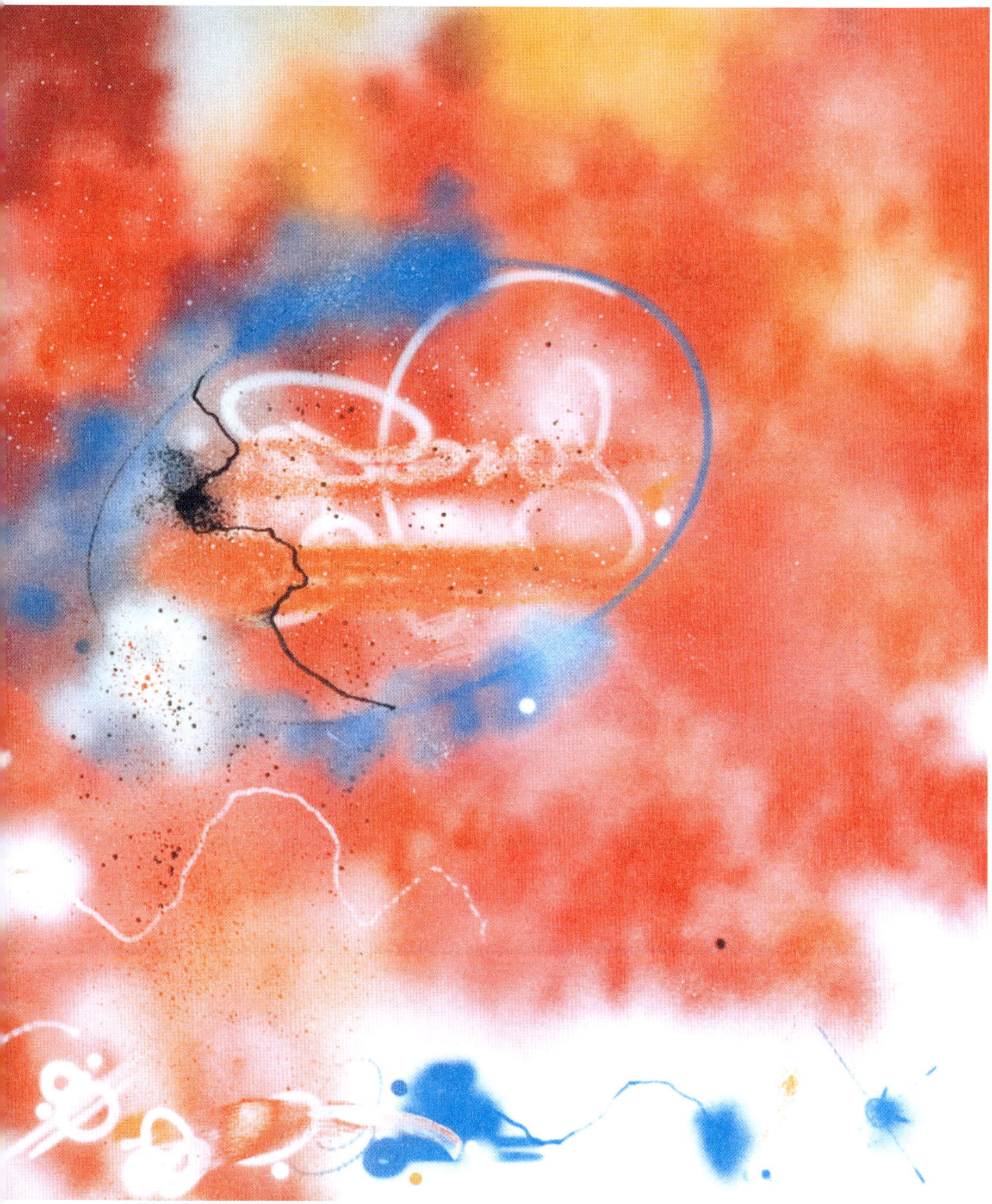

Moreover, he was one of the taggers to have given a significant amount of theory to his style. Over time, he expanded his explorations, making his writing more or less intelligible as well as working on links between letters and the symbols surrounding them.

The beginning of artistic recognition

At the end of the 1970s, all New Yorkers were the day-to-day viewers of an art that was starting to assert itself. At the time, FUTURA still thought that "it is difficult to call graffiti art because it was created to work outside the system." But at the beginning of the 1980s, everything changed. Over time, the MTA's aggressive cleaning squads gradually meant that graffiti artists had to leave the subway platforms and to seek new horizons. On the one hand, they moved on to walls, which themselves were quickly cleaned. On the other hand, having unquestionably become artists in the eyes of some people, they sought a way to leave a real mark on their times and their environment. To do so, they needed their works to remain in place longer.

Art galleries began to take an interest in this creative outpouring as early as 1979. That year, for example, LEE and FAB 5 FREDDY were presented at the Claudio Bruni in Rome. For non-New Yorkers, this was a first encounter with graffiti. In 1980, alternative places such as Esses Studio, Fashion Moda (Stefan Eins's gallery) and Patti Astor's Fun Gallery opened their doors to graffiti.

Moved by the massive cleanup operations launched by the MTA in 1978, the collector Sam Esses decided to finance a workshop project that allowed many street artists to work in peace, which meant moving from the street to canvas—and acquiring the status of visual artists. This initiative greatly increased solidarity between certain figures in the graffiti scene. BLADE recalls, "That was the first place that I actually sat down and did a spray painting on canvas and concentrated on it. To me it was just sort of an experiment."
Born in 1958 in the Bronx, Steven Ogburn, aka BLADE, was only fifteen years old when he founded his group the Crazy Five Crew. A crew is a group of young graffiti enthusiasts. Such an informal organization enabled them to better organize their artistic activities, to help each other when being chased by the police and to take control of a neighbourhood and claim it visually, thus increasing their impact and recognition of them. Strength in unity!
BLADE was known as a specialist in "blockbusters", a technique that involves covering entire trains in graffiti. The proclaimed "king of whole-cars" reigned on lines 2 and 5 of the New York City subway from 1975 to 1980. He is a true legend. Some people credit him with painting more than 5,000 train cars.

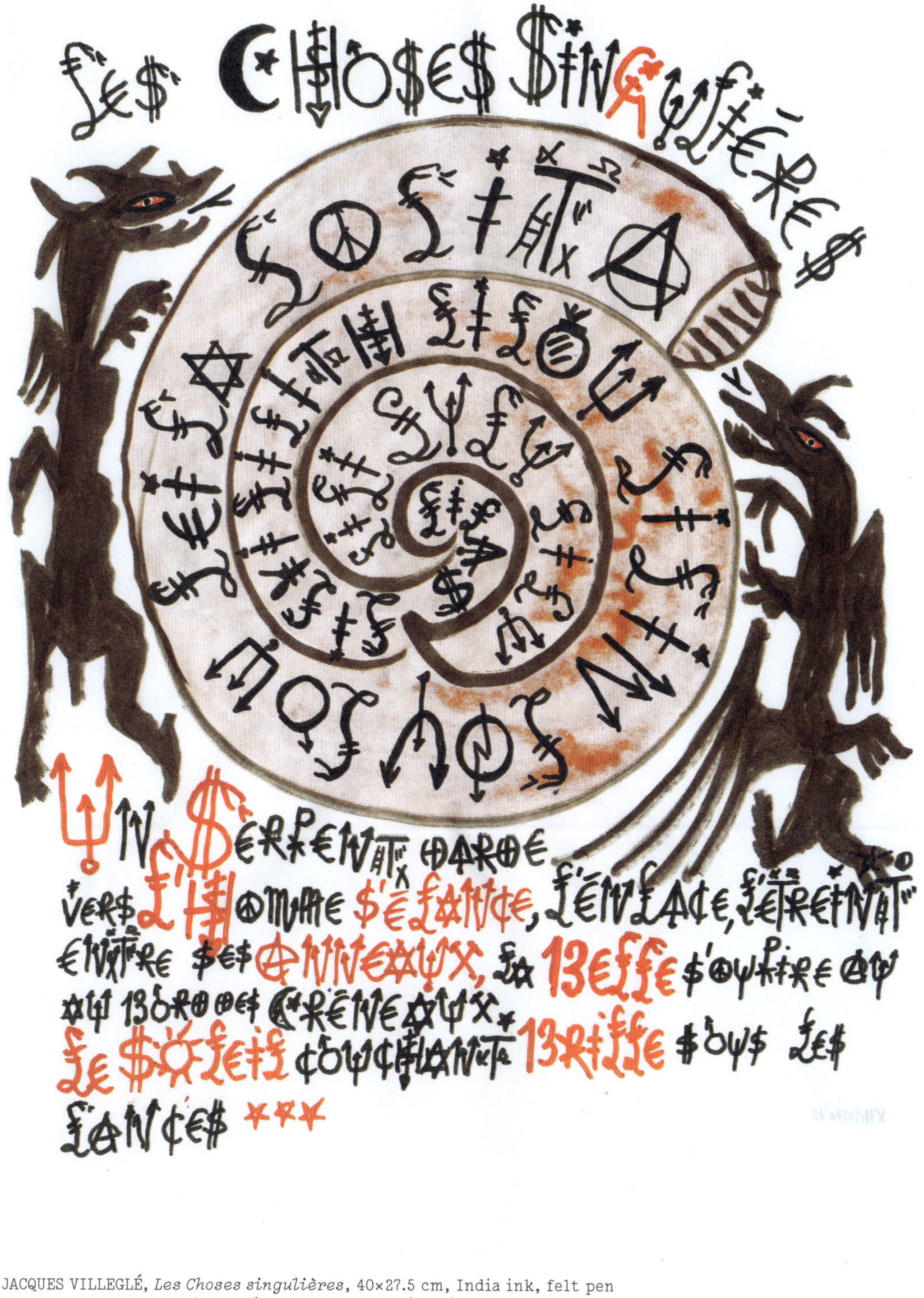

JACQUES VILLEGLÉ, *Les Choses singulières*, 40×27.5 cm, India ink, felt pen on paper, anonymous photo. With Fonds de donation Villegle's kind permission.

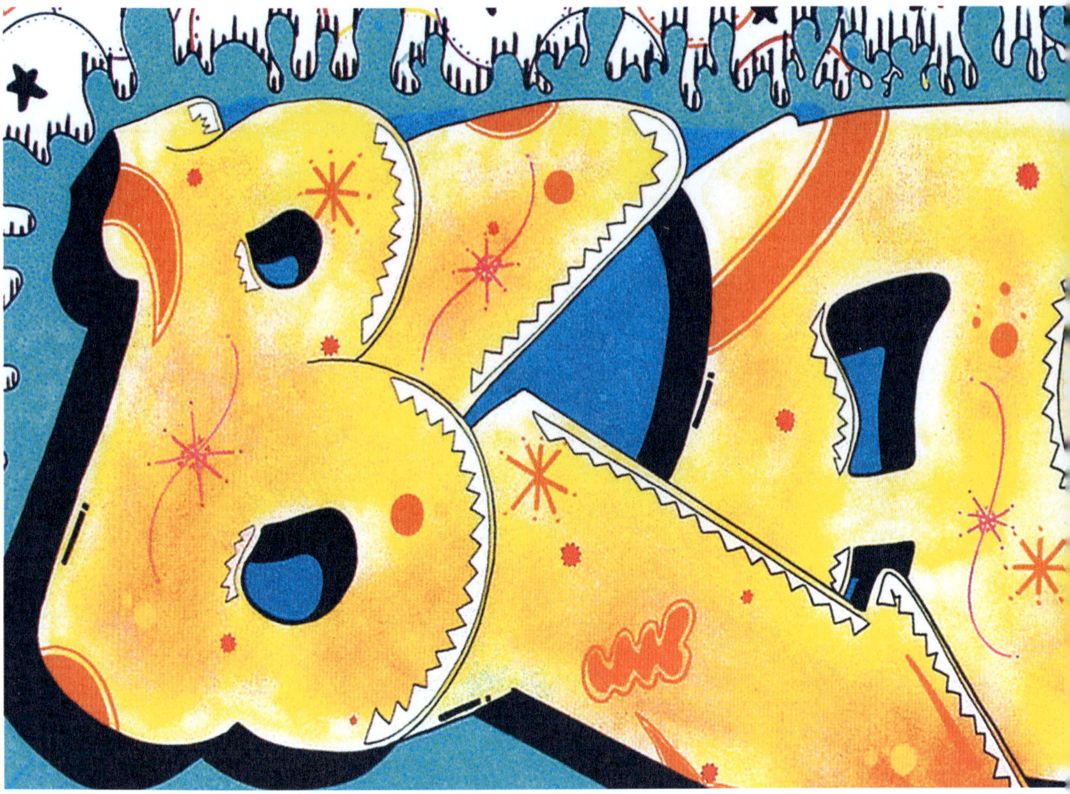

BLADE, *Images*, spray paint and marker on canvas, 60×206 cm, 1986, Henk Pijnenburg collection

In a style that was often very playful and colourful, he combined lettering with a taste for perspective and geometry. At the time, many of his competitors strongly emphasized that this was a departure from pure graffiti. However, the originality of his style was what led Diego Cortez to invite him to participate in the *New York / New Wave* exhibition at the PS1. He was also one of the first to be spotted by Europeans and exhibited on the other side of the Atlantic. Producing many works on canvas, he was stigmatized as an outsider by his peers. However, the infinite variations on the letters of his name are proof, if any was needed, of his innovative talent. With more than a hundred exhibitions worldwide, BLADE is one of the most prolific and enduring urban artists, always ready to serve the cause of traditional graffiti.

In 1979, Stefan Eins, a Vienna native turned New Yorker, opened an art space in the South Bronx called Fashion Moda. The initial objective of Fashion Moda was to invent a cultural concept that was different from classical art galleries. He imagined it as "a collection of science, invention, technology, art and fantasy." He presented many artists from all walks of life. Some of them, from Jenny Holzer, Sophie Calle and Louise Lawler through to Jean-Michel Basquiat and Keith Haring, would become key figures. CRASH and DAZE were among the first graffiti artists whose work he exhibited.

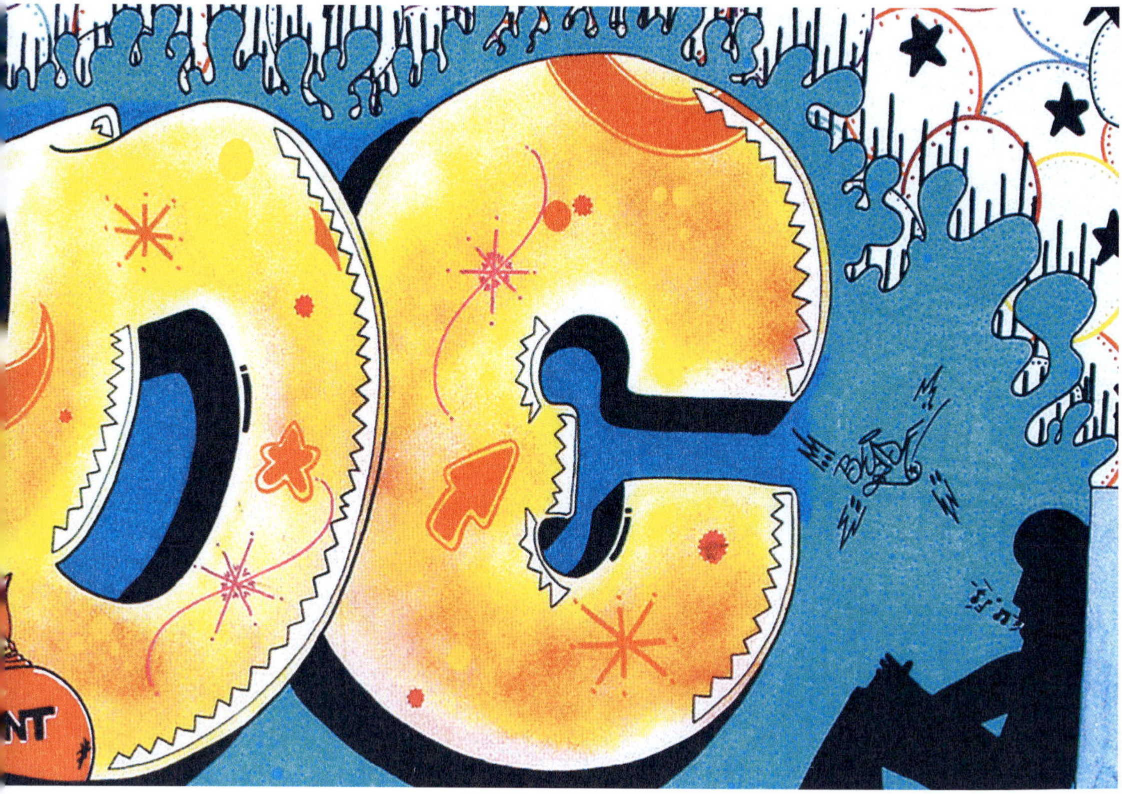

In January 1981, the famous *Artforum* magazine published an article about Fashion Moda, describing its creation and its rise. A month later, another article in the *Arts and Recreation* section of the Sunday edition of the *New York Times* also mentioned the gallery, which soon became a central spot in East Village, an area with links to New Wave Punk. Because it was a nonprofit initiative, Fashion Moda struggled to survive, and it closed its doors in 1993.

Discovering the graffiti movement in the 1980s, KEITH HARING was ecstatic about what he saw. "Graffiti were the most beautiful things I ever saw... These kids, who were obviously very young and from the streets, had this incredible mastery of drawing which totally blew me away. I mean, just the technique of drawing with spray paint is amazing, because it's incredibly difficult to do. And the fluidity of line... And always the hard-edged black line that tied the drawings together! It was the line I had been obsessed with since childhood!"

KEITH HARING was born in 1958 in Reading, Pennsylvania. At a very young age, he developed a taste for drawing, and his father taught him the cartoonist's basic skills. In 1976, he joined the Ivy School of Art in Pittsburgh, which specialized in applied graphic arts. Although he soon realized that he did not have the right motivation to follow a career as a graphic designer, he stayed at the school for two and a half years before

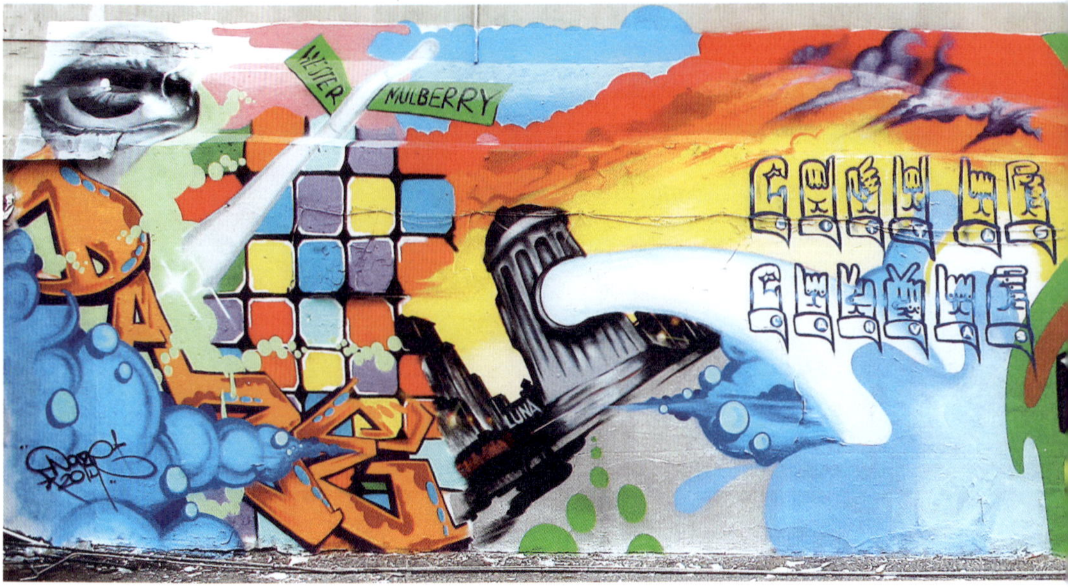

CRASH, *Wall (the L.I.SA. Project)*, Mulberry Street, Little Italy, 10×50 m

CRASH, *The Popeye Wall*, Houston Street, 2013, 20×66 m

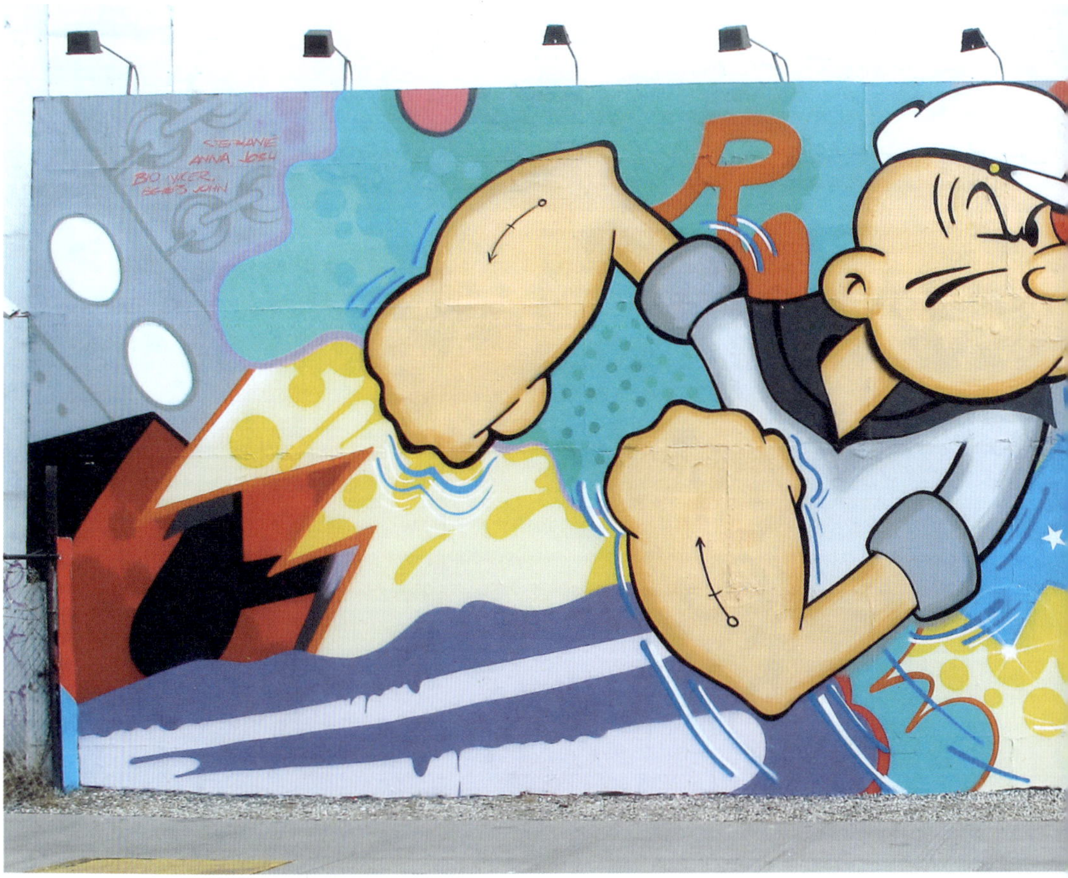

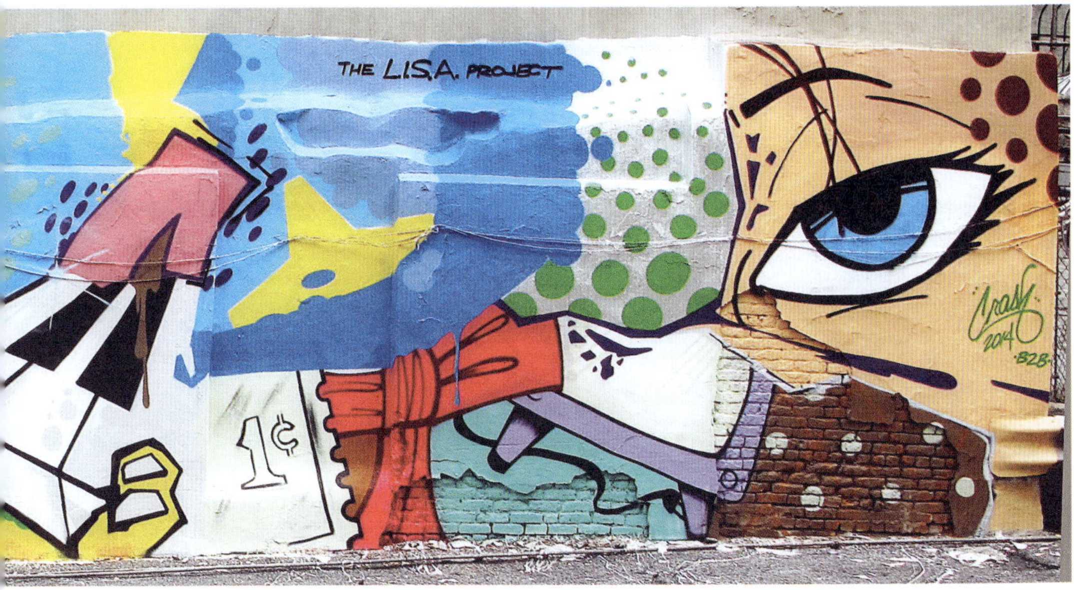

The wall located at the intersection of Houston and Bowery in New York is one of the hot spots of street art. From 1982, it became the focus of artists, such as CRASH here in 2013.

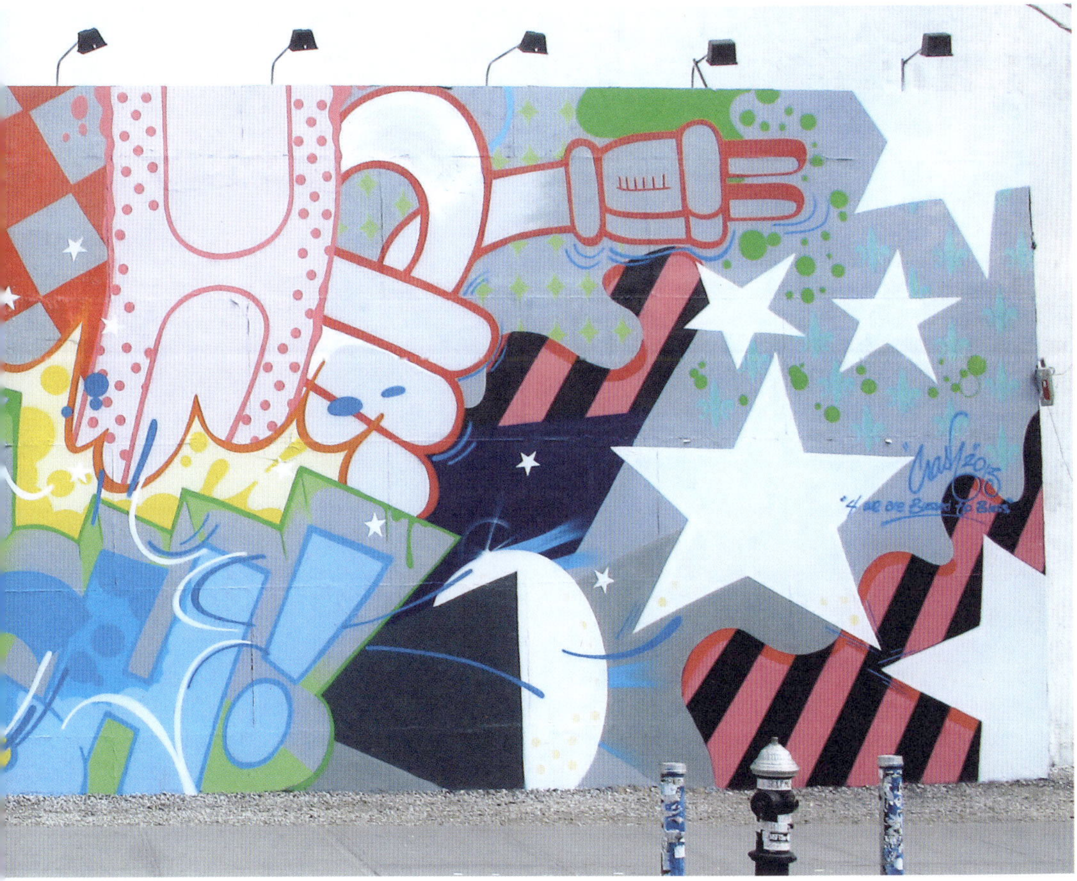

leaving, while at the same time pursuing his personal career ambitions. 1978 was a big year for him: not only did the Arts and Crafts Center of Pittsburgh offer him his first solo exhibition, but he also moved to New York. Upon his arrival, he was fascinated by the graffiti that he discovered in the street, and he began to draw his characters on New York subway billboards with white chalk.

In addition to drawing, he experimented with performance, video, installations and collage during his studies. He soon struck up a friendship with artists like Kenny Scharf and Jean-Michel Basquiat, as well as with musicians, performers and writers. At the heart of the whirlwind New York scene of those years, HARING was an active component of the city's artistic life, through his exhibitions, performances and alternative meetings.

His first New York solo exhibition was held in 1982 at the Tony Shafrazi Gallery. It was a massive public success. That same year, he also exhibited in Rotterdam in the Netherlands. The following year, he was part of a collective exhibition on the graffiti scene at the Fun Gallery. From that moment onwards, his international fame would only continue to grow. Between 1980 and 1985, he was offered twenty-two solo exhibitions, including one by Leo Castelli himself. At the same time, he continued to produce hundreds of drawings in the street—sometimes up to forty a day. For him, the urban universe was a giant laboratory for experimentation: the subway, wooden and metal fencing, dumpsters, unusual objects—everything became a potential canvas for creation and poetry. His meteoric career ended far too early: on 16 February 1990, Keith Haring died of AIDS. He was thirty-one. His urban poetry used graffiti's *modus operandi* of speed. Like street artists who were shaped through painting trains, KEITH HARING expressed himself with simple and precise motions. His personal touch resided in the infinite repetition of forms outlined with a black line and featuring bright, vibrant colours. He developed an aesthetic composed of obvious symbols. For example, a flying saucer represented superior power; Mickey Mouse was synonymous with popular culture; and a red cross meant death and a green one life. The "radiant baby" became his signature and logo. He was above all a reference point for life force, and he had an energy tinged with joy and an almost childish inspiration.

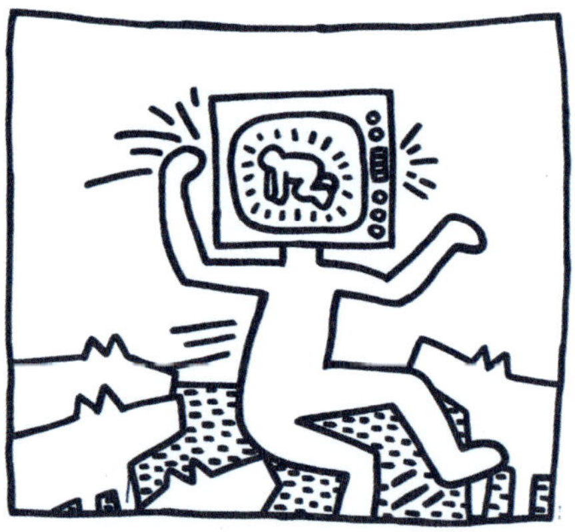

KEITH HARING artwork © Keith Haring Foundation with their kind permission.

CRASH, real name John Matos, was born in 1961 in the Bronx. Following the previously mentioned successful debut at Fashion Moda, he has had a prominent artistic career, exhibiting throughout the world. His style is inspired by the visual environment in which he grew up: the America of the 1960s and 1970s. Patchworks of pop and ad imagery (logos, close-ups of faces and so forth), his works echo the art in vogue at the time.

Following double-page spreads: graffiti in New York City. Photos © Stéphane Bisseuil

Film star Patti Astor launched the Fun Gallery in East Village, creating a bridge between the posh environments of the art scene and the graffiti of the Bronx and Brooklyn. Jeffrey Deitch, a key figure in the art world, would declare it "one of the hottest galleries in the city." In 1980, CRASH was chosen to curate one of the first graffiti exhibitions organized there. He invited eleven friends to create works either on the walls or on canvas. Among those chosen were: MITCH, KEL, 139th, DISCO 107, FUTURA, ALI, ZEPHYR and LADY PINK. Over the years, the Fun Gallery would host the street artists FAB 5 FREDDY, FUTURA, DONDI, KENNY SCHARF, SHARP, A-ONE, LEE, RAMMELLZEE and many others. The exhibitions had important repercussions on the international scene and gave graffiti the beginnings of legitimacy in the eyes of the authorized art world. For many artists presented there, it was an unexpected opportunity for solo exhibition.

In February, the art critic and curator Diego Cortez presented the *New York / New Wave* exhibition at PS1, one of the main centres of contemporary art in New York. The exhibition highlighted in particular works by unknown young artists such as Jean-Michel Basquiat. The publication of a highly comprehensive catalogue seized the attention of critics around the world. The exhibition also gave rise to controversy. The *Village Voice* critic Peter Schjeldahl deplored the exhibition's "participatory narcissism." Critics denounced what they considered a recapturing of a free movement by the fashion industry. In spite of all this, the exhibition was a historic one owing to its billing of star artists and creators such as Jean-Michel Basquiat, William Borroughs, Henry Chalfant, Larry Clark, CRASH, DONDI, FUTURA, Nan Goldin, KEITH HARING, Joseph Kosuth, Robert Mapplethorpe, QUIK, Kenny Scharf, SEEN, Andy Warhol and Lawrence Weiner. In April, FAB 5 FREDDY was so inspired by his participation in the Fashion Moda exhibition that he organized his own at the Mudd Club entitled *Beyond Words*. Through it, he introduced the work of Afrika Bambaataa. As the name of the exhibition indicates, for these artists the idea was now to go "beyond words" and the simple tag. The diversity of artists was such that FAB 5 FREDDY would produce a collaborative piece in 1981 with Olivier Mosset, a Swiss contemporary artist and founding member of the BMTP group along with Daniel Buren, among others.

One year later, Fashion Moda had acquired such fame that the gallery and its artists were invited to Documenta 7 in Kassel, Germany, which was organized by Rudi Fuchs[3] and considered to be one of the most prestigious contemporary events in the world. For the event, the gallery was faithfully rebuilt on site and there were editions and t-shirts by artists such as Jenny Holzer, KEITH HARING, Kenny Scharf, Mike Glier, Tom Otterness, Kiki Smith and Louise Lawler. In addition, many video works by Charlie Ahearn, Jane Dickson, Dieter Froese, Joseph Nechvatal and Glenn O'Brien were presented and offered for sale. Art critic Benjamin Buchloh welcomed the exhibition as "one of the few courageous curatorial choices" on Documenta's part.

[3] Rudi Fuchs: this Dutch historian and art critic, who was born in 1942, became the director of the Van Abbemuseum in Eindhoven in 1975. In 1982, he became artistic director of the essential meeting place for contemporary art: Documenta 7 in Kassel, Germany. He then took charge of the Gemeentemuseum in the Hague and then the Stedelijk Museum in Amsterdam.

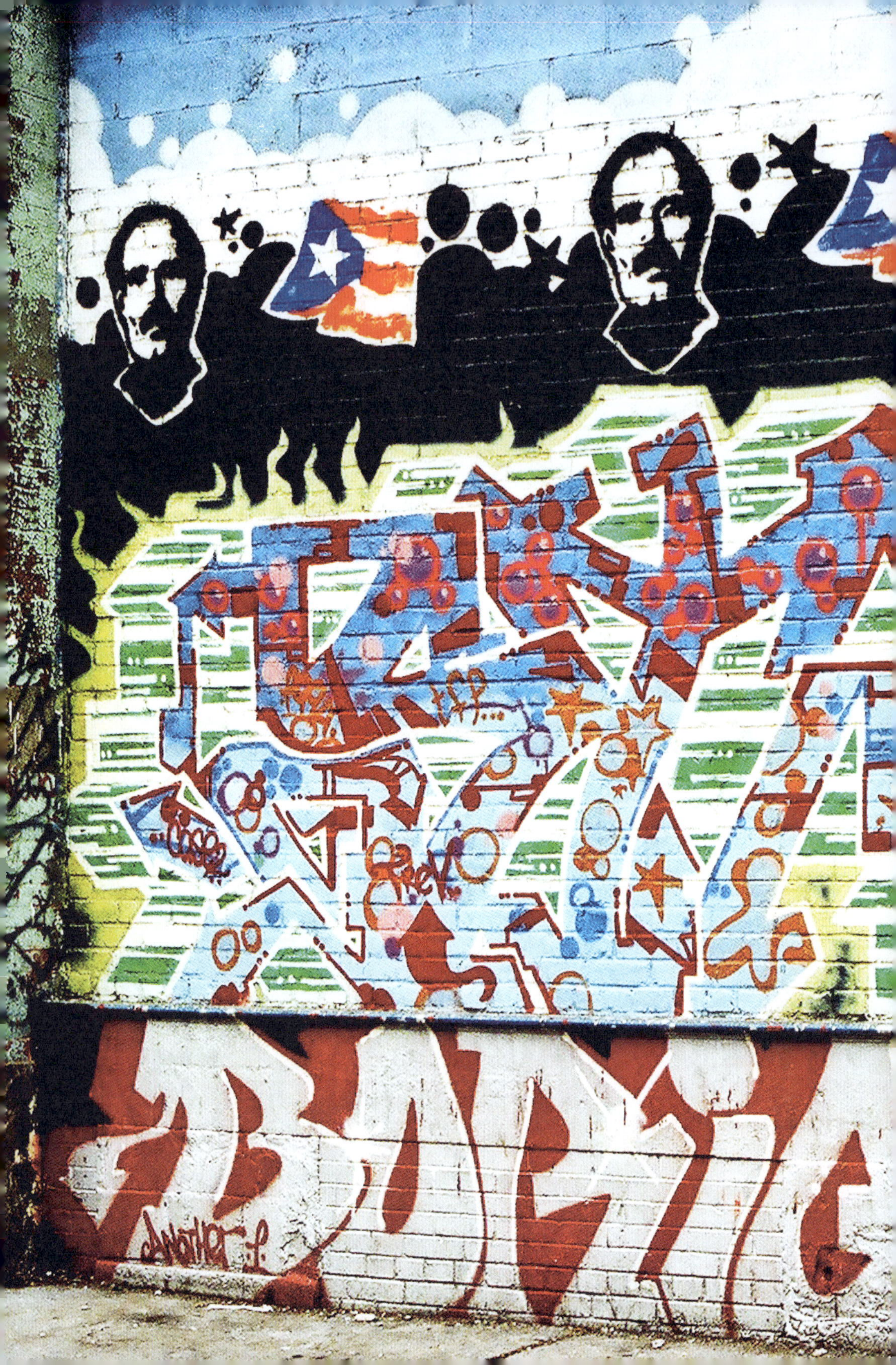

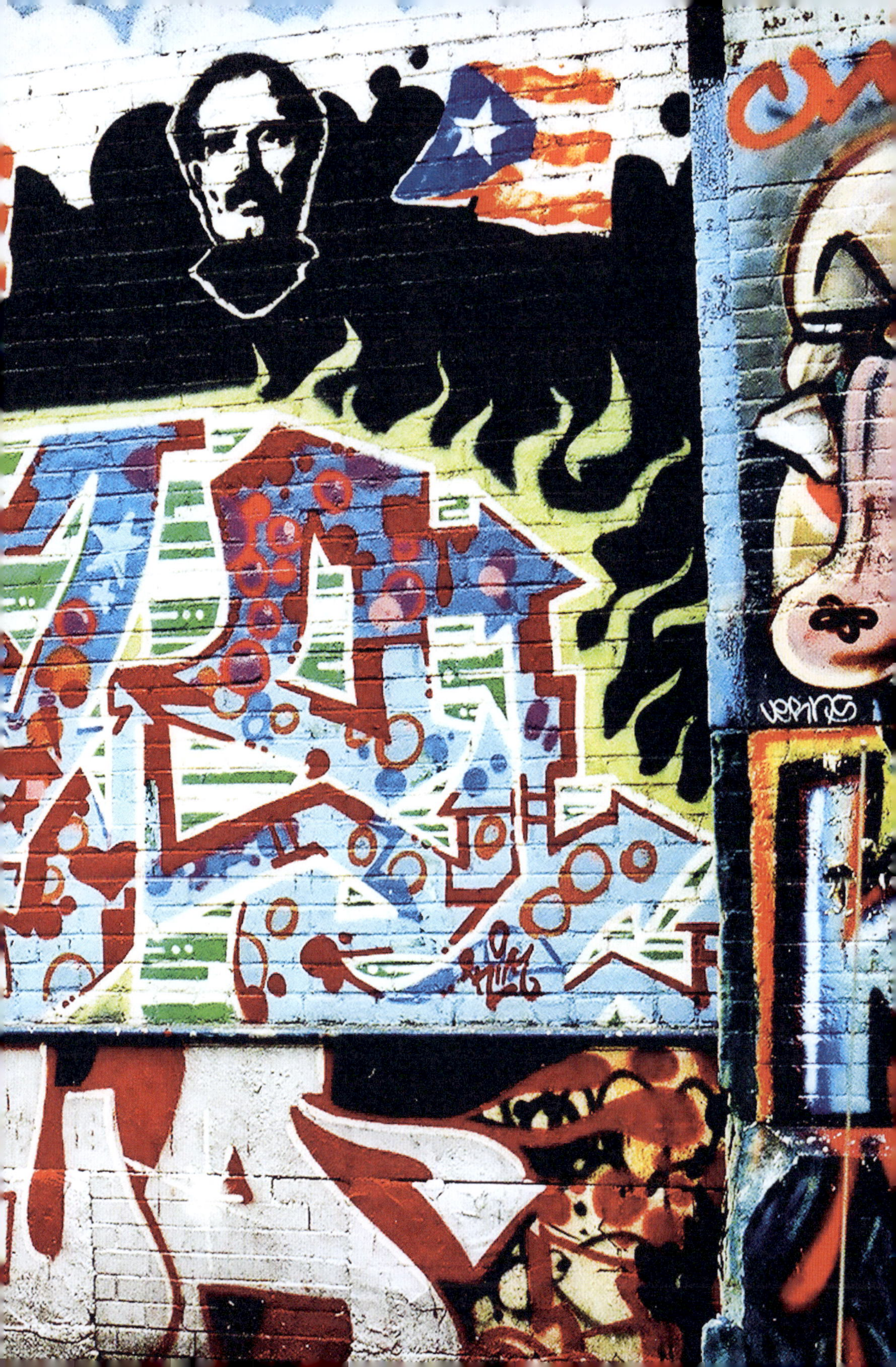

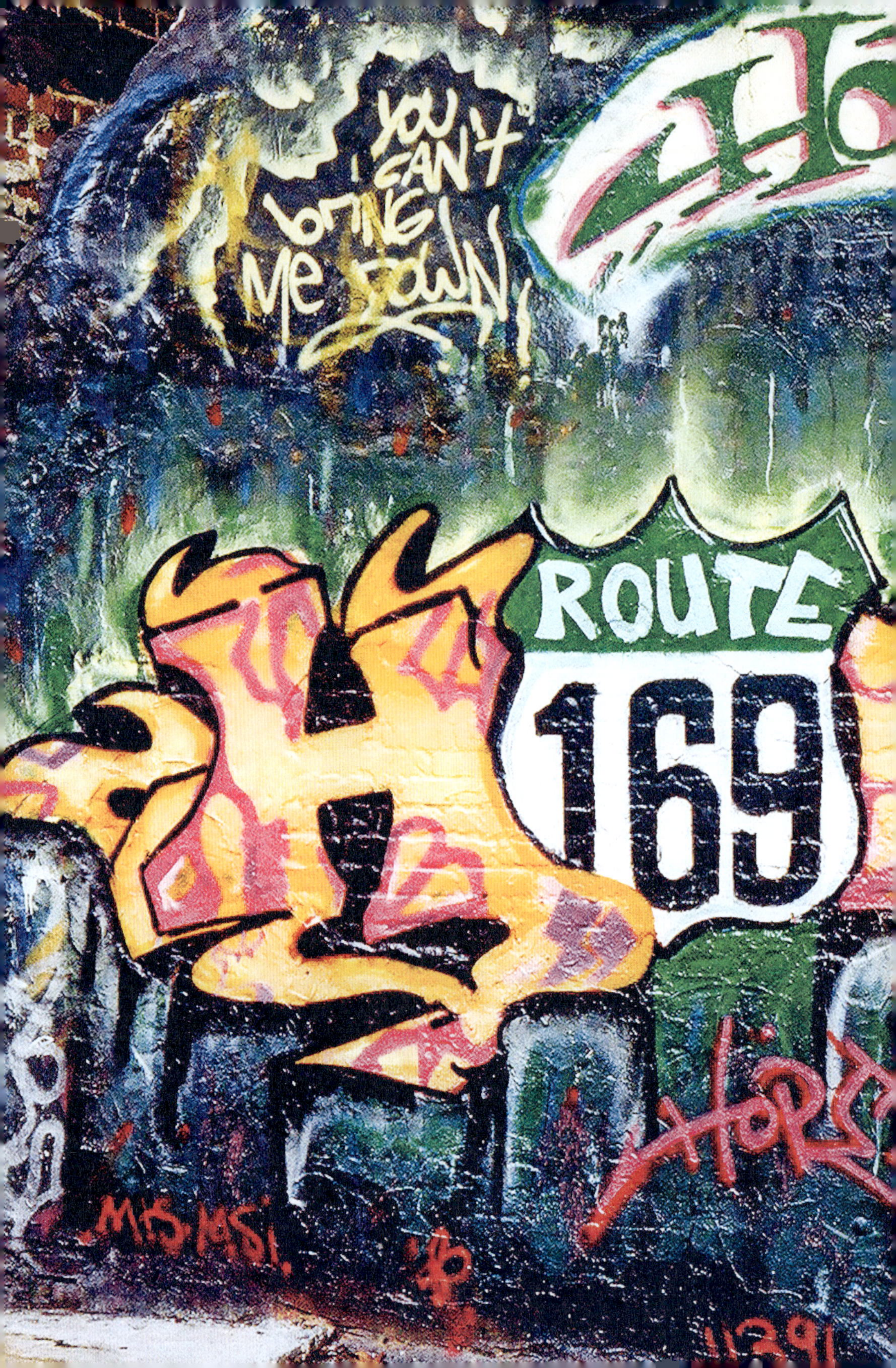
YOU CAN'T
BRING
ME DOWN
ROUTE
169

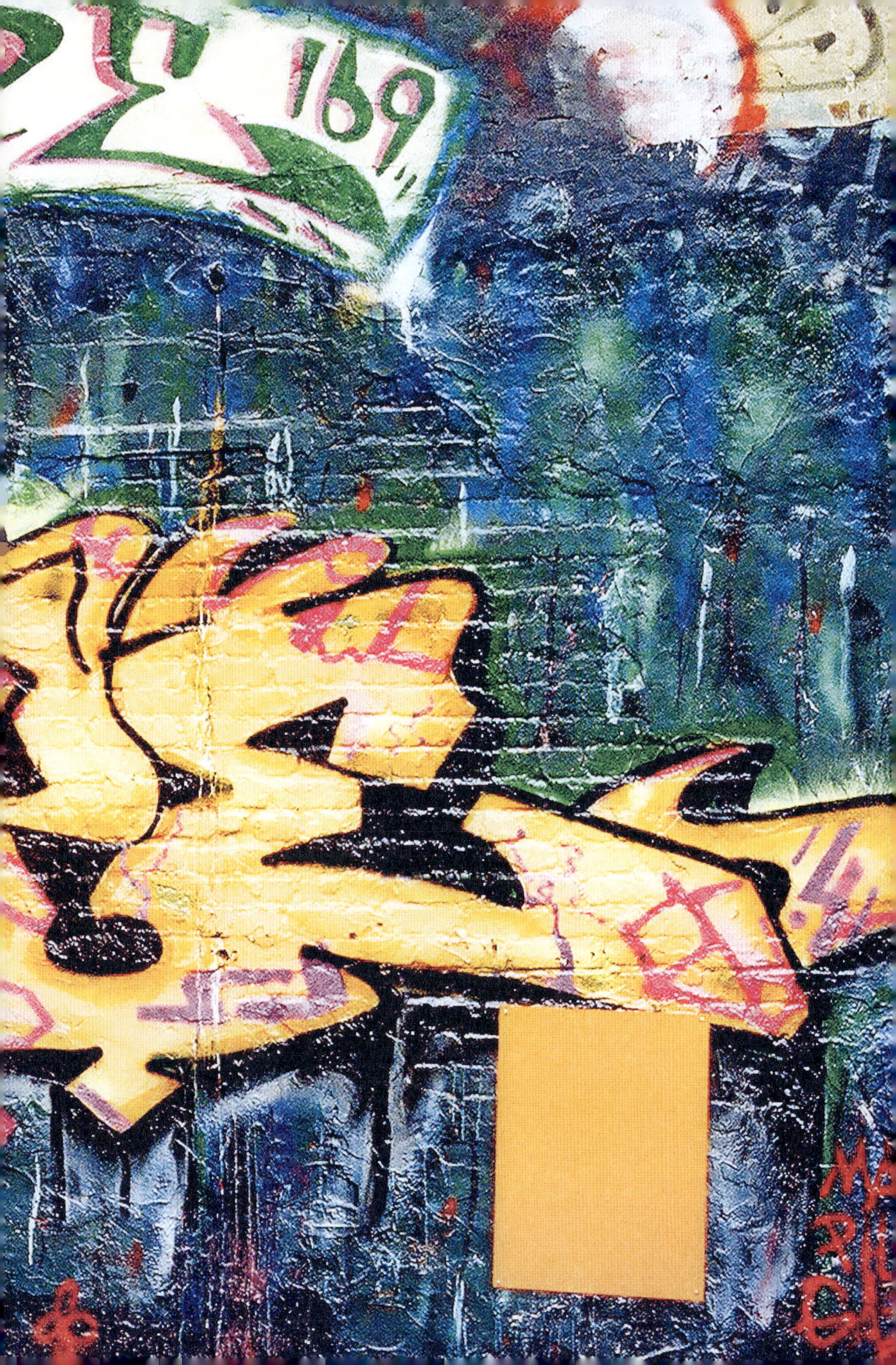

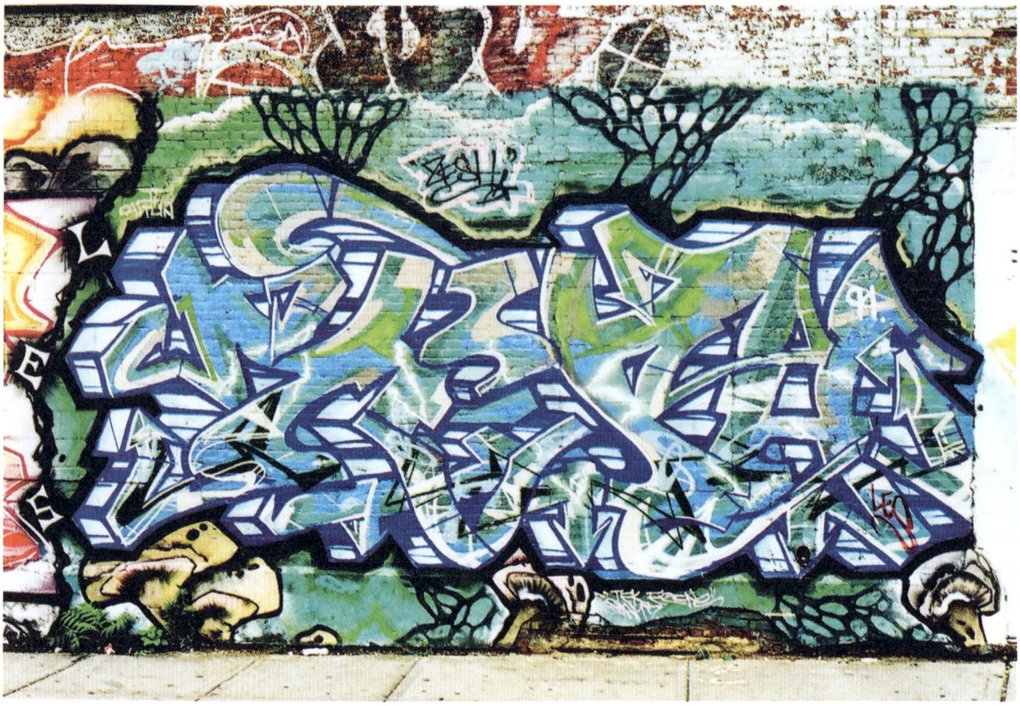

Graffiti in New York. Photo © Stéphane Bisseuil

Graffiti in New York. Photo © Stéphane Bisseuil

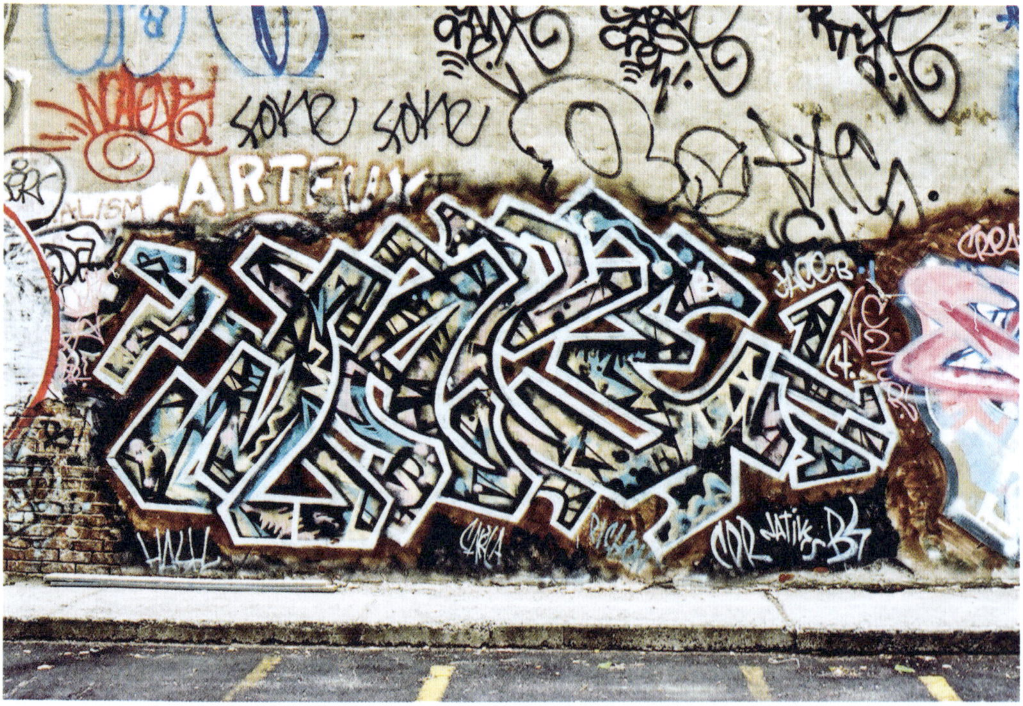

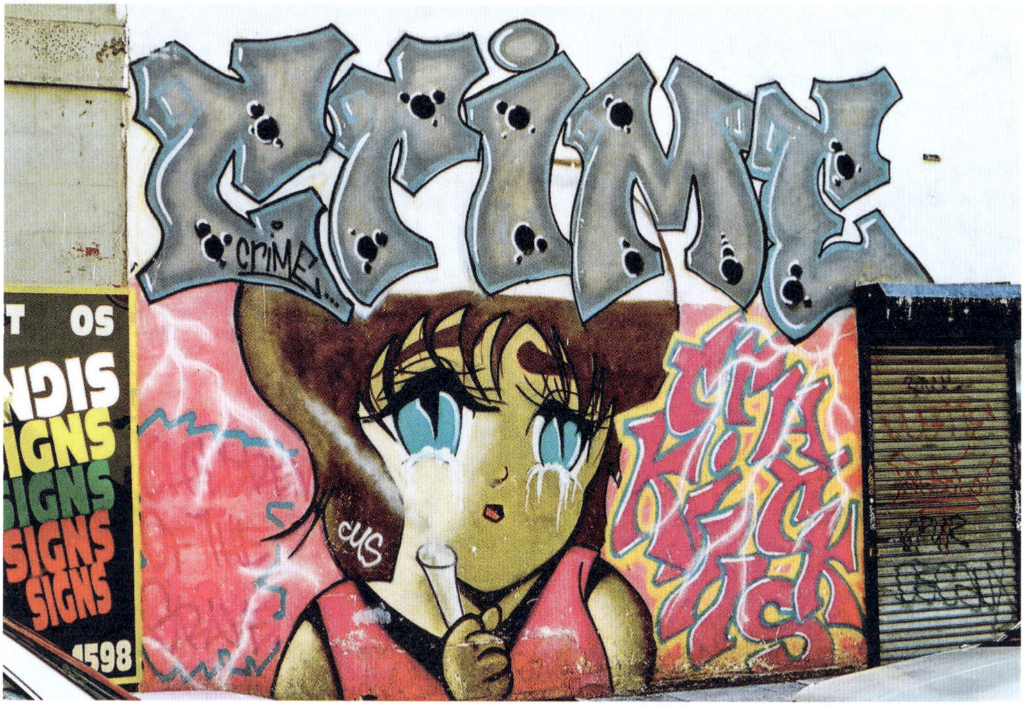

Graffiti in New York. Photo © Stéphane Bisseuil

Graffiti in New York. Photo © Stéphane Bisseuil

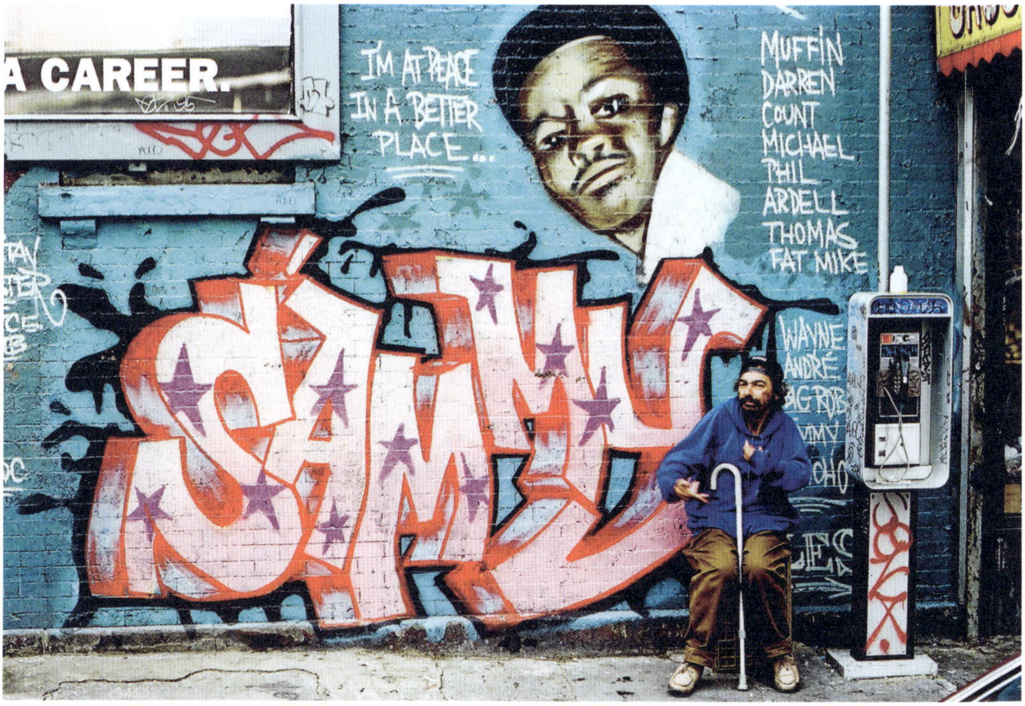

Between 1980 and 1989, LAME, DAZE, SEEN, CRASH and FUTURA were the stars of more than two hundred exhibitions across the world. Besides Fashion Moda and the Fun Gallery, more so-called mainstream New York galleries like those of Sidney Janis and Tony Shafrazi exhibited graffiti.

Cinema also contributed to increasing the fame of many of these artists. Many of them were consulted during the production of videos and films that talk about New York's culture and urban environment of the time. For example, RAMMELLZEE was involved as an actor, though playing himself, in Jim Jarmusch's film *Stranger Than Paradise* (1984). LEE, FAB 5 FREDDY and Jean Michel Basquiat contributed to Blondie's video for "Rapture". LEE worked on the Susan Seidelman movies *Smithereens* (1982) and *Desperately Seeking Susan* (1985).

In addition to many one-off projects, two films would anchor the movement in the film world.

Wild Style, released in 1983 and produced by Charlie Ahearn, is often regarded as the first hip-hop movie. It includes the greats of the time, from FAB 5 FREDDY to LEE, LADY PINK and RAMMELLZEE. DONDI painted the title of the film on the subway. The logo that he created would be the basis for the poster for the film. Along with LADY PINK, his on-screen and lifelong companion, and actress Patti Astor, LEE practically played himself in a very free storyline. This cult film above all captured the atmosphere of the time. It demonstrated the interconnection between different hip-hop practices and also highlighted issues inherent in the movement: being exhibited in a gallery and the future of this artistic practice.
The second film, Tony Silver's *Style Wars*, is usually regarded as a documentary. Produced in 1983 with the help of Henry Chalfant, the photographer who captured the first moments of graffiti, the film explores graffiti practice in depth. It showcases the history of young graffiti artists and describes the difficulties that they experienced. Among other artists, DONDI and SEEN appeared in it. Although it was originally created for television, it nevertheless won the Grand Jury Prize at the Sundance Festival and also became a manifesto film for the movement and this generation of artists, some of whom displayed a truly artistic approach from very early on and would soon stand out from the crowd. Like DONDI or FUTURA, A-ONE also left an enduring mark on the movement.

Anthony Clark, aka A-ONE, was born in Manhattan in 1964. At the age of six, his artistic talent was clear to all. But like many self-taught artists, the street was his true classroom. It would only be much later that he would study architecture, an area in which he developed a strong interest. Despite being the target of criticism from other street artists, A-ONE chose for a long time to not paint trains, preferring instead to express himself on walls and canvas.
Regardless of his preferred medium, he stood out owing to a style that was particularly expressive and abstract—or even wild, in the view of some.

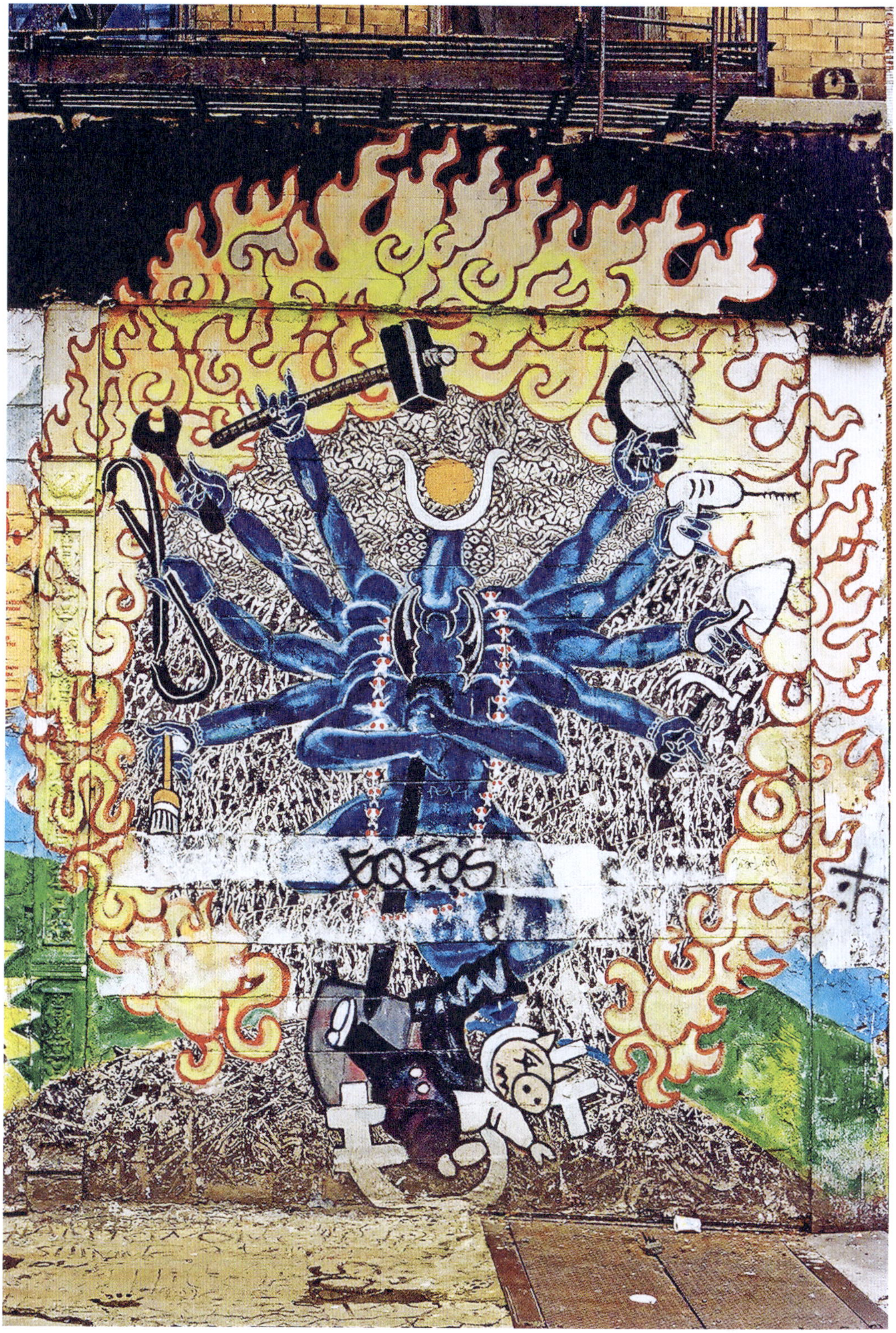

Graffiti in New York. Photo © Stéphane Bisseuil

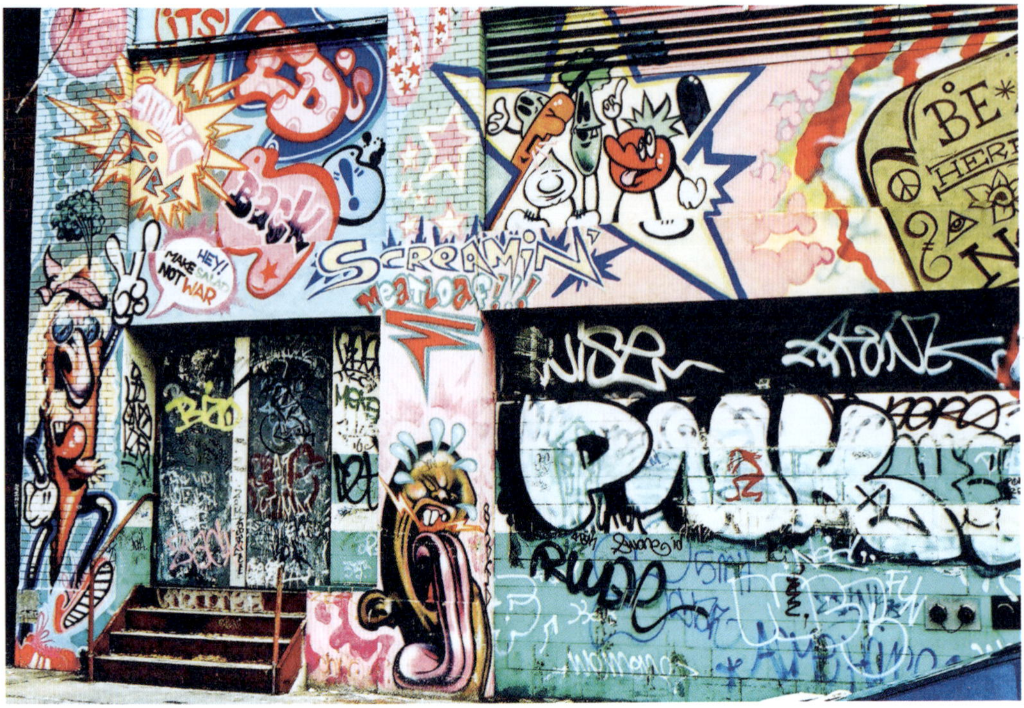

Graffiti in New York. Photo © Stéphane Bisseuil

Graffiti in New York. Photo © Stéphane Bisseuil

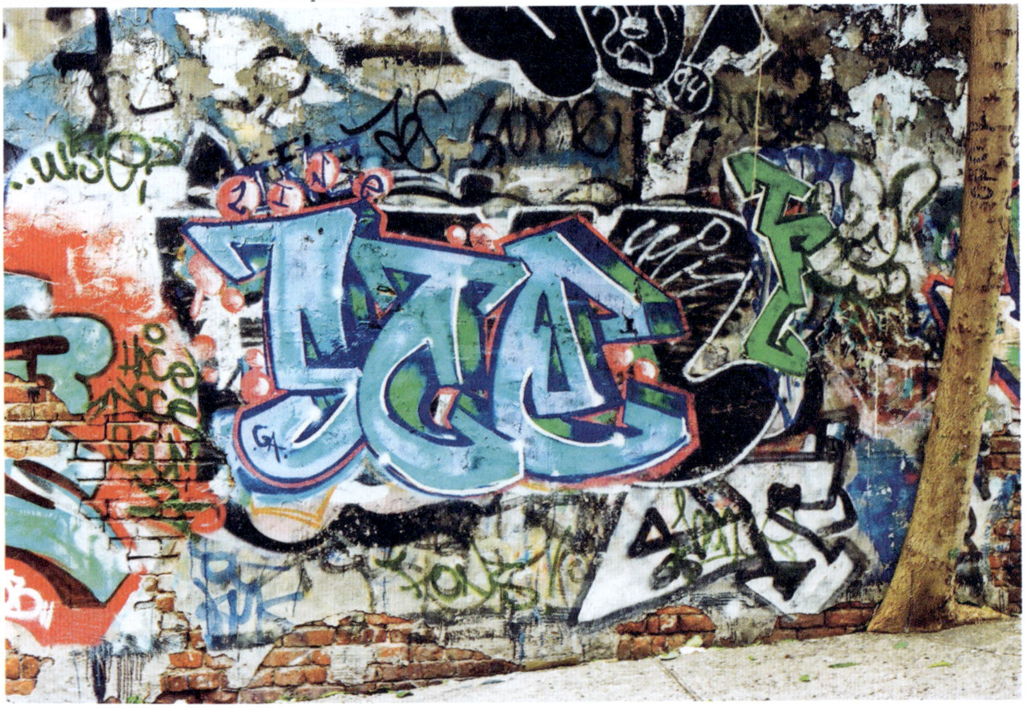

A key fixture in the nascent graffiti scene, and exhibited in galleries and museums from Fashion Moda (in 1982) to the Venice Biennale (1984), A-ONE emerged from the beginning as a full-fledged artist, an identity that he was proud of asserting: "I look at myself as an artist or better, an aerosol expressionist, not as a graffiti artist. Everyone can call it graffiti, I don't mind, I know what I'm doing." His highly abstract painting is charged with energetic lines that blend and overlap in a kind of secret language where it is possible to decipher here and there a symbol, a hidden sentence or a portrait of Rasta character. His work reflects the quest for a symbiosis between American culture and that of his African roots. Fighting against "Babylon the Great," described in the Bible's Book Of Revelation as "the mother of prostitutes and abominations of the earth," A-ONE preached a certain urban mythology. He peppered his works with mystical spiritual and Rasta references, highlighting a certain cultural plurality similar to that of Jean-Michel Basquiat, his friend and adviser. He died in Paris in 2001, leaving behind a body of work and a career that, although often cryptic, were coherent and an innovative part of the movement.

Meanwhile, JEAN-MICHEL BASQUIAT, born in Brooklyn in 1960, was perfectly at one with this group of friends. His first pseudonym was SAMO, for "Same Old Shit." While the rise of graffiti was in full swing, SAMO followed his own path, not normally partaking in traditional graffiti other than on a solo basis. He independently found his own way and artistic style. In 1979, he covered the SoHo neighbourhood with the inscription "Samo is dead."

Whether or not to include this unique figure in the history of graffiti is a thorny question. Although he undoubtedly knew graffiti artists, started at sixteen with his artist street friends and followed them for a while, BASQUIAT always had a style that was his own, and in which graffiti was one component among others. He never boasted of having done this or that train, and nor did he seek to make murals in the same way as his peers. And he had little involvement in the style war that prevailed in the 1970s, having already found himself on an artistic level and having taken his own path.

But no one can deny, upon studying the styles of FUTURA, A-ONE or RAMMELLZEE, that the creative exploration of these artists—from the symbols used (crowns, stars, writing and so on) to the intended symbolism (the issue of an American counterculture in opposition to conceptual art and pop art)—had many points in common.

Following double-page spread:
A-ONE, *The Babylon System, The Prophet Rides Again*, spray painting on canvas, 205.5×254 cm, 1985, private collection

The issue of American counterculture is essential for understanding the importance of graffiti in the history of art. Although sociologically speaking it is accepted in the United States that the "centre" is the dominant thinking of the time, and that the "fringe" is the "underground," it seems that the former inevitably feeds on the latter. At a time when pop art in particular reigned supreme in the United States—and a more conceptual kind of art dominated in Europe—graffiti was the "underground." This

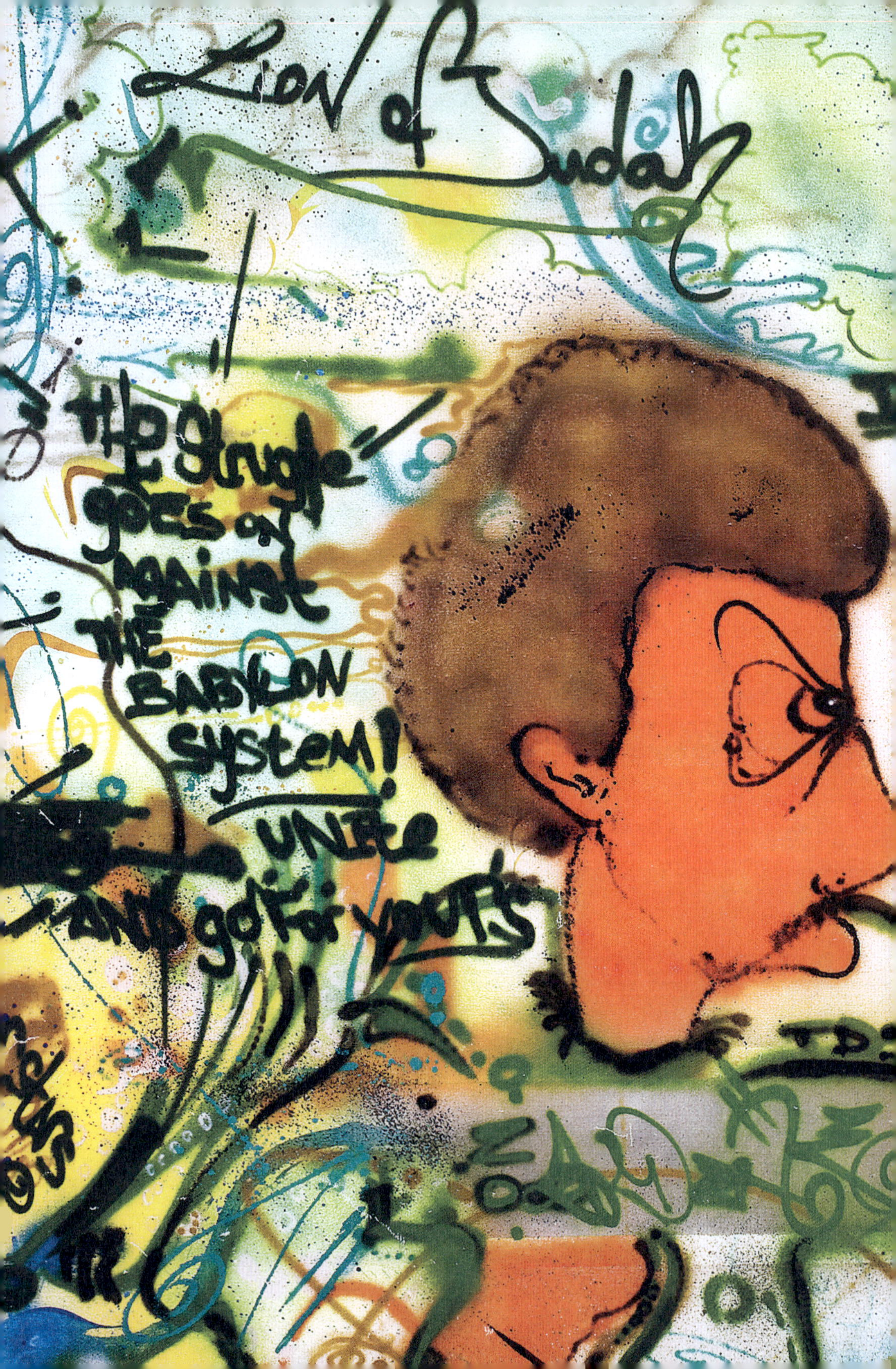
Lion of Judah
The struggle goes on against the Babylon system!
Unite and go for your's

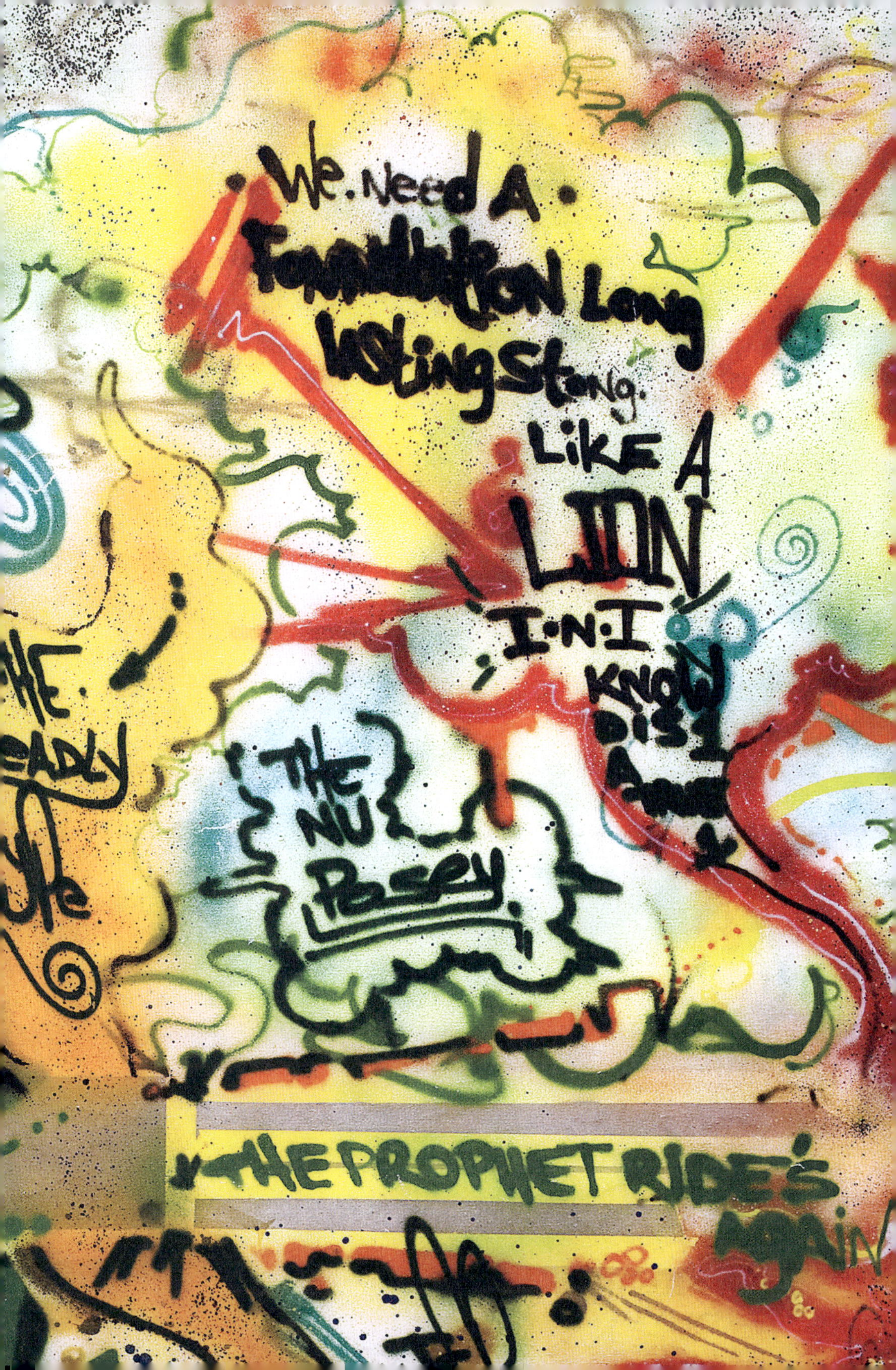
We. Need A
LIKE A
LION
I.N.I
KNOW
DIS 1
THE NU Posey
THE PROPHET RIDE'S AGAIN

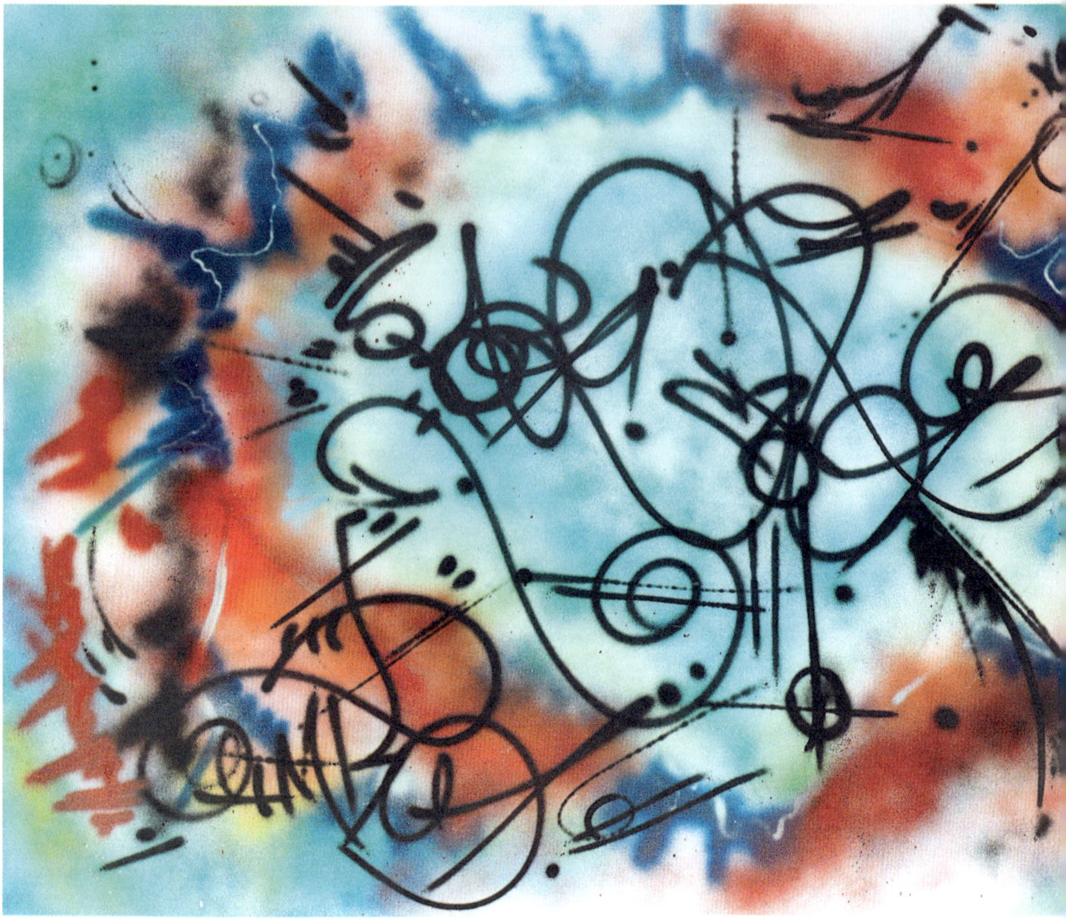

A-ONE, *The Overture Explosion (The Wall)*, spray painting on canvas, 129.5×230cm, 1983, private collection. Photo © Michel Gurfinkel

counterculture quickly became the centre of attention. Exhibitions in East Village or at the PS1 from the beginning of the 1980s testify to this.

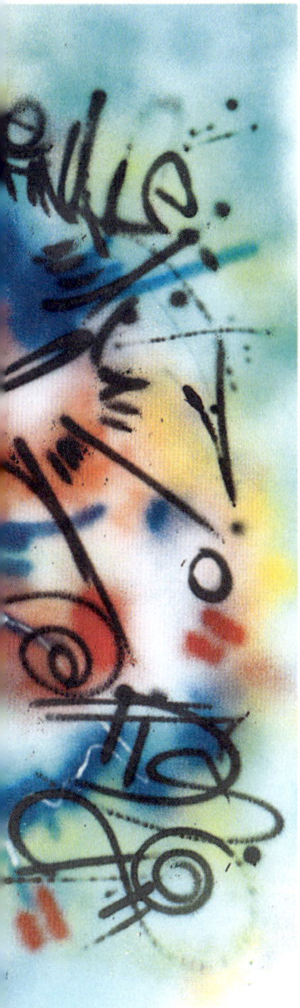

Although in France the history of urban art comes from other sources, it is also undoubtedly contained in the history of official art, as evidenced by the practice of figures such as VILLEGLÉ or DEGOTTEX. In May 1968, for example, DEGOTTEX, an internationally recognized abstract painter, stopped giving classes at the Beaux-Arts in Paris to teach his students about making posters to put up in the street.
These different relationships to art show that from very early on street art and urban art belonged to a movement that was committed to having an artistic existence. Its legality would be a different matter, with the invasion of the street being problematic in more than one respect for the authorities.

THE RENEWAL AND ROOTING OF URBAN ART

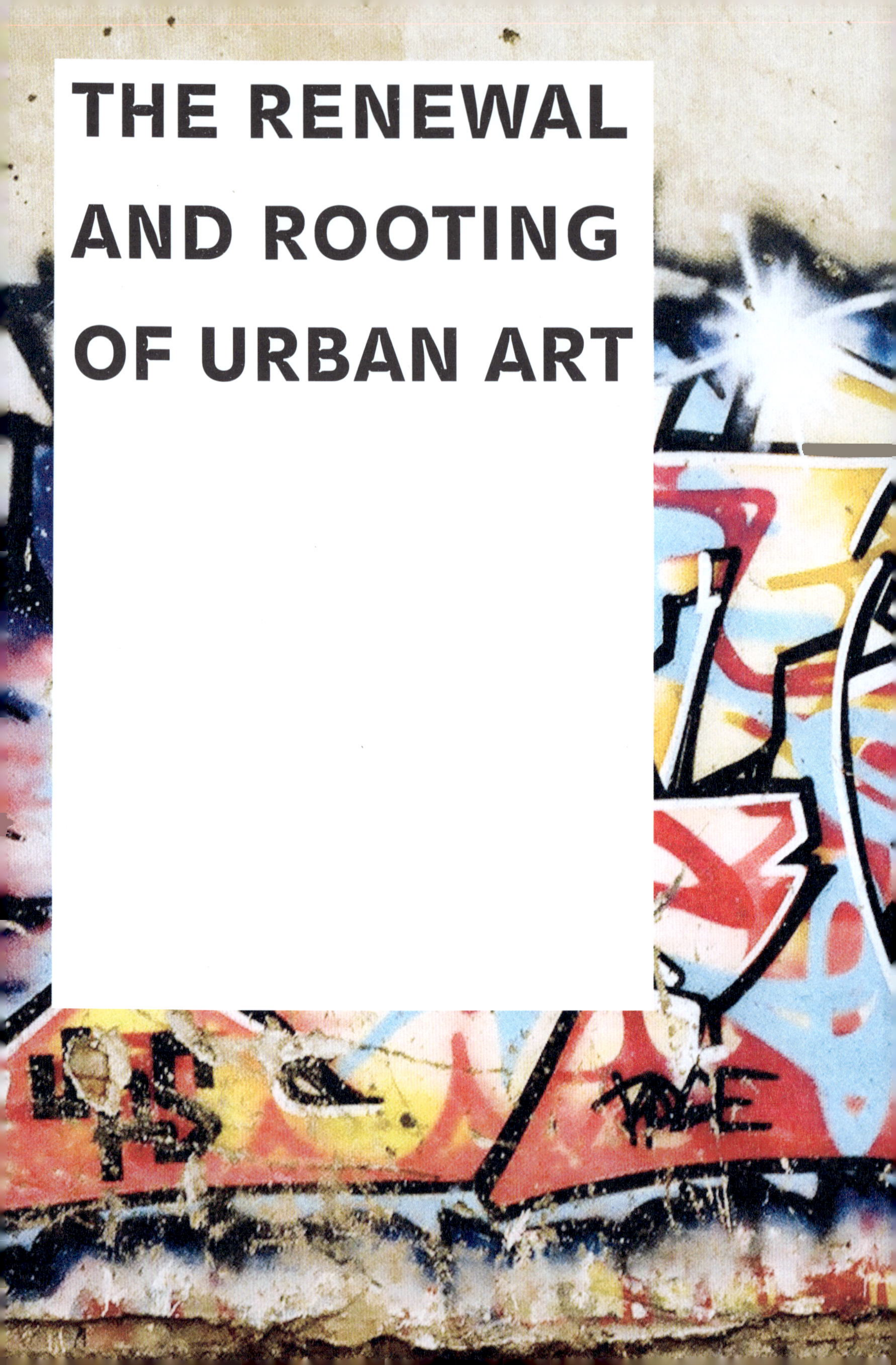

A CONTEXT OF RETREAT AND REPRESSION 77

The war against graffiti 77

Graffiti, cause of all society's ills 78

Learning and documenting 79

The race to survive 80

A WORLDWIDE OUTBREAK 83

The new playing field 83

The crossover with Europe 85

The European scene's first steps 92

Stalingrad, the cradle of European graffiti 104

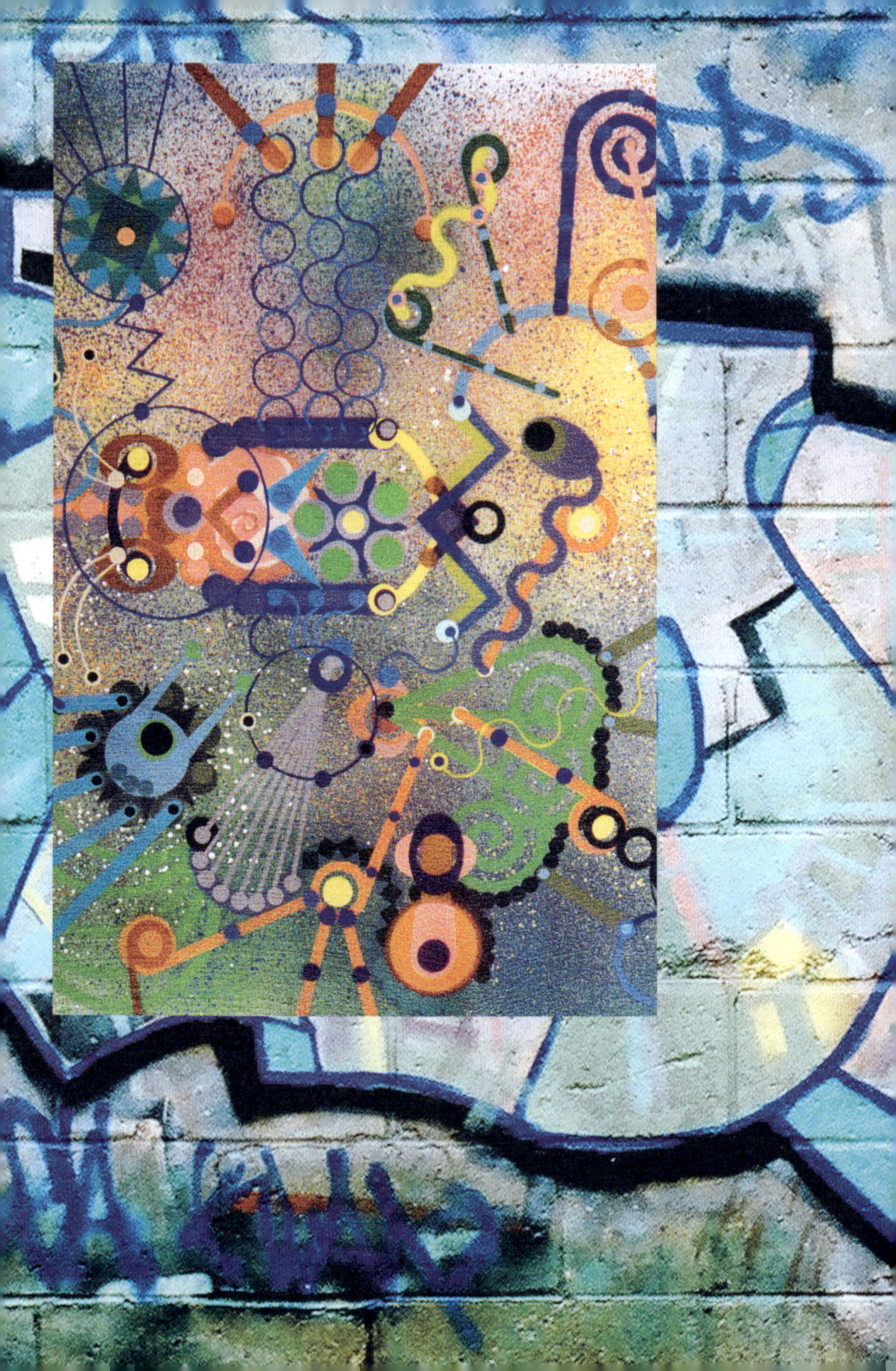

A CONTEXT OF RETREAT AND REPRESSION

The war against graffiti

In 1972, New York City mayor John Lindsay officially declared a "war on graffiti." This phenomenon would continue intensify as the years passed. The movement came under great threat, and not only from the outside in the form of stronger laws to target it directly, but also from the inside, with the rise of crack and arms trafficking gnawing away at it from within. Philadelphia, the cradle of graffiti, was also one of the first cities to implement a network to repress it, the PAGN (Philadelphia Anti-Graffiti Network). A link between the war against graffiti and the war against gangs was established, and repression raged. Paradoxically, the PAGN was also responsible for the Mural Arts Program, which was behind the commissioning of many legal murals.

With the advent of the movement and its media coverage, controversy raged over whether the development of this form of expression that was blossoming on subways and walls was art or a form of vandalism. *The New York Sun* spoke of a "generation that refuses to grow up" and even likened graffiti's spread to metastasis. It denounced the position of the *New York Times*, which viewed the phenomenon as an artistic movement.

ASH, Untitled, Spray paint on canvas, 90×120 cm, 1992 (detail) © A.R.R.

Behind: graffiti in New York City. Photo © Stéphane Bisseuil

Ed Koch, mayor of New York from 1979 to 1989, advocated zero tolerance. Graffiti was identified as causing decay in poor neighbourhoods. Antigraffiti budgets climbed in order to bring about systematic eradication. Works that once had a lifespan of several weeks were erased after a few days, clipping the wings of the artists who produced them.

Graffiti, cause of all society's ills

Antigraffiti advertising campaigns were launched. In 1982, New York City invited local celebrities —from boxers Hector Camacho and Alex Ramos to actors such as Irene Cara and Gene Ray from *Fame*— to deliver the on-air slogan "Make your mark in society, not on society." In this context, graffiti artists became more organized. New techniques that were more difficult to erase emerged, such as markers made using paint and polish. Style wars and aesthetic exploration became ancient history; leaving a mark became the sole priority.

In the history of graffiti, the years 1984 to 1989 were ones of intense repression. Nearly a thousand employees set about cleaning the 6,245 subway cars and the 465 stations of the network, drawing on an annual budget of $52 million. Security was tightened around railway stations, which were encircled with barbed wire and transformed into fortresses. Punishments were so heavy that some street artists went as far as changing their names. Many of them became disheartened and gave up. In 1989, the MTA officially announced its "victory" over graffiti.

The "broken windows theory" developed by the mayor of New York Rudolph Giuliani (elected to his first term in 1994) gained popularity across the United States. According to Giuliani, a single broken window in a neighbourhood contributed to increasing feelings of insecurity by giving the impression that it had been abandoned by the authorities and that it would therefore attract crime, which would feed a vicious cycle. Paradoxically, graffiti was directly implicated as a factor in the impoverishment of neighbourhoods.

Jurisdictions faced with the problem of street art are able to set up their own legal response. In some places, there has been a crackdown on even the act of walking around with spray paint. In Los Angeles, a system named TaggerTrap has been tested out. It is based on the fact that spray cans emit a specific sound and has the potential to lead to a large number of arrests. Companies that specialize in the archiving of the data, especially photographs of tags, have helped to fatten the case files against arrested artists. Special units have been put in place. More so than ever, anonymity is a guarantee of survival.

In terms of legislation, street art, and in particular graffiti, has raised many questions about both the degradation of private and public spaces and individual freedoms and freedom of expression. Facing a phenomenon that seemed to be growing in an uncontrolled fashion and to be unstoppable, authorities have attempted to limit its scope and ban it, without making any distinction between vandalism and creation.

Many street artists have thrown in the towel, but others persevered. They have changed their habits and risen to the challenge. And although the question of territory has always provided an underlying impetus to graffiti, in this context it has really come to the fore. A corollary to increased risk is a flow of adrenaline and the feeling of freedom. In seeking to suppress the movement, to a certain degree authorities have made it more virulent. For some, illegality would become the norm, and danger and prohibition their sources of inspiration. Purists came to view any work produced within a legal framework (legal walls, exhibitions) as an illegitimate form of practice, feeding an endless debate and putting in danger the artistic part of graffiti.

Learning and documenting

However, nothing seemed to be able to stop a movement that was both emulated and organized around codes respected by all. The first street artists were followed by new generations who tirelessly practised their art. The graffiti tradition spread through an extremely codified and intense form of learning.

The older artists reminded new entrants of the need to learn the fundamentals. And as they had done in their early days, they advised the newcomers to undergo a demanding process of exploration before making an outdoor work.

Thinking that graffiti is essentially made outdoors is to forget that before painting a train or a wall, a graffiti artist must carry out numerous studies on paper and fill in many books—the famous "blackbooks"—in order to develop style, precision and dexterity. Working indoors is not a contradiction, but rather one of the steps that demonstrate that true works come about within a great tradition. In an immutable order, the preparation of a mural or a train work involves:

1 - preparation on paper (sketches, lines, fluidity of the lettering and so on);
2 - preparation of equipment and supplies;
3 - choice of the place;
4 - production *in situ*;
5 - immediate documentation (photographic records).

Documenting is a critical stage in street art practice and an integral part of the approach. Whatever the outdoor space chosen and the impact sought by ephemeral art, documentation remains the main means of sustaining and sharing the approach.

Photographic records, the only evidence of the exploits carried out, also bear witness to a context: they allow us to understand why the artist chose to operate in this or that place. Context is an integral part of the work, making it resonate as much from an aesthetic point of view as from a symbolic one.

Since the beginning of the movement, street artists have jealously kept their photos, and they sometimes take along photographers who document their creations as comprehensively as possible. Henry Chalfant and Martha Cooper published the first books revealing the "liveliness" and the dexterity of the scene, and their images have become emblematic of the richness of the first years of graffiti.

Many hand-printed fanzines were released and quickly changed hands, allowing a wider audience to be reached.
This documenting, at a time when graffiti was being threatened by the authorities, became the bulwark of street art culture and its history. The strength of people's first-hand testimonies was just as important. Oral transmission of a common history and values made the movement stronger. Codes, whether behavioural, artistic or semantic, involved precision, and a true community emerged. Paradoxically, the intensity of the crackdown only strengthened the feeling of belonging to a worldwide movement. On one side was the law; on the other was a repressed generation that found common codes, mutual support and admiration. It was a community of actors who saw themselves in one another and respected each other even though they were in permanent competition. Those not considered worthy of respect came to be labelled "toys." It became permissible for artists to "toy" these individuals' works—that is, to write the word "toy" on them. This ultimate act of disavowal reflects a system of values that allows the quality of works to be judged. A work of high quality would be preserved, and few would dare to defy its creator by painting over it.

The race to survive

Slowed by the increasing difficulties and debates that they saw as vacuous, some of the greatest street artists decided on a change of horizons and left New York. They went to seek opportunities in cities where their work was authorized, respected and even admired. Across the United States —whether Los Angeles, Washington or the museum of the university in Iowa City— and in institutions in Europe, artists found a haven of peace where they could create with more freedom, and as a result they propagated their practice and their culture beyond the borders of its birthplace. Across the world, the movement grew massively, as it had done in the streets of New York ten years earlier.

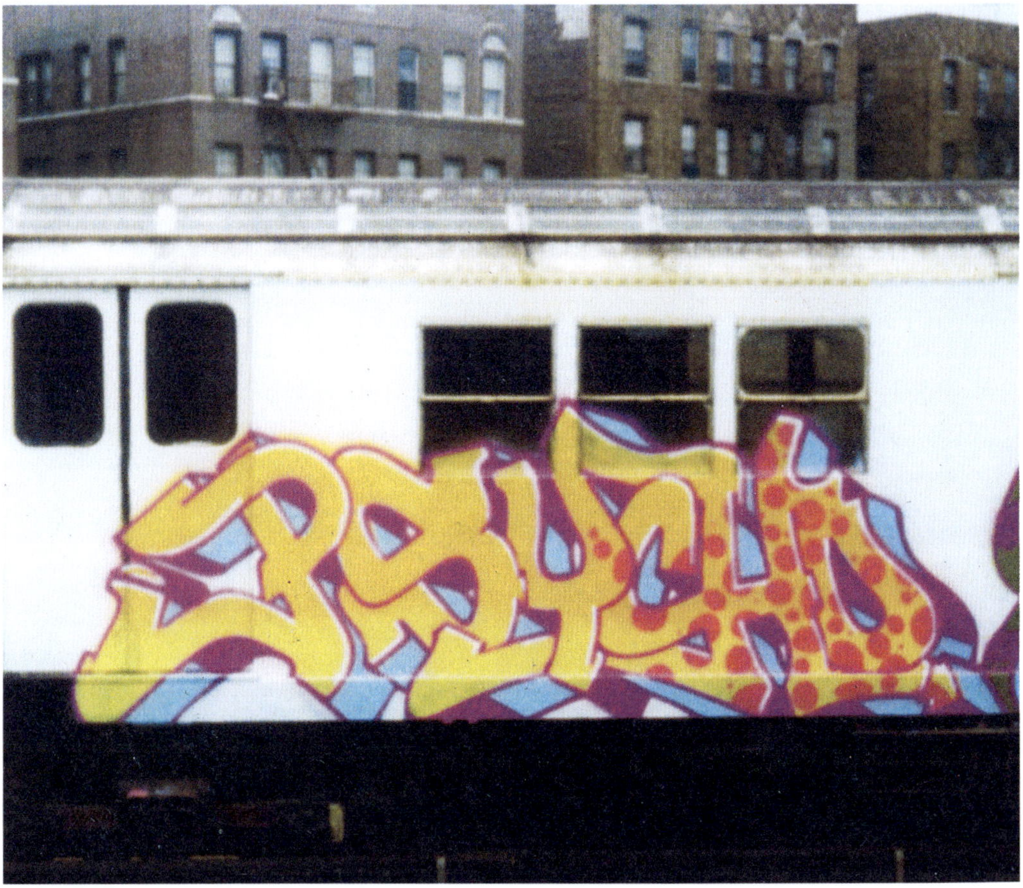

SEEN, spray painting on New York subway
Contemporary photograph of a train piece in New York by SEEN, who occasionally signed as PSYCHO in his early days. © Seen Studio

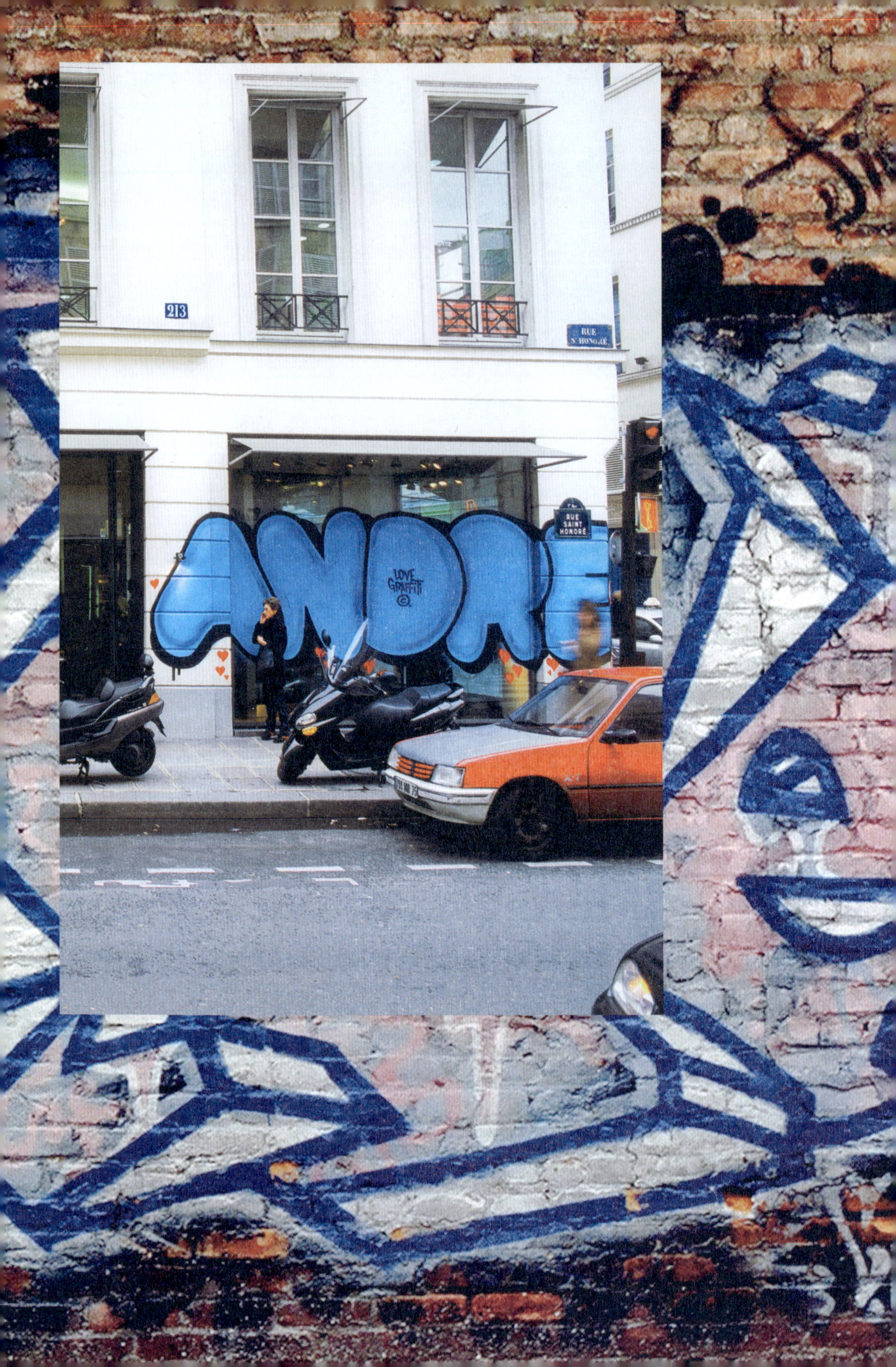
213
RUE SAINT HONORÉ
ANDRE
LOVE GRAFFITI

A WORLDWIDE OUTBREAK

The new playing field

That New York is seen as graffiti's home is due to its historical weight within the movement. Major figures still live there and some of them carry the flame of this culture. However, while New York has remained the hub of the world of urban art, it is not always the city in which artists gain recognition. From the 1980s, other cities emerged, feeding new energy into the moment. This is the case, for example, of San Francisco and more particularly of Los Angeles.

Indeed, the City of Angels has been fertile ground for murals, linked particularly to the very strong presence of "chicano" muralism, a direct heir of Mexican muralism and a part of the cityscape since the 1930s. Its impact on graffiti is a particular feature of the city. The tradition of introducing art and murals into public spaces continued just as strongly in the 1970s, well before graffiti arrived on the West Coast. In the climate of protest against the Vietnam War that characterized this period, 82 walls were painted in Los Angeles between 1972 and 1978.

Many local street artists have said that the first graffiti involving writing with a spray can, which previously had been left by gangs to mark their territory, date back to 1983. Without the phenomenon yet going by the name "graffiti," local styles quickly appeared. They were the product of a mixture of New York influences and the Mexican cultural presence.

ANDRÉ, *Olympia Love*, Colette, Paris, 2009 (detail) © A.R.R.

Behind: graffiti in New York City. Photo © Stéphane Bisseuil

In his book *The History of Graffiti in Los Angeles*, REKAL recalls how it all began: "Before 1983, I only saw writing by gangs. But in 1983, I started

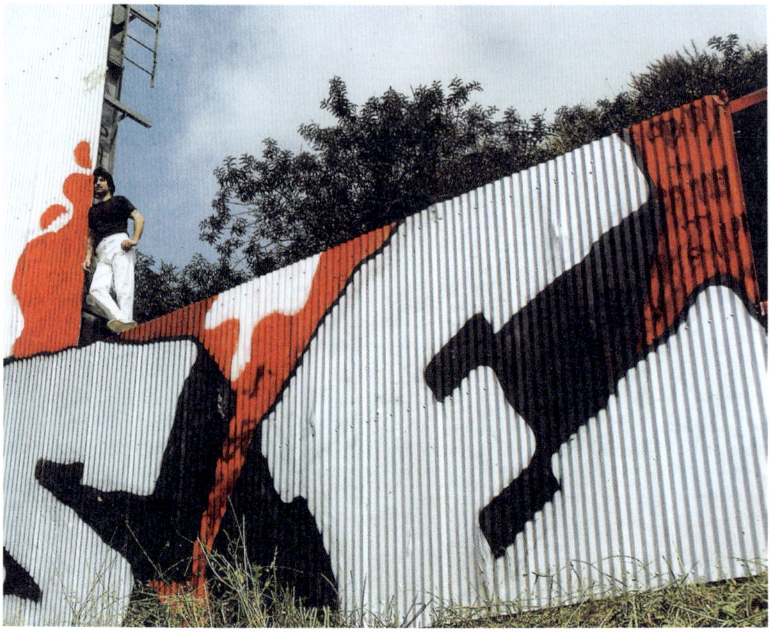

SEEN standing on the L of the Hollywood Sign, which he had just painted on, in the mid-1980s. © Seen Studio

noticing something that turned out to be graffiti from hip-hop culture. It wasn't about promoting a gang or a neighbourhood any more, but yourself."

Some of the legends of New York graffiti who were discouraged by its repression turned up in Los Angeles, hoping to find fresh walls. And in 1984, SEEN organized an attack on the highly symbolic Hollywood sign. It's an escapade that he still vividly remembers: "In 1984, BLADE and I went to Hollywood, California, on a mission to leave our mark. We bombed the city from Venice Beach to Sunset Strip. We even decided to do a little something extra by painting each side of a tour bus from Star Tour Bus Hollywood... But I could only think about one thing: the Hollywood sign. As I was leaving, I knew that my adventure was unfinished. A few months later, I returned to Hollywood just to put that icing on the cake. My only mission this time was to paint the Hollywood sign. I had planned to complete my mission from my first night on the spot so as not to waste any time. I had chosen my tools and my colours: red, black and chrome. Chrome would allow me to quickly fill my lettering, because I was not sure how much time I would have... I was in the middle of working when I suddenly heard the noise of helicopters. I had to run away again with that sense of leaving something unfinished. I ripped the film from my camera to avoid having incriminating evidence on me... Back at my hotel, I slept for a while, and then I returned for one last go and finally made my work."

From its beginnings, the movement in Los Angeles seems to have remained somewhat underground until an article in the *Los Angeles Times*: "New York's graffiti work moves to West." Published on 10 November 1984 and written by Robert L. Pincus, the story highlighted graffiti's growing importance. Some local collectors began to take an interest, such as Elli Broad and Frederick R. Weismann. And some galleries hosted the first exhibitions. The Michael Kohn Gallery invited FUTURA in 1985, and the Tamara Bane Gallery opened its doors to DAZE in 1988 and CRASH in 1989.
However, following the same impulse as on the East Coast, repression was not long in becoming unleashed. In 1992, the city registered a charge of an additional $ 3.7 million for cleaning up graffiti. The sale of spray paint to minors was banned, and penalties against graffiti artists were passed in 1993.

The crossover with Europe

The summers of 1983 and 1984 marked the beginning of an intense artistic dialogue between the two sides of the Atlantic. A number of young Europeans attracted to America made the trip to New York, where they discovered the energy of a unique artistic output. Individuals met and friendships were formed, and this artistic form was exported to the Old Continent, where it spread like wildfire. Invitations were extended to graffiti artists such as JONONE. Having revealed the New York scene to BANDO, he in turn discovered Paris, further encouraging the spread of the movement.

Born in New York in 1963, John Andrew Perello, alias JONONE, began to tag his name on the city's walls and subway cars in the late 1970s. During this time, he met A-ONE, who used to hang out with Jean-Michel Basquiat. "A-ONE was the link between the street and the art world. He had travelled to Europe and come back with lots of money, just through his art. I listened to stories of his travels with wide-eyed envy," he remembers. In 1984, he founded the Group 156 All Starz, after his street number. He became JON156 and then JONONE.
In 1985, he began to paint on canvas, persisting in his attempts to reproduce the founding element of his style: a graffitied subway train whose acceleration produces streaks of colour. What distinguished him from the other graffiti artists was his attention to restlessness and movements of colour rather than to figuration. That same year, gallery owner Rick Librizzi exhibited his work in New York. Following an invitation from BANDO, he moved to Paris in 1987. France gave him the opportunity to "continue his personal enrichment."
In turn, then, Americans found breathing space and a certain level of recognition in Europe. This phenomenon was reinforced by the rise of hip-hop culture on the Old

JONONE, store front with the artist's signature, Paris Artist's archive © A.R.R.

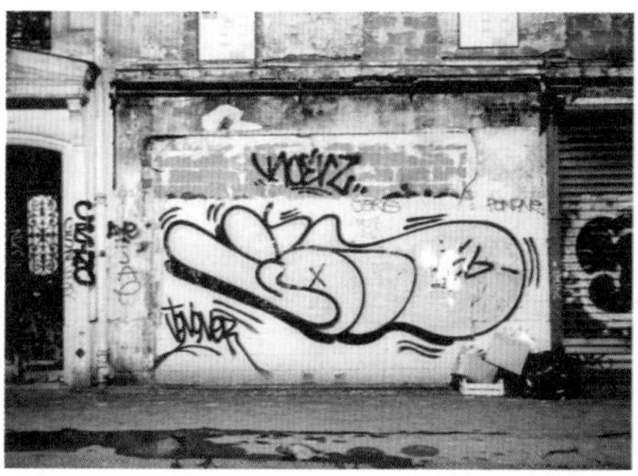

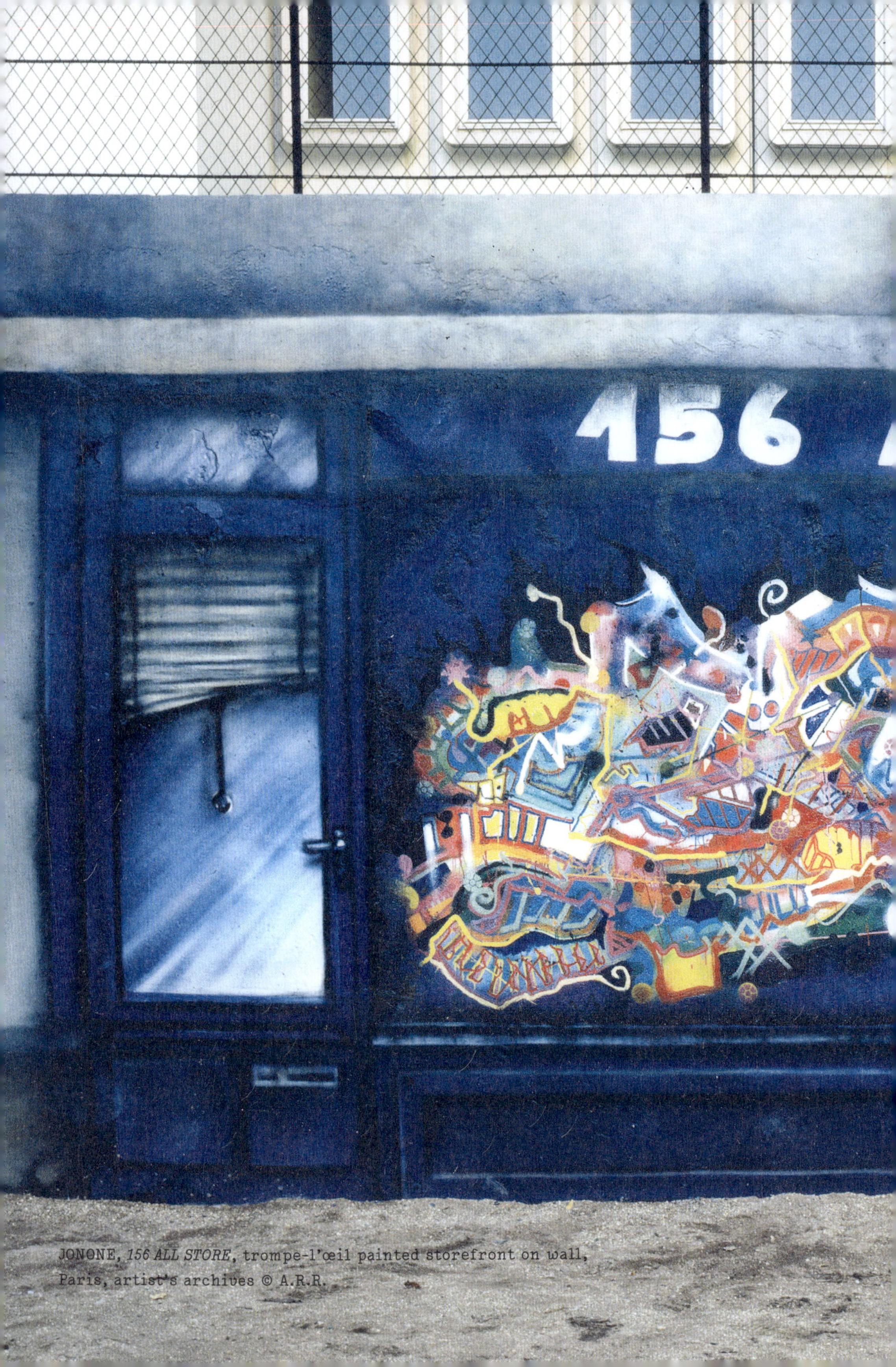

JONONE, *156 ALL STORE*, trompe-l'œil painted storefront on wall, Paris, artist's archives © A.R.R.

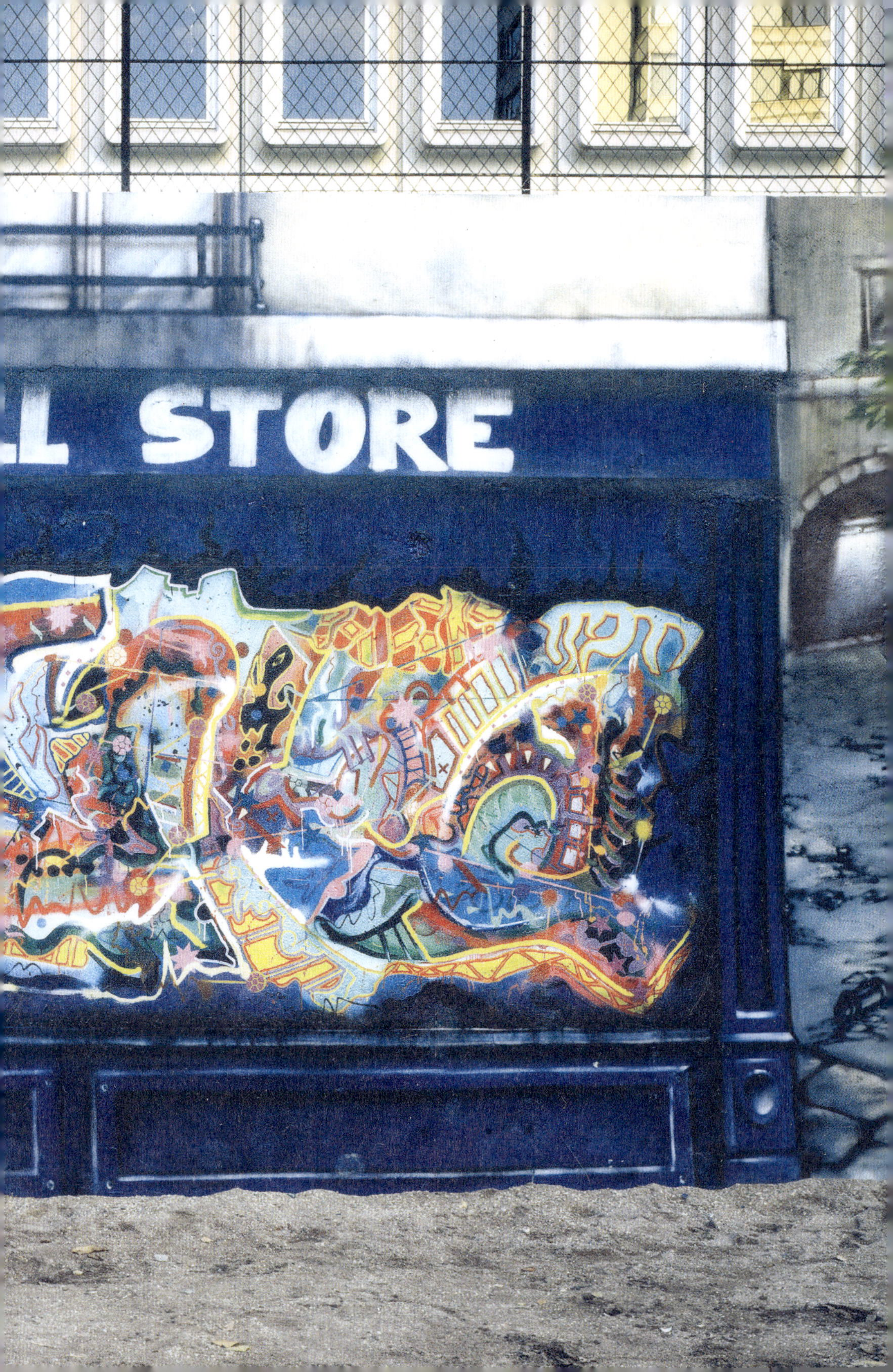
STORE

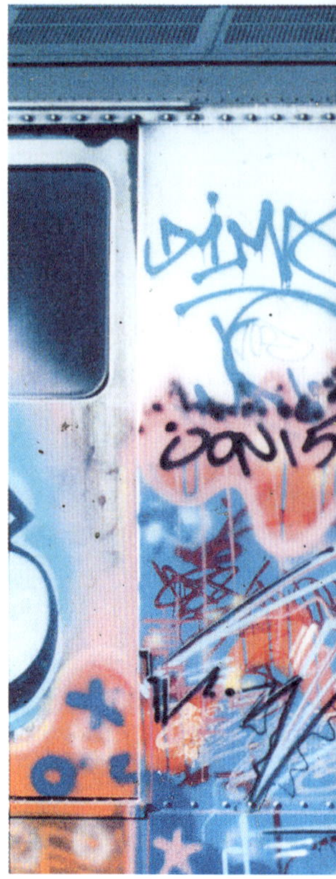

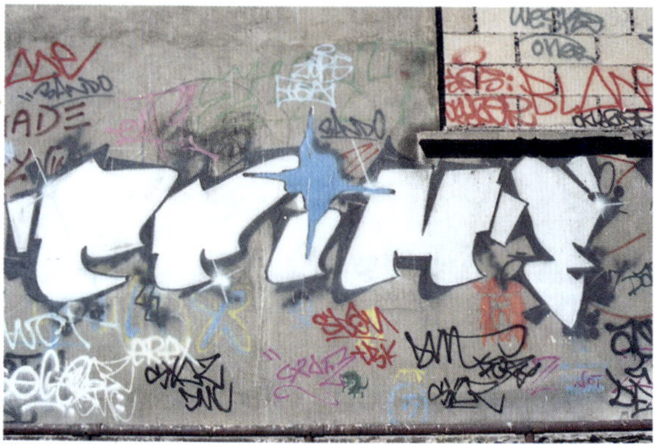

BANDO, *Crime*, 15th arrondissement, Paris, 1980s. © Tarek Ben Yakhlef

JAYONE, *Stalingrad wasteland*, 1980s. © Tarek Ben Yakhlef

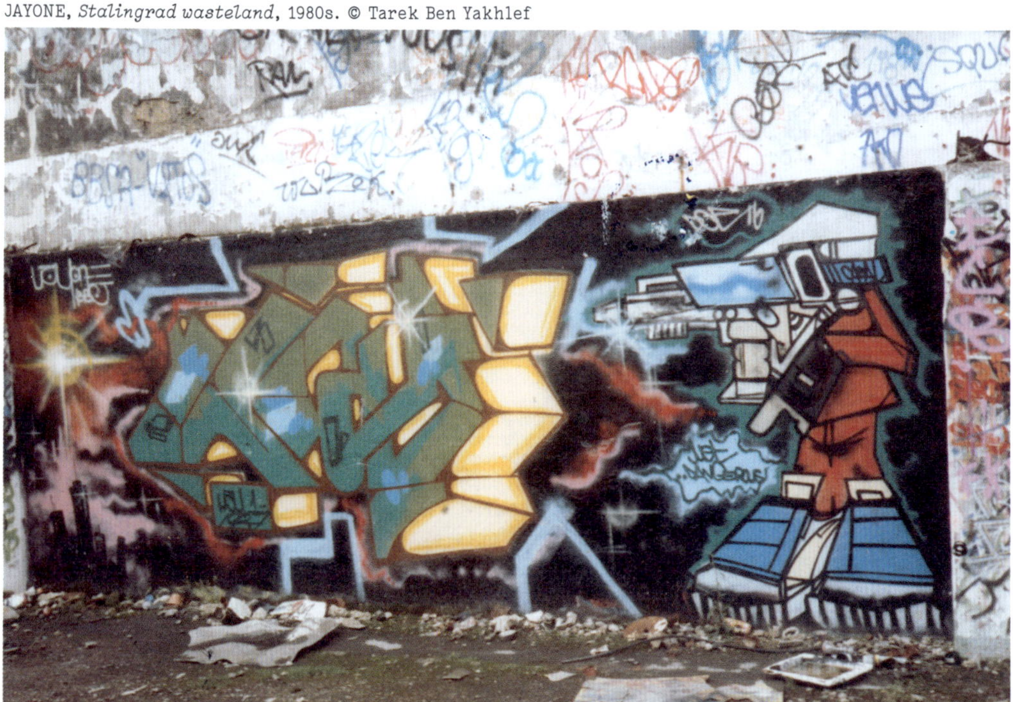

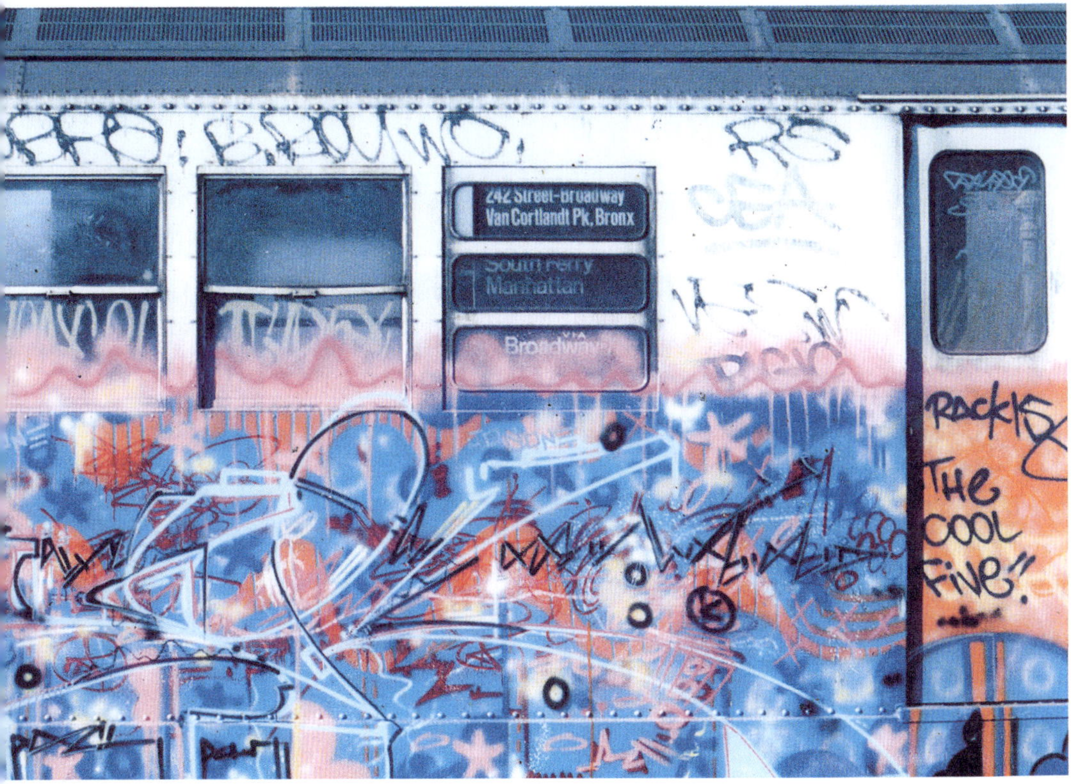

JONONE, subway painted by the artist.

VEASONE, 93NTM, exterior wall, Stalingrad wasteland, 1990. © Tarek Ben Yakhlef

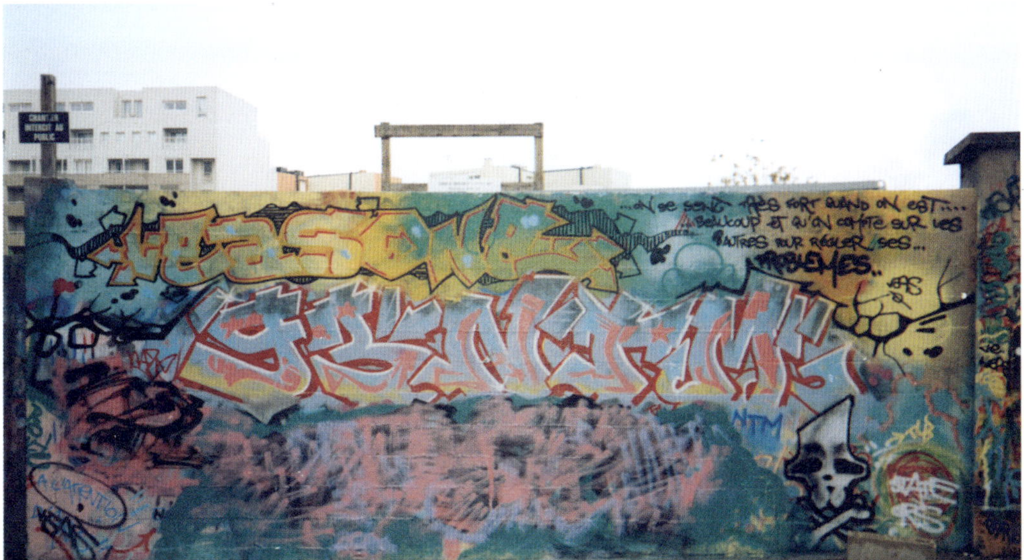

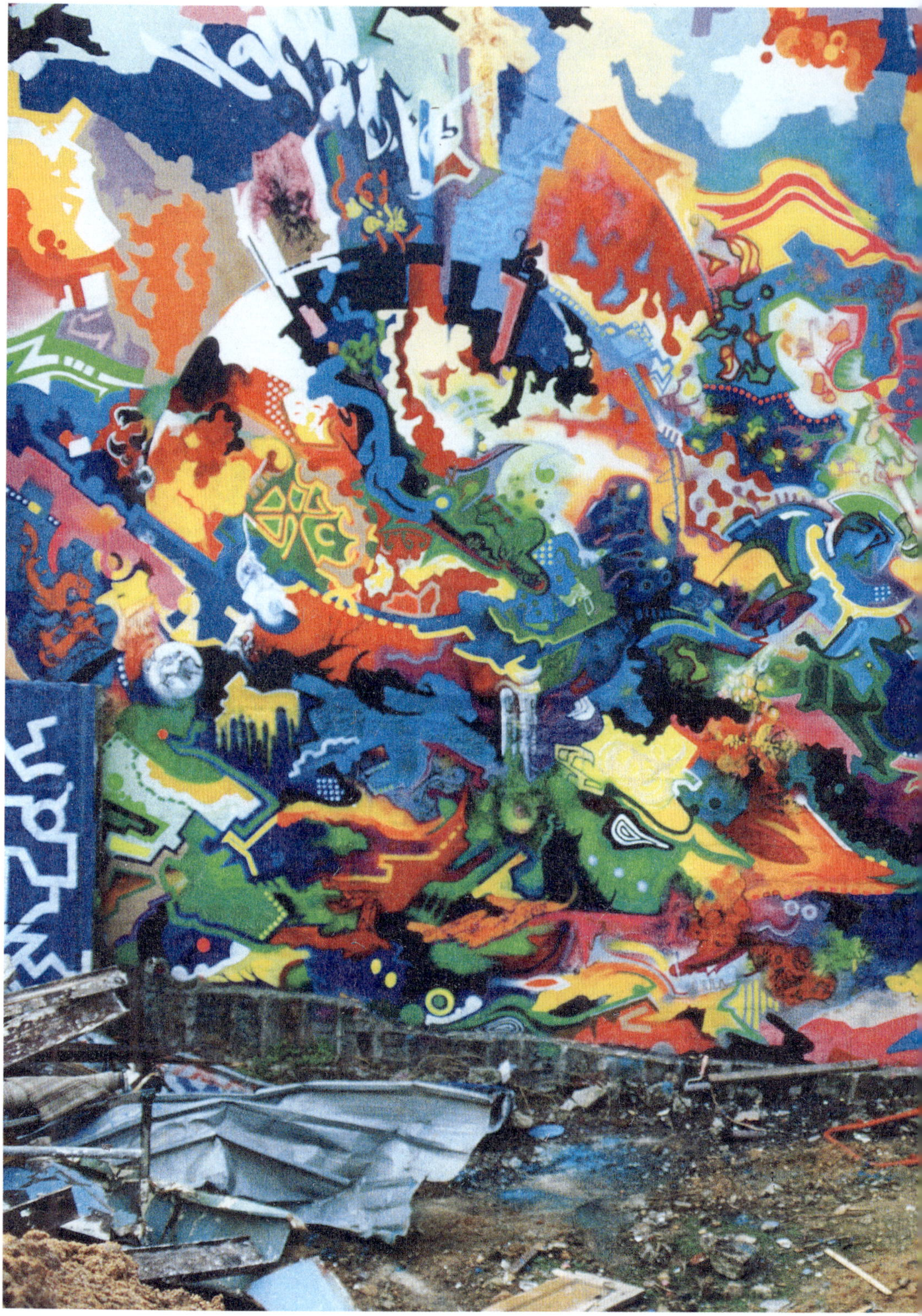

JONONE, around the artist's studio, April 1999. Archives of the artist © A.R.R.

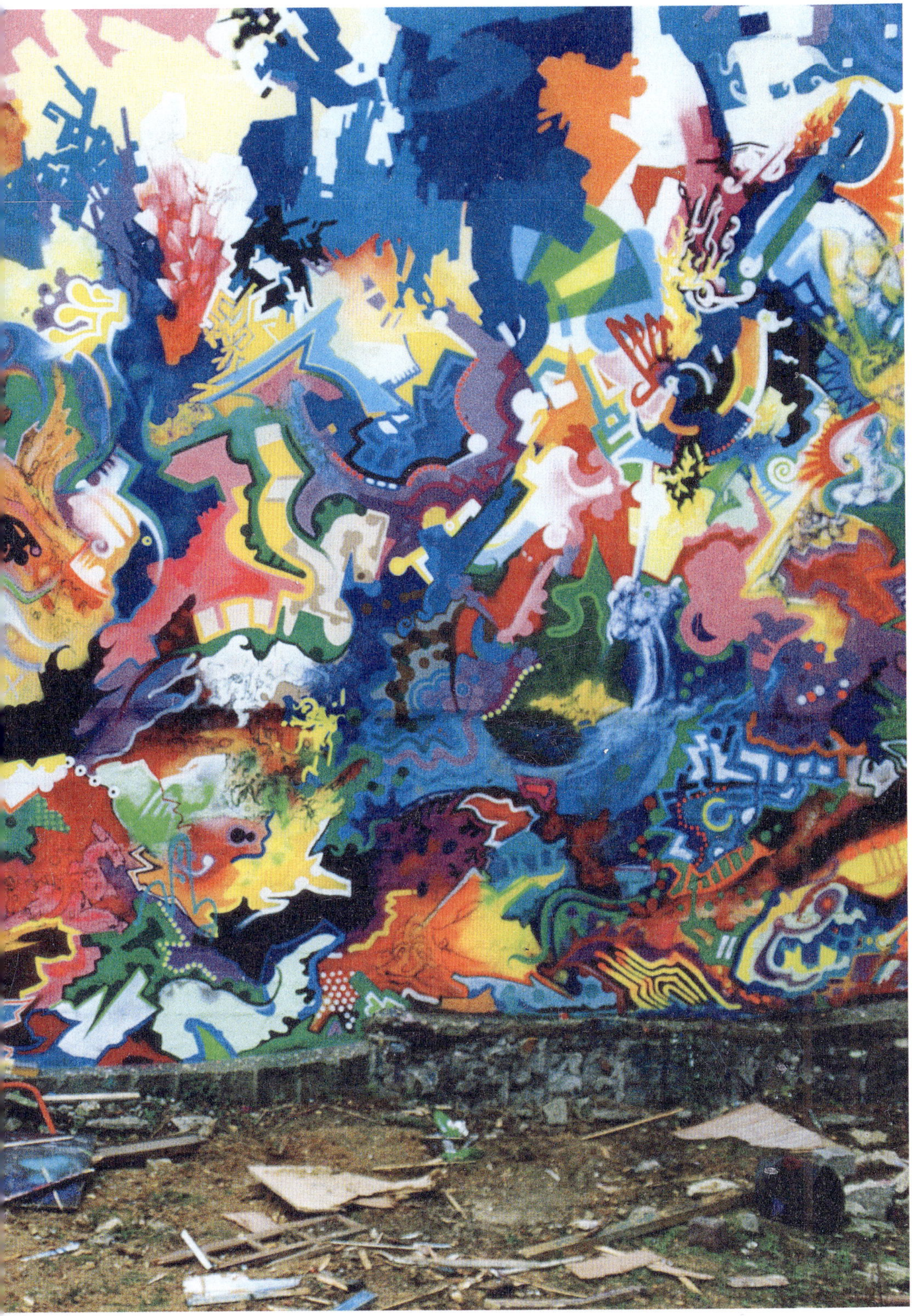

Continent. Promoted by the media, many figures pledged allegiance to the Zulu Nation[1] and, like Afrika Bambaataa, became stars. As a member of the Rock Steady Crew, DOZE toured Europe and helped to propagate the graffiti legend. From Spain to France and England, there were many who dreamed of also belonging to the Zulu Nation. Although films like *Beat Street* were closer to Hollywood than they were the street, they contributed to the legend. In Vienna, Düsseldorf, Munich, Copenhagen, Paris and London, trains were soon covered with graffiti. With their own histories and contexts, each of these cities became a fertile playground.

1 International organization founded in 1973 by Afrika Bambaataa, an American musician and one of the creators of hip-hop. Originally, the Universal Zulu Nation was called the Organization and proposed a peaceful alternative to the various violent gangs that controlled most of New York's deprived neighbourhoods. Renamed Zulu Nation in 1975, it brought together young and peaceful individuals whose means of expression were dance, graffiti, rap and deejaying.

The European scene's first steps

In Germany, historical context played a key role, in the form of the Berlin Wall, which was built to stem the exodus of inhabitants of the East to the West in 1961. Nobody on the East side of the wall was allowed to approach it. In the West, on the other hand, artists decided to use it to express themselves. Extended to a height of 3.60 m in 1976, the wall would attract well-known and anonymous artists alike. Coming from around the world, they began to paint the Western side from 1980, transforming it into a giant canvas that was open to all. In 1986, KEITH HARING produced a work on it. From 1987, the French artists JAYONE, SKKI and ASH took their turns. Because of the occupation by American troops of the Western zone, the practice was all the more tolerated; graffiti was seen as an element of American culture. A highly symbolic bastion of graffiti, the wall became a page in the history of this culture, with most of the stars of the time having visited it. In 1989, in the aftermath of its downfall, 118 artists from 21 countries left their mark there, giving birth to a true open-air museum: the East Side Gallery.

Due to the increasingly frequent visits of leading American artists to Europe, a real scene developed. Some German museums and galleries began to present these artists from across the Atlantic. DONDI had a solo exhibition in Düsseldorf at the Art in Progress Gallery (1983) and then at the Galerie Thomas in Munich (1984), and his work was part of the *Graffiti* exhibition at the Leopold-Hoesch Museum (1986).

Curiously, at the beginning of the 1980s, American street artists found particular recognition in the Netherlands. In 1983, the art dealer Yaki Kornblit returned from New York with an obsession: to import into Amsterdam the fruit of his New York discoveries. He therefore brought together several famous artists, including DONDI, CRASH, RAMMELLZEE, ZEPHYR, FUTURA, QUIK, LADY PINK, SEEN, BLADE and BIL BLAST, in an ambitious exhibition entitled *New York Graffiti* at the Museum Boijmans van Beuningen. The Yaki Kornblit Gallery stood out as one of the pioneers for graffiti in Europe, presenting solo exhibitions from each of the big American names in Amsterdam. As a result, throughout this period, numerous historical works by artists such as BLADE, QUIK, DONDI and SEEN entered Dutch private collections. In parallel, the exposition of the Museum Boijmans van Beuningen in Rotterdam (The Netherlands) would be presented at the Louisiana Museum in Humleboek (Denmark, 1984), then again at the Groninger Museum in Groningen (The Netherlands, 1984), at the Gemeente Museum in The Hague (The Netherlands, 1985), and at the Stedelijk Museum Helmond in Amsterdam (The Netherlands, 1985)...

At the other end of Europe, in Italy, following Raffaele Garrucci's[2] study on graffiti in Pompeii, art critics had been busy deciphering these signs left in the street since 1854. In the context of May 1968, through its art critics Italy played a leading role in defining a politicized reading of urban writing. Some also conducted in-depth analysis beyond European borders. Gusamo Cesaretti moved to Los Angeles in 1969 and studied Cholo Writing[3] thanks to Chaz Bojorquez, one of the major representatives of this current. *Street Writers: A Guided Tour in Chicano Graffiti* was published in 1975. In the early 1980s, Bologna and its region became the point of entry for graffiti from the United States. In 1981, gallery owner Emilio Mazzoli invited Jean-Michel Basquiat to Modena. He exhibited in Rome the following year. New York legends such as LEE QUINONES and RAMMELLZEE would then follow. Around the same time as the *Graffiti* exhibition at the Museum Boijmans Van Beuningen in Rotterdam, *Arte di Frontiera: New York Graffiti* was in preparation. The exhibition began in 1984 and travelled through Bologna, Milan and Rome. If it had not been for the premature death of its curator, Francesca Alinovi, in 1983, this museum exhibition would have been the first in Europe to cover the phenomenon.

2 Raffaele Garrucci (1812-1885), author of the work *Inscriptions gravées au trait sur les murs de Pompéi calquées et interprétées par Raphaël Garrucci*, which was published in 1854 and is still studied today.

3 Graffiti from *cholo* culture, a term used in Latin America, initially to designate people belonging to street gangs. By extension, the term applies to graffiti from the Hispanic neighbourhoods of Los Angeles.

Street art in France was not born yesterday, having been practised since the 1950s by artists like VILLEGLÉ, Gérard ZLOTYKAMIEN and Ernest PIGNON-ERNEST.

Jacques VILLEGLÉ (born in 1926 in Quimper) began in 1949 with his art school companion Raymond HAINS (born in 1926 in Saint Brieuc) to work with urban materials by collecting ripped posters. He underpinned his approach with theory by viewing himself as a mere collector of posters, with the real artist being the "anonymous ripper." This appropriative behaviour, closer to the *readymade* than what would become street art, extracted urban materials from their context more than it played with them. His motto of "ravish it rather than make it" shows his willingness to question the position of the creator.
VILLEGLÉ creates works from posters that have been ripped by passers-by or damaged by weather conditions. He takes them from the surface that they were attached to in the street and rebuilds them before smoothing them down on canvas. He creates abstract works that reveal fragments of logos from the consumer society's advertising posters or political slogans from posters that address current affairs,

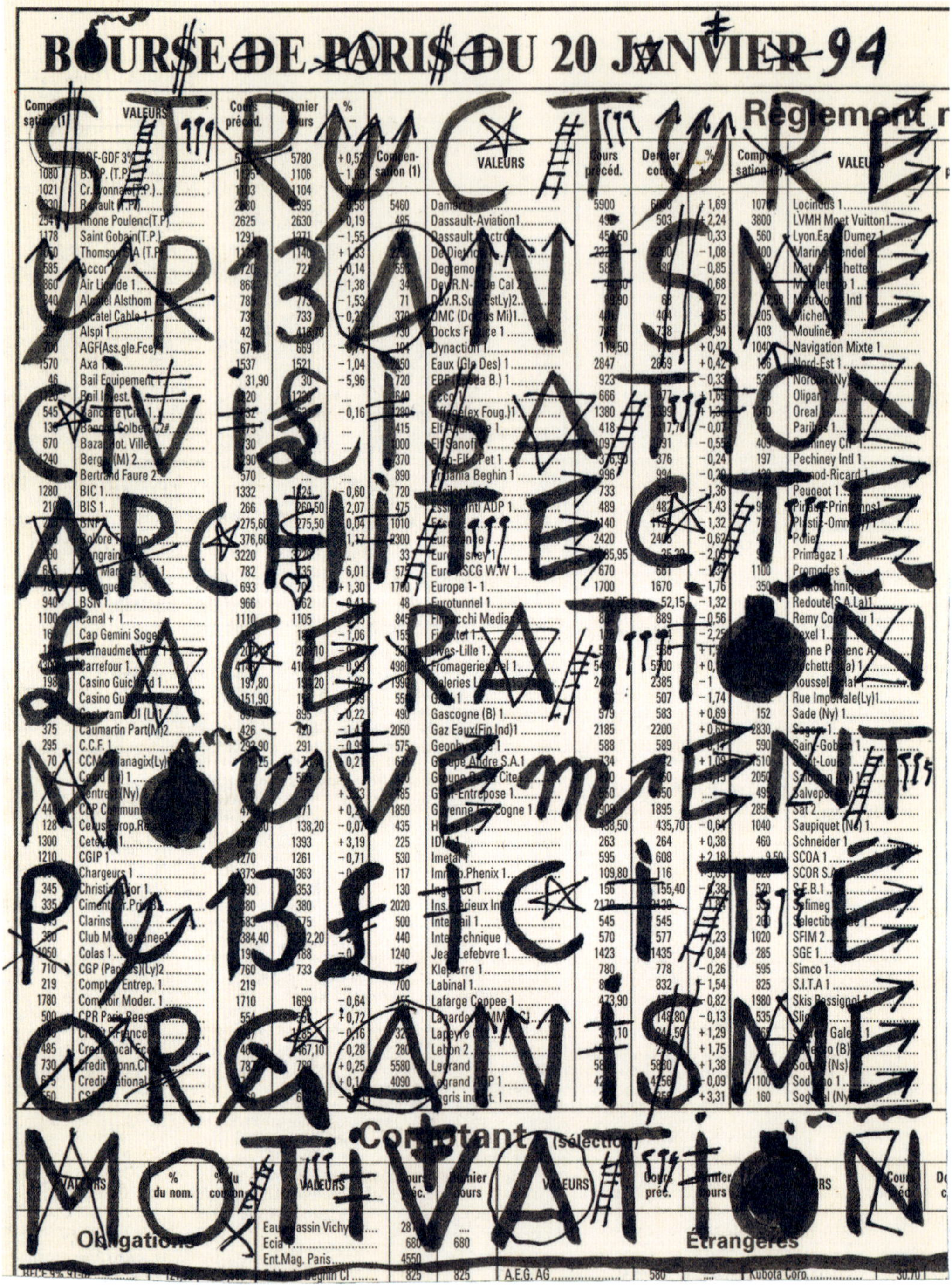

JACQUES VILLEGLÉ, *Bourse de Paris*, 19.8×15 cm, felt tip on newsprint, anonymous photo. With Fonds de donation Villegle's kind permission.

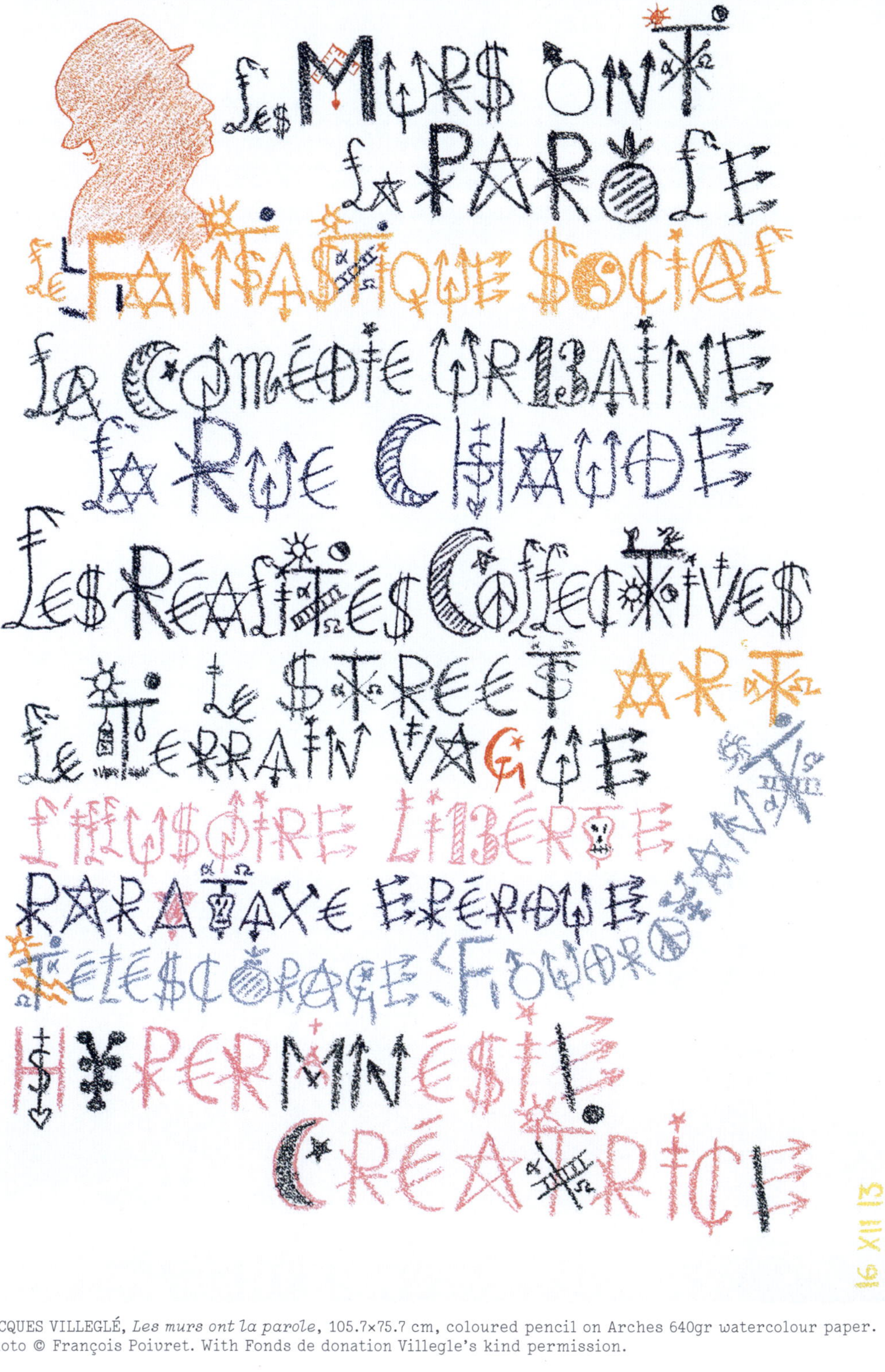

JACQUES VILLEGLÉ, *Les murs ont la parole*, 105.7×75.7 cm, coloured pencil on Arches 640gr watercolour paper. Photo © François Poivret. With Fonds de donation Villegle's kind permission.

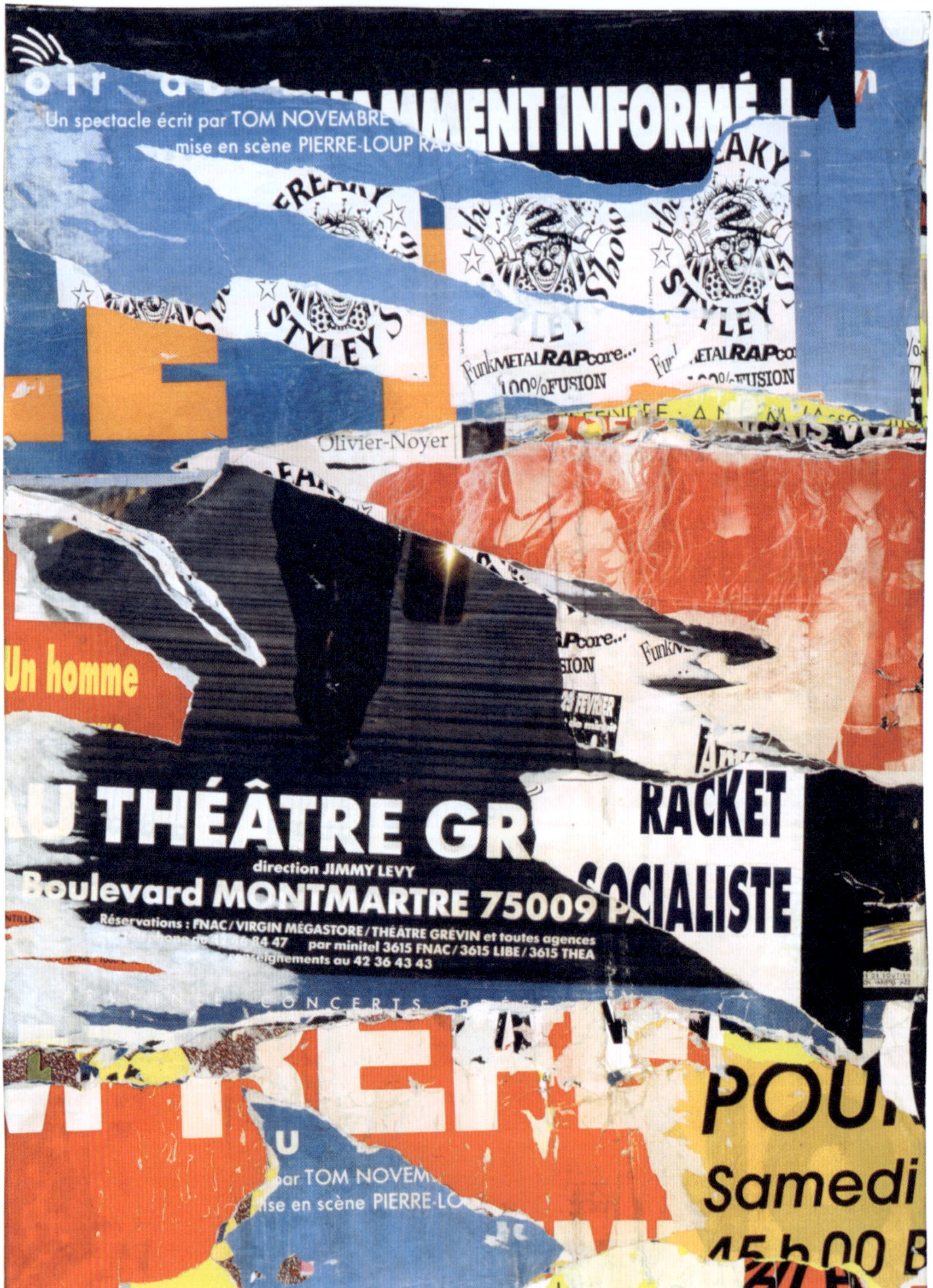

JACQUES VILLEGLÉ, *Saint-Séverin - Saint-Jacques*, 100×81 cm, ripped posters pressed onto canvas. Photo © François Poivret. With Fonds de donation Villegle's kind permission.

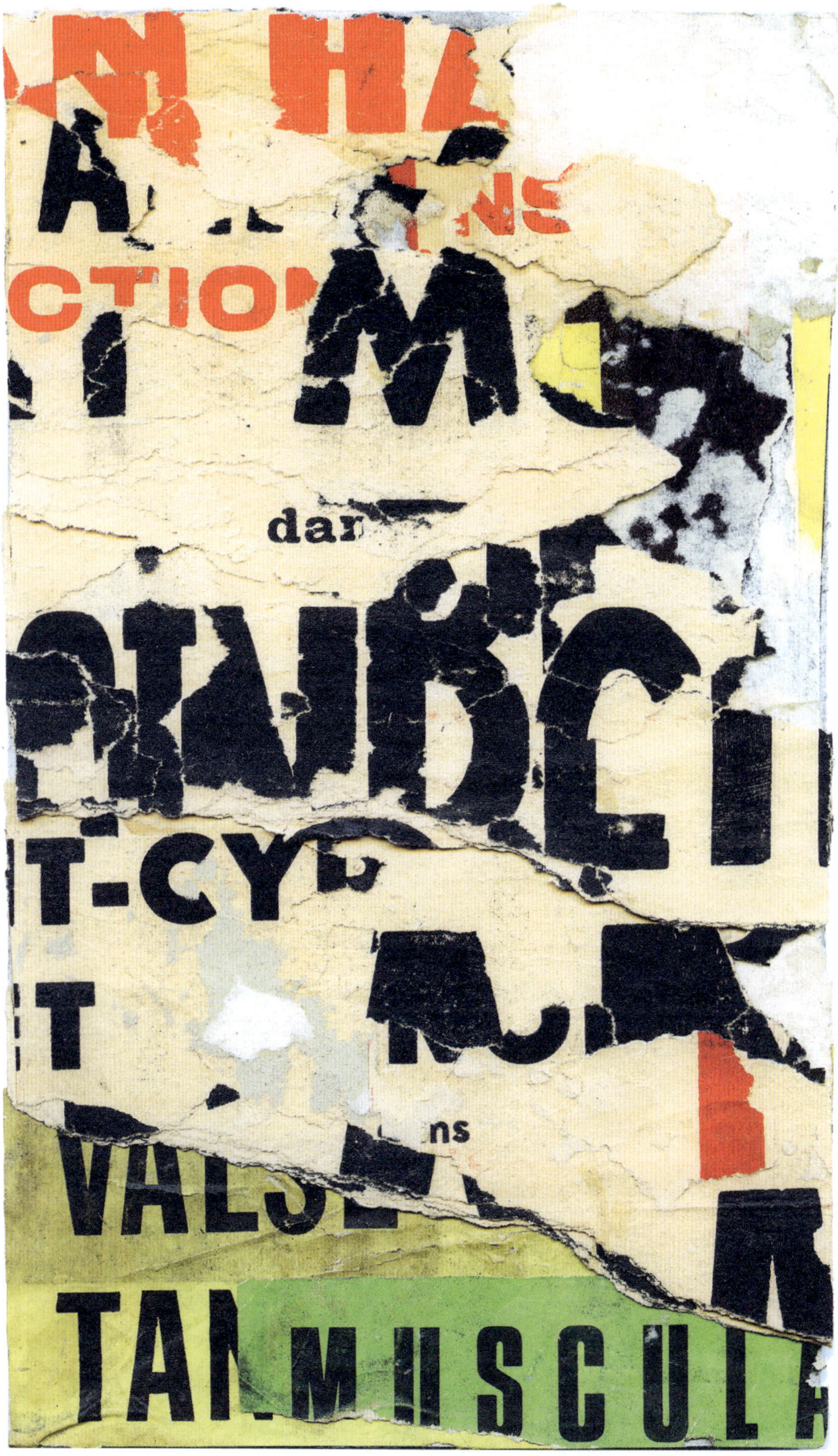

JACQUES VILLEGLÉ, *métro Saint-Sulpice*, 27×15.8 cm, ripped posters pressed onto cardboard, anonymous photo. With Fonds de donation Villegle's kind permission.

from the Algerian War (1954-1962) to the presidential election battles between Giscard and Mitterrand (1971 and 1981). Through this practice, VILLEGLÉ has defined himself more as an archaeologist of the street.

Among the many artistic explorations that the artist has undertaken is the "sociopolitical alphabet" that he imagined from 1969 in tribute to Sergei Chakhotin,[4] author of the 1939 essay *The Rape of the Masses; the Psychology of Totalitarian Political Propaganda*. In the sociopolitical alphabet, each of the letters of the Roman alphabet takes on another dimension with the addition of signs that often carry totalitarian or authoritarian meanings. For example, two coupled Ds form the basis of the Celtic Cross; the V represents the Cross of Lorraine; the F is transformed into a swastika. On a more complex level, the name of Nixon is composed of the letter N with three arrows, referring to the old Socialist Party; the X is a swastika; the O is a circle enclosing a Celtic Cross. The S is replaced by the $ symbol, which itself sometimes encompasses a snake's body and head. He presented his creation as a poster or applied it using painting and aerosol in the form of full quotations. Although the appearance of this alphabet came about completely independently from the graffiti movement—at that time in its infancy across the Atlantic—it cannot be viewed as an isolated phenomenon. The work of lettering and the search for additional meaning in words are common points between VILLEGLÉ's explorations and those of graffiti artists who were constantly reinventing their style and transforming the Roman alphabet.

4 Sergei Chakhotin (1883-1973) was a German sociologist and microbiologist of Russian origin. He is known for his *The Rape of the Masses; the Psychology of Totalitarian Political Propaganda*. In 1932, he invented the three-arrowed symbol that became the symbol of the Iron Front (1931-1933). The use of the three arrows is theorized in his book. Placed on a wall after or before another symbol (for example, a swastika), they are supposed to cancel it out.

These different graphical explorations were deeply related to the simplicity of this alphabet. In contrast to Asian calligraphy, for example, no letter has an illustrated meaning. Western artists have lacked ideographs, carriers of a semantic supplement, and they have therefore been obliged to reinvent them, making writing become a question of rebuses, composition and inventiveness. Playing with words has also been accompanied by playing with images.

ERNEST PIGNON-ERNEST, *Hommes bloqués*, Palais de Tokyo, Paris, 1962

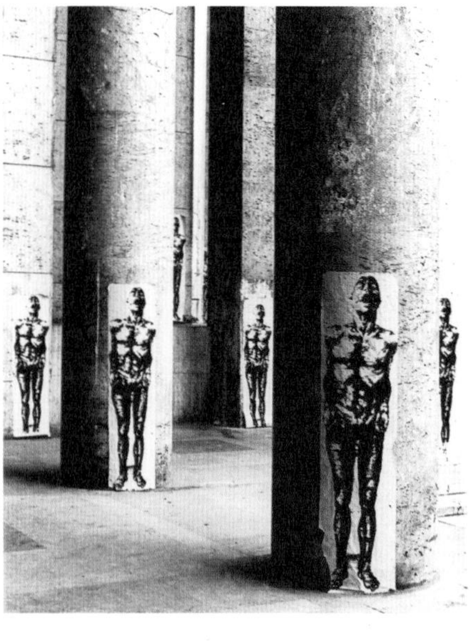

Gérard ZLOTYKAMIEN, who was born in 1940, began painting in 1955. In 1963, he made his first street piece with his *éphémères*, febrile and flickering black silhouettes painted with spray paint through no more than a freehand line. They recalled Hiroshima's radiation and the human shadows printed on walls after the nuclear explosion. In the 1970s, he painted his creatures at the Les Halles building site, an area of Paris then in the midst of reconstruction. A manager in the Galeries Lafayette by day and a painter by night, he was on the fringes of the art scene and put his *éphémères* in many cities across the world.

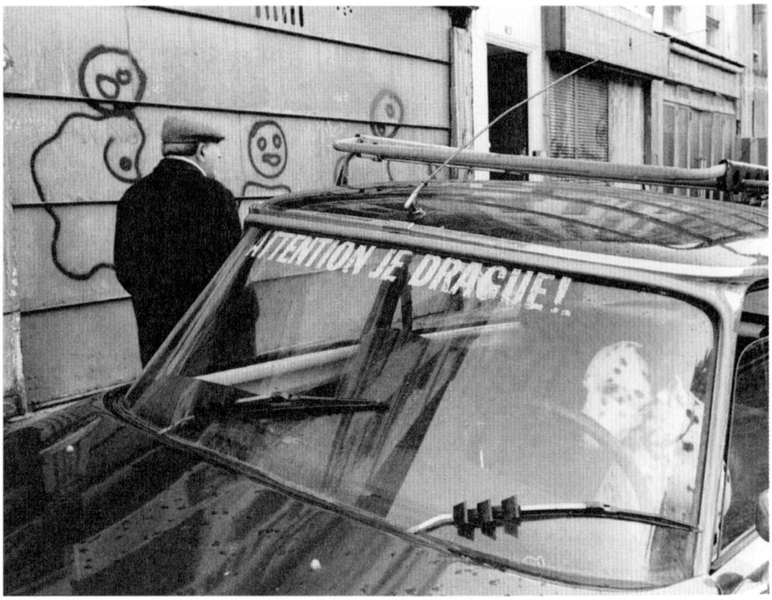

ZLOTYKAMIEN, rue Saint-Merri, Paris, 1978. Photo © Jacques Faujour

The shadows of Hiroshima also left a mark on Ernest PIGNON-ERNEST (born in 1942 in Nice)—so much so that he began painting on rocks and the roads of Vaucluse. "After a lot of trial and error on canvas," he recalls, "I was convinced that I could not evoke these thousands of potential Hiroshimas encysted under the lavender with paint. (...) [It] became clear that it was the places themselves that were infected with this threat, this suggestive load, and they were what needed marking out and needed seizing as both visual and symbolic material. Based on the silhouette of a charred body, I cut out a stencil and drew these imprints from Hiroshima on walls, rocks and roads leading to the Plateau d'Albion as a signal." A number of his series comprised silhouettes applied to the ground.

At the beginning of the 1960s, then, the historical and political context created a unique scene. Inscriptions on walls, and then, in a more elaborate way, slogans and stencils, were soon seen as a form of artistic expression that, in spite of some critics, became a movement. Towards the end of the decade, graffiti in its classic sense (writing and stencils) carried an intellectual value that was strongly inspired by the political ideas of the time. Often filled with humour and poetry, plays on words and double meanings, catchy slogans on walls flourished.

As a result of these pioneers, a new generation of urban activists emerged. This is the case of BLEK LE RAT and Jérôme MESNAGER, who continued to stimulate the urban art scene in the footsteps of their predecessors.

Jérôme MESNAGER, born in 1961 in Colmar, founded the Zig-Zag group in 1982, which brought together around ten young artists, and decided to occupy the street through graffiti. A year later, he invented his White Man, "a symbol of light, strength and peace." It stormed the streets, first in Paris, and then in towns around the world.

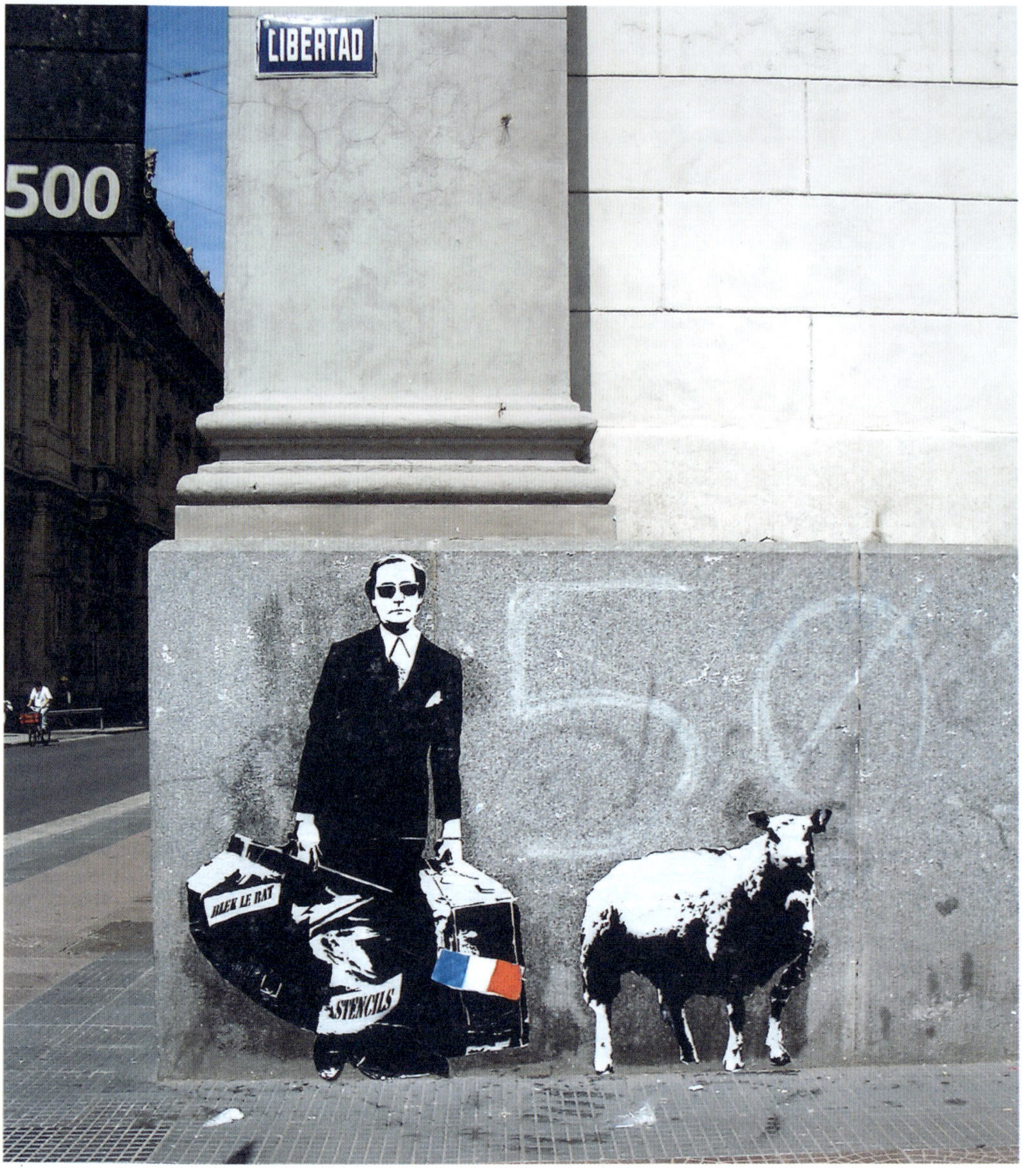

BLEK LE RAT, *Libertad*, Argentina
Archives of the artist © A.R.R.

Blek le Rat is one of the pioneers of stencils in France. He has been populating cities with his painted characters for more than thirty years. He has placed his iconic figures in countries all over the world.

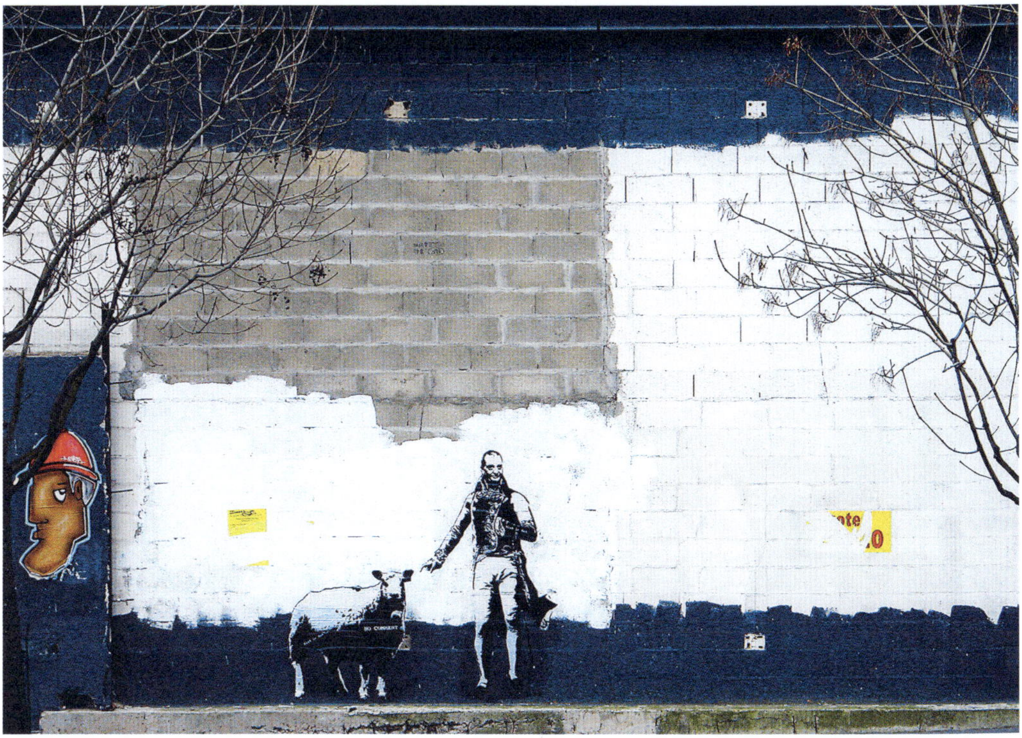

BLEK LE RAT, *Napoléon et mouton*, Paris. Archives of the artist © A.R.R.

BLEK LE RAT, *Check point Charlie*, Berlin, 2003. Archives of the artist © A.R.R.

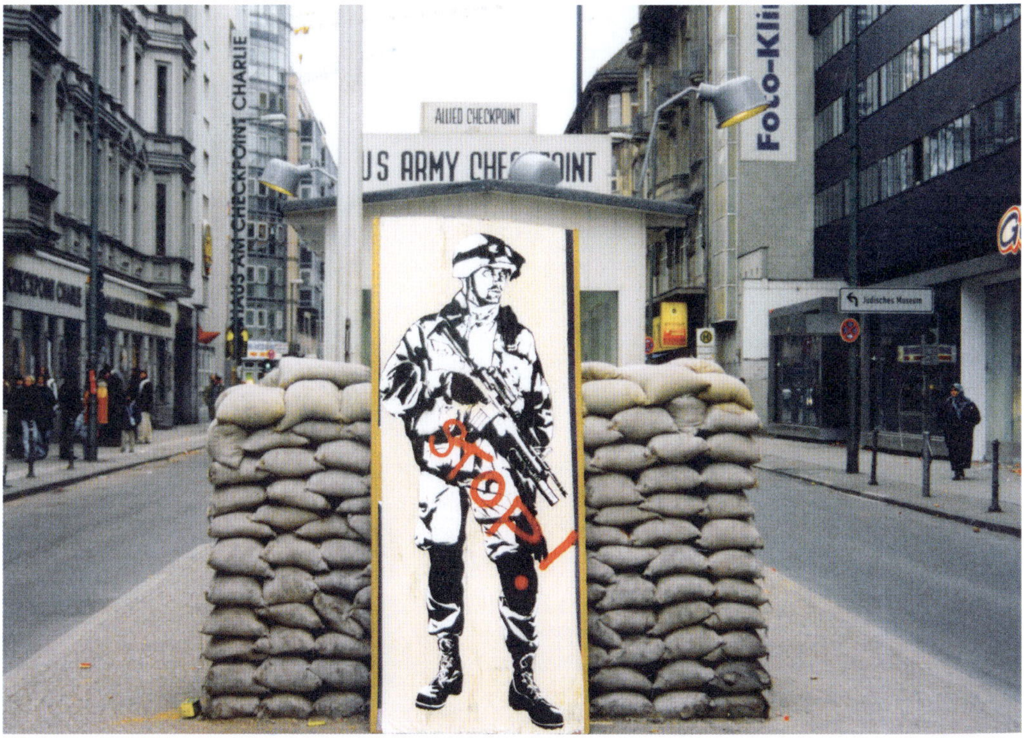

BLEK LE RAT, born in 1951 in Boulogne-Billancourt, was one of the first figures of French urban art to have been really inspired and motivated by the nascent American scene. While still a student, he discovered New York's subway graffiti for the first time while on a visit there during the summer of 1971. Although he had already encountered graffiti and political posters in France, what he discovered there impressed him. However, it would only be ten years later, having studied at art and then architecture school, that this inspiration was turned into a reality. He attempted the American style with coloured lettering, but he was not satisfied with the results. He also drew inspiration from his European travels, where he encountered a lot of propaganda stencil works. He came to favour a similar technique. "Stencils worked well with the spray paint. You could prepare them in your studio. In the street, when doing graffiti, you have to be quick and effective. The image left by the stencil was impeccable. Stencil and spray paint were a perfect technique for this kind of expression," he recalls. An exclamation of identity and a desire to exist in the urban jungle, his signature asserted itself quickly with a symbol—a mundane one at the time—of urban life: the rat. "It pleased me to leave an image on the street when I knew thousands of people would see it the next morning and certainly talk about it and ask themselves: but who made it?"
In 1981, he came into contact with art's sacred world by bombing the neighbourhood of Beaubourg, the fiefdom of the museums and galleries of contemporary art, and graffitiing the esplanade of the Musée d'art moderne (Centre Pompidou). Building on the motivation that this adventure gave him, he then continued to use stencils in the street. His works generally depict anonymous figures or famous ones, in life size. He has often drawn inspiration from characters from daily life and the urban reality.

That same year, the Pompidou Centre organized its *Graffiti and Society* exhibition, which focused on redeeming graffiti's status and adopted a historical perspective. This newly acquired prestige was a key factor in the development of the use of stencils. "Street designers" at the time received relatively benevolent treatment from the police over their illegal activities. This conducive environment was what American street artists were met with upon their arrival in France. Finding a positive response to their approach in the country, they fuelled the New York myth and allowed the urban art scene to find new momentum and grow. France, and Paris in particular, played a significant part in nurturing street art. It did not merely welcome the movement from New York; it also contributed new inspirations and challenges to it.

In its early days, French graffiti found space on the walls alongside the Seine. BANDO, some of whose family lived in the United States, was one of the first to import the graffiti that he discovered in New York. Back in Paris in 1981, he began to paint. BANDO and SCAM followed one another. They produced graffiti in the French capital from 1981. A year later, the Englishman MODE 2, already known in the London scene despite his

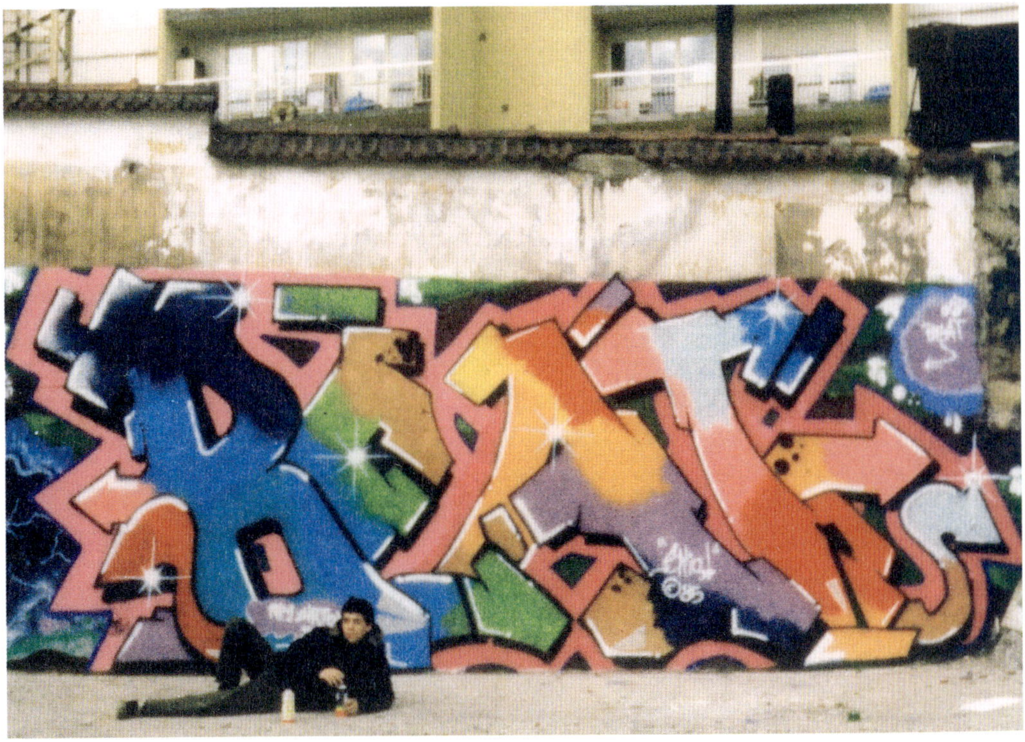

ASH posing in front of his fresco, *Beat*, at the wasteland of Stalingrad (metro), Paris, 1985.

ASH, 1985. Stalingrad was considered to be the Hall of Fame of European graffiti in the 1980s.

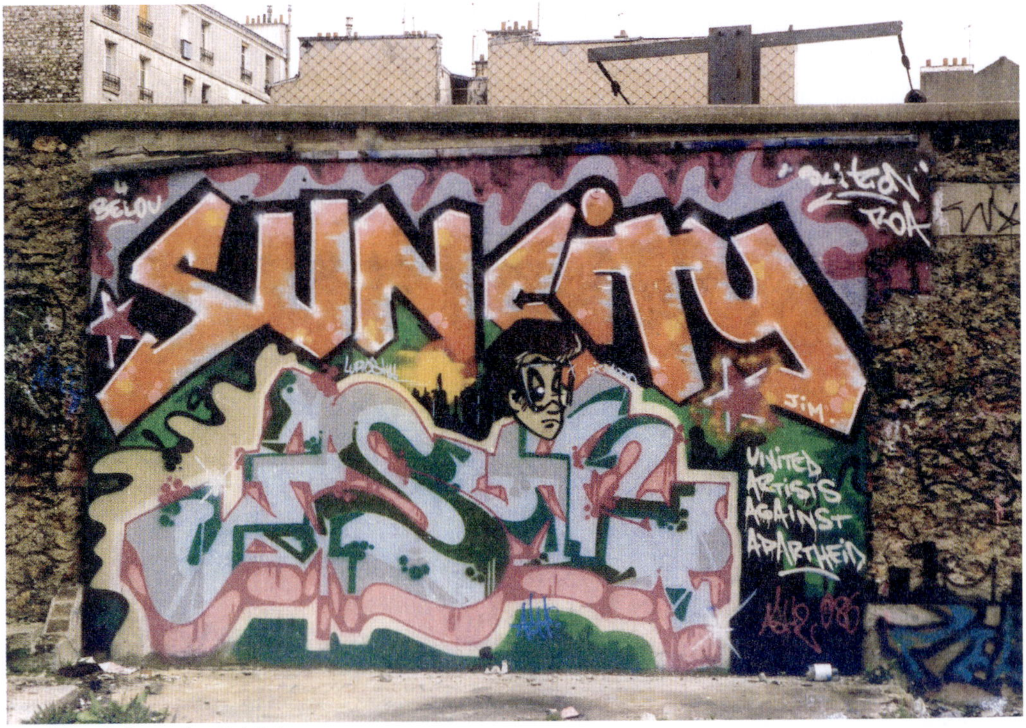

Archives of the artist © A.R.R.

young age —he was just 14 years old at the time— was introduced to them and joined BANDO on these same walls. Together, BANDO and MODE 2 created the earliest masterpieces. MODE 2, whose stylistic inventiveness was already winning admiration, was seen as a character specialist, while BANDO's forté was lettering. They produced many pieces, including some works on the fencing around the Louvre, which was under renovation at the time. The combining of these two English and French figures was probably the founding of the European branch of graffiti. Having heard of this Franco-British coupling, the Dutchman SHOE from the United Street Artists (USA) in turn went to Paris and took them on. This artistic duel led to a friendship that took the whole team through Europe. Collectively, they became ambassadors for European graffiti.

Stalingrad, the cradle of European graffiti

In the history of graffiti, the wasteland of Stalingrad, located in the north of Paris, is crucial. In the 1980s, it was considered to be the genre's hall of fame. Surprisingly for this ephemeral art, this urban wilderness would enjoy an artistic output that would last more than ten years, from 1982 to 1993. Here BANDO would discover the graffiti of one SAHO, who was none other than ASH.

Victor Ash, aka ASH, was born in Portugal. In 1972, his family left the Portuguese countryside and emigrated to the Parisian suburbs. As a teenager, he was immersed in the electro funk scene and hip-hop. Like all the other emerging graffiti artists, he sought to stand out from his peers. With JAYONE and SKKI, he founded the BBC (Bad Boy Crew), a pioneering group in Europe. Between 1983 and 1986, he also signed his name as SAHO and ASH2. His work was photographed and published by Henry Chalfant in the cult book *Spraycan Art*. Because of his origins, ASH was confronted with diverse environments, something that he cultivated in his works. In his creations, the abstract meets very lifelike everyday objects, which are

Fencing at the Louvre © A.R.R.

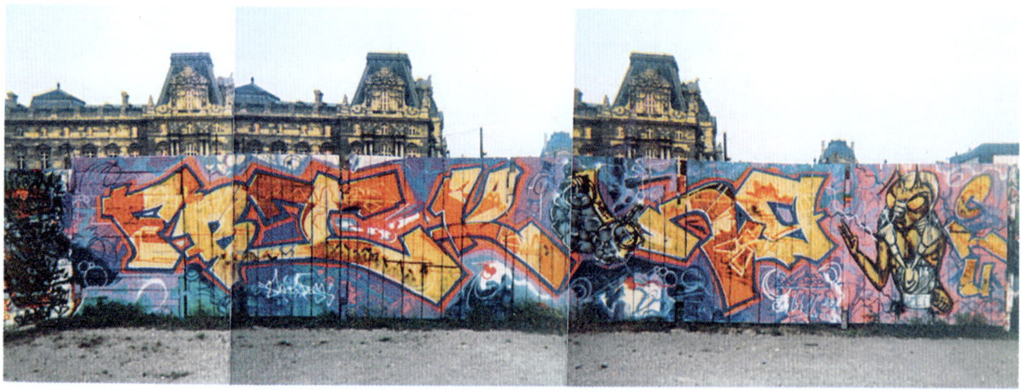

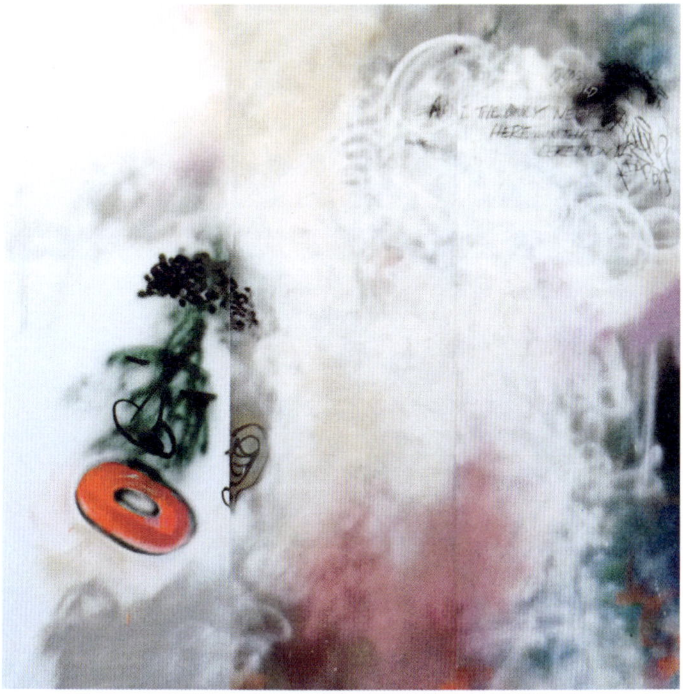

JAYONE, *Am I The Only Nigger in This Here*, spray paint and acrylic on canvas. Photos: archives of the artist © A.R.R.

JAYONE, *Power to Conquer*, acrylic and chalk on canvas

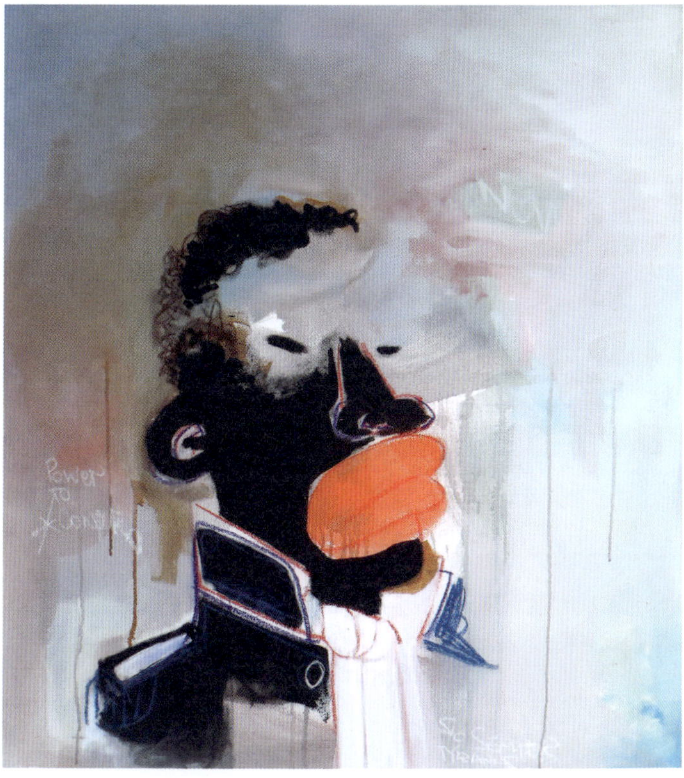

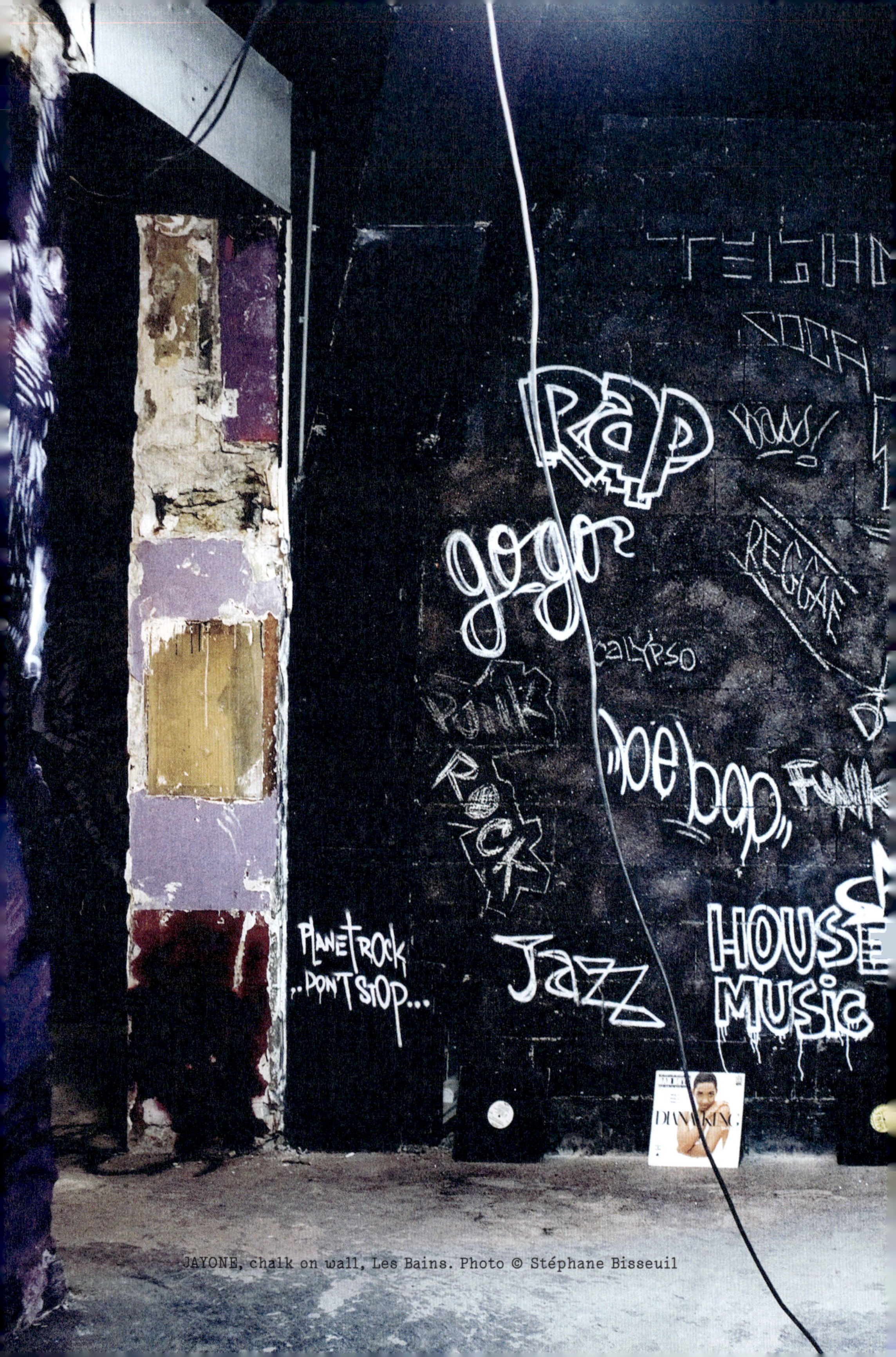

JAYONE, chalk on wall, Les Bains. Photo © Stéphane Bisseuil

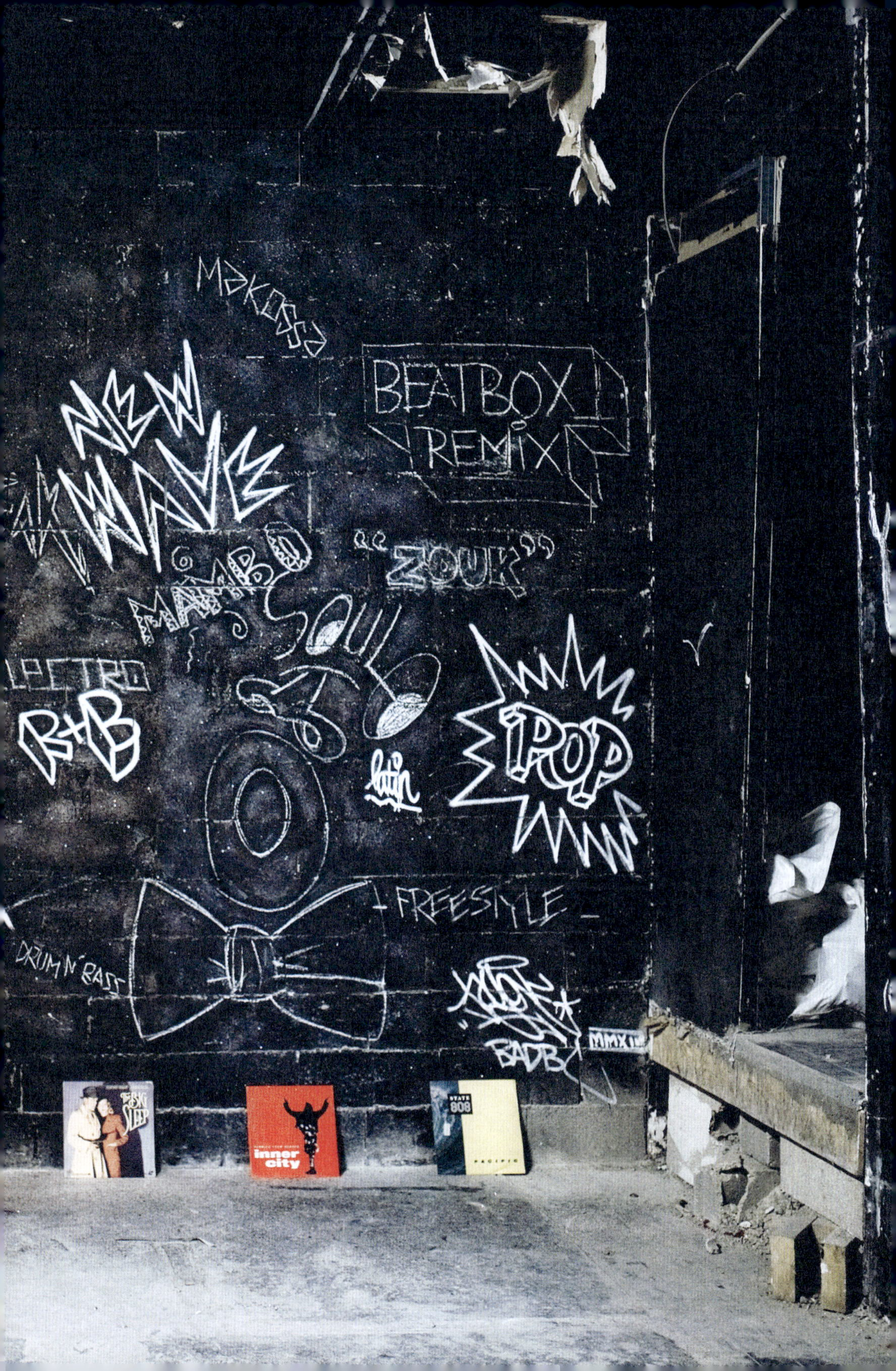
MAKOSSA
BEATBOX
REMIX
NEW WAVE
"ZOUK"
SOUL
LECTRO
R+B
latin
POP
FREESTYLE
DRUM N' BASS
BADB
The Big Sleep
inner city
STATE 808
PACIFIC

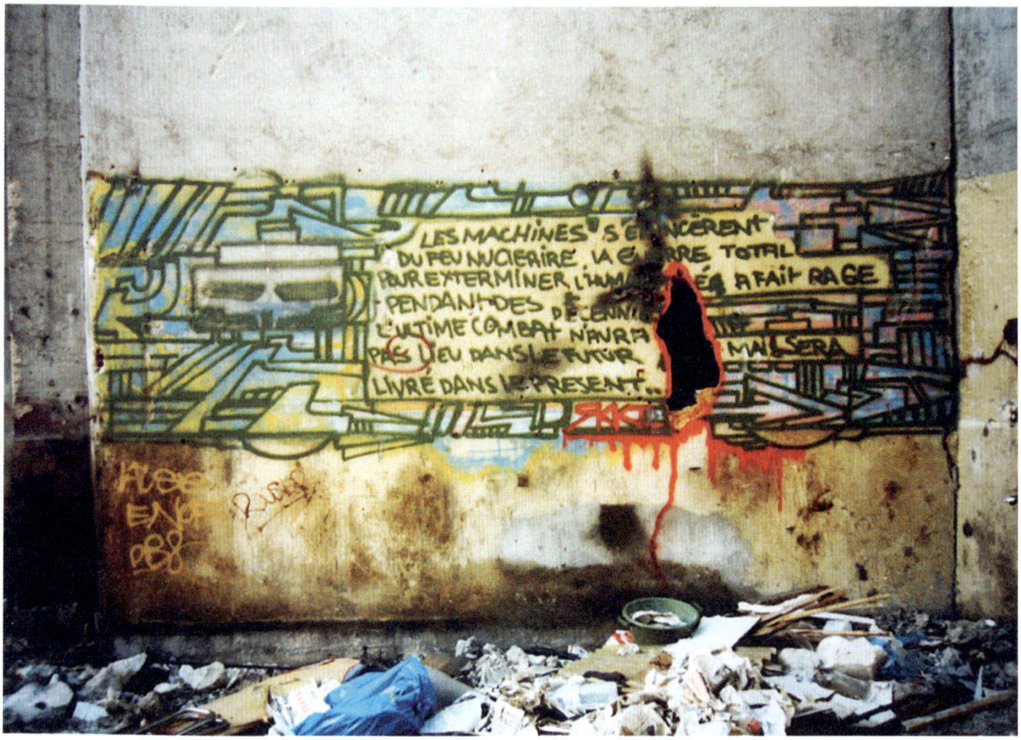

SKKI, *Terminator*, 1989. Photo © SKKI

SKKI, *Barcelona*, 1989. Photo © SKKI

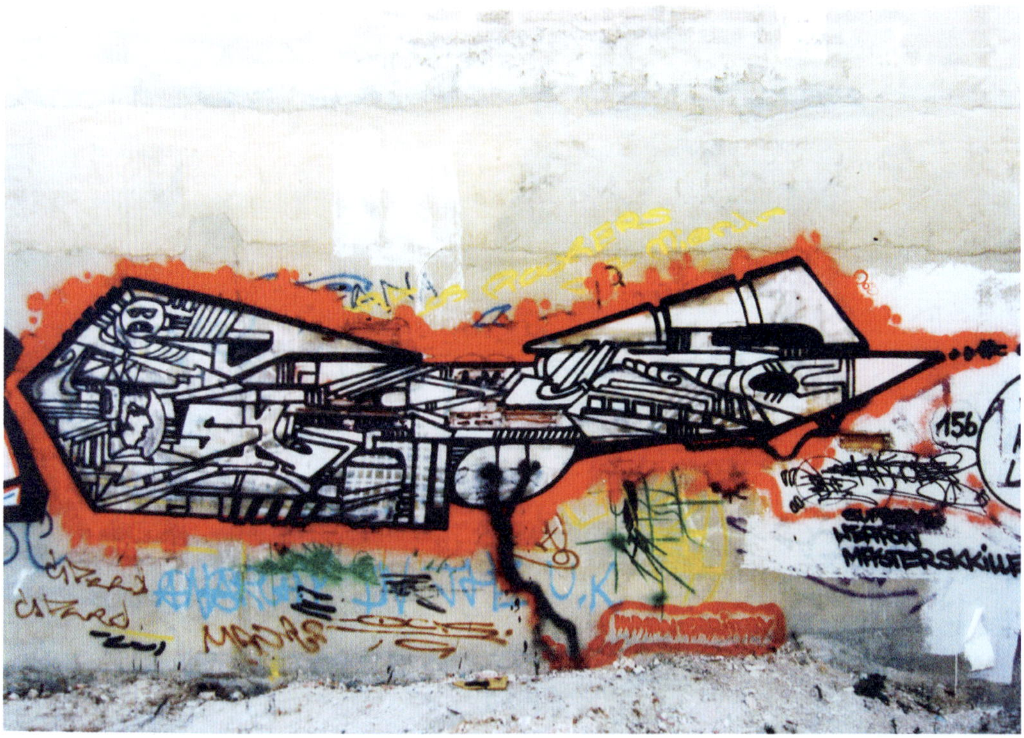

always executed with a precise sense of detail. The forms that he likes to integrate into his paintings are organic and mechanical. They are like elements of a toolbox that he combined to develop a personal, authentic visual language.

In terms of references, ASH mixes elements from the past, present and future, emphasizing formal contrasts. Sciences, communication, technology, architecture, graphic design and photography are among his many sources of inspiration. ASH sees himself as a chameleon, blending traditional painting with collage and stencil techniques.
In a process similar to that of a DJ, he mixes the elements of his painting. Although his universe is very graphical one, he prefers to use simple colours. Over time, he has devoted himself more and more to monumental murals works that increasingly are produced in black and white.
In Stalingrad, he cleared away for himself part of the site and painted it with the other BBC members: JAYONE and SKKI. SKKI also drew parallels between the original organic and plant environment of the land, which inspired him, and the manner in which graffiti "grew" there.

Because the embankments of the Seine were becoming increasingly unsuitable due to the speed with which graffiti was covered up, many—such as PSYCHOZE NO LIMIT and members of FORCE ALPHA—turned to Stalingrad. Most of the big European street artists have produced many murals there: MODE 2, BOXER and LOKISS joined BANDO, SKKI, ASH and JAY, and from 1985, they were joined by New York's JONONE.

Jay Ramier, aka JAY, born in 1967 in Morne-à-l'Eau in Guadeloupe, grew up in France. He drew a great deal during his childhood. He soon became fascinated by street art, and as a teenager he admired BLEK LE RAT's stencils. In 1983, he tried street art for himself and made his debut with his friend SKKI. This was the time when hip-hop was sweeping across Europe.

JAY was active in his own neighbourhood, near Jaurès and Stalingrad. He also worked in the vicinity of the Trocadero, where all the first local breakdancers would meet. It was also where he met ASH. Alongside SKKI, he produced pieces on the fencing around the Louvre and the Royal Palace, where BANDO and BLITZ of the Force Alpha group were already very active. These formative years were critical. SKKI remembers: "I'm lucky to have started with graffiti. I do not think that I could have experimented with as much artistic practice with a formal education from an art school, where it is the teachers who make the art while the students watch. Whether it's music, painting or dance, there is no better way to learn than to practice."

SKKI, La Chapelle Stalingrad wasteland, 1989. Photo © SKKI

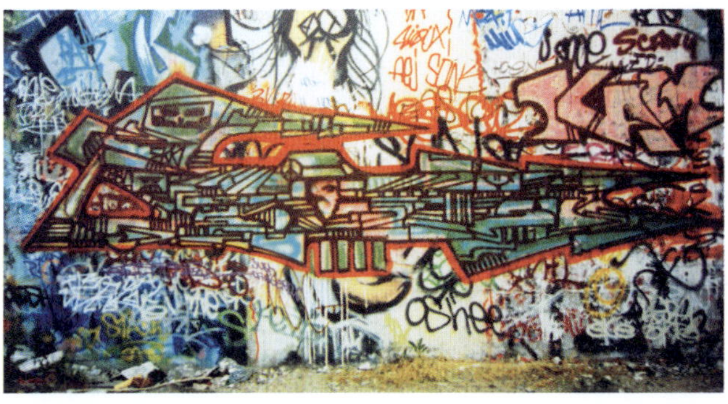

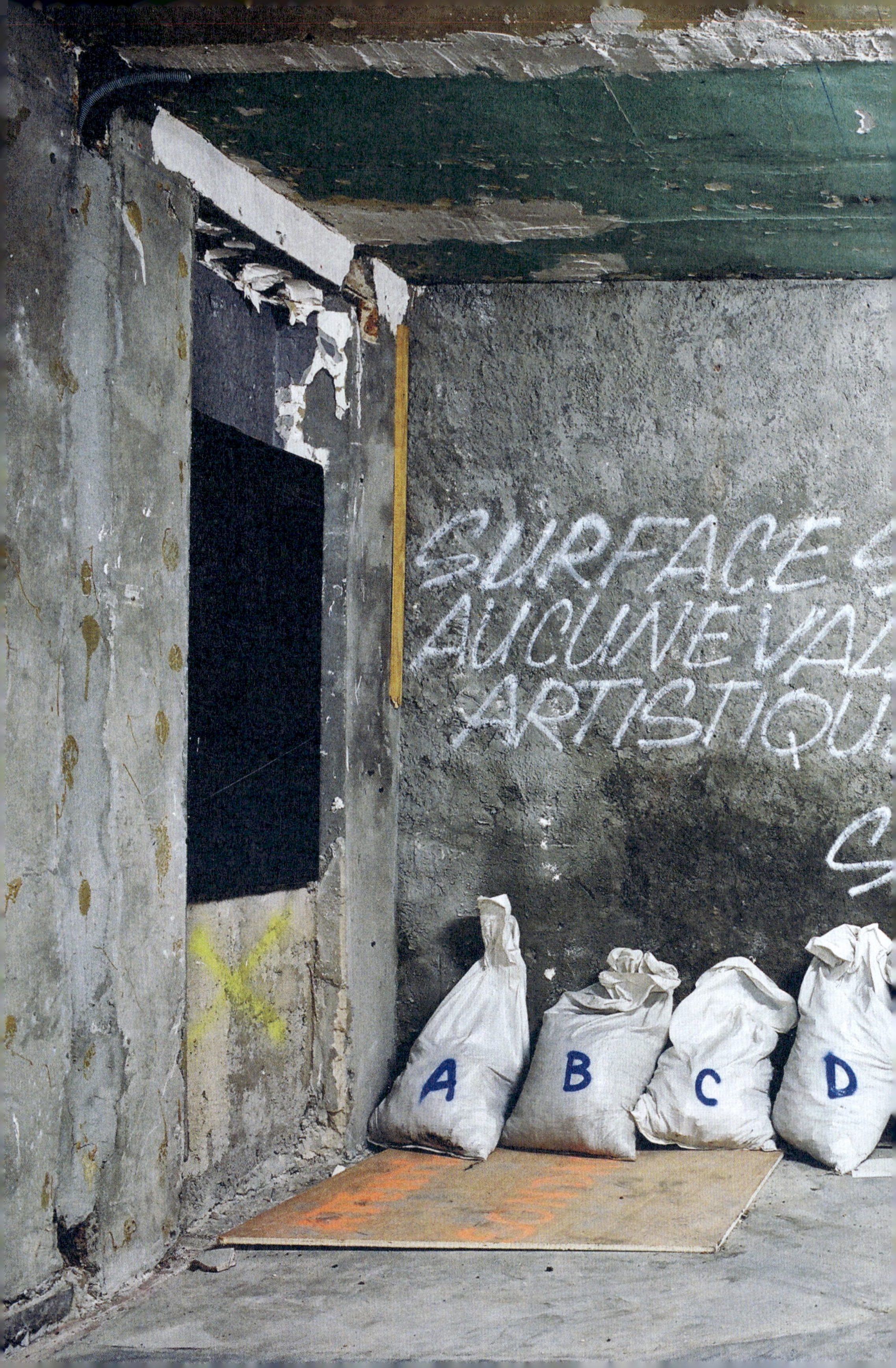
SURFACE
AUCUNE VAL
ARTISTIQU
A
B
C
D

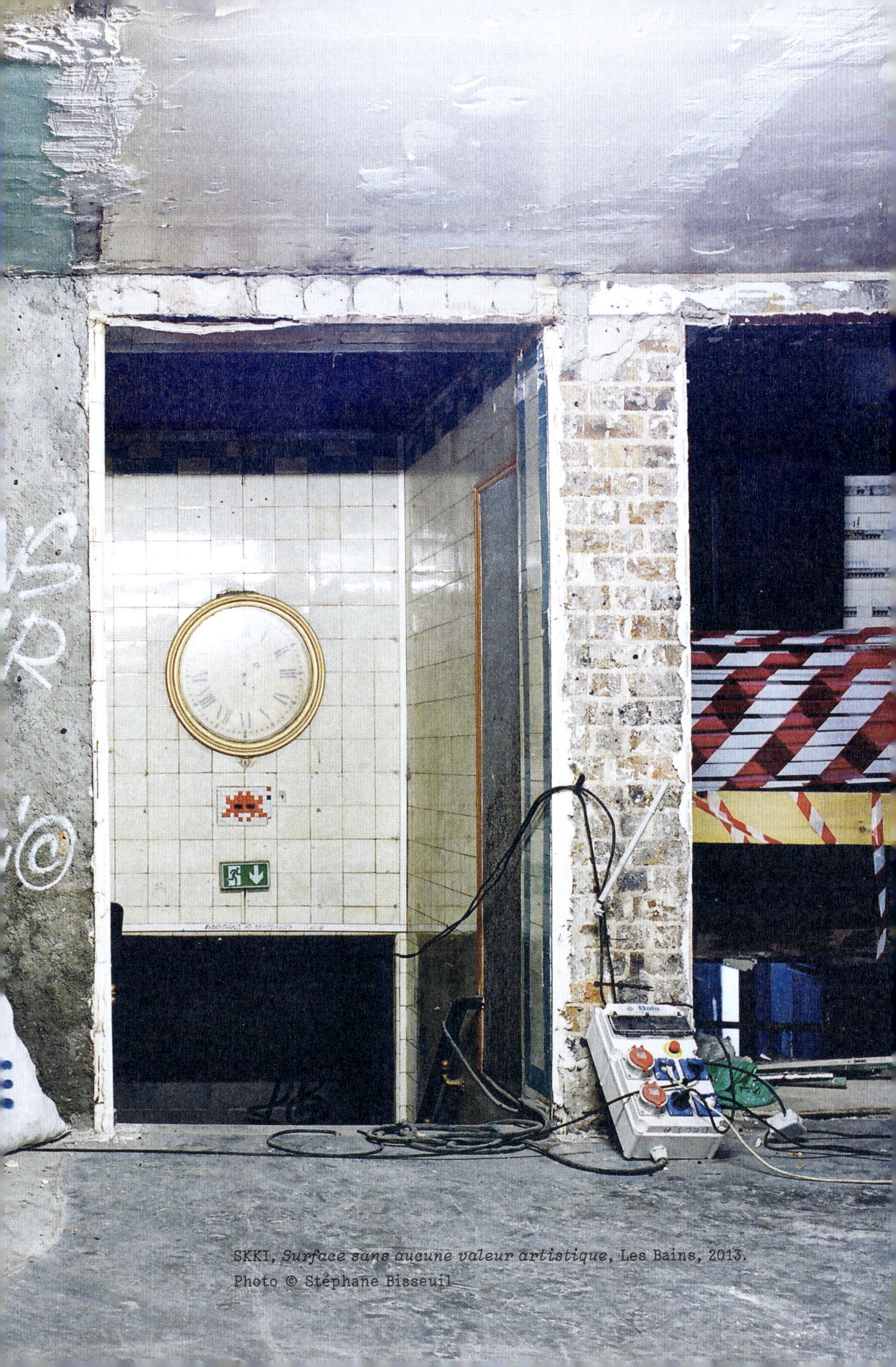

SKKI, *Surface sans aucune valeur artistique*, Les Bains, 2013.
Photo © Stéphane Bisseuil

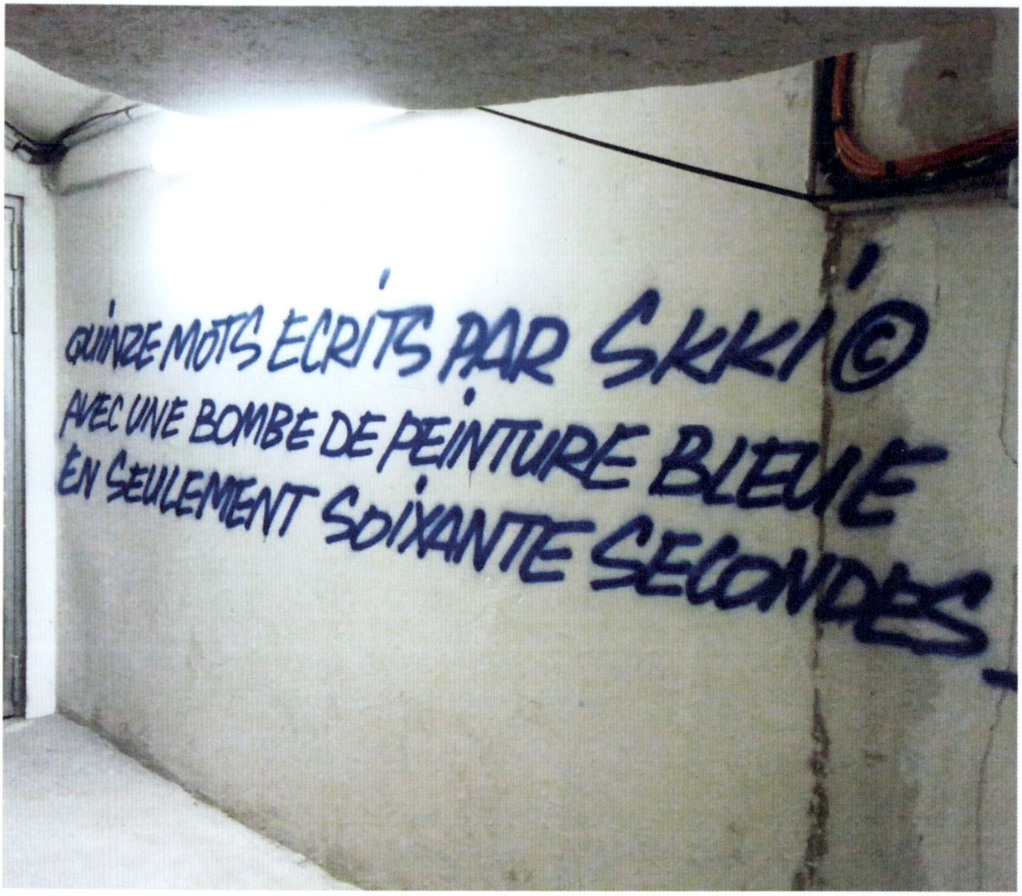

SKKI, *Quinze mots pour Lasco project 2*, Palais de Tokyo, November 2013
Photo © SKKI

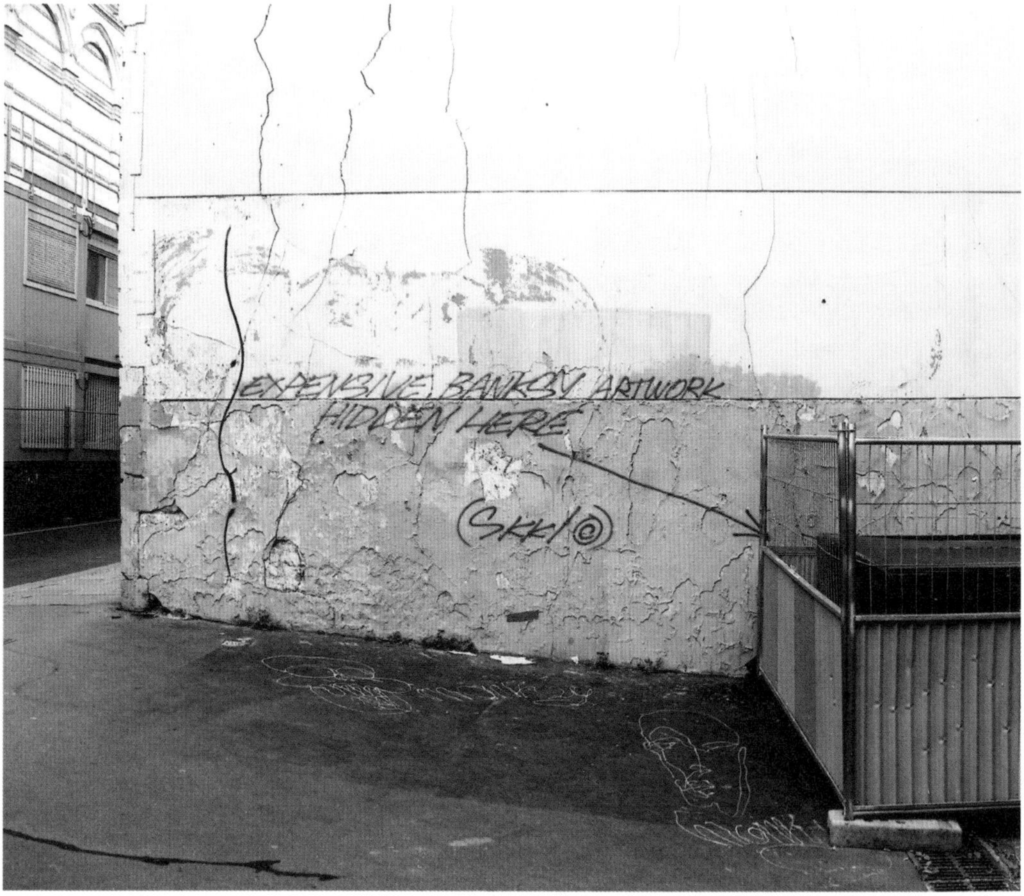

SKKI, *Expensive Banksy artwork hidden here*, 2013. Photo © SKKI
SKKI adds more conceptual references, or tagged sentences that are almost philosophical in nature.

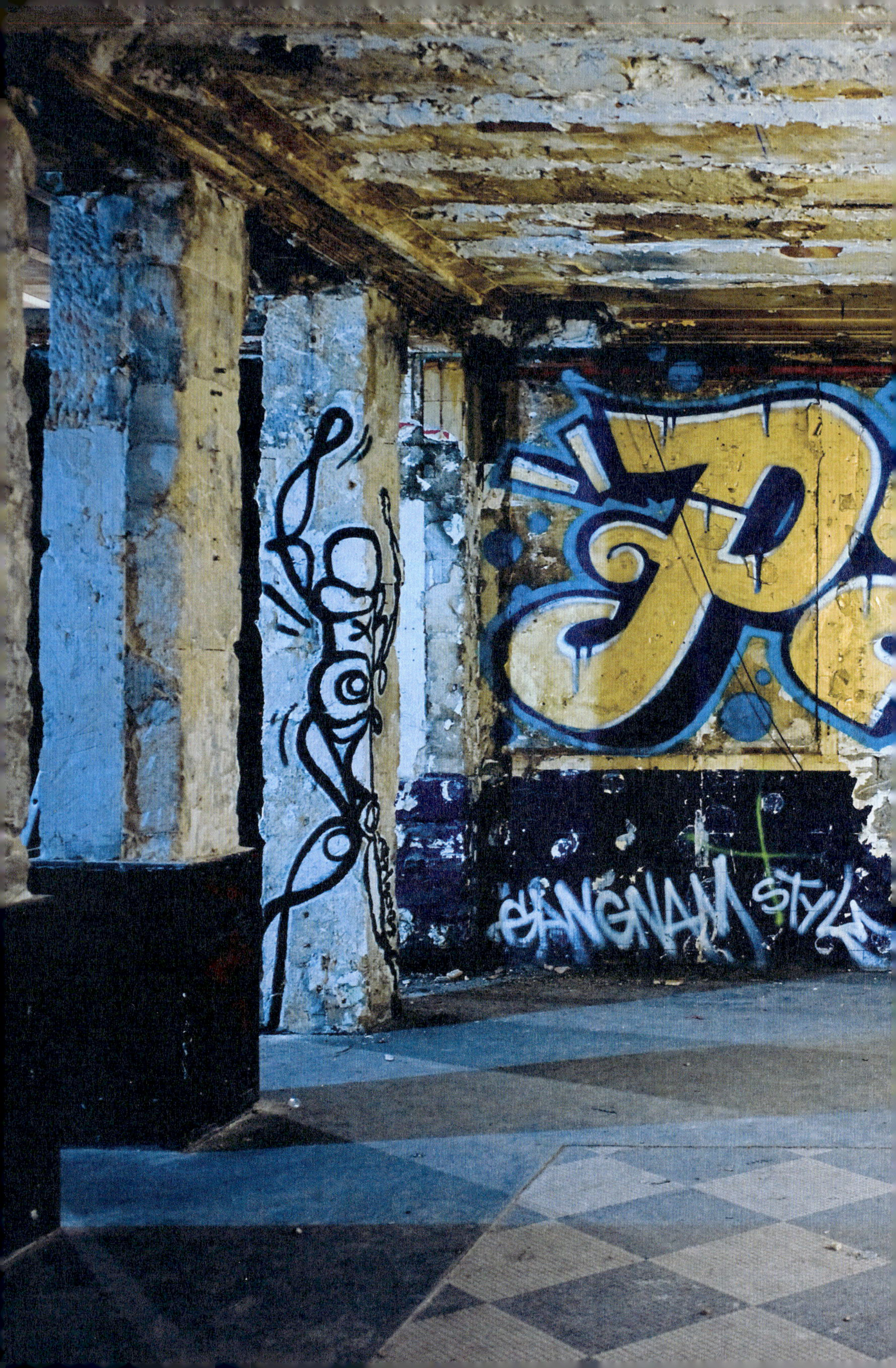
GANGNAM STYLE

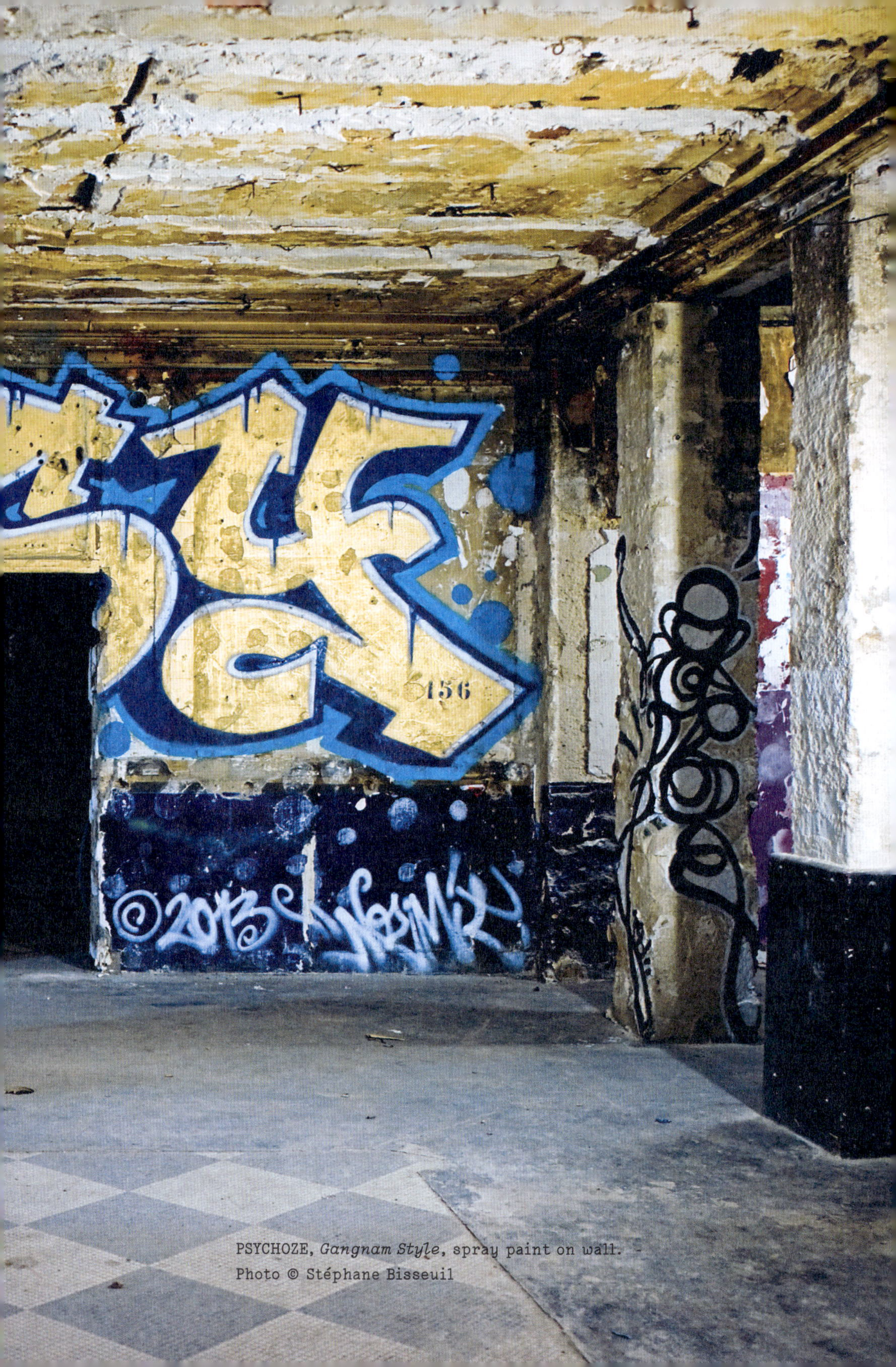

PSYCHOZE, *Gangnam Style*, spray paint on wall.
Photo © Stéphane Bisseuil

Berlin was undoubtedly a major influence on JAY's career. In parallel to painting outdoors, he was soon organizing workshops. In New York, he met graffiti artist RAC 7, as well as the mother of the young MEO (named Myles Carter and close in terms of style to JONONE). Their conversations on Haitian art shaped his work. "I do not really have a style... But my approach before starting any piece is simple and direct to avoid easy repetition. Something close to DADA." Harmonious clouds of colours and a mass of symbols are among his trademarks. His work was also influenced by artists like Jenny Holzer, Richard Prince, Raymond Pettibon, Kenny Scharf and the sculptor John Ahearn. But the street artists DOZE GREEN, SKKI, JONONE, TKID, LEE, TOXIC, SHARP, and A-ONE also played a role in his production, each for different reasons. Some of them inspired him through their painting approach, others in terms of technique or themes. And some simply provided advice. Art critics quickly nicknamed him the "Black Picasso," but JAY humbly declares himself "not to be among those who are technically qualified. In this battle with the canvas and the pigment, the energy required to give a soul to my work is humanity in all its grandeur and its weaknesses."

SKKI, born in 1967 in Paris, is an artist whose parents are of Polish origin. His pen name, as he likes to call his tag, comes from "ski," a nickname given to him by his classmates because of his unpronounceable Polish family name. He added a second K and later © for "copyright," as if his artist name was turning into a brand or a logo. "The use of pen names is very common in literary or artistic circles... Interestingly enough, most of the Russian revolutionaries also used them: Vladimir Ilyich Ulyanov (Lenin), Lev Davidovich Bronstein (Trotsky) and Skki ©!" At the time when he started, he listened to a lot of punk music, including the emblematic Clash. His first link with the graffiti scene came from there and came about in 1982 while he was watching the video for "This Is Radio Clash," in which FUTURA spray painted. What he calls a "cultural chemical reaction" changed how he saw things. In 1983, he painted his name in the streets of Paris, especially in the Stalingrad area, with his classmate JAY. They quickly moved on to complex murals, where SKKI added more conceptual references, or tagged sentences that were almost philosophical in nature.

The territory was crawling with artists who competed in artistic battles. To begin with, French street artists above all sought visibility and recognition from their peers, hence the desire to compete openly. This distinction between illegal painting on the metro and the more tolerated use of abandoned land was one of the keys of their expression. From their earliest days, street artists who preferred working on such land asserted a more artistic approach. The media soon focused on the Stalingrad phenomenon, placing the movement under the spotlight.

At this stage of development, it is interesting to note that artists were already planning their approach in a contextual art. Indeed, the wasteland of Stalingrad enjoyed a doubly favourable location: it was visible

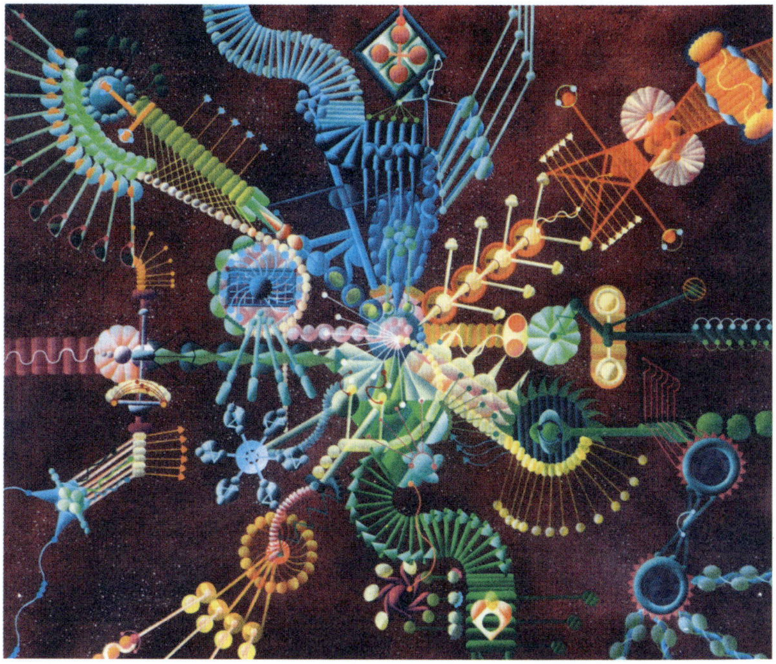

ASH, *Rayons series*, 155 × 150 cm, spray paint and acrylic on canvas, 1993
Archives of the artist © A.R.R.

from both the street and the overhead metro. This "open-air gallery," as SKKI called it, soon became essential, and a great number of young people went there to soak up the new culture of hip-hop.

On the back of the success of his legendary book on graffiti on the New York subway, *Subway Art,* photographer Henry Chalfant answered BANDO's invitation to document the European scene. The resulting book, *Spraycan Art,* immortalized the first steps of European graffiti. Upon discovering this scene centred on Paris, he was struck by the inventiveness of the style, which, at the same time as incorporating American codes and precepts, reinvented this writing and made its reading even more complex, thereby fully affirming its singularity.
A master of tangled letters and of wild style, French graffiti artist LOKISS (born in 1968) astonished people with his dexterity and the level of abstraction that he was able to achieve in making his handwriting illegible to the neophyte's eye.

A style war raged once more, with two schools asserting themselves and competing.
On one side, the group gathered around BANDO extolled lettering work as a meaningful object whose lines must be perfect and legible. The concept of construction was key. As in architecture, each element and each letter should find its form and its balance, then fit perfectly into a whole.

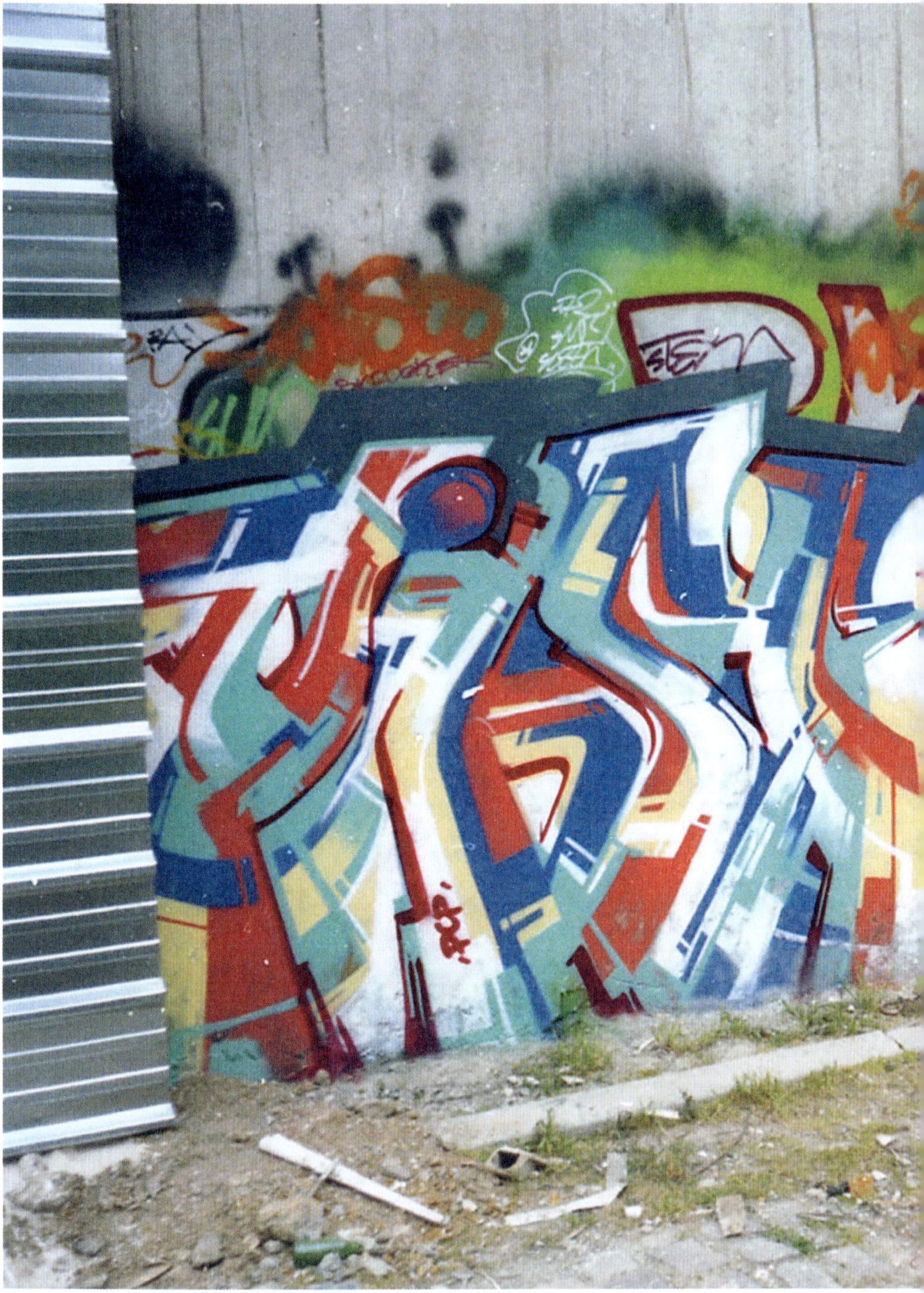

DISCO PCP on wasteland in the 14th arrondissement, Paris, 1990.
Photo © Tarek Ben Yakhlef

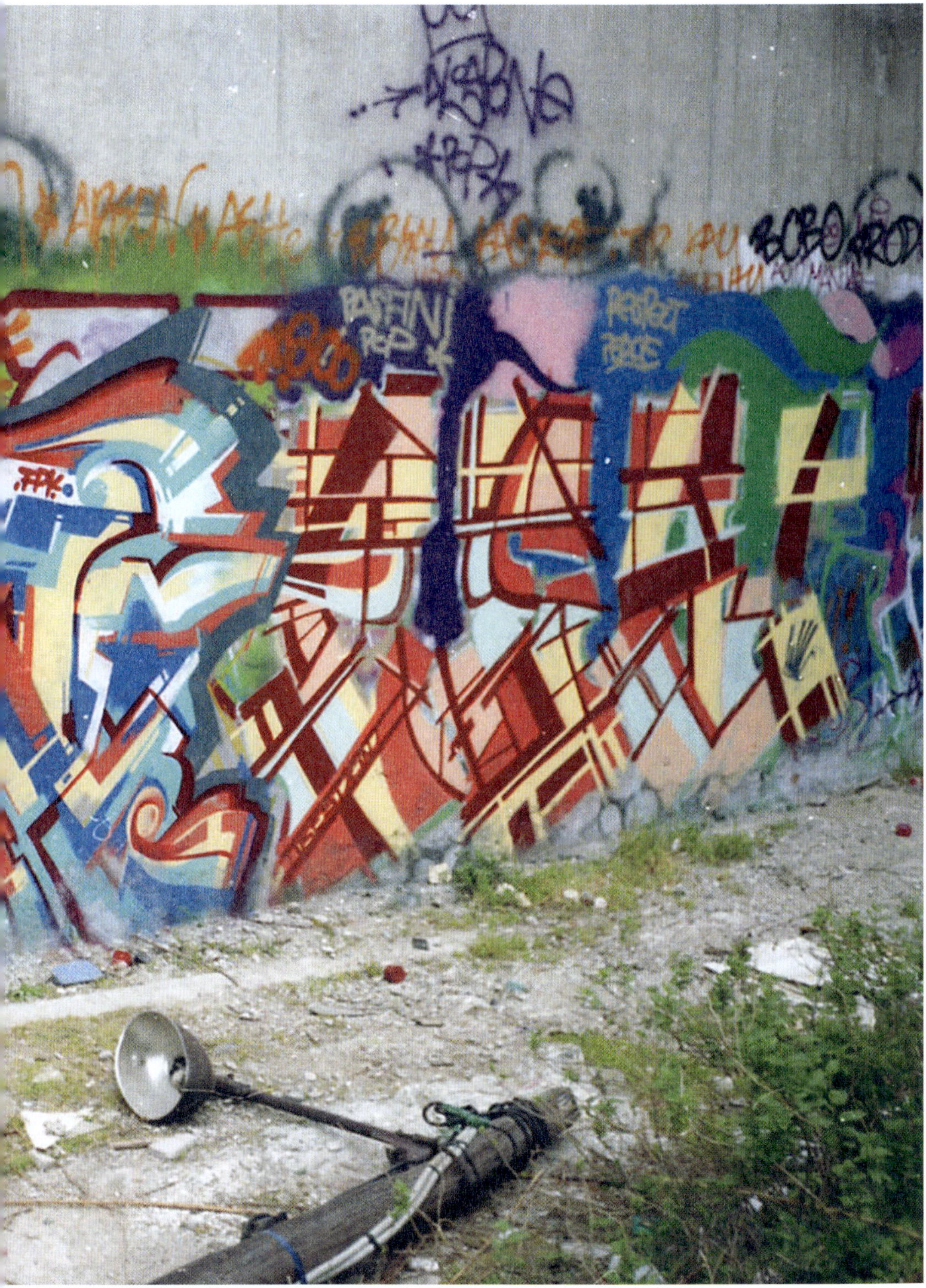

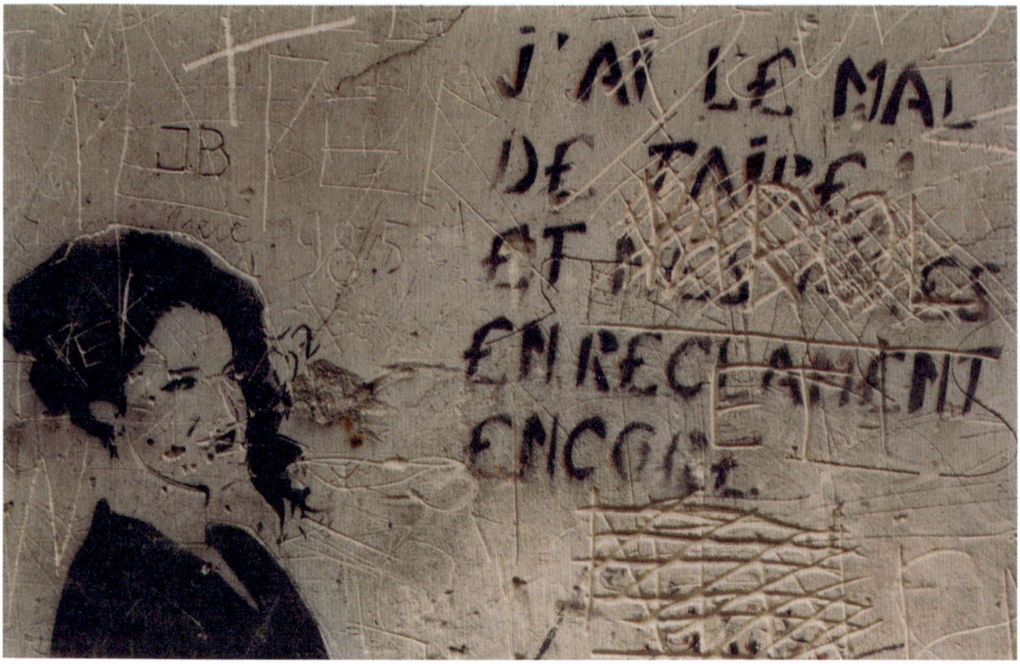

MISS.TIC, "I have trouble keeping quiet and my wings are begging for more", Paris, 1986. © A.R.R. Courtesy of the Miss.Tic estate.

BANDO even went as far as separating letters so that each came to life autonomously, independently of the word, the name and the signature. In this sense, BANDO was influenced by his American precursor DONDI, while still creating his own style: sharp letters with fine connections between them, as well as sophistication and complexity. On the other, the BBC understood things in terms of the form as a whole. They sometimes did not even give letters an outline, and their writing became illegible. They wanted to work more on composition than on technique.
It is in this frenzied atmosphere —in this French English, Dutch, German and American melting pot— that graffiti would take a decidedly artistic turn.

The years 1985 and 1986 marked Stalingrad's heyday, but creative outbursts also flourished throughout the city. Illegal graffiti spread like wildfire. Graffiti artists "massacred" the walls of the city and "tore" whole metro cars, as they described their activities. And they constantly sought the best spots—that is, the most visible ones. Public opinion was angered. The rail operators RATP and SNCF and Paris's local government hired specialist brigades in charge of monitoring sensitive locations. They made a show of publishing press releases containing alarming details of the cleaning costs that graffiti required. Punishments became more severe, reinforcing the fratricidal debate between artists who backed an illegal approach to tagging and those who wished to explore a more artistic world of murals. The distinction between taggers and graffiti artists remained difficult because of their common culture and sometimes shared practices; the conflict gave rise to thorny semantic debates.

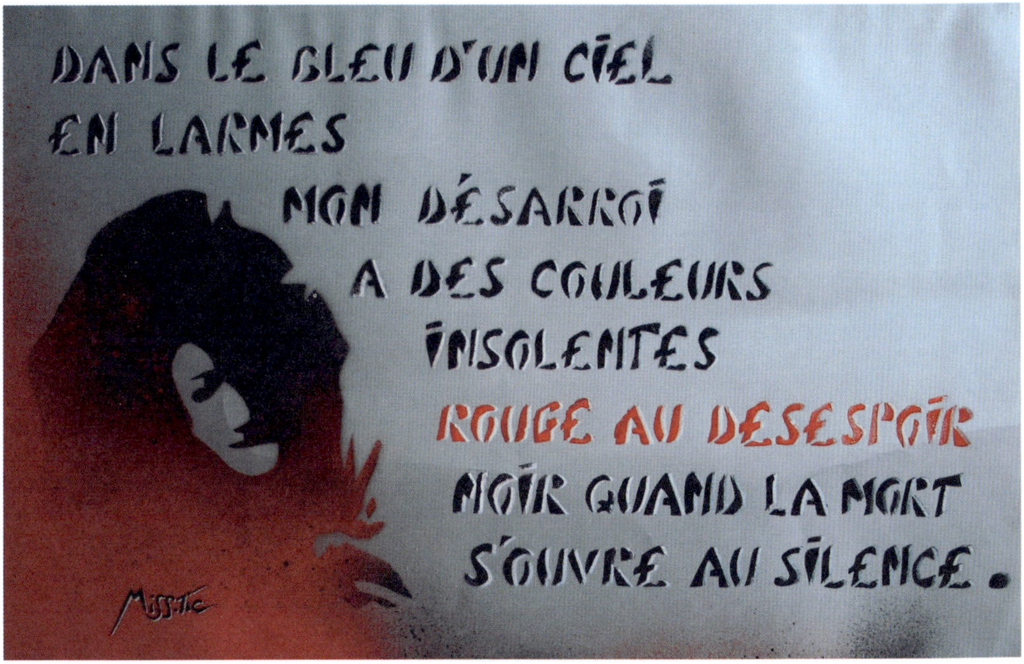

MISS.TIC, "*In the blue of a weeping sky...*", Paris, 1986.

But the Parisian scene was not just Stalingrad. Elsewhere, street artists' creativity was developing just as greatly. Standing out from the tags and frescoes of graffiti artists, the works of the stencil artist MISS. TIC (born in 1956 in Paris) appeared in this urban pictorial landscape from 1985. One of the few well-known female stencil artists, she produced her work on walls. She mixes stencil and poetry through subtle word play that complements her imagery. Embodying above all the free woman, she plays on stereotypes of attractive and seductive women to better question them. Outwitting the false perfection found in advertising and the redundancies of its slogans, MISS. TIC appears where she is not expected—that is, everywhere.

In January 1992, hip-hop and graffiti culture reached its peak with the exhibition *Graffiti Art – Artistes américains et français – 1981-1991* (*Graffiti Art – American and French Artists– 1981-1991*), which was held at the Musée des Monuments français in Paris and brought together the biggest names of the time, including CRASH, DONDI (whose work graced the cover of the catalogue) and SEEN. This monumental exhibition reversed scenographic codes by letting the artists produce works on large indoor fencing, present huge installations, and project documentary videos. Cut-out figures straight from the world of graffiti accompanied the public throughout their visit. The exhibition raised once more the eternal debate: where do tags end, and where does graffiti begin?

For many young graffiti artists, the beginning of the 1990s coincided with the peak of their feats. NASTY captured the attention of eyes and minds by spray painting an RATP advertising slogan on a whole car of the overhead metro.

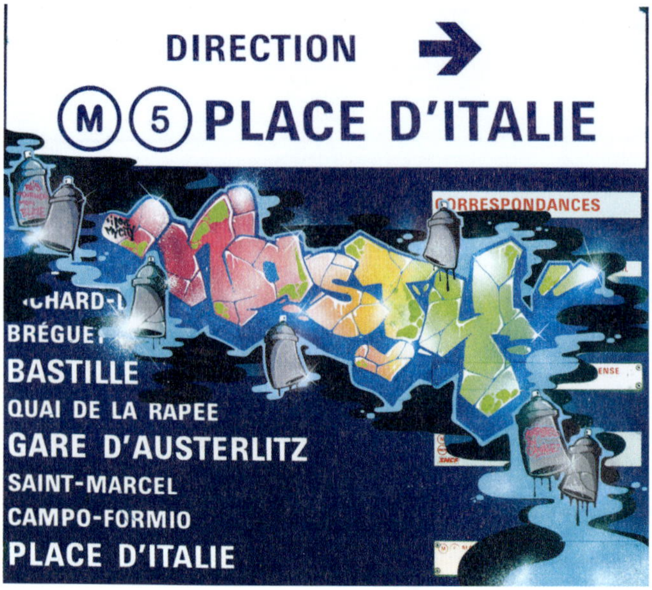

NASTY, *Place d'Italie*, spray paint on metro sign © A.R.R.

NASTY, *T'as le ticket chic*, 1990. By borrowing the RATP's famous advertising slogan, NASTY produced one of his most emblematic works. © A.R.R.

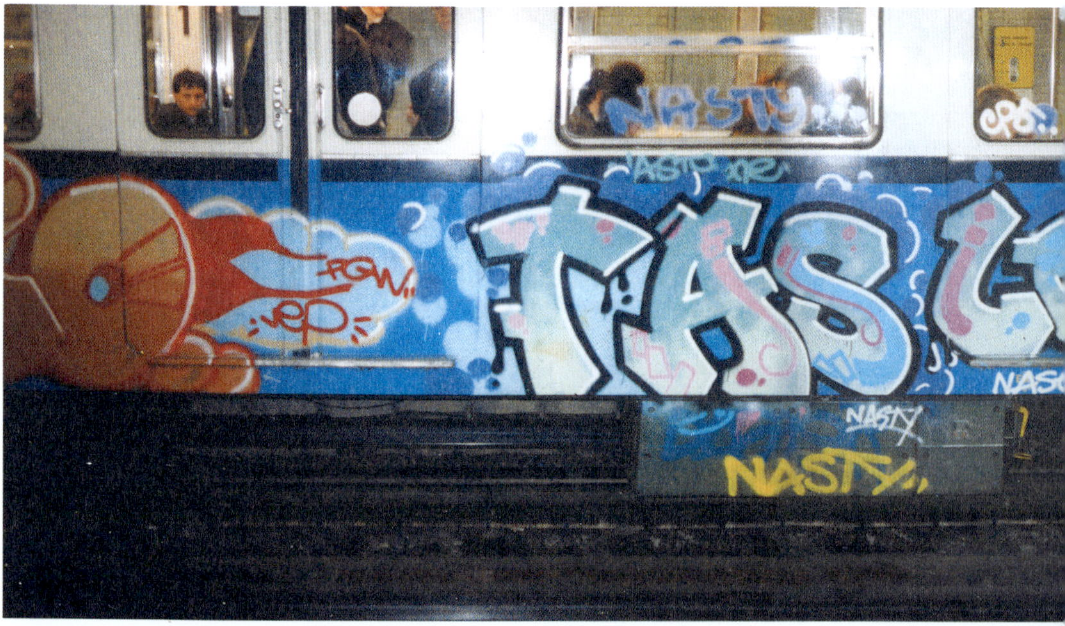

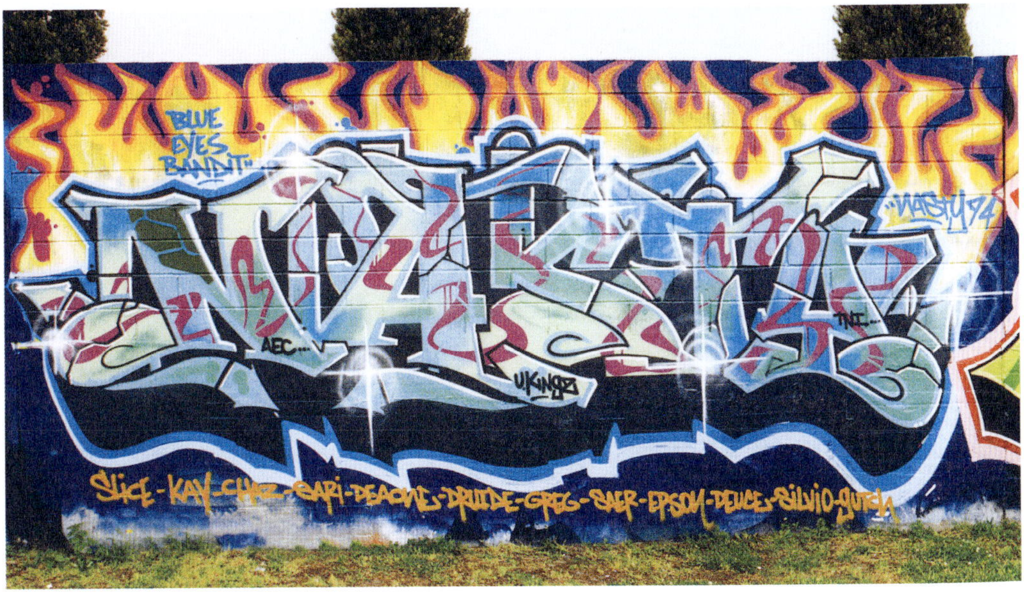

NASTY, Bobigny, 2001 © Gaut

"I always told myself that graffiti borrowed its codes from advertising: repetition, strategic locations, slogans and so on. So one day, I borrowed the RATP's slogan, hijacking it for my benefit. Everyone loved this nod, and it remained in people's memories." NASTY

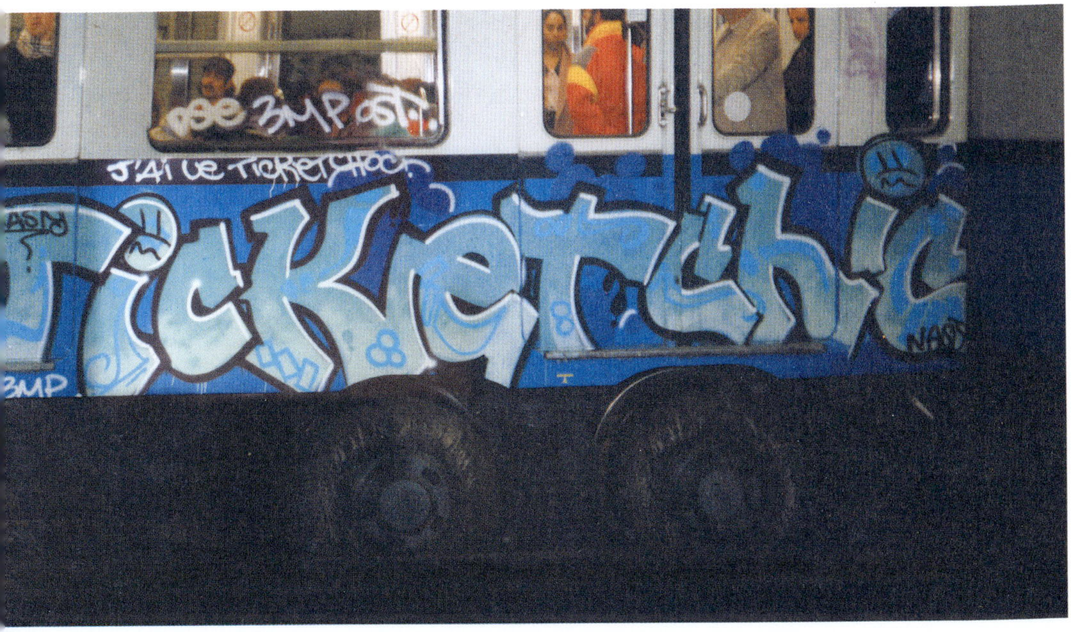

André Saraiva, alias ANDRÉ, born in 1971, started doing graffiti in 1985. He felt inspired by seeing the mysterious names of BOXER and BANDO. For this fan of Brassaï, taking possession of walls was a major artistic gesture. In place of a signature, he spray painted his character Mr A, who was recognizable to all through its asymmetric eyes: one round and the other a cross. ANDRÉ was a forerunner of the drawing of characters within a postgraffiti approach. He painted hundreds of thousands of them. This conceptualization of the signature was also the mark of a looming artistic turn.

The movement extended across all of France. In Marseille, FORCE ALPHA was the group that took the city's façades by force. In Toulouse, *la Ville Rose*, graffiti sprouted in the mid-1980s among the young punk and skate ranks, before developing into a truly creative practice at the beginning of the next decade. At this time, the eighteen-year-old Miss Van started to paint in the street. Her innovative style contrasts with traditionally masculine urban art. She stood out through a style of her own, in which lettering was abandoned in favour of figuration. The currents that have influenced her work range from *figuration libre* to 1950s pin-ups, comics and religious imagery.

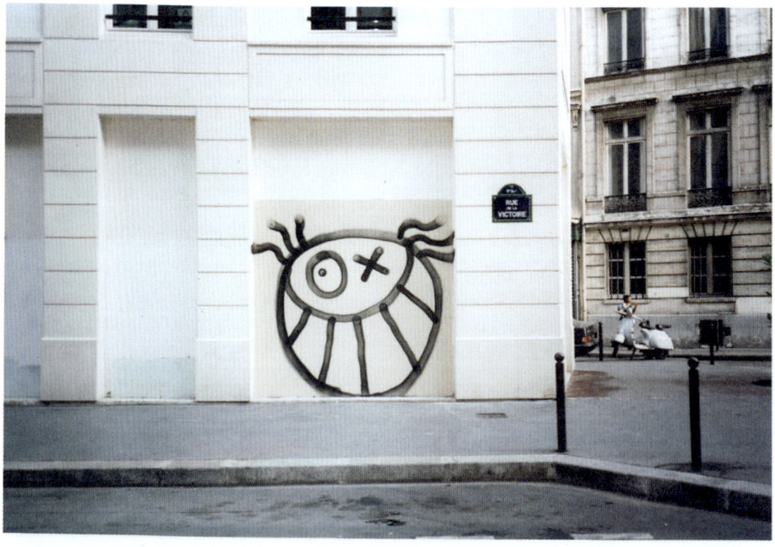

ANDRÉ, *Mister A,* his alter ego, became his signature.

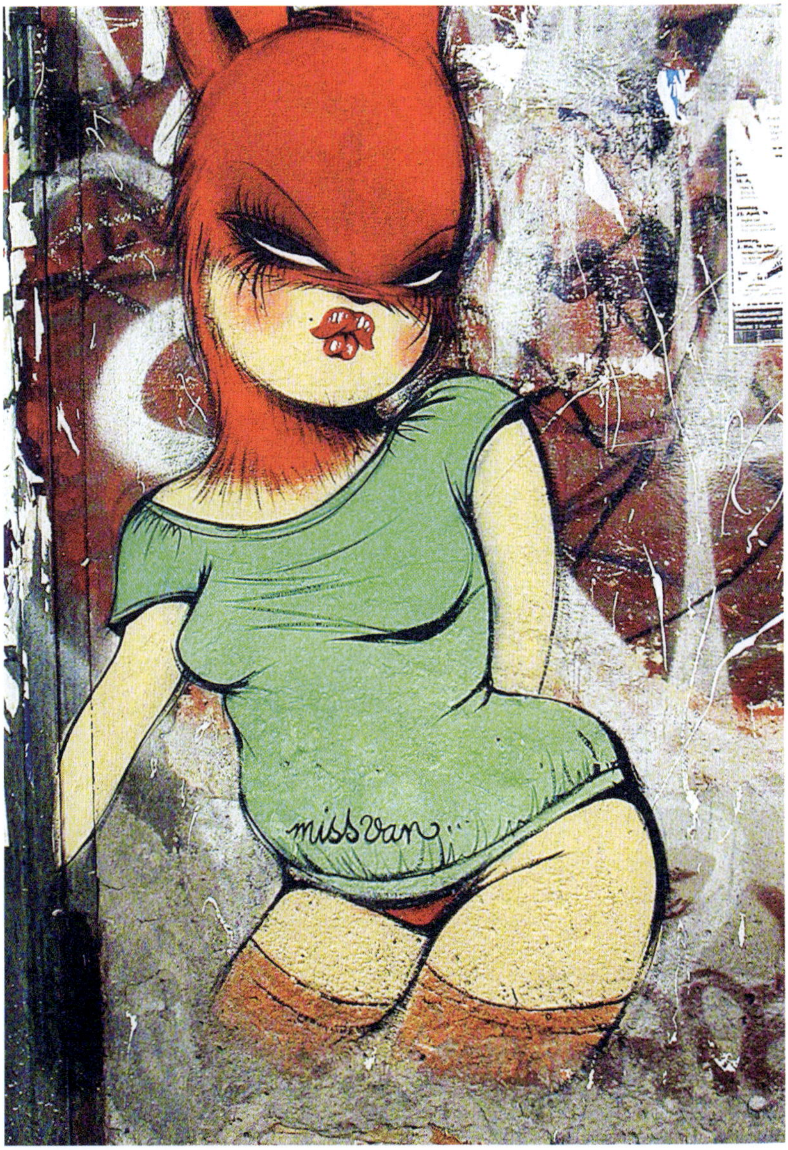

MISS VAN, Berlin, 2004 © Miss Van

THE ADVENT OF A CONTEXTUAL ART

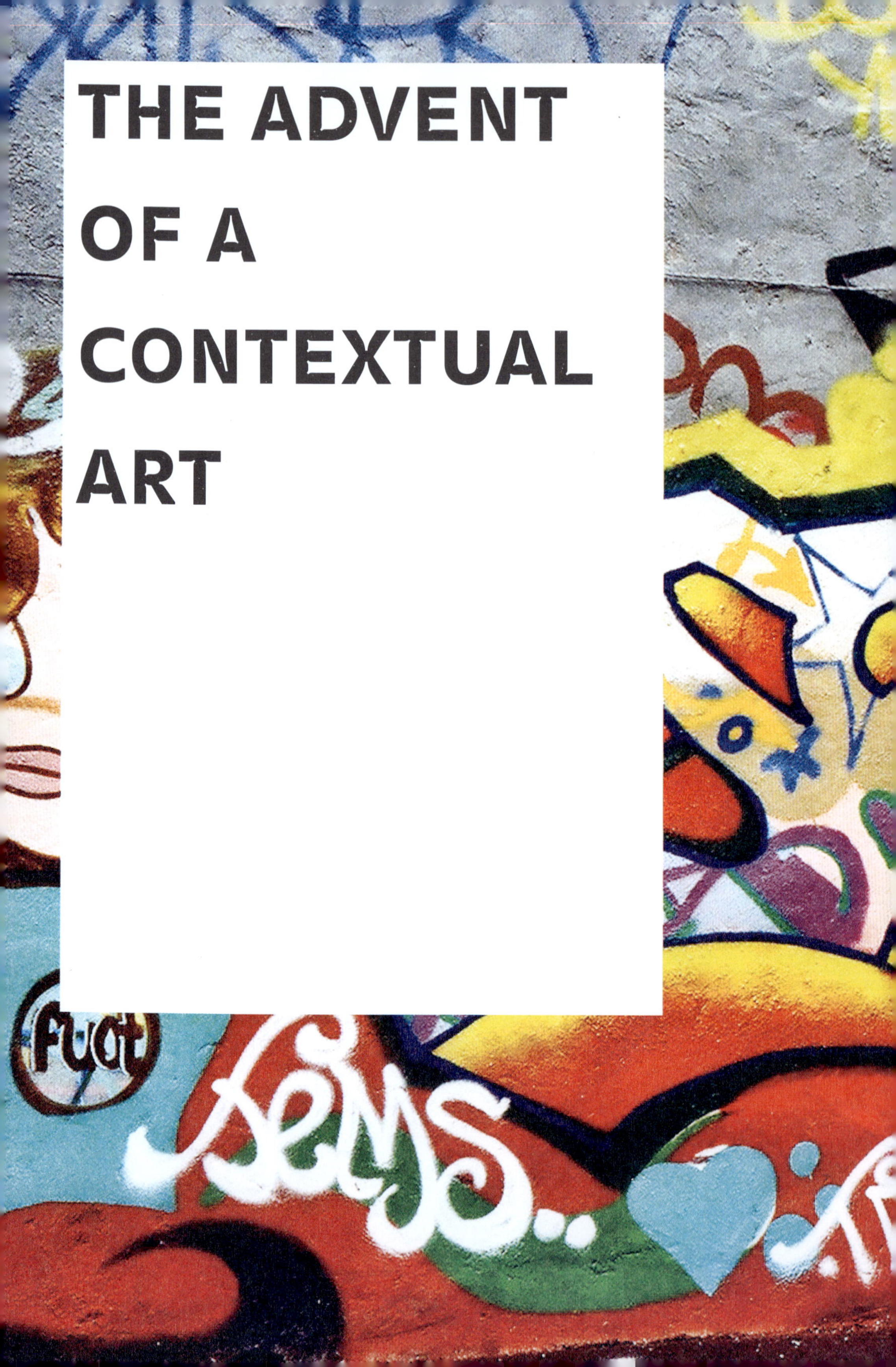

CHANGING COURSE 129

A guerrilla war that gave birth to street art 129

The stencil 130

Enrichment of the movement through contact with other practices and cultures 136

The strength of the message 156

STREET ART IS EVERYWHERE 165

The success of the cult of anonymity and pervasive art 165

Turning the street into the world's biggest gallery 181

Secret exploration and Urbex 187

A writing of the illegible 188

The hypervisible and its context 200

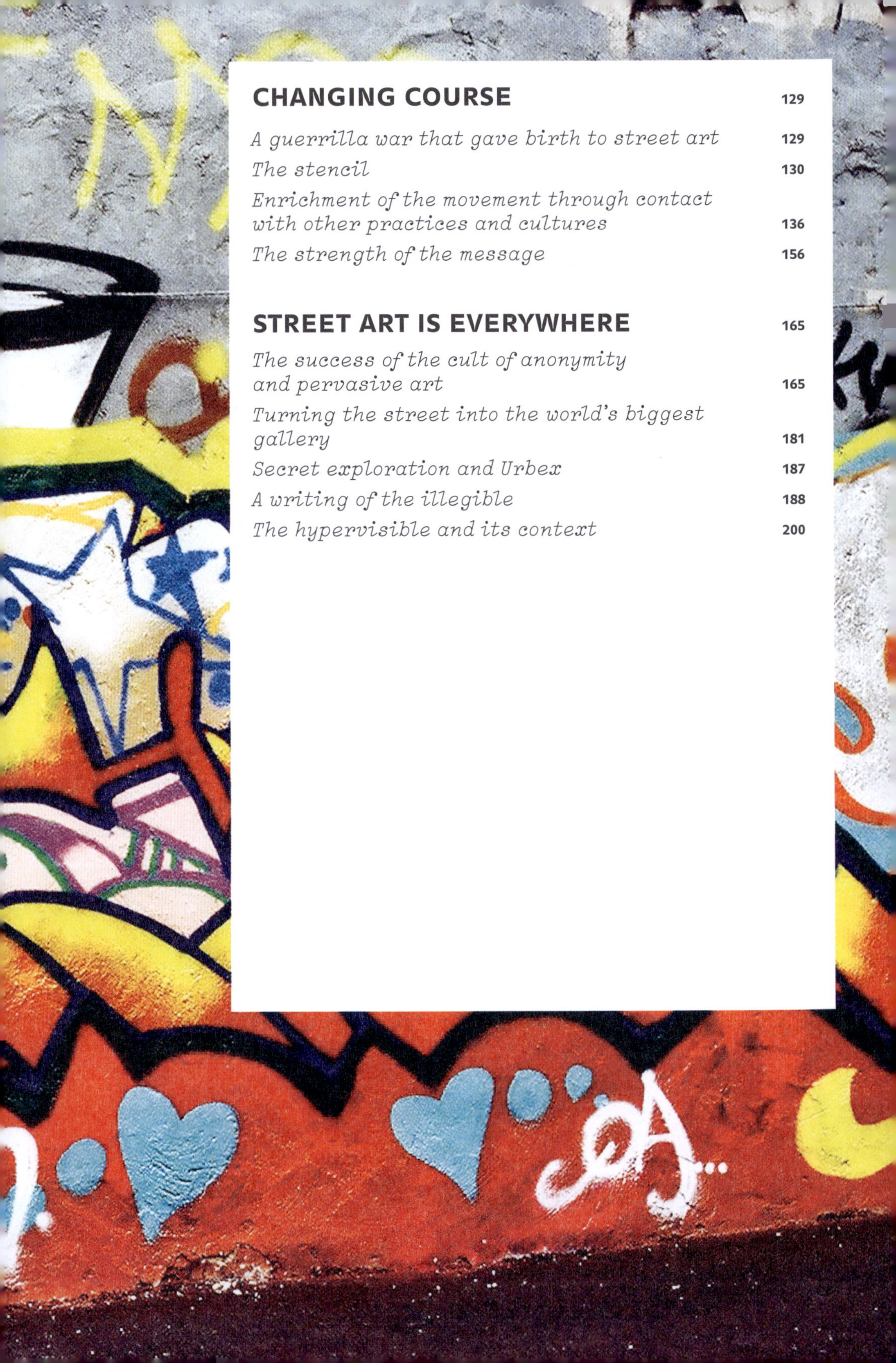

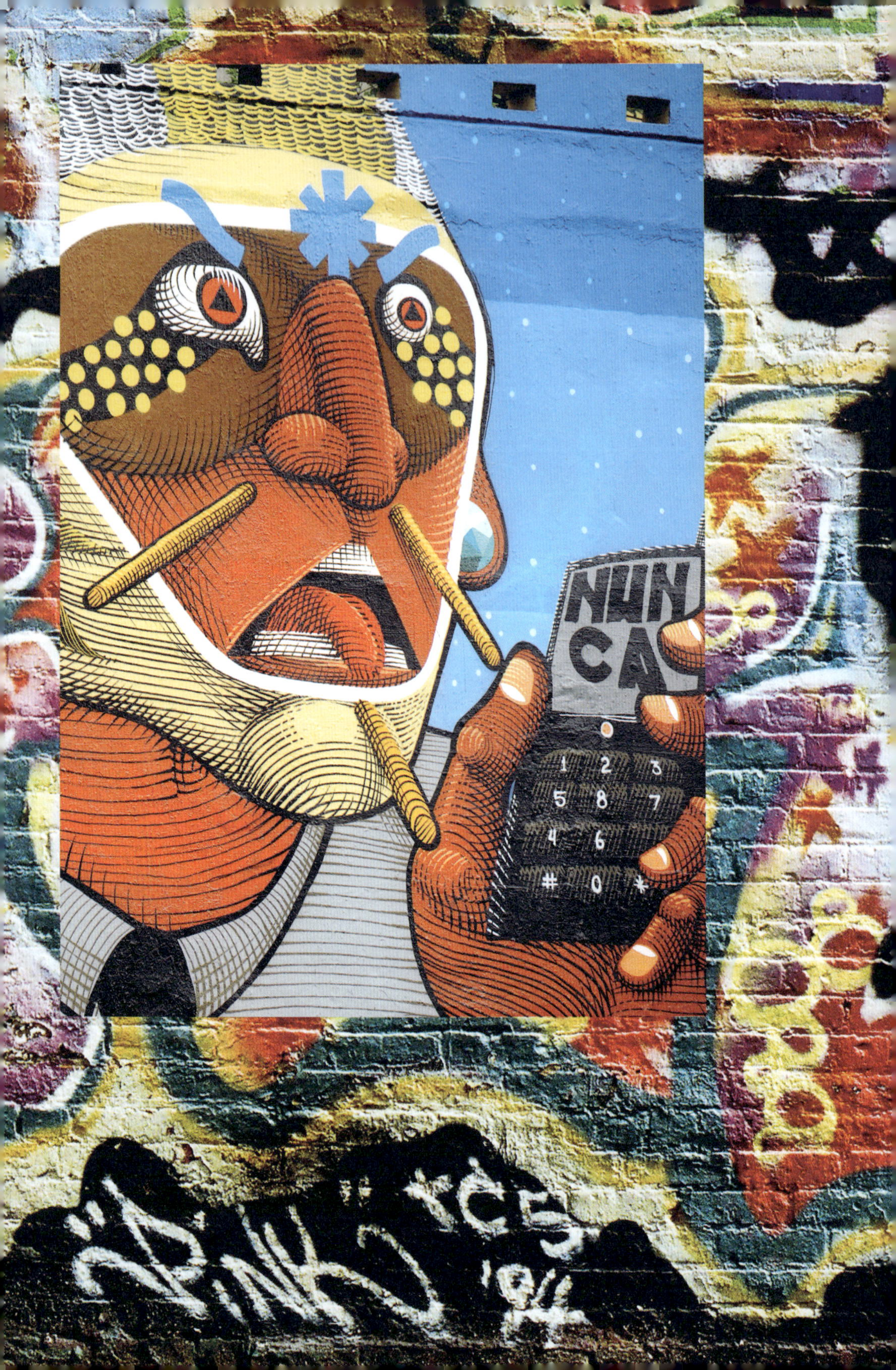
NUN
CA

CHANGING COURSE

A guerrilla war that gave birth to street art

At the dawn of the new millennium, urban art experienced a revival. Enriched with new practices, the movement became stronger at a time when it could have faltered or disappeared under the weight of repression. After American graffiti and then its European disciples, a third generation was born. This inventive and cosmopolitan bunch marked a new milestone for the movement.

The main causes of this renewal can above all be found in a context that was both very coercive and fiercely competitive, with originality bringing recognition. In addition, the advent of the Internet generated rapid dissemination and even stronger emulation. From this, a renewed creativity and increased activism came about. Work in itself was now assumed to convey a message.

The legal reprisals handed down to street artists everywhere in Europe produced a form of guerrilla warfare that made it necessary to reinvent both how to work and the shape that pieces took. The increase in constraints in competition between street artists and in the surfaces on which creations were produced led to major artistic breakthroughs. The context of each country, especially that of France, where urban art existed before graffiti, gave impetus to artists in substantial and singular ways. As the 1990s began, encounters with other artistic techniques and cultural movements proved to be extremely fruitful.

NUNCA, wall, (detail) © A.R.R.

Behind: graffiti in New York. Photo © Stéphane Bisseuil

This is the time when street artists who were just starting out became increasingly involved in art schools, seeking to pursue their passion while distinguishing themselves from their forerunners who had established their reputations two decades before. Being different, finding one's own style as well as a new mode of expression, and at the same time remaining consistent with the movement's principles were key priorities. In response to this evolution that was worthy of a revolution, many debates have raged. The term "graffiti" has ceased to be appropriate for referring to the practices of new artists. They do not necessarily confine themselves to spray paint, even if they respect the concept of the signature and virality— one of the engines of graffiti and street art. The virus-like proliferation of *in situ* works is paramount. Whether they work with spray paint, stencil or postering, street artists seek above all to spread their creations everywhere, on as many walls and in as many cities as possible. We can see this in SPACE INVADER's mosaics representing the characters from the namesake video game. This new type of signature has pushed some to say that it no longer belongs to the same artistic movement. However, all these artists, including Space Invader, share the same culture and reality. Following the terms "graffiti" and then "postgraffiti," the expressions "urban art" and then later "street art" have progressively become more widely used to refer to the movement in its entirety, regardless of whether or not the works are carried out with spray paint or involve lettering.

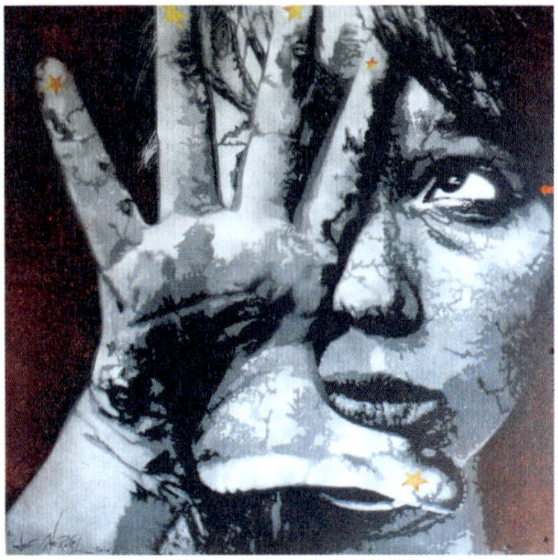

JEF AEROSOL, *Melanie*, cardboard stencil, 100×100 cm © A.R.R.

The stencil

The stencil is probably the perfect example of these branches of street art that did not specifically begin in New York and that existed before graffiti. This practice focuses just as much energy from the street and shares a common history. However, it has experienced a much more prudent and humble rise, and it has also been enriched through contact with pop, rock and punk influences. Beyond its inspirations, its specificity lies in the technique itself, which is one of contrasts. Stencils are prepared in the studio, and they are the result of careful cutting. This gives rise to a thick, lace-like paper template. Then, this initial laborious work having borne fruit, the artist can quickly apply her or his stencil to the often rough surface of a wall.

The great stencil artists of the 1980s —for example, BLEK LE RAT, MIX MIX, MISS. TIC, MARIE ROUFFET, JEROME MESNAGER, EPSYLON POINT, PAUL ETHERNO, HERVE MORLAY (known as VR) and JEF AEROSOL— were followed in the 1990s by NEMO, the SPLIX collective (Pixal Parazite, Spliff Gâchette), LASZLO, MOSKO and C215.

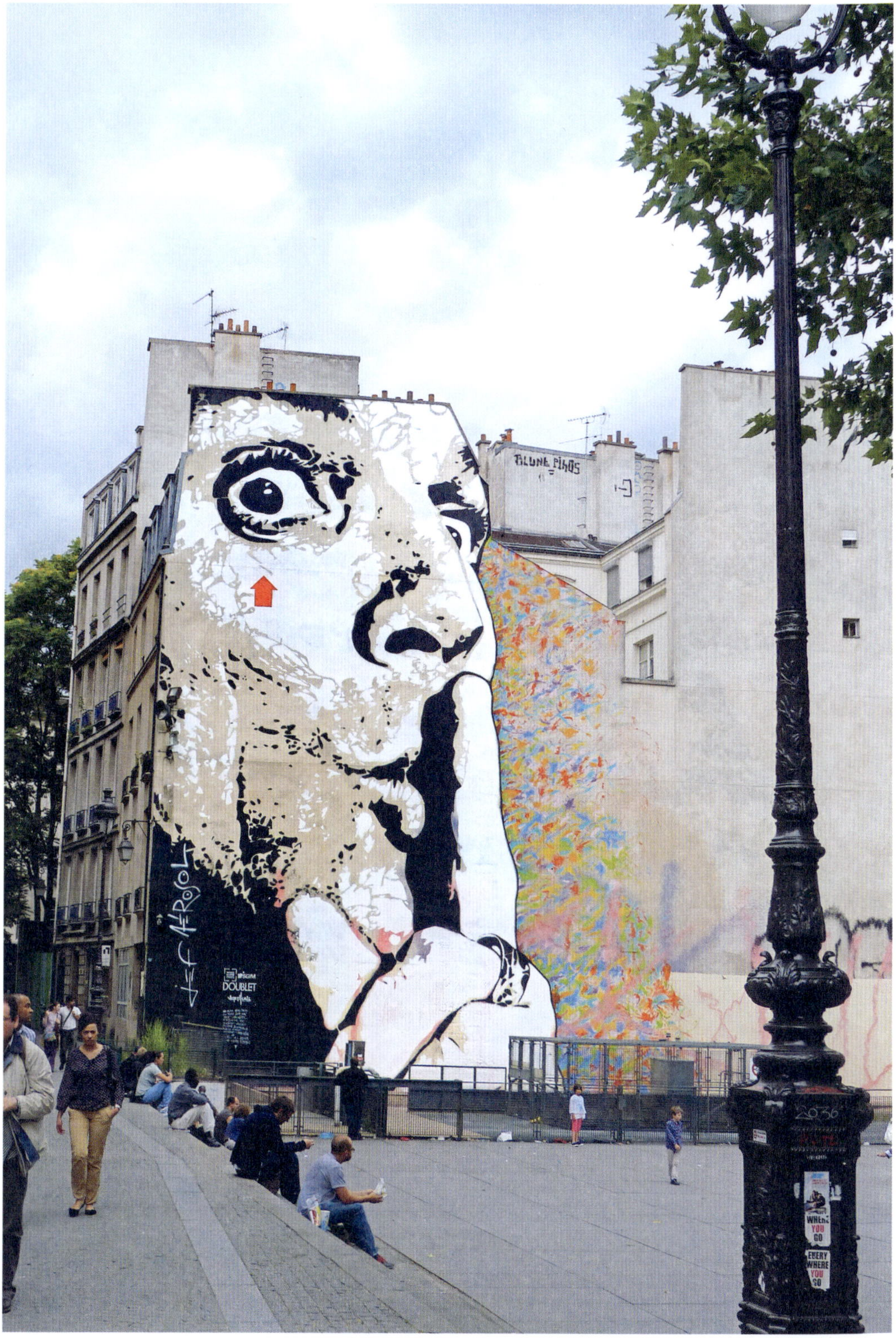

JEF AEROSOL, *Chuuuttt!!!*, Paris, 2011 © A.R.R.

JEF AEROSOL demonstrates the contrast between thoroughness of preparation and urgency of application. Born in 1957 in Nantes, he was one of the main proponents of stencil graffiti. Jef Aérosol often creates portraits of celebrities, including Elvis Presley, John Lennon, Hendrix, Basquiat and Dylan. The jukebox-like artistic approach that he has adopted owes much to the visual culture of record sleeves, which he began collecting early on in life. Conversely, another part of his work is devoted to the streets' anonymous figures, such as musicians, bystanders, beggars, children and pets—frequent themes for many stencil artists. Over the course of his travels around the world, Jef Aérosol has perfected his silhouettes and the outlines of his characters, making them more expressive. And in tirelessly refining his work, he has added extra detail to his stencils and increased the number of layers that form the final work. He has gone far beyond a simple stencil cut-out and a single layer of black. Anthracite, pearl grey, light grey and white offer new dimensions to the painted subjects. The more stencil layers, the more realistic the subject becomes. The texture of the skin, bits of clothing, a bird's plumage: all these elements will become increasingly visible. The artist explains his approach: "I start out with black and then go lighter. First you see the overall silhouette, and bit by bit you can make out the face, the body and finally the eyes. This is also how we meet people deep down... Friendships are first made in a blur, and little by little light is cast on what they really are. I like my shadows to be vivid ones: even if people died a long time ago, I revive them and give them life on the wall, and once again they belong to the street. They mingle with the stream of passers-by, because they are fixed, a freeze frame of the film of life, or of the city. There is a mirror or identification effect." The accumulation of minute details and levels enriches the meaning of Jef Aérosol's works. He has combined the strength of urban stencil and the subtlety and patience of the cut-out to reveal human mystery in the light of his spray cans.

In his own particular way, C215 (who was born in 1973 and whose real name is Christian Guémy) has contributed since 2006 to refining the use of stencils by adding energy and colours that are particular to graffiti. C215 has left his emotion- and poetry-filled mark on walls across the world. On the back of his university studies in art history, his work features many nods to Renaissance paintings. He gladly talks about Caravaggio as his source of inspiration for "his light and the subversion inherent in his work"; he calls Botticelli the "ultimate Illustrator"; he talks about Veronese and his "mastery, academicism and absolute classicism"; and he references Dürer's portraits. On the street art side of things, his references are ERNEST PIGNON ERNEST, BANKSY, EL MAC, DAN23, ARYZ, BLU and SWOON. With C215 having usurped the use of just black and white, he has not hesitated to increase the detail level in his works, combining colours and making increasingly large stencils in the urban environment.

Since its inception, the stencil has been a practice that has not ceased to evolve and grow. In this guerrilla environment, it has developed its full meaning. It allows works to be produced and repeated in record

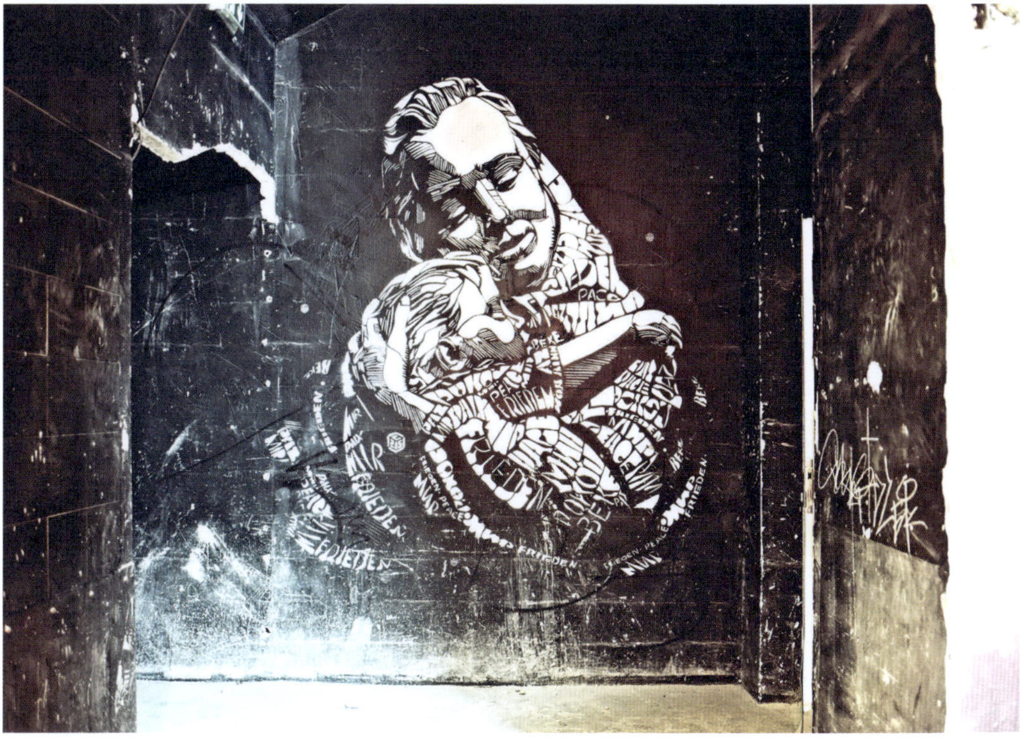

C215, *Les Bains*. Photo © Stéphane Bisseuil

C215, São Paulo © A.R.R.

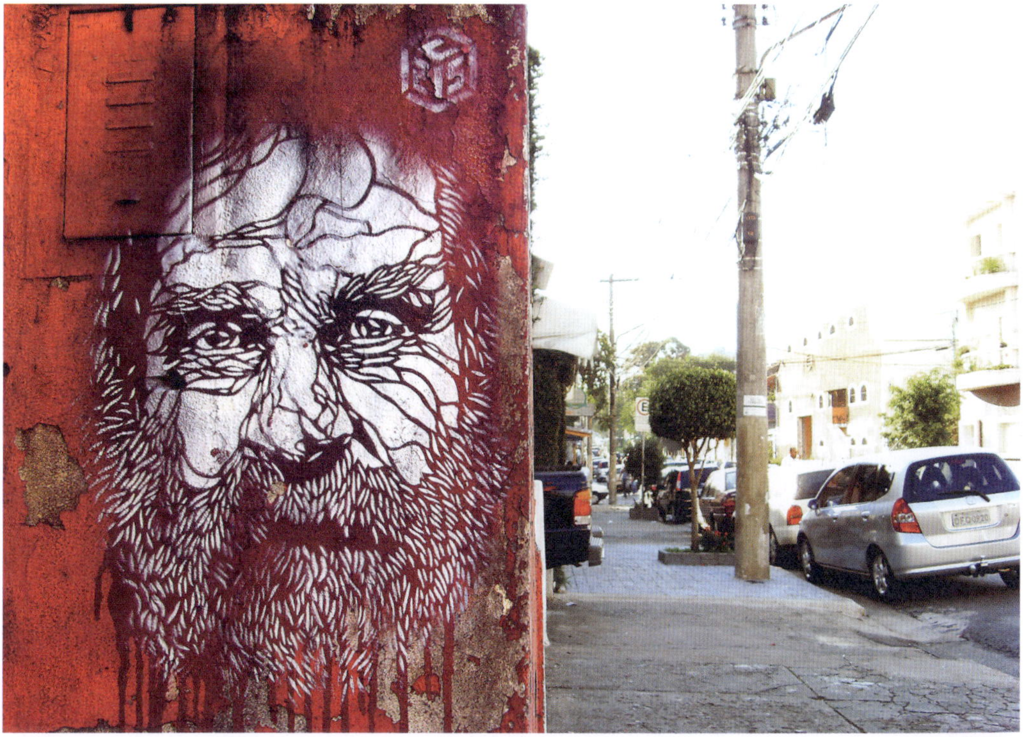

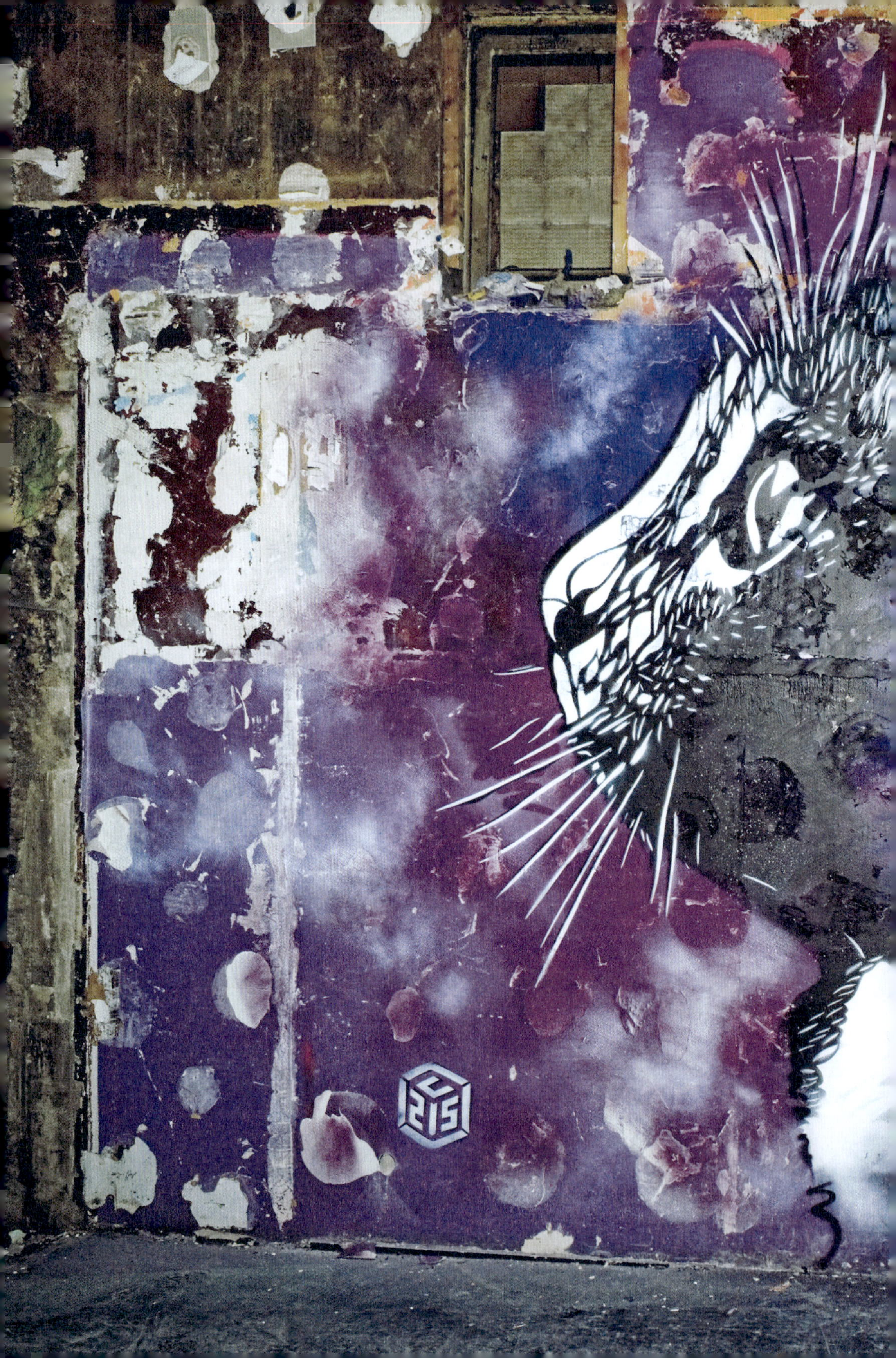
C215

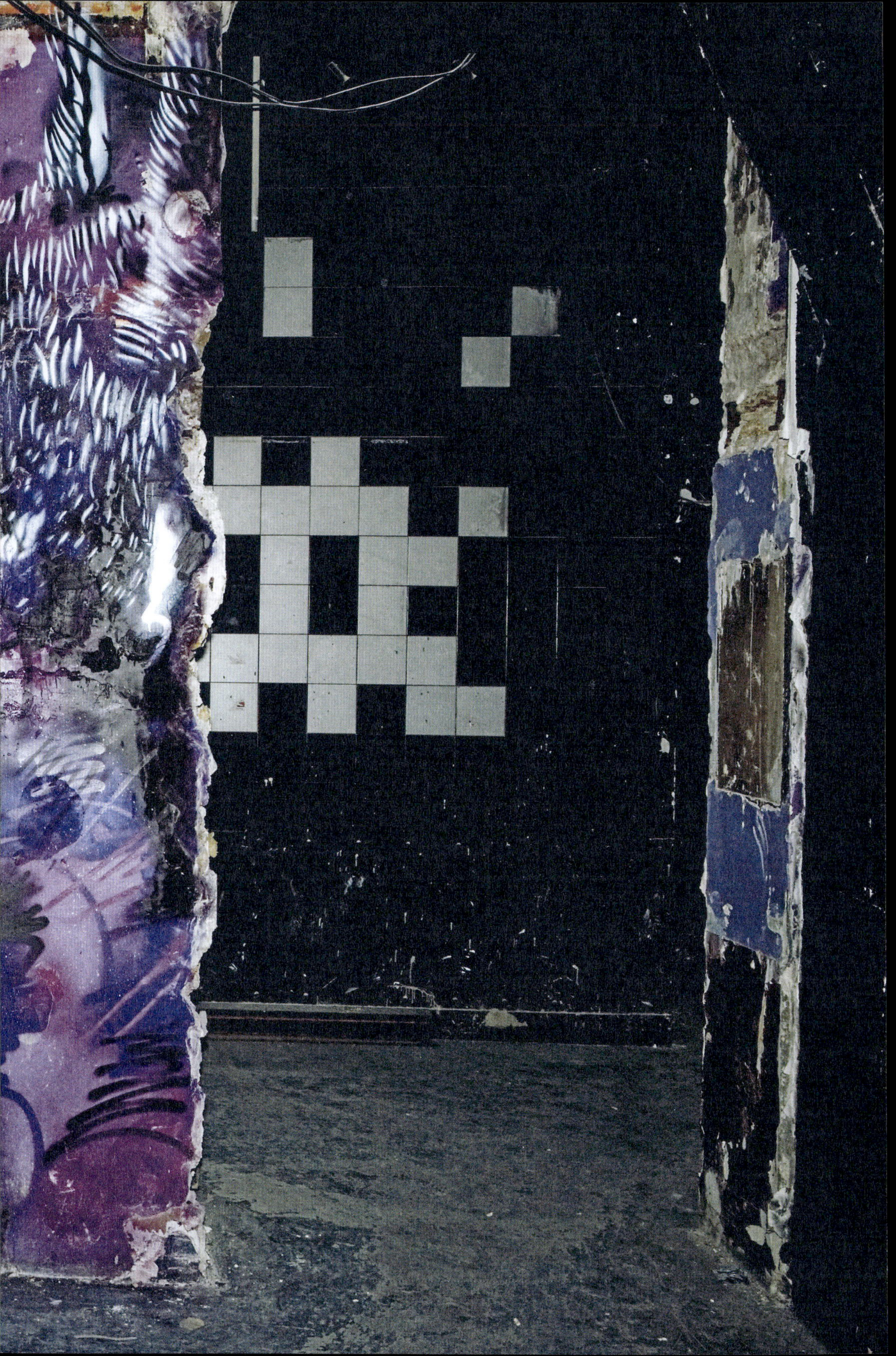

time, substantially reducing the risk of being arrested. At the start of the twenty-first century, BANKSY, SPEEDY GRAFFITO, JÉROME MESNAGER, MISS. TIC, NEMO, JEF AEROSOL, BLEK LE RAT, C215 and LOGAN HICKS were among the most well-known stencil artists.

Enrichment of the movement through contact with other practices and cultures

One of the other effects of ubiquitous repression has been to bring to the fore techniques for executing a work quickly—as is the case with collage. In urban areas, artists can prepare their works at their convenience beforehand and quickly apply them on the wall of their choice. Moreover, legislation on damaging public property is more lenient on collage than it is on spray paint, which is far more expensive to clean up.

For example, Shepard Fairey, alias OBEY, began his eponymous collaging and postering campaign in Los Angeles in 1989, railing against this superficiality of advertising communication in our societies.

For these same reasons of logistical ease, stencils have become more popular than ever. New generations of stencil artists have paid tribute to the previous generations and further improved the technique.
From the beginning of the 1990s, the emergence of these various intersecting techniques and branches would mark the end of New York's supremacy. In the United States, the West Coast took over in terms of innovation with new talents such as Barry McGee, alias TWIST, in San Francisco, and Shepard Fairey in Los Angeles. In Brazil, twin brothers OS GÊMEOS brought a revival to the concept of mural painting. In Europe, the works of ZEVS and SPACE INVADER also opened up new perspectives.

While traditional graffiti is still active, the movement has found new life and developed in different spheres. This unprecedented proliferation is evidence of a fertile dynamism. This already global movement has only continued to grow. More than ever, the participants in this movement feel entitled to go beyond the work of their predecessors with a unique style of their own. Although some of this generation barely experienced the graffiti years and have moved on from old school techniques, they have continued to seek out fresh artistic challenges, and as a result the scope for their art is wider. To convey this creative abundance, the term "branches" seems appropriate. At this stage, the movement can be represented in the form of a tree. If American graffiti is the roots (1970s), and European graffiti (1980s) the trunk, the third generation's street art (from the end of the 1990s) has added many branches that have kept growing. Roots, trunk and branches are the three essential parts of this living movement.

Previous double page spread:
C215, Les Bains.
Photo © Stéphane Bisseuil

As it has become bolder, it has also reflected at a fundamental level on the power of its message. Nurtured and hardened by advertising codes, the new generation enjoys deliberately subverting procedures and codes to attack them better. Is the message a means or an end in itself? The saturation of the visual space by advertising's commercial communication has encouraged in a more or less conscious way a whole generation to actively defend the spaces of visual freedom. A form of rebellion through images has begun anew.

In this context of heightened creativity, in which a willingness to deliver a message is growing, new practices and techniques are emerging. Street art sheds new light on a number of traditional techniques. From frescoes to mosaics and stencils or simple posters, each artist seeks in these other practices to produce a new offshoot within the movement that will allow him or her to be recognized as the creator of a new style. Likewise, new technologies have inspired a set of new approaches, from sticker art to video projection and LED art.

Among the traditional arts, mural art has had an astonishing revitalizing effect on street art. Although inseparable from the beginnings of the movement, the history of murals is itself very rich and stretches back much further. Art as we understand it in our modern society was born on walls with the cave painting of prehistoric times. The wall-painting tradition has its roots in the history of humanity and has been renewed during our societies' great artistic revolutions. Later, the term "mural" would refer to a specific practice known as *fresco* in Italian.

It is astonishing how the mural has reflected the concerns of each age, whether in public or private, secular or religious, and popular or elite form. It has also often played a social or even political role. Closely linked to architecture, it has employed perspective and touches on 3D techniques, with some artists having shifted from pure mural paintings to outdoor installations. This art form is by turns popular, modest and ambitious. Over time, it has earned some form of public recognition, while remaining largely underestimated and often ignored by the cultural authorities.

OS GÊMEOS, wall, East Houston and Bowery Street, New York. Photo © Stéphane Bisseuil (detail)

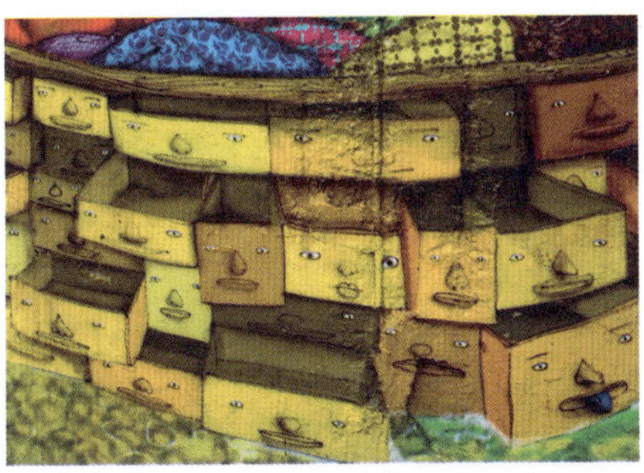

Depending on the context, murals are based on the need to voice the concerns of everyday life, on political activism or on a pure need for artistic expression. The Lascaux caves are a perfect example of creativity, and they tell us much about the use of wall painting in another time (or by another civilization). From Ancient Egypt's Valley of the Queens to cathedrals around the world, religious murals have always impressed through their size and impact. The most recent murals have often been produced to glorify the products that they advertise or, at the other end of the spectrum of communication, for political propaganda purposes. In South America since the beginning

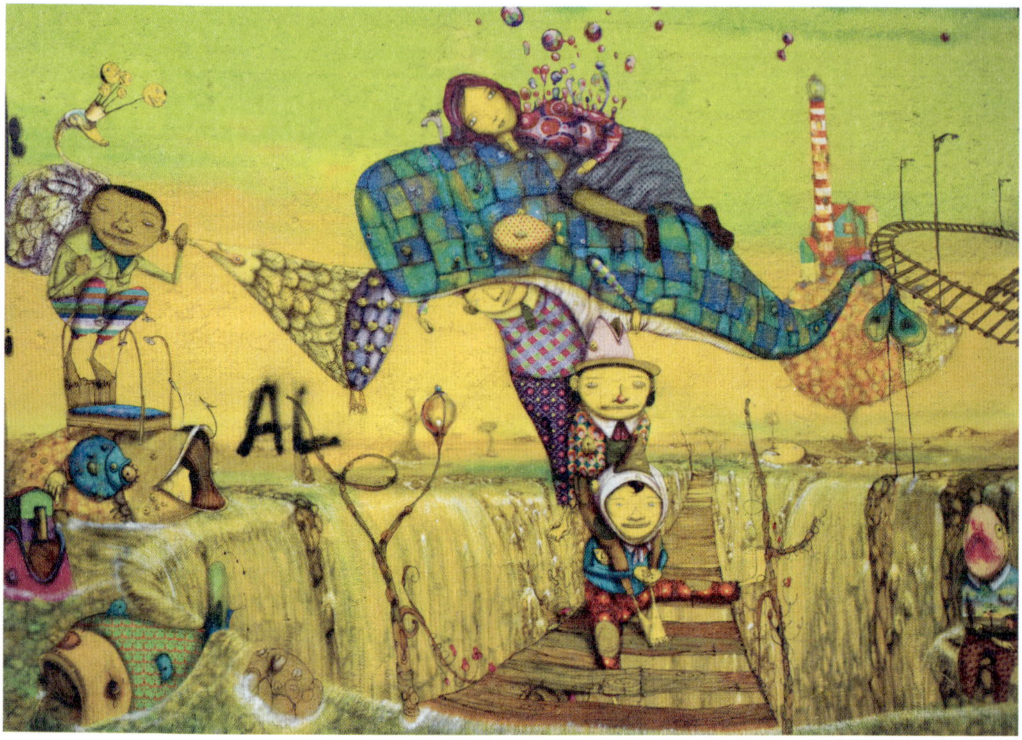

OS GÊMEOS, wall, East Houston and Bowery Street, New York. Photo © Stéphane Bisseuil (detail)

OS GÊMEOS, wall, East Houston and Bowery Street, New York. Photo © Stéphane Bisseuil (detail)

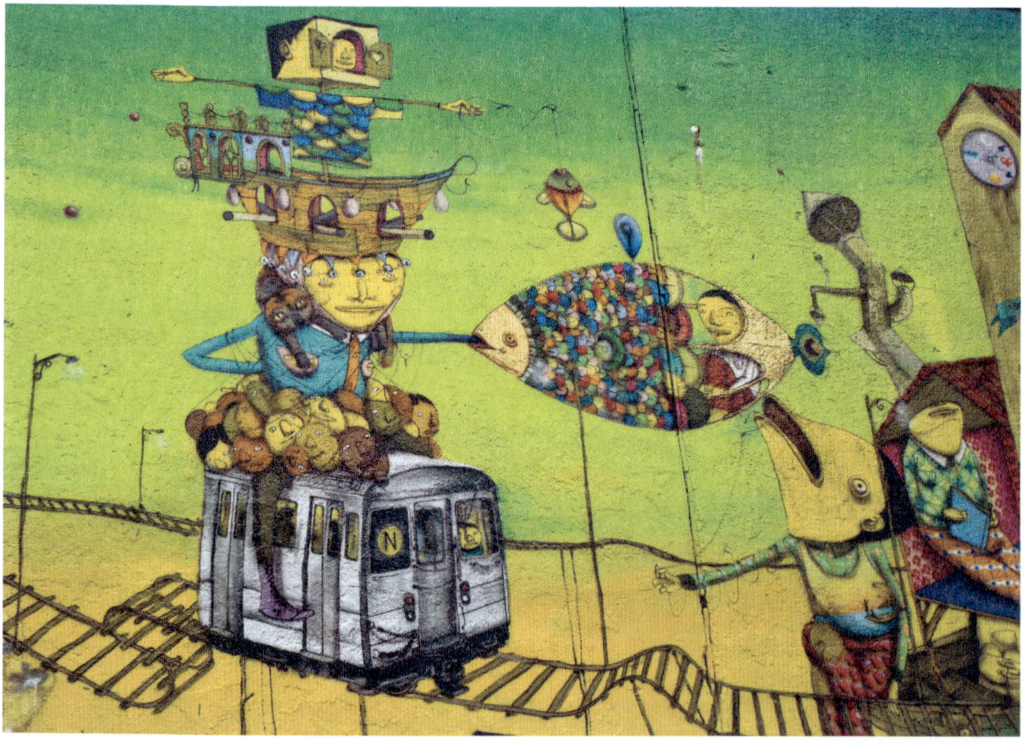

of the 1920s, muralists like Diego Rivera have mainly focused on political issues and tried to create their own style, whether Mexican or indigenous. Closer to us, whether on the Berlin Wall, the walls of May 1968, or even those of Northern Ireland, murals are legion. They have become a "normal" element of the cityscape in many places.

In its earliest days, graffiti sought to continue this heritage. Many artists abandoned the subways where they began as artists to express themselves on walls. For obvious geographical reasons, the Los Angeles and Brazilian scenes are among the strongholds of graffiti imbued with influences from the South American muralists. Specific styles have therefore emerged in these places.

OS GÊMEOS (literally, "the twin brothers"), from São Paulo in Brazil, were born in 1974. In 1985, hip-hop culture came to Brazil, and the two brothers immediately embraced it. "We lived in a district where hip hop culture was very strong in its beginning. We went to the street and saw our neighbors break dancing on the sidewalk. All night they practiced and we fell in love with this universe," they recall. They naturally moved from break dance to graffiti, and they began to produce their first works in 1987. Although they accept that they initially followed American inspirations, the lack of interaction with New York artists at the time led them to explore new dimensions and integrate Brazilian elements and cultural influences. They quickly became key figures in South America, encouraging the emergence of a true Brazilian style.

The key event that moved them on from old school graffiti (an influence fuelled by cult books and films like *Style Wars, Subway Art* and *Beat Street*) was a fortuitous encounter with BARRY McGEE. This American travelled from San Francisco to Brazil in 1993 for an academic exchange program. He would bring the work of the two Brazilians to the attention of the United States. "At first we were the same as the others, painting b-boys and generally staying close to the themes in hip hop culture. As time passed, naturally things changed. We never forgot the roots, but we decided to go our own way. Perhaps because we had no information about graffiti in the beginning, it helped us a lot. We never watched anyone else painting. The only things that we had were some flicks and a piece of film that showed us graffiti. So we tried to discover how these things were done. We think we ended up discovering other things as a result." OS GÊMEOS are among the standard bearers of a revived graffiti from the 1990s. Since 1999, they have participated in collective exhibitions around the world.

Recognizable by their yellow characters, the works of OS GÊMEOS are surprisingly complex. There are references to their own family portraits, but also more broadly to São Paulo's social conditions and politics, or to national folklore. And their style is also influenced by traditional hip-hop and Brazilian culture. In terms of techniques, the twins were also pushed to innovate and find their own way. From very early on, they

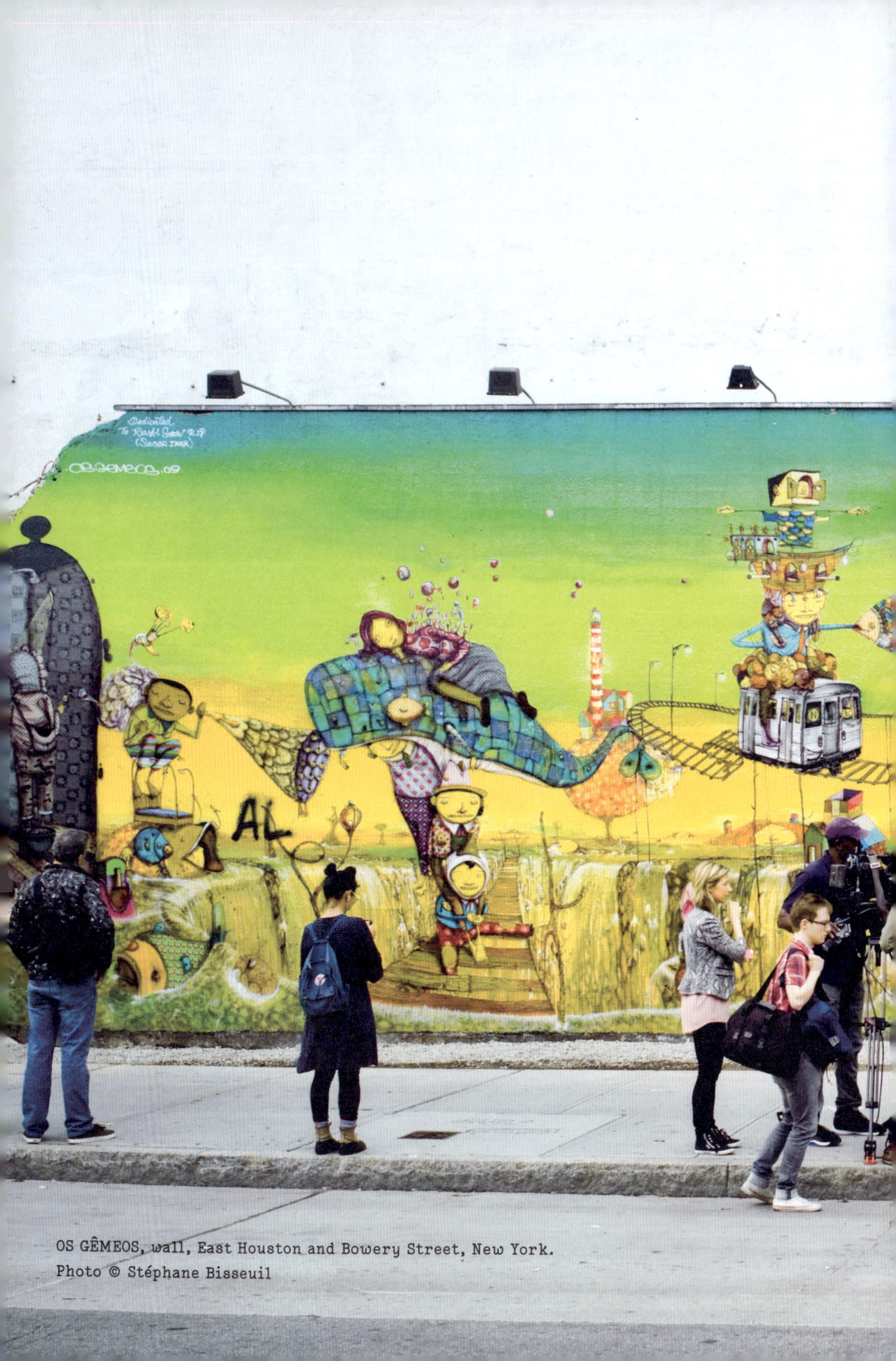

OS GÊMEOS, wall, East Houston and Bowery Street, New York.
Photo © Stéphane Bisseuil

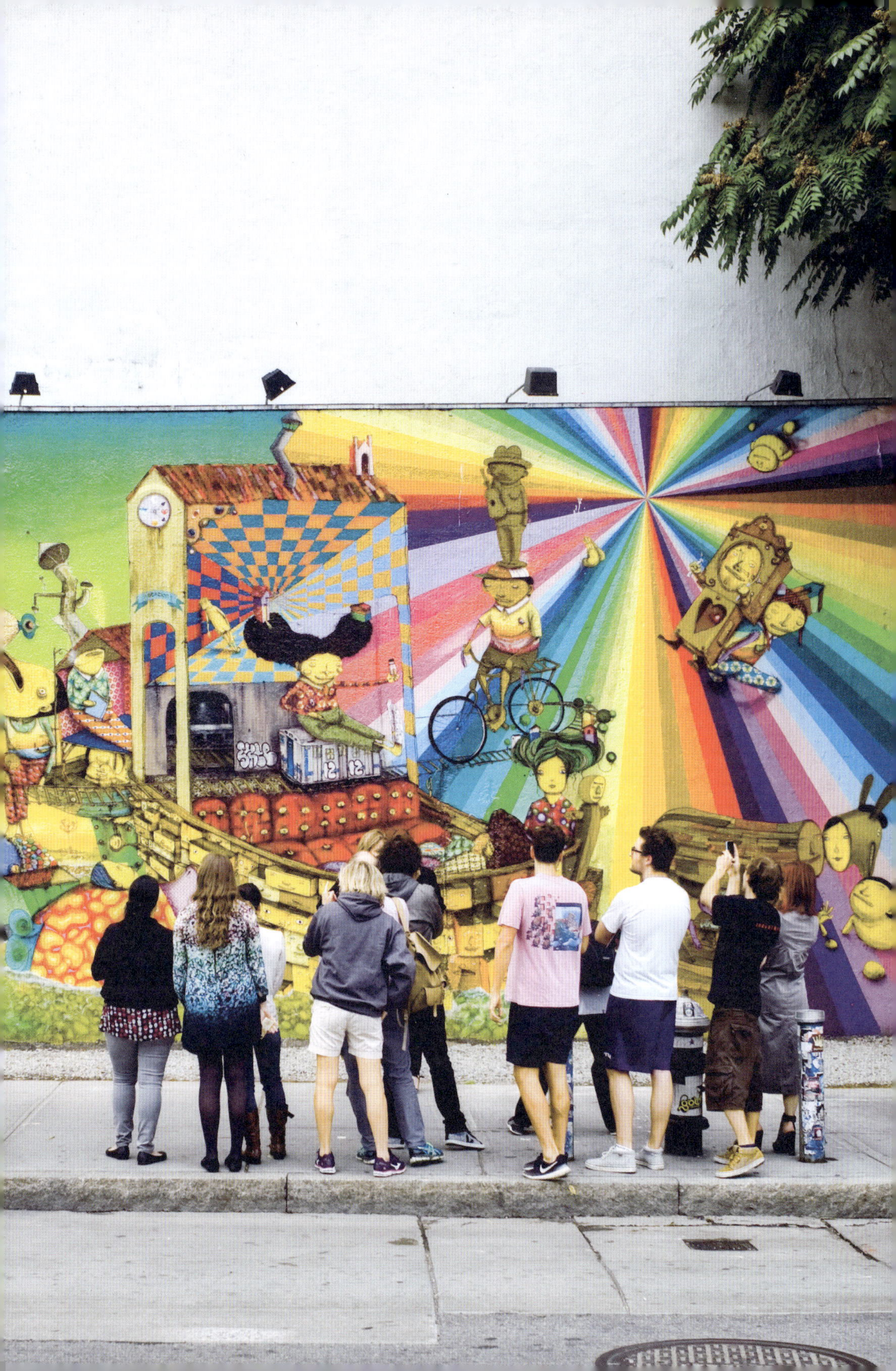

opted to use various products in addition to spray paint—for example, latex paint, which is cheaper and very effective in covering surfaces.

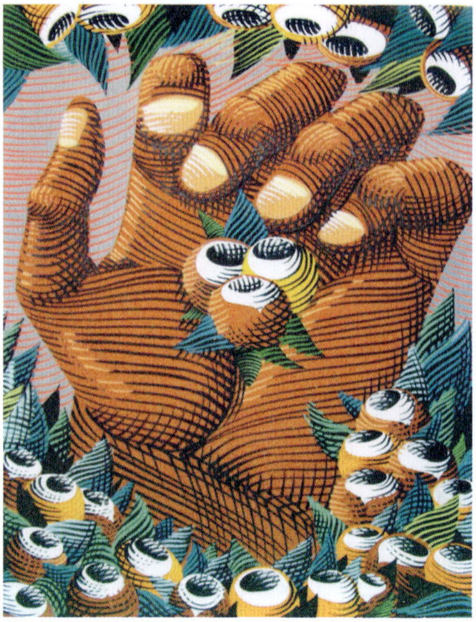
NUNCA, work on paper

Their monumental frescoes are very colourful —their favourite colours of yellow and brown complement their use of blue, green and purple— and replete with characters in often surreal situations. At first glance, their painted scenes, which are made up of a collection of short stories linked by natural elements such as the sea or by amazing constructions such as psychedelic spirals or rails, seem to be the products of a dreamlike and childish universe. Although characters remain central to their works, often these characters' clothes or accessories comprise a world of their own. In fact, each element is rich in meaning and contains other details within it. They serve as pretexts to develop another world—an almost endless pictorial mise en abyme.

Often use transformations as a theme. A boat turns into a fish, a character wears a mask, and animals are purely fantastical. Their humour-filled creations do not lack depth or clarity about the problems facing society. For example, they denounce the segregation established by the ghettos and favelas. As Jeffrey Deitch[1] points out, "An art intellectual, an art historian can appreciate their work, but a kid on the street can, too." Brazilian artists like NUNCA have since followed in their path, creating even more lively and expressive murals.
Among the other elements that have played an undeniable role in spreading graffiti, skateboarding culture, which exploded in the 1990s, has been especially important. Having emerged at the end of the 1930s, the first "scooters" mutated into skateboards twenty years later. The phenomenon spread from California and became global in the 1970s, at a time when graffiti was beginning to appear. The conjunction of these two developments gave rise to a new visual subculture, in which urban art and skateboarding mixed. Moreover, emerging from the deeply rock 'n' roll surfing, skateboarding developed in the street, which from the outset brought it closer to rap and therefore to graffiti. The two worlds were destined to meet, as the career of a great name from the genre shows.

Frank Shepard Fairey, alias OBEY, was born in 1970 in Charleston, South Carolina, a city that he left at the age of seventeen. "I was not really exposed to graffiti culture," he acknowledges. "Instead, I fell into skateboarding and punk rock." Although he dreamed of becoming a professional skateboarder, his parents pushed him to pursue his studies. He was accepted to the Rhode Island School of Design. "I'm glad I went there, because when I got there, we were pretty close to New York.

[1] Director of MOCA LA between 2010 and 2013. A graduate from Harvard's class of 1978, he opened his first gallery while still a student in 1972 at the Curtis Hotel. From 1979 to 1988, he was an art consultant at Citibank and columnist for *Flash Art*. Between 1988 and 1996, Deitch became an art dealer and private advisor to a number of collectors, including Jose Mugrabi. In 1996, he opened the Deitch Project in Soho, which showcased stars like Vanessa Beecroft, Jocelyn Taylor, Nari Ward and Mariko Mori. He was also one of the first people to defend graffiti in the 1980s.

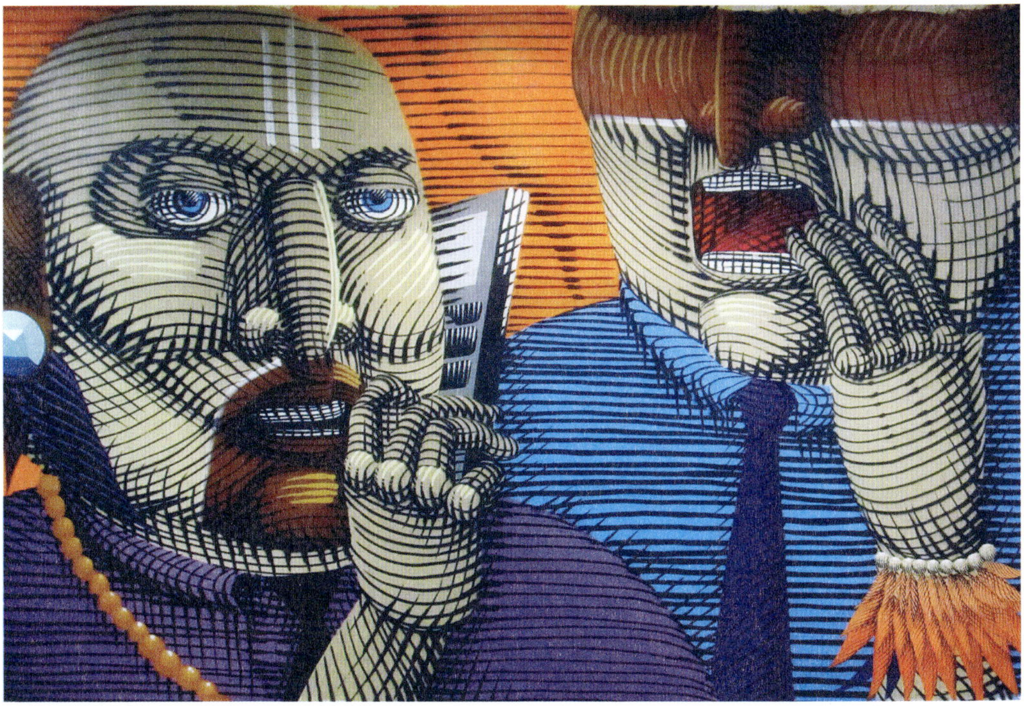

NUNCA © A.R.R.

NUNCA, mural, São Paulo © A.R.R.

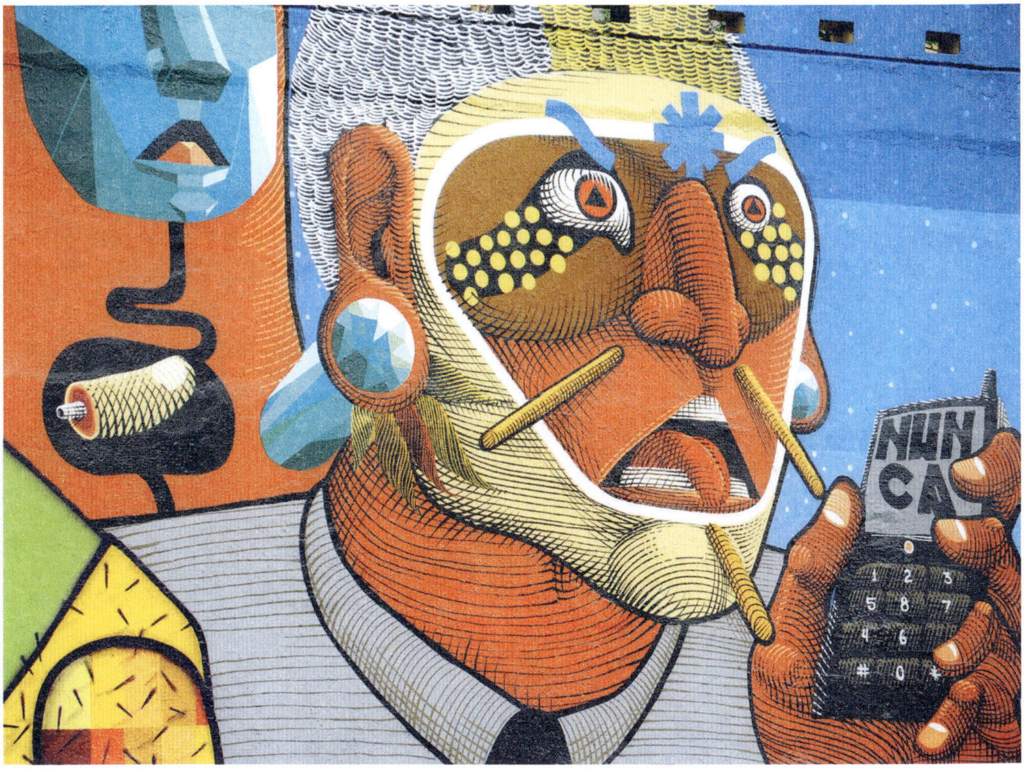

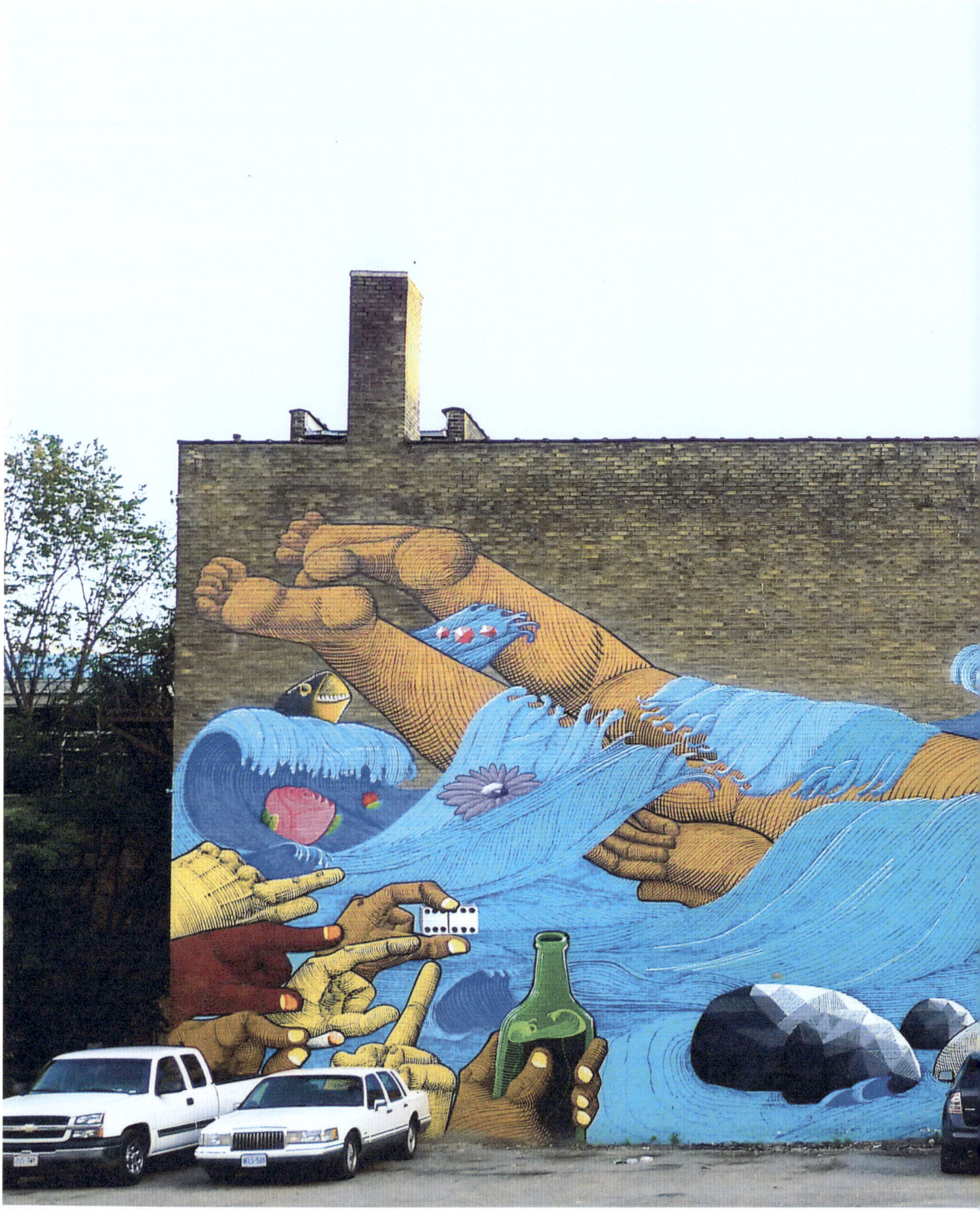

NUNCA, *Mutual Street*, Montreal, Canada © A.R.R.

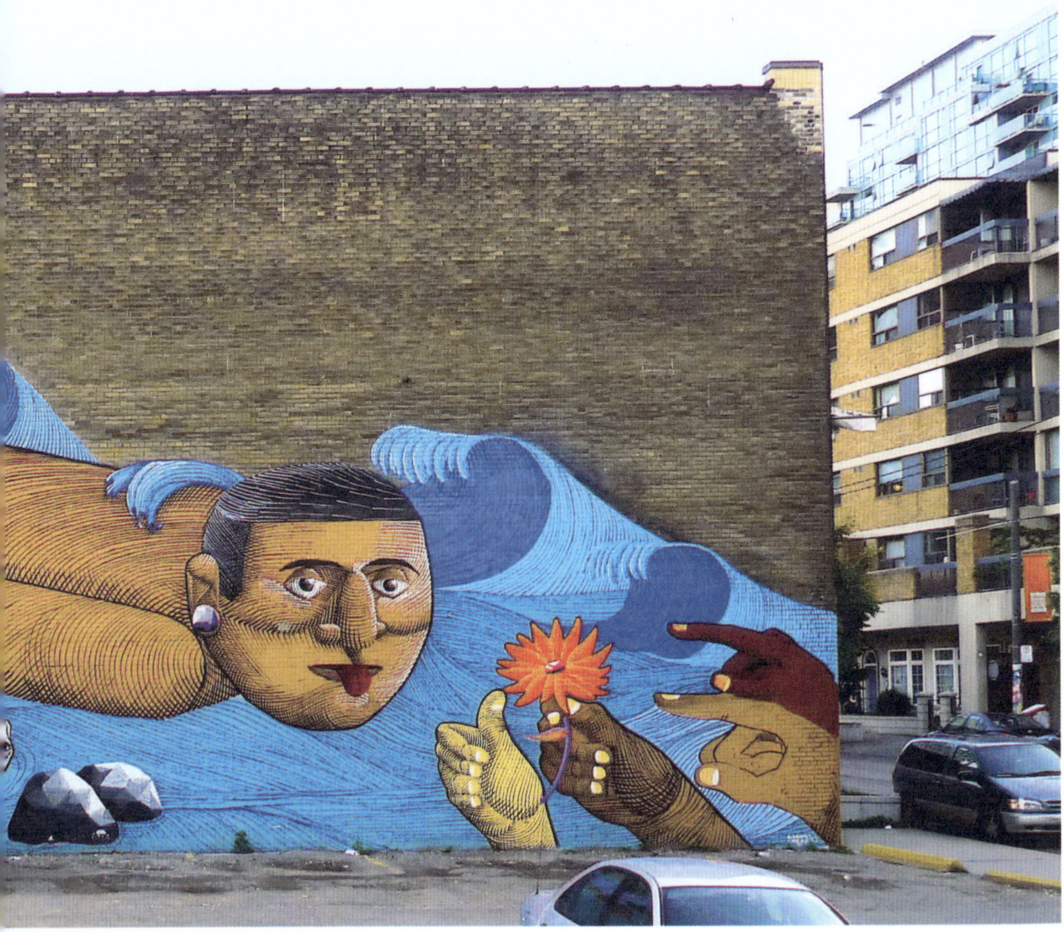

NUNCA has developed his own style, mixing colours and lines where Brazilian tradition and modern demands intersect.

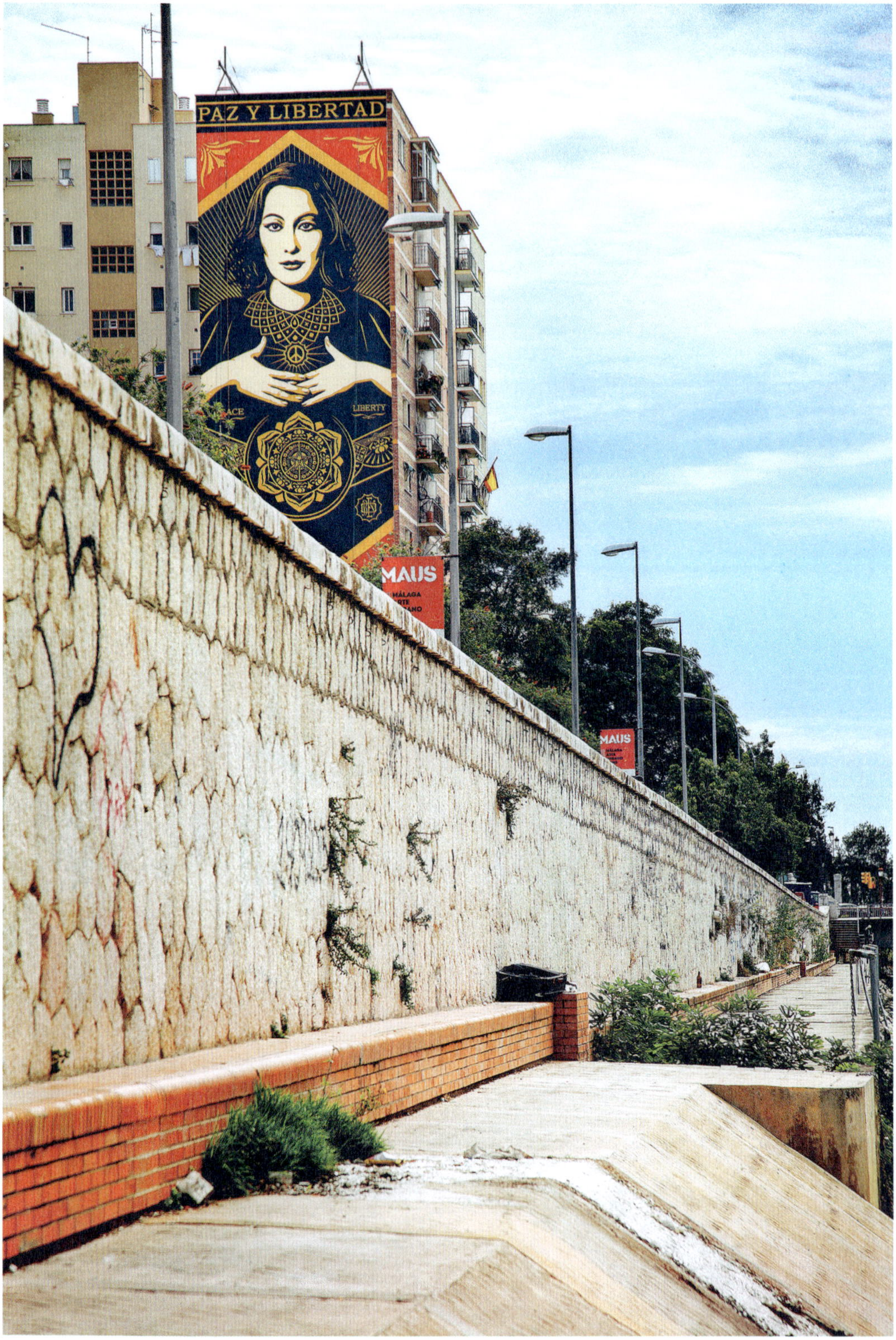

SHEPARD FAIREY aka OBEY, *Paz y Libertad*, Malaga © Obey giant art and John Furlong

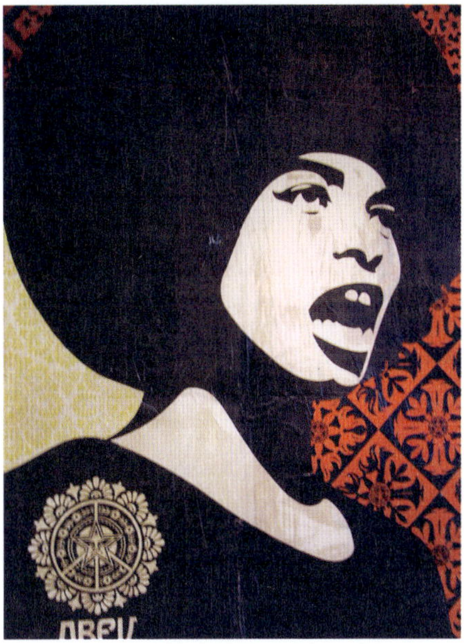

SHEPARD FAIREY aka OBEY,
Revolutionary woman, mixed technique

Seeing graffiti pieces across the Bronx Expressway, just getting your name out there, inspired me." His studies allowed him to learn silkscreen and to discover sticker art.

In parallel with his job as a salesman in a skate shop, he developed his technique of stencil and silkscreen by creating t-shirts of his own. And in 1989, while still a student, he created, somewhat by accident, his icon, André the Giant—the wrestler arrested in 1989 for assaulting a cameraman. This figure would accompany him throughout his career. "One evening, while I was making my t-shirts, a friend who was bored stiff of watching me wanted to learn how I made them. So I looked for a visual in the newspaper to show him the technique of silkscreen printing, where I stumbled upon a story with a picture of André the Giant." Once it had been hijacked in this way, the visual, a succinct black-and-white portrait, became a great source of inspiration. Shepard Fairey made many stickers of it, which he distributed to his friends with the goal of affixing them everywhere they could. This invasive phenomenon that was worthy of street art soon became huge.

In 1990, Shepard Fairey produced a manifesto to explain his work that connects it to Heidegger's phenomenology: "Phenomenology attempts to enable people to see clearly something that is right before their eyes but obscured; things that are so taken for granted that they are muted by abstract observation," he explained. The manifesto then called for "visual disobedience," a key concept for this artist. Borrowing Marshall McLuhan's slogan[2] of "the medium is the message," he invaded the city with his stickers and then posters of André the Giant. In so doing, Shepard Fairey denounced the omnipresence of advertising. In interfering with advertising spaces by sticking his own posters on them, his work acted as a parasite in an urban space saturated with messages: "Why should we accept the growth in the number of billboards and other types of ads in public spaces where people have no other choice than to look at them, just because you have money?"

[2] Marshall McLuhan: an English literature professor and communication theorist who was one of the founders of contemporary media studies. Studying the cultural changes that printing brought about in the Western world, he considered the medium of communication to be more important than its contents, as he stated in the formula "the medium is the message."

His degree in his pocket, SHEPARD FAIREY continued his urban invasions in San Diego for a time, and then in Los Angeles from 1998 after he moved there. His area of expertise became guerrilla marketing applied to street art. Wherever he went, he affixed or had affixed the refined version of the portrait of André the Giant in sticker or screen-printed poster form. He endlessly adapted and reinterpreted this stylized icon, creating large posters that were either placed next to each other in large numbers or used to create a single monumental piece. Mainly in black and white, and more rarely with a hint of red, the

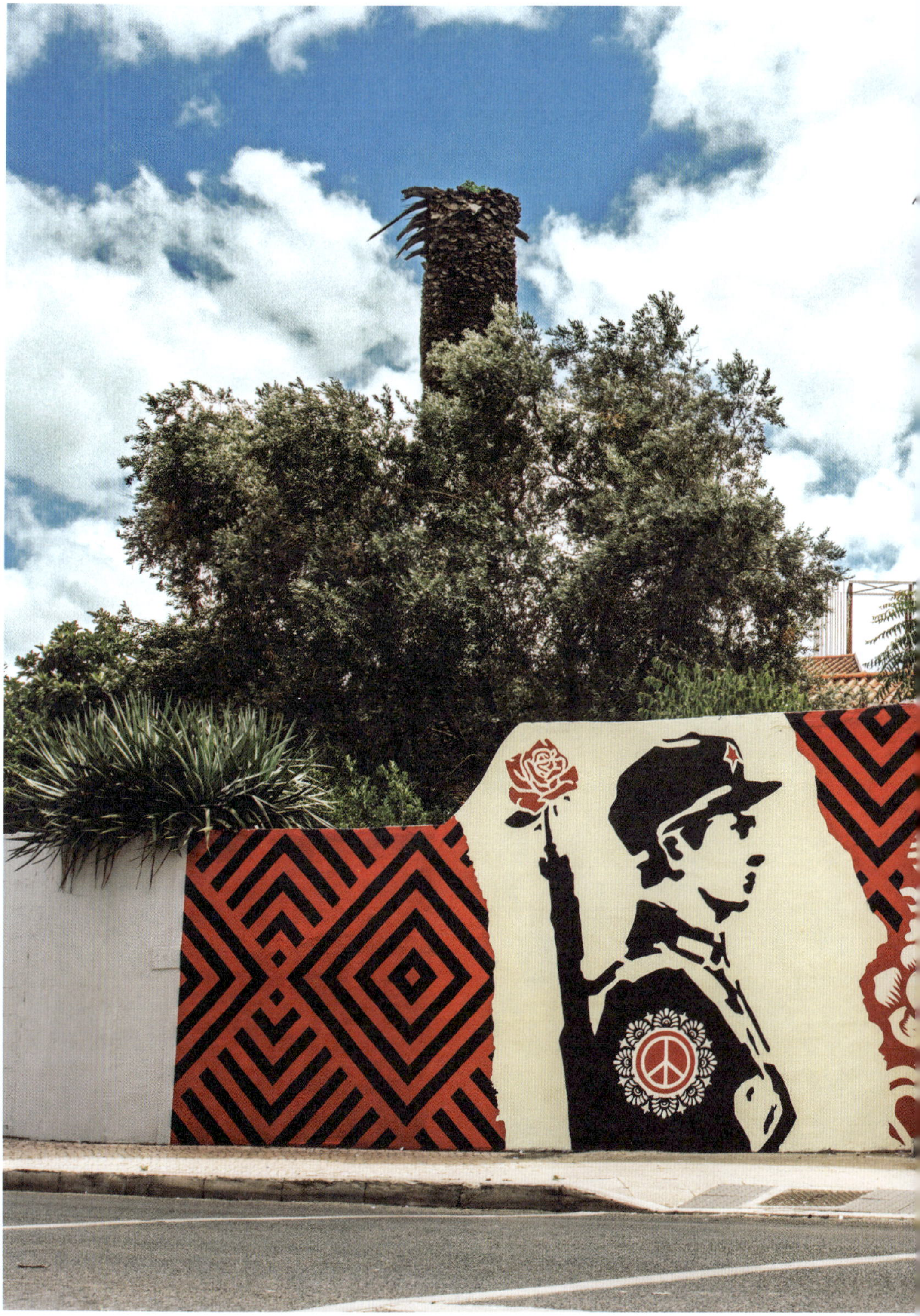

SHEPARD FAIREY aka OBEY, *Peace Guard Mural*, Lisbon, Portugal, 2017. Photo © Jonathan Furlong

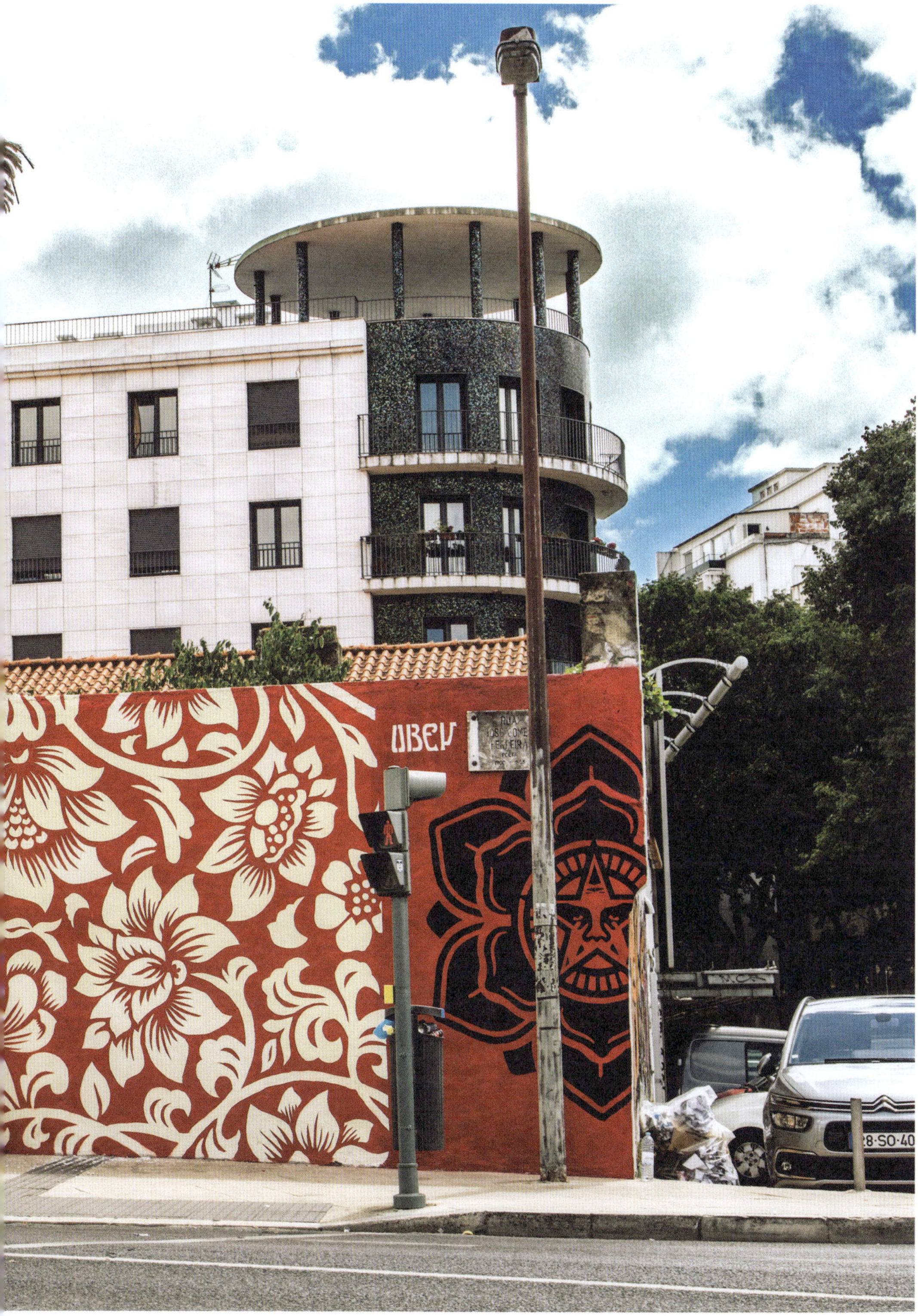
OBEY

face is surprisingly simple and the message an energetic one: OBEY. It's a reference to John Carpenter's 1988 film, "They Live" ("Invasion Los Angeles" in France), where billboards conceal subliminal messages calling for submission. The artist says, "People go through life like sleepwalkers, and Obey is my way of throwing cold water in their faces".

Little by little, his visual world has incorporated other elements that are often inspired by the codes prized by Communist propaganda or advertising. He therefore denounces the pervasive forms of indoctrination in all societies and calls on everyone to develop their own critical spirit. He has created hundreds of silkscreen posters that are based on slogans and are direct, powerful and full of hidden meaning.

Simplicity of forms is a key element of his work, both for accessibility and for visual impact. Collage is his weapon. Following a tradition from graffiti, he places posters of an impressive size in the most unexpected places. However, he believes that he is "not just a graffiti artist. My practice has, at least, I hope, greater social relevance by being more punk and antagonistic than most classical street artists." He deliberately distinguishes himself from the graffiti and spray paint schools, claiming to have never really practised such forms: "The closest thing to graffiti that I have done is stencilling, which I have used because it is quick and permanent." This admission is shared by many other street artists, but despite this, everyone, including SHEPARD FAIREY, is part of the same culture of invasion, signatures and urban expression.

Through his distinctive work, SHEPARD FAIREY is one of the pioneers of a form of art directly linked to graphic design, which he explores in a still more complex manner in his workshop pieces. The fruit of overlaying many concrete or abstract symbols, these pieces mix several techniques, including silkscreen printing, collage, stencil and painting. But the purpose remains the same: that of an artist who, almost with the eye of a sociologist, tirelessly analyses images and the mechanisms of propaganda, whether they are of American, Soviet, Maoist or some other origin.

At the same time, urban art has met yet another unexpected cultural area: video games. The history of video games stems from the 1950s, the time of their appearance, and the 1970s, when the commercial sale of arcade terminals, games and consoles began.

In 1951, the game *Nim* made its appearance on computer. It was one of the first attempts at human-machine interaction, as was *OXO* one year later, a noughts-and-crosses game in which one of the players is controlled by the computer. In 1958, a game called *Tennis for Two* allowed two opponents to play one another. Because of the complexity and the cost of computers at the time, it was not until 1972 with *Pong* and the *Magnavox Odyssey* that this entertainment genre truly took on a practical and marketable form. A phenomenon was born. A veritable world made entirely from pixels would develop. In terms of content, there were characters that were initially simplistic and rules that were often inspired by

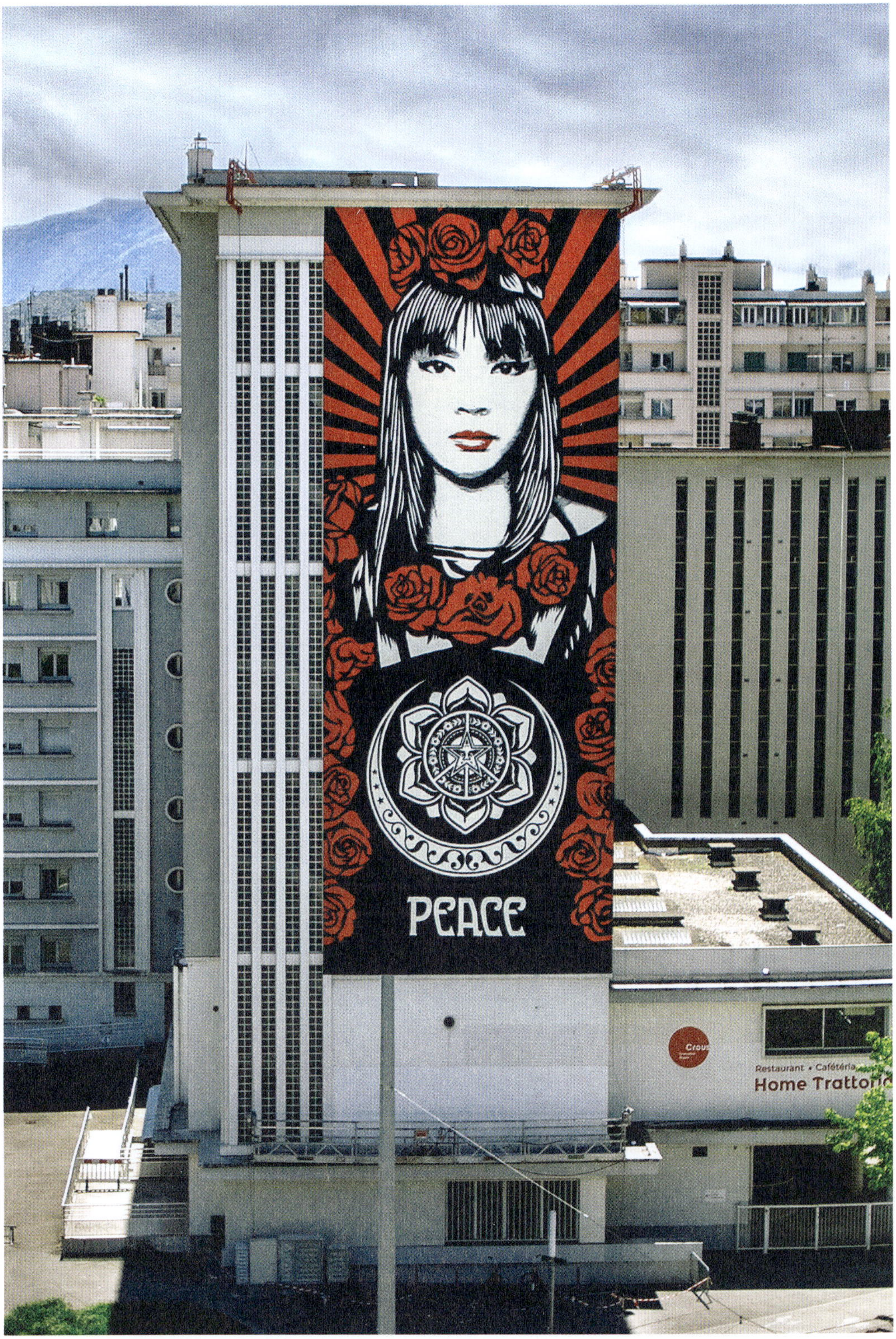

SHEPARD FAIREY aka OBEY, *Rose Girl mural*, Grenoble, France, 2020. Photo © Jonathan Furlong

war or competitive sports. Created in 1980, *Pac Man* and *Space Invaders* encountered almost immediate worldwide success. Although virtual, these characters and worlds became a reality for a large number of young people and became an integral part of the world surrounding them.

The meeting of graffiti and video games was not only related to the temporal coincidence of the 1980s. In both phenomena, the language used was international and even universal, and it was shared by "players" who met and understood one another. The characters depicted renewed an image that had initially come from the world of comics. And there are parallels here with the quest for new territories. It is about winning by playing, but also about building up renown, in the form of recognition of one's pseudonym. The best player is the one who is most present on the ground, whether it is real or virtual. Virality and infiltration are two motivations related to street art culture. The artist SPACE INVADER is emblematic of the union of these two worlds.

Born in France in 1969, SPACE INVADER made his first mosaic on the walls of his home town of Paris in the 1990s. "It all started when I put my first Invader in a Paris alley. It was like a sentinel, and it stayed in place for a few years. The invasion as such only began in 1998, when I activated the Space Invader programme." The propagation occurred on a massive scale, with mosaics inspired by the video game swarming across the world. These unsigned and enigmatic specimens have created a buzz from London to Los Angeles, Tokyo, New York and Bangkok: "I kept the name of the game as an alias," he explains, "because it is a perfect definition of my work. I am an invader of space. It is very binary."
SPACE INVADER's approach is based on combining mosaics and squares to create pixels. "I like to consider this work as a project around the world in which the notions of the infinitely small and the infinitely large are in constant confrontation," he adds. His thoughts on art and its intrusive potential are interesting in more than one way, feeding what is today among the most effective approaches in street art.

Mosaics are unaffected by the damage caused by weather or the ravages of time. The works are cemented on the walls of cities in the most unexpected and hard-to-reach places. They have a longer life than ephemeral graffiti, and their colours remain bright. The use of mosaic is rare and original in the world of street art. The parallel between a representation from antiquity—mosaic—and a technological element—the pixel—is a metaphor that highlights the artistic aspect of new technologies. Moreover, by choosing this ancient medium, SPACE INVADER not only anchors his output in an artistic tradition that has survived over the centuries, giving his work an extra resonance, but he also creates a bridge between two historic and cultural moments that are a priori antagonistic.

INVADER, *Pong*, ceramics and pâte de verre on wooden board, 147×122 cm, 1999, private collection. Photo: Weltkulturerbe Voelklinger Huette - Merkel © A.R.R.

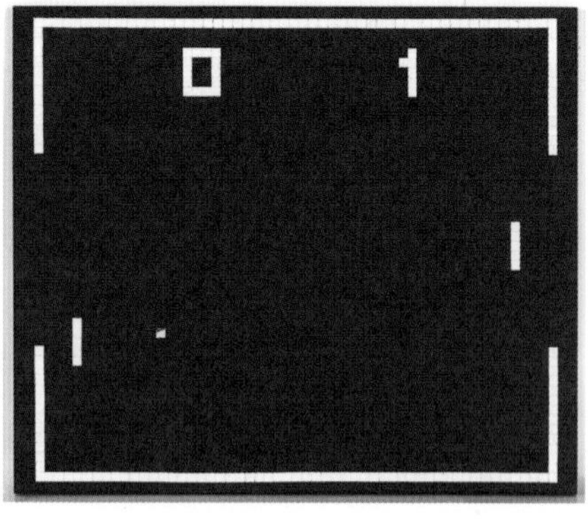

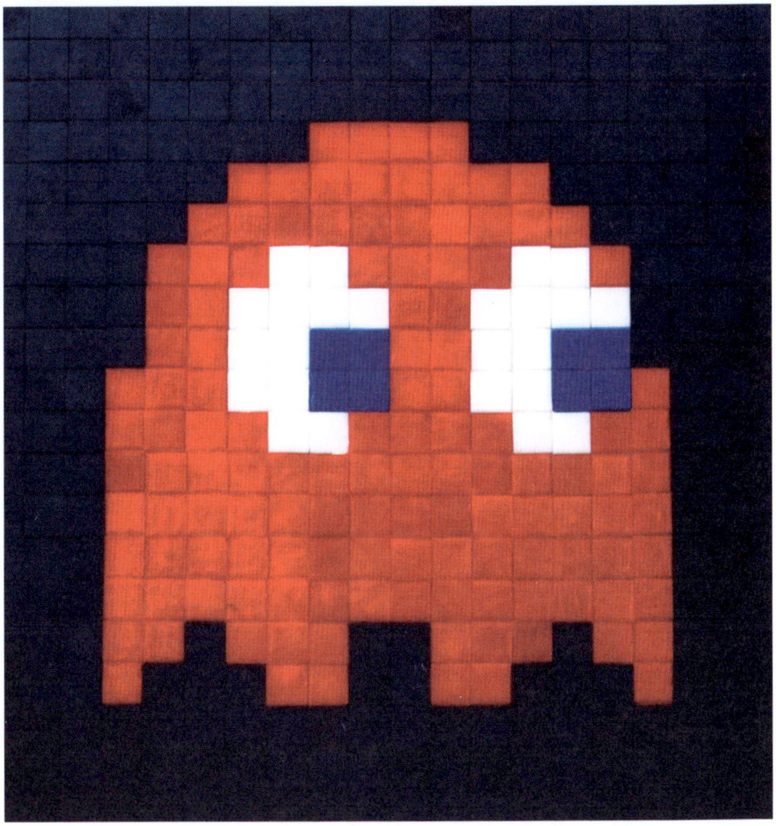

INVADER, *Alias*, ceramics and pâte de verre on wooden board © A.R.R.

In a similar way to SHEPARD FAIREY in Los Angeles, SPACE INVADER's work is controversial among the first generation of graffiti artists. Purists only accept spray paint works. However, the works of this French artist are at least as effective as a tag in the city. They put in place a parallel network, like a patiently woven canvas, that only insiders know how to decipher and follow. As SPACE INVADER says about graffiti culture: "I found a lot of energy and life in this culture, as well as a family... It has brought friendships and interesting references." The positioning of his mosaics is never accidental. Each new location is carefully selected, perpetuating the contextual element that is so highly valued by urban artists, regardless of their practices. Furthermore, consistent with the graffiti and street art approaches, SPACE INVADER meticulously documents every step of the creative process. Adopting the entomologist's approach, he catalogues and photographs all of the Invaders. Echoing video games, he even creates maps identifying them in each city and awarding points for each of them.

This low-tech artist bases his work on a playful paradigm and a principle of simple repetition. Just as video gamers accept the challenges thrown down to them by the machine in front of them, SPACE INVADER accepts challenges from society. The game and its rules are not only part of our

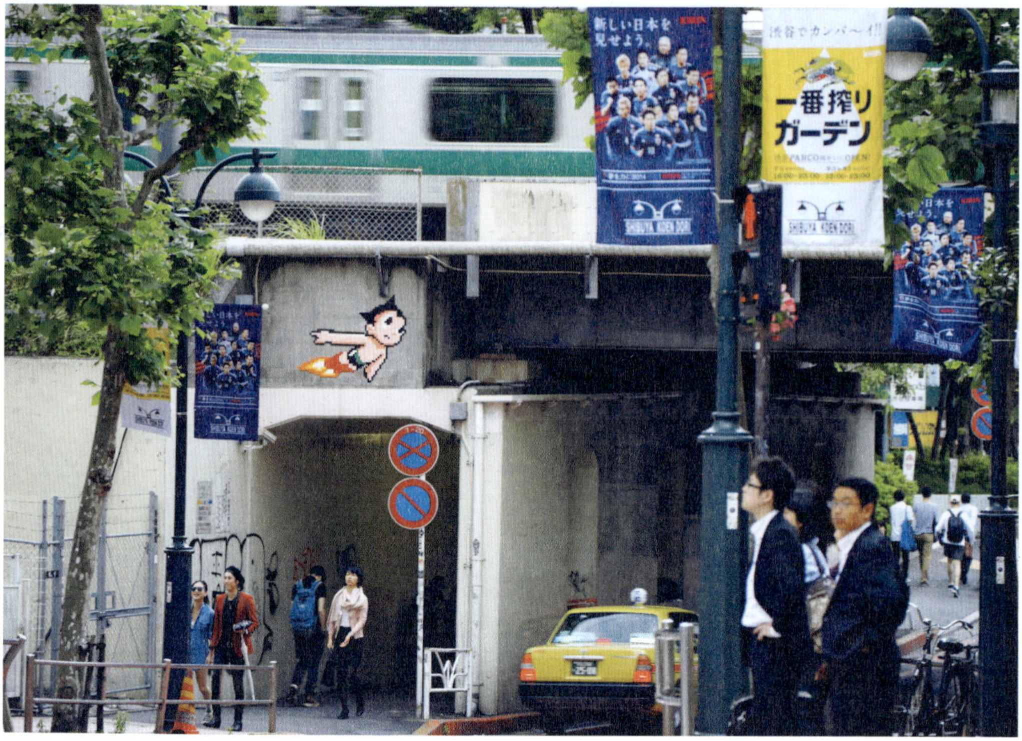

INVADER, Tokyo, 2014 © Invader

INVADER, Paris, 2013 © Invader

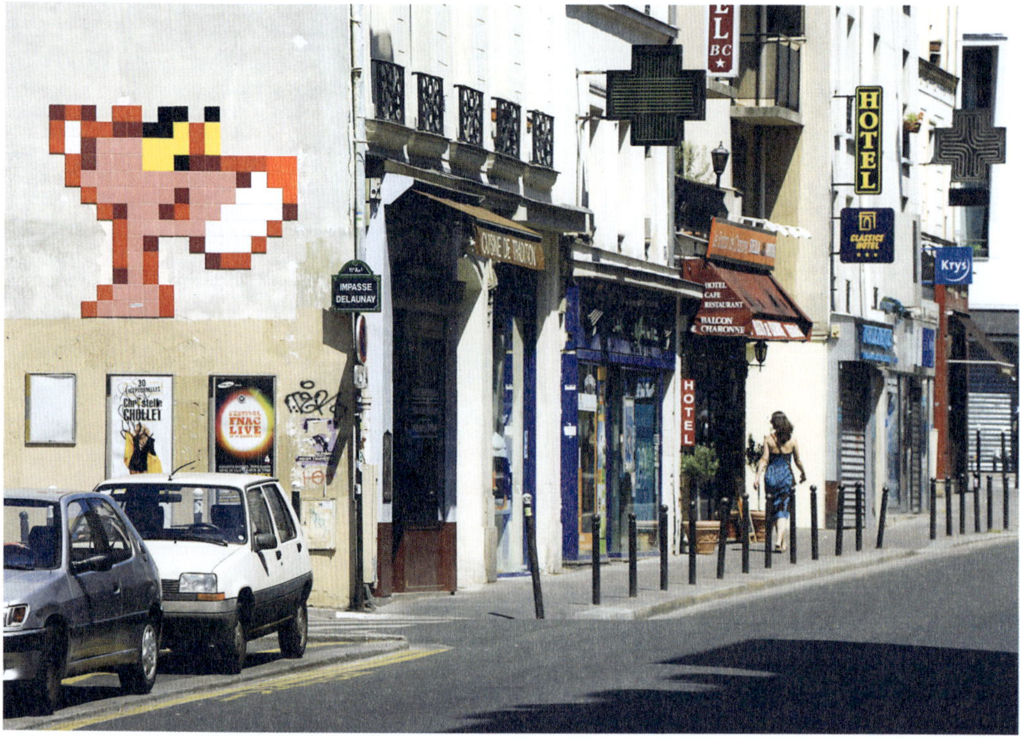

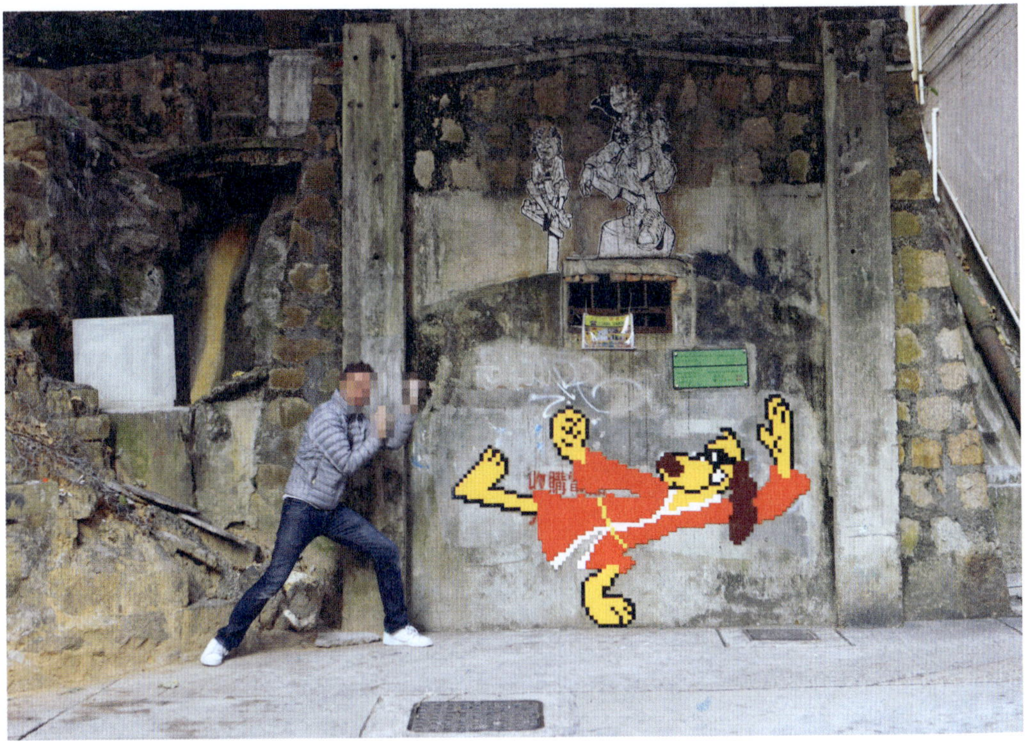

INVADER and HK_53, Hong Kong, 2014 © Invader

INVADER, New York, USA, 2007 © Invader

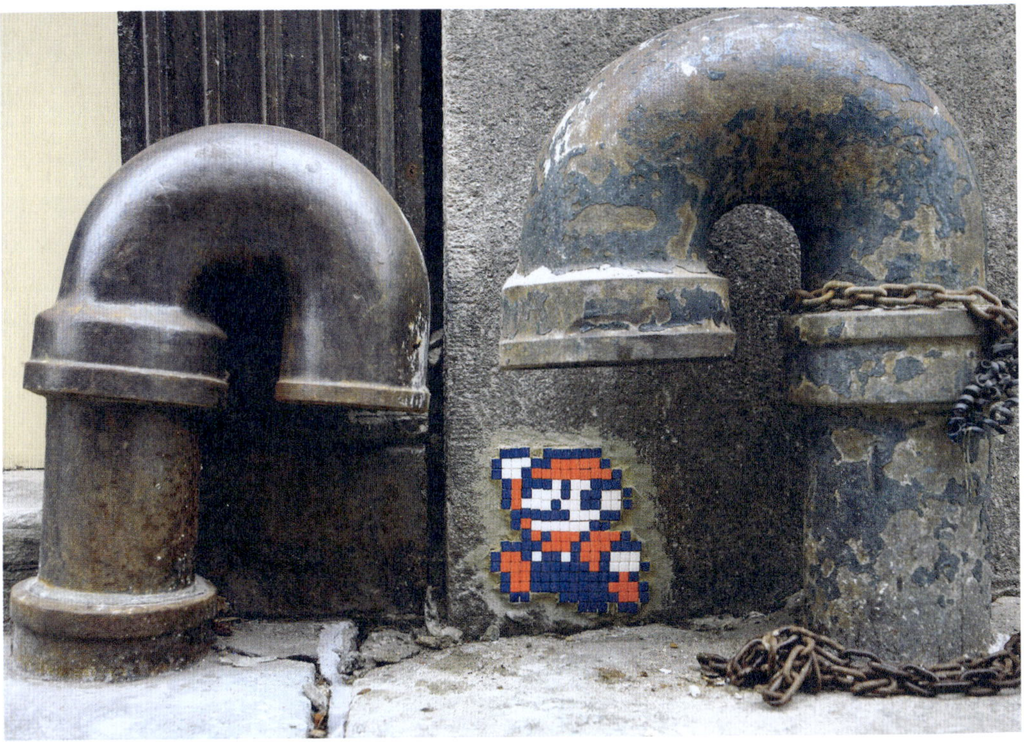

leisure culture. Far from being "just a game," this approach is a deep and constructed one. It deals with a serious part of ourselves and of the urban and programmatic aspects of our nature and its subjection to artificial intelligence.

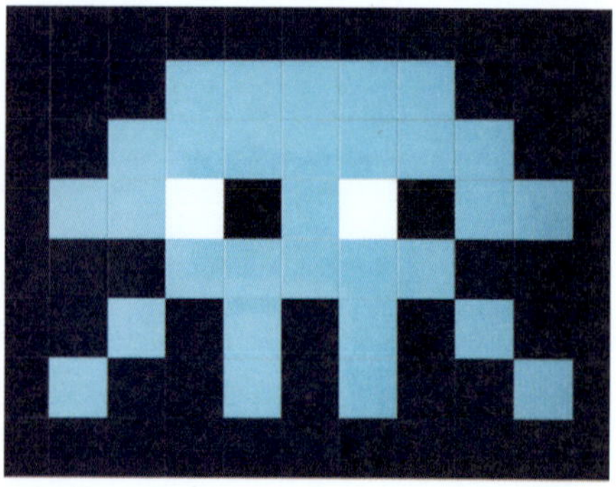

INVADER, *Alias*, ceramics and pâte de verre
© Invader

In this context, the artistic output becomes a virus. SPACE INVADER's proliferation of works is a step-by-step process that has spread from city to city around the world. So far, sixty-five urban centres have been contaminated, from the largest megalopolises and capitals (including New York, London, Bangkok, Tokyo, Hong Kong and Los Angeles) to smaller cities (including Avignon, Grenoble, Montauban and Nîmes) and places that usually do not appear on the artistic map (for example, Dhaka, Ljubljana, Mombasa and Perth). Since 2015, there has even been an Invader mosaic floating above the Earth in the International Space Station.

"Invading a city is a very intense experience. I completely immerse myself in the role of the invader. I prepare my templates in advance, and I travel with them. Once I'm there, I move fast, but at the same time I feel that it is like a performance distributed over a period of several days, because it takes me at least a week. I divide the city into squares... I have my own map for each invasion. It is the first thing I do when I arrive in a new city: I get a map that allows what will follow to take shape. [I then redraw it, and] I print several thousand copies of it. These maps are very important because they are the synthesis of the whole process. Each tells a story that you need to break the code. The maps are then distributed throughout the invaded city."

The strength of the message

Other artists have freed themselves from the North American tradition of pure graffiti during this era. At the same time as claiming an allegiance with graffiti culture and its history, they have renewed it with a tradition that has links to the poster artists of May 1968. The message has become as important as the form.

Before its encounter with the New York graffiti scene, political graffiti involved writing on walls and direct messages. BRASSAÏ was the first to catalogue its works. In the 1930s, at a time when he was already an inveterate flâneur, though not yet a photographer, he observed and noted traces of a rapidly changing society, whose darkest corners he loved to explore: "He hunted down wastelands, which were the favoured spots for lovers and children. There they would leave on the walls marks of their love and their games. He observed condemned buildings as he searched for the limbo of a city abandoned by its former inhabitants.

And his curiosity led him to follow the blackened trail left by chimney pipes. But above all, as a butterfly hunter for whom the quest of fragile and fleeting life remained just as much a scientific principle as a philosophical one, for nearly forty years he flushed out Paris's graffiti."[3] He soon realized that his notes and drawings may not be enough to show the transience of his graffiti, and so he decided to capture them in photographs. In 1933, he published several of these photos in Minotaure, along with a text entitled "Du mur des cavernes au mur des usines," in which he described his approach. He highlighted graffiti's natural and almost primal side: "Antiquity was its prime, the stone age its mindset." In his eyes, graffiti had not been distorted by a more adult world of propriety. This state of mind would be reborn during the events of May 1968, when walls were given the kind of voice of freedom of expression and thought that Brassaï had recorded and been fascinated by.

[3] Agnès Gouvion Saint Cyr, *Jacques Villeglé: graffiti politiques / Brassaï: graffiti*, exhibition catalogue, Galerie Vallois (2014).

But in the 1990s, political messages also reverberated among some artists, who took on the task of putting their talents to use to defend their beliefs.

This was particularly the case for SHEPARD FAIREY. He began to integrate satirical posters of George Bush into his collages and tirelessly denounced the confused objectives of a Gulf War that called America's political class into question. He reaffirmed his creative engagement through a series of posters promoting Barack Obama's candidacy in the 2008 election—in part at the request of the campaign team. At his expense, he distributed 300,000 stickers and 500,000 posters during the election campaign. The future president of the United States sent a letter of thanks for his support, in which he said: "The political messages involved in your work have encouraged Americans to believe they can help change the status quo. Your images have a profound effect on people, whether seen in a gallery or on a stop sign."

On the other side of the world in China, other voices have also made themselves heard. Foremost among them, the King of KowlooN, whose real name was TSANG TSOU CHOI and who was born in 1921, began covering Hong Kong's walls with graffiti that denounced British imperialism in 1956. It was an activity that he would continue with until his death in 2007. Described by Hans Ulrich-Obrist as an "urban poet," TSANG TSOU CHOI would put fragments of sentences, the name of his ancestors and slogans into Chinese ideograms. Through his approach, he asserted his family's lawful ownership of a territory that was controlled by the British Crown. He proclaimed himself the "King of Kowloon" and made his title known on all of the city's walls.

ZHANG DALI, who was born in 1963 in northern China, is one of the few Chinese artists to have been immersed in graffiti culture since the late 1980s. During a trip to Bologna —one of Italy's active graffiti scenes— in 1984, he discovered the power of this art form. He was attracted to the

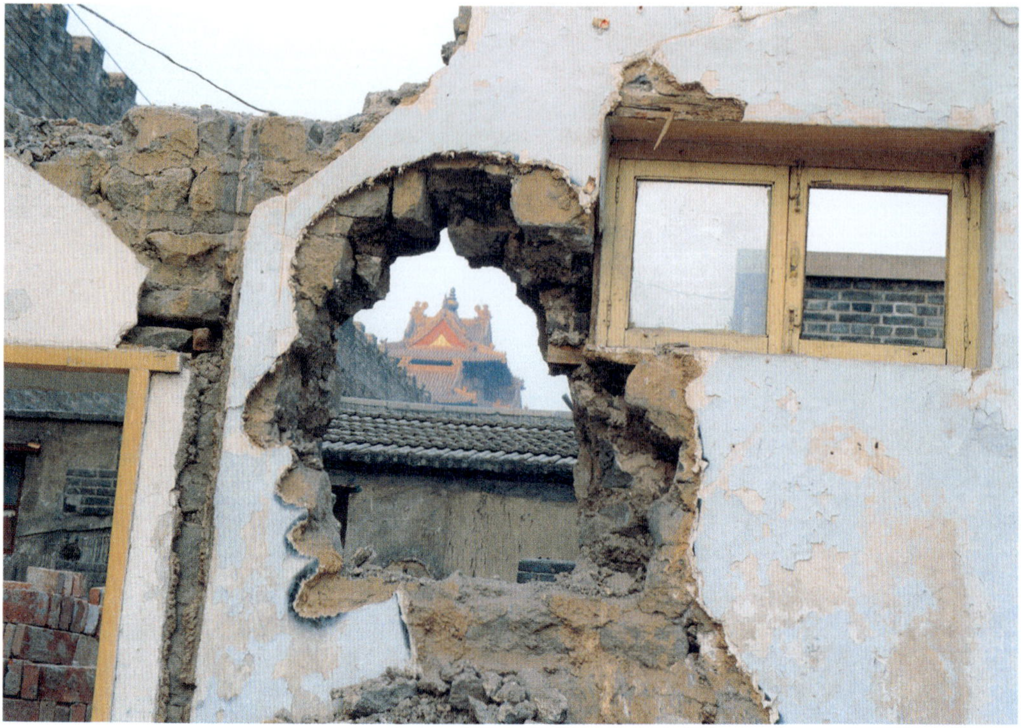

ZHANG DALI, *Demolition: Forbidden City*, Beijing, 1998 © A.R.R.

opportunity that it provides to speak out from behind a form with a simplistic appearance. "As an artist, I felt that I had to create something outside the studio. Graffiti combined both speed and power in this respect." ZHANG DALI, who received his training at Beijing's Central Academy of Art and Design, chose the pseudonym AK-47 and at the beginning of the 1990s became the only graffiti artist in Beijing. Between 1995 and 1998, he painted more than two thousand giant profiles of his bald head on condemned buildings in black spray paint. His icon and signature became a cry in response to the "chai," an ideogram painted by municipal authorities to indicate buildings selected for demolition. He also expressed his opposition to runaway and forced urbanization of this ancient city. He called this series Dialogue: "When people look at it, I want them to think: 'What happened here?' I want them to be able to express themselves."

In addition to politics, consumer society and its absurdities have also become subjects for some artists. Whether it is BANKSY's cynical take on the excesses of our society, or ZEVS's direct targeting of advertising, these artists try to raise awareness through lucid expression and humour. Both of these artists are the product of old school graffiti culture, a genre into which they have breathed new life by lending it a certain subtlety of tone. They often opt for an economy of form in order to make their messages have a greater impact. ZEVS tenaciously adopts an approach of diverting and systematically undermining consumerist codes.

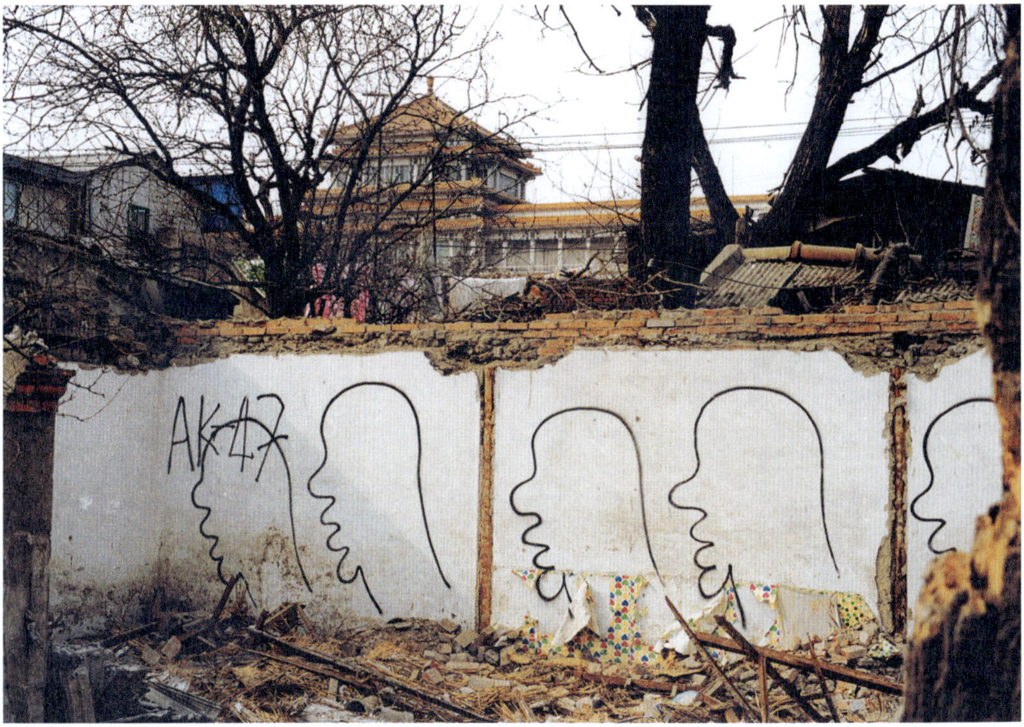

ZHANG DALI, *Dialogue*, Beijing, 1999 © A.R.R.

ZEVS was born in 1977 in eastern France but chose to settle in Paris. Like most graffiti artists, he began to cover the walls of the capital at a relatively young age. His artist name came about owing to the fact that in 1992, having been active for a few years on the graffiti scene, he was nearly hit by a commuter train. The names of the carriages in the Paris region, called "assignment codes," are displayed in bright letters on the front carriage. The one that almost killed him was "called" ZEVS, and so it became his pseudonym. To assert his own identity in the blossoming world of Parisian graffiti, he then began to systematically add a cloud and lightning bolt to his tag. This leitmotiv and logo of sorts, positioned on the top of Paris's buildings, quickly became famous.
In the late 1990s, ZEVS started his *Ombres urbaines* (*Urban Shadows*). Using white paint, he would make an outline around the shadows cast on the pavement by letter boxes, benches, parking meters and other pieces of urban furniture. The resulting silhouettes, which spoof the outlines placed around bodies during murder investigations, create strange effects depending on the time of day. They represent an original attempt to move graffiti from walls to other surfaces—in this case, the pavement.

For his next series, 2001's *Attaques visuelles* (*Visual Attacks*) he focused on the huge advertising posters that cover the walls of the metro. According to his own terminology, he "murdered" all of the people that they featured using red spray paint. In the middle of each individual's forehead, ZEVS left a dripping, "murderous" mark that resembled a blood spot.

ZEVS is emblematic of the recent changes in the graffiti scene. His actions are the result of the movement's transformation and evolution. His strategy of urban guerrilla warfare echoes the work of artists such as SPACE INVADER and SHEPARD FAIREY. After *Attaques visuelles*, he continued to take on the advertising world. This time he did so with a new weapon, swapping his spray paint for a scalpel. It is worth noting that his abandoning of the movement's key tool was quite exceptional at the time. In 2006, the Liquidated Logos series aimed to distort the logos of major companies by literally liquefying them. Created using paint, the logos seem to melt before our very eyes... Between ephemeral art and political action, ZEVS has found his own position and chosen to develop his artistic process in the battlefield of the street, with protest and advertising strategy as his weapons.

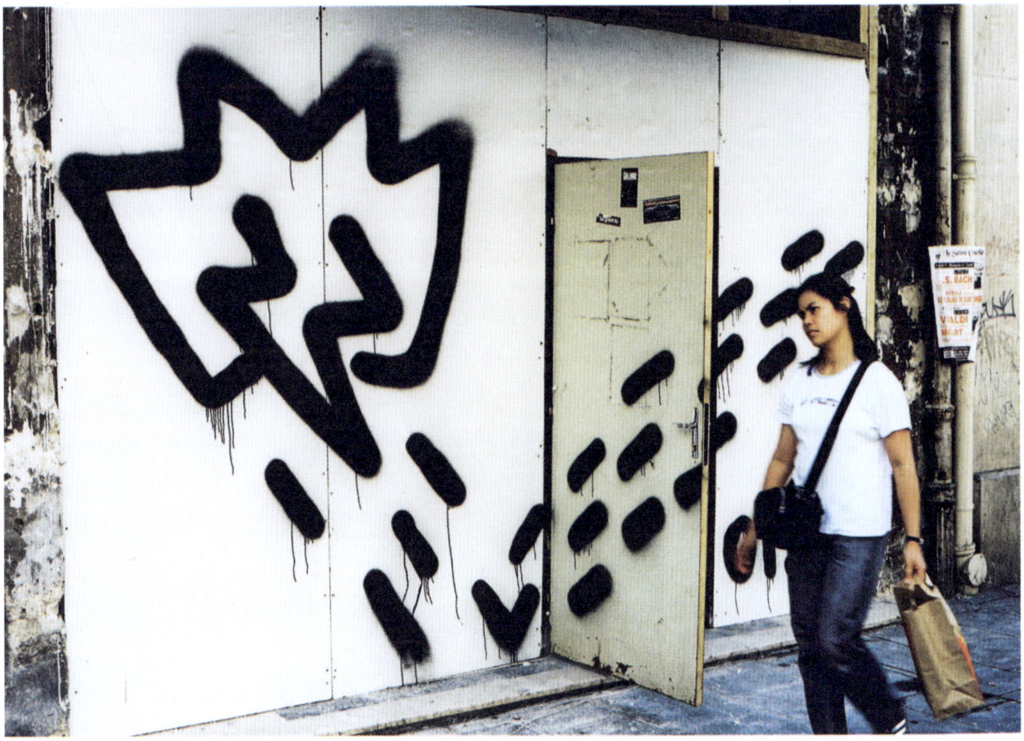

ZEVS, *Fatcap graffiti*, cloud and bouncing rain, Paris, 1998 © A.R.R.

ZEVS, *Ombre électrique*, bench, Montmartre, Paris, 2000 © A.R.R.

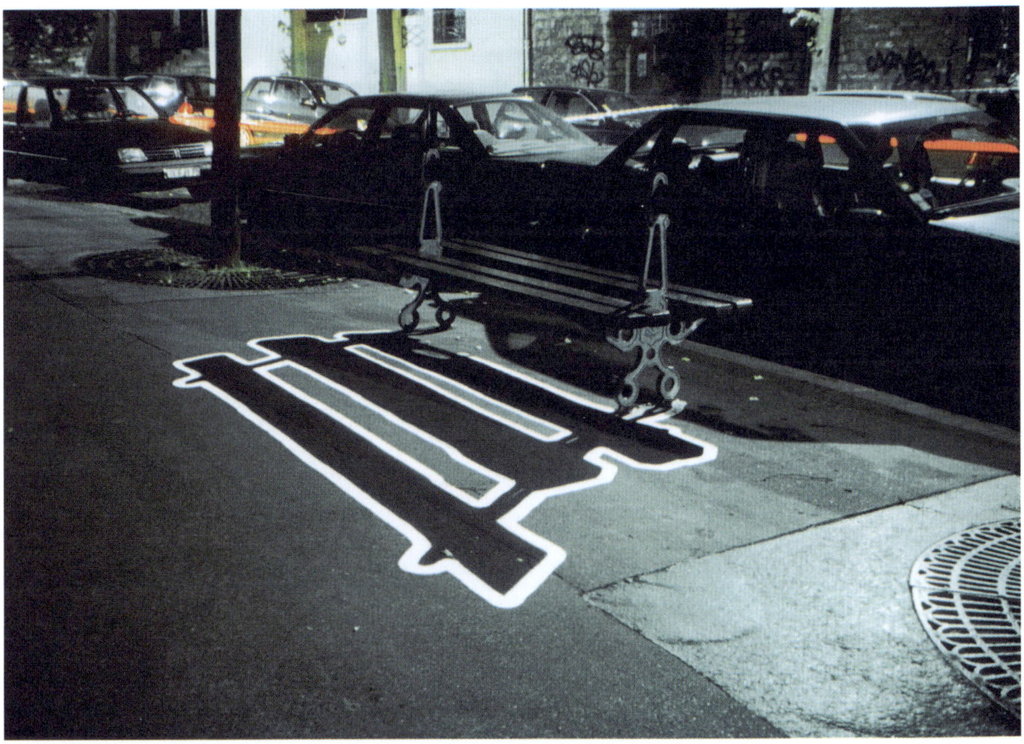

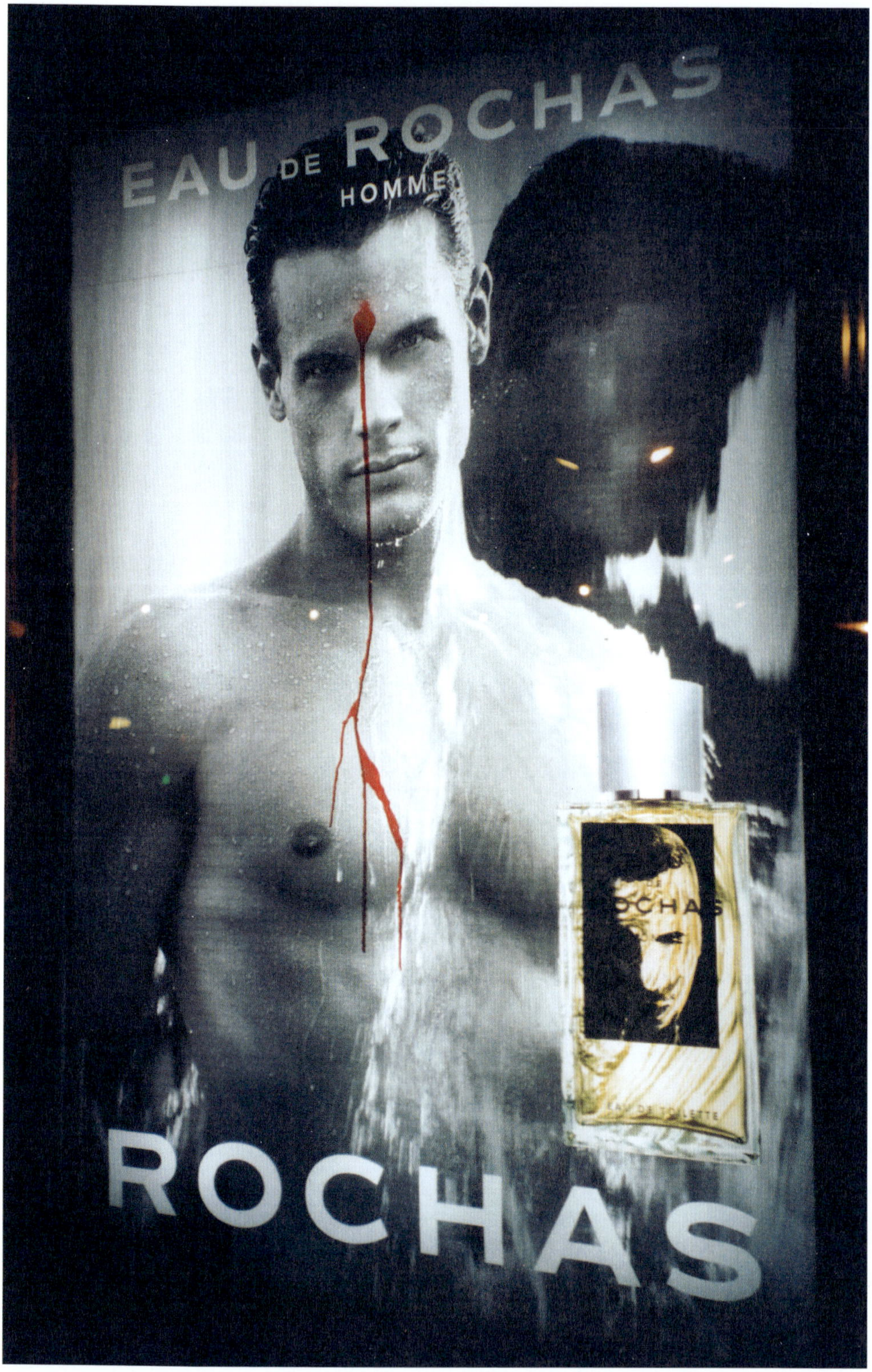

ZEVS, *Kidnapping visuel*, Berlin, 2020 © A.R.R.

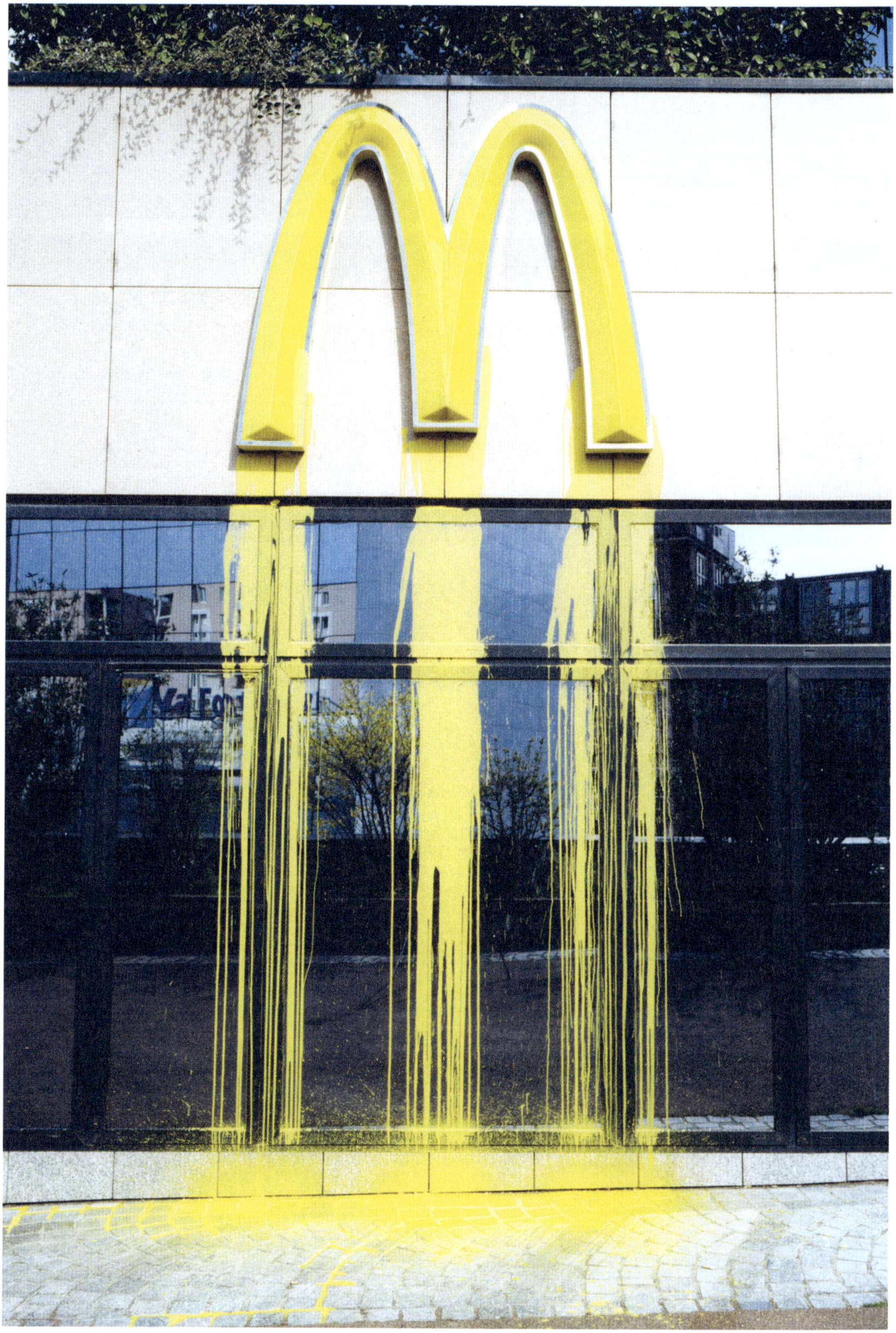

ZEVS, *Liquidated McDonald's Logo*, Parisian suburb, Paris, 2006 © A.R.R.

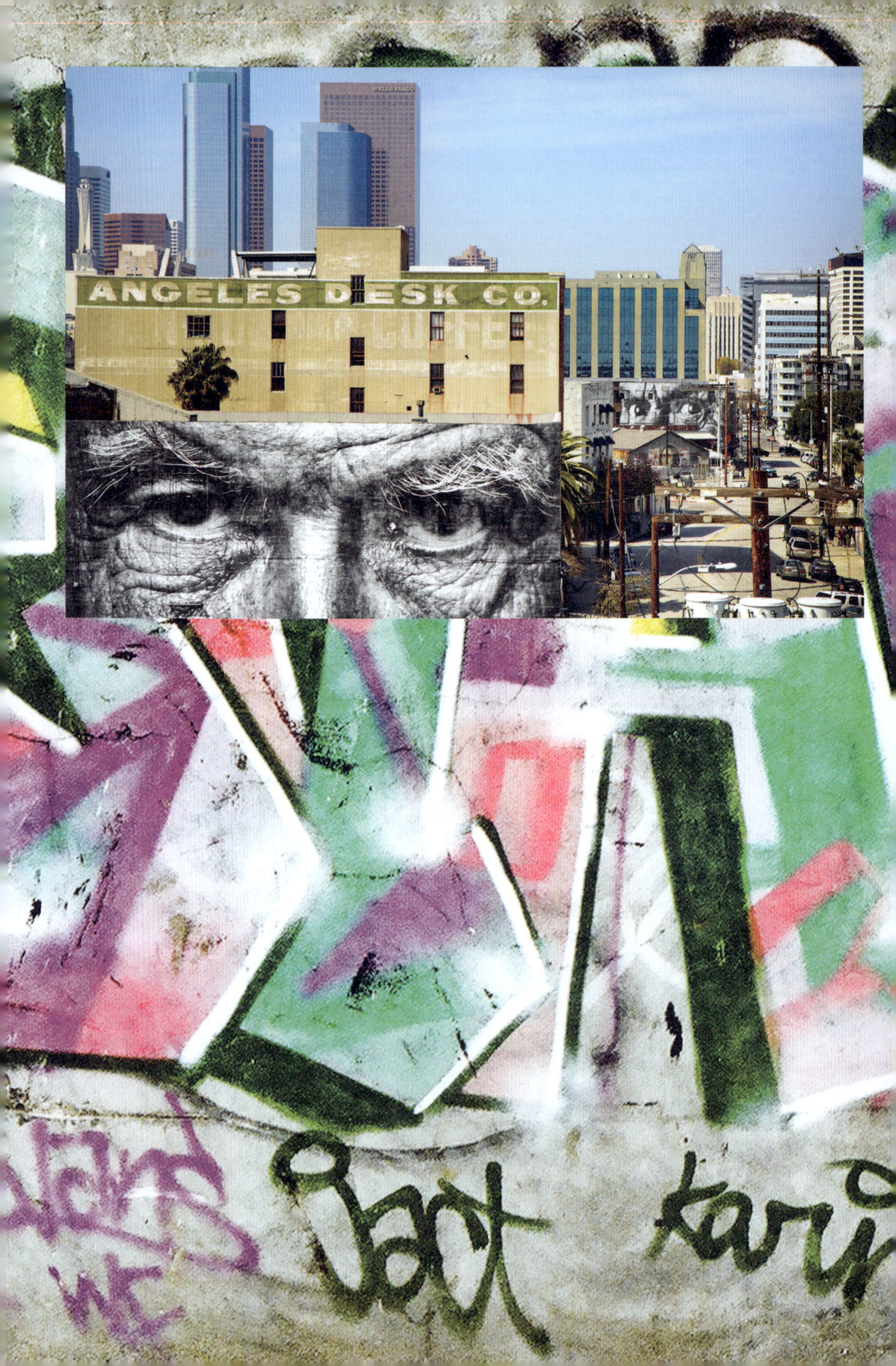
ANGELES DESK CO.

STREET ART IS EVERYWHERE

The success of the cult of anonymity and pervasive art

At present, BANKSY is the most famous stencil artist in the world. He rose to prominence through the excesses of his 2006 *Barely Legal* show in Los Angeles. But like many of his peers, he fiercely protects his anonymity. Originally, artists followed this practice to protect themselves from the authorities, who could charge an offender for all the works that he or she had produced in the past. The taste for the criminal act, the adrenaline that it produces, and the common culture from which it emerged are all factors that push the movement's participants to maintain an illicit side to their activities. However, for some artists, anonymity is not only a means to escape justice. Like BANKSY, SPACE INVADER has, since his first organized exhibition in a restaurant in 2000, made anonymity an essential component of his artistic identity, and he never derogates from this sacrosanct rule. But BANKSY is without a doubt the great champion of this game. He is all the more attractive to the general public because no one—or almost no one—really knows who hides behind his works. An aesthetic of anonymity has therefore emerged.

JR, *The Wrinkles of the City*, Los Angeles, Michael Downtown, USA, 2012. Courtesy JR

Background image: graffiti in New York. Photo © Stéphane Bisseuil

Placing one's signature in a city to get noticed is therefore no longer sufficient—or this is at least what someone like BANKSY obviously thinks. For him, more is required. The goal is no longer to hide behind a pseudonym, but instead to be "recognized" not physically but artistically.
The boundary between anonymity and popularity is not a particularly tangible one, and it contributes to the myth. BANKSY has understood

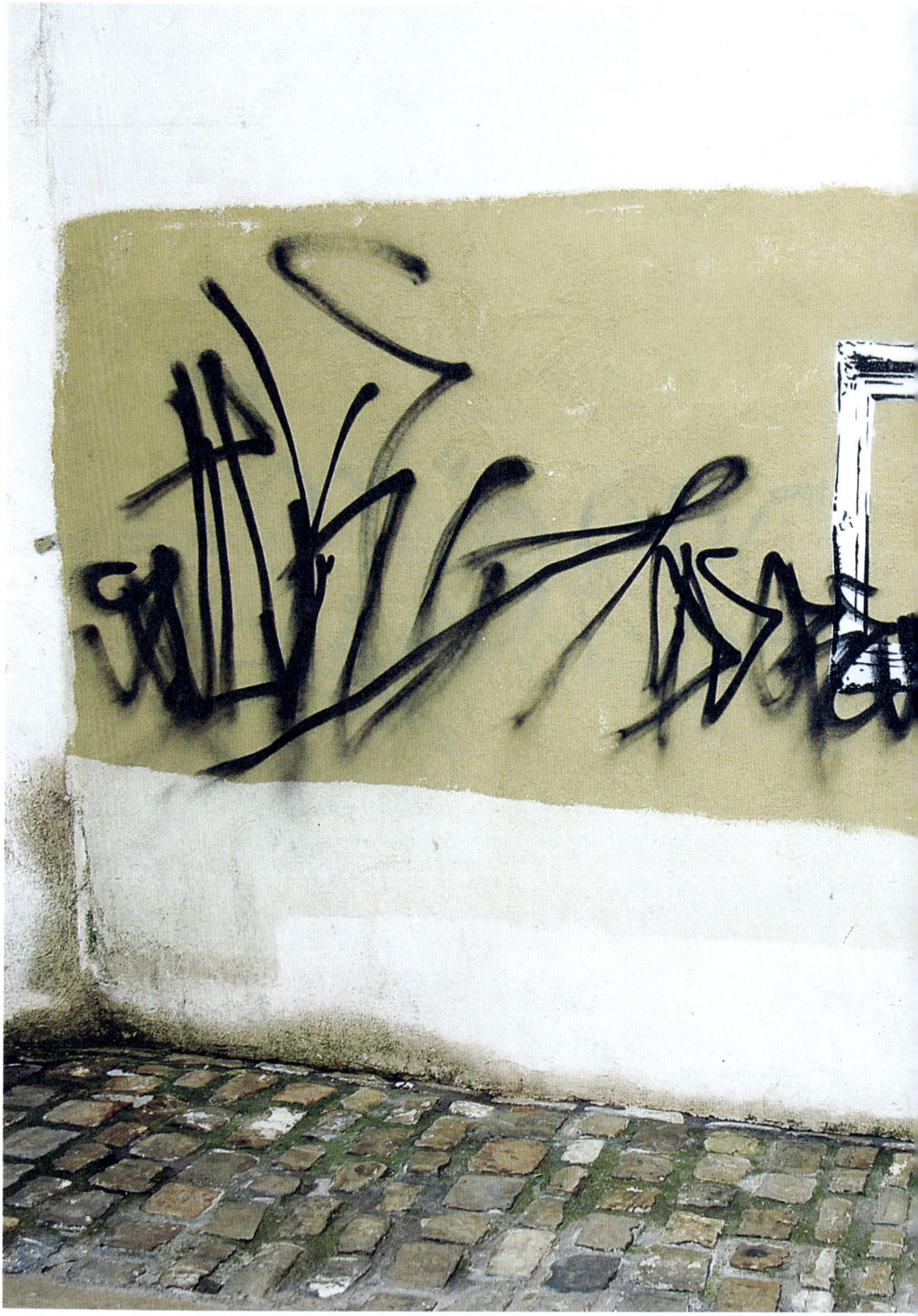

BANKSY, San Sebastian. Photo © Macu Masari

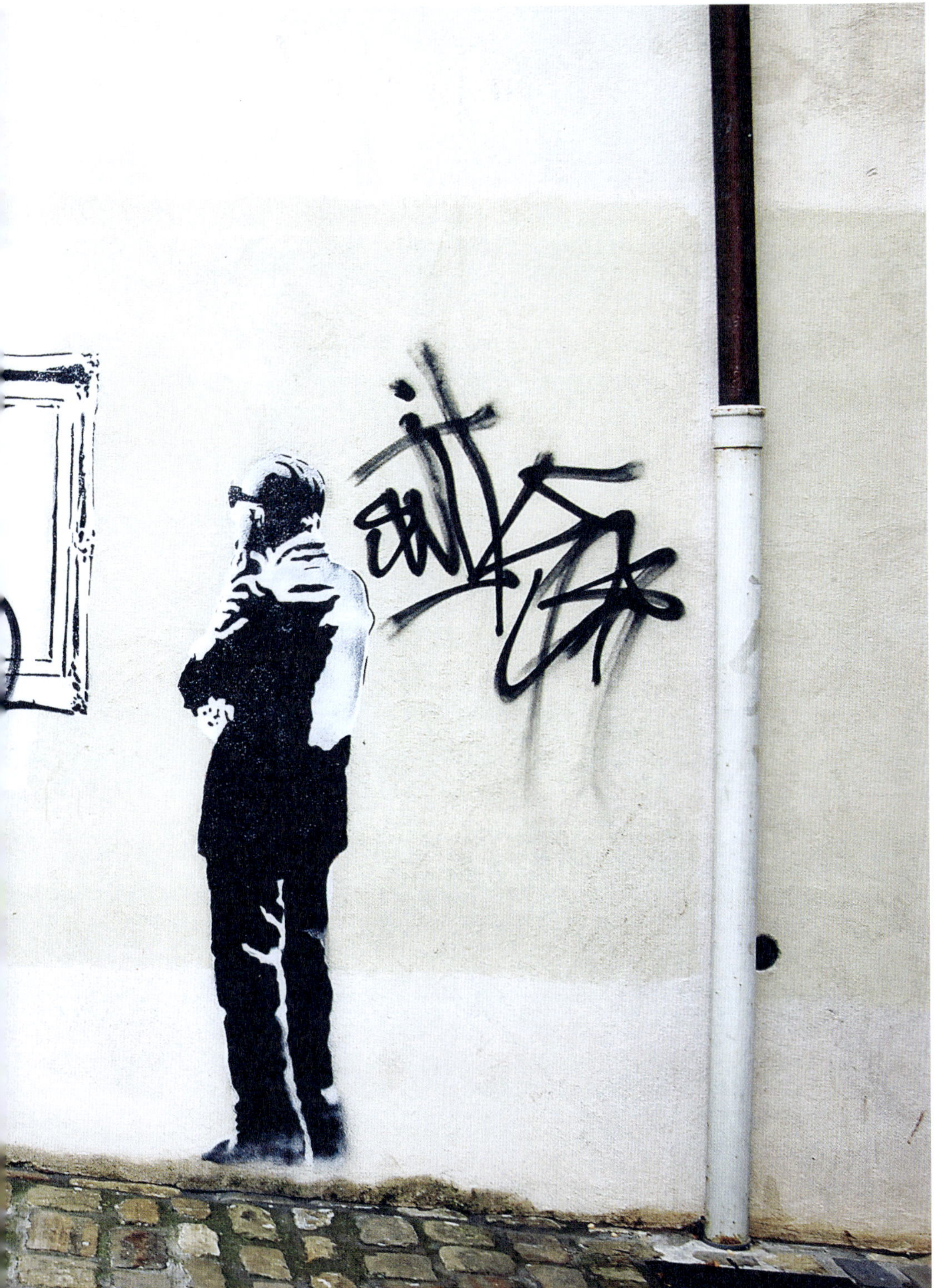

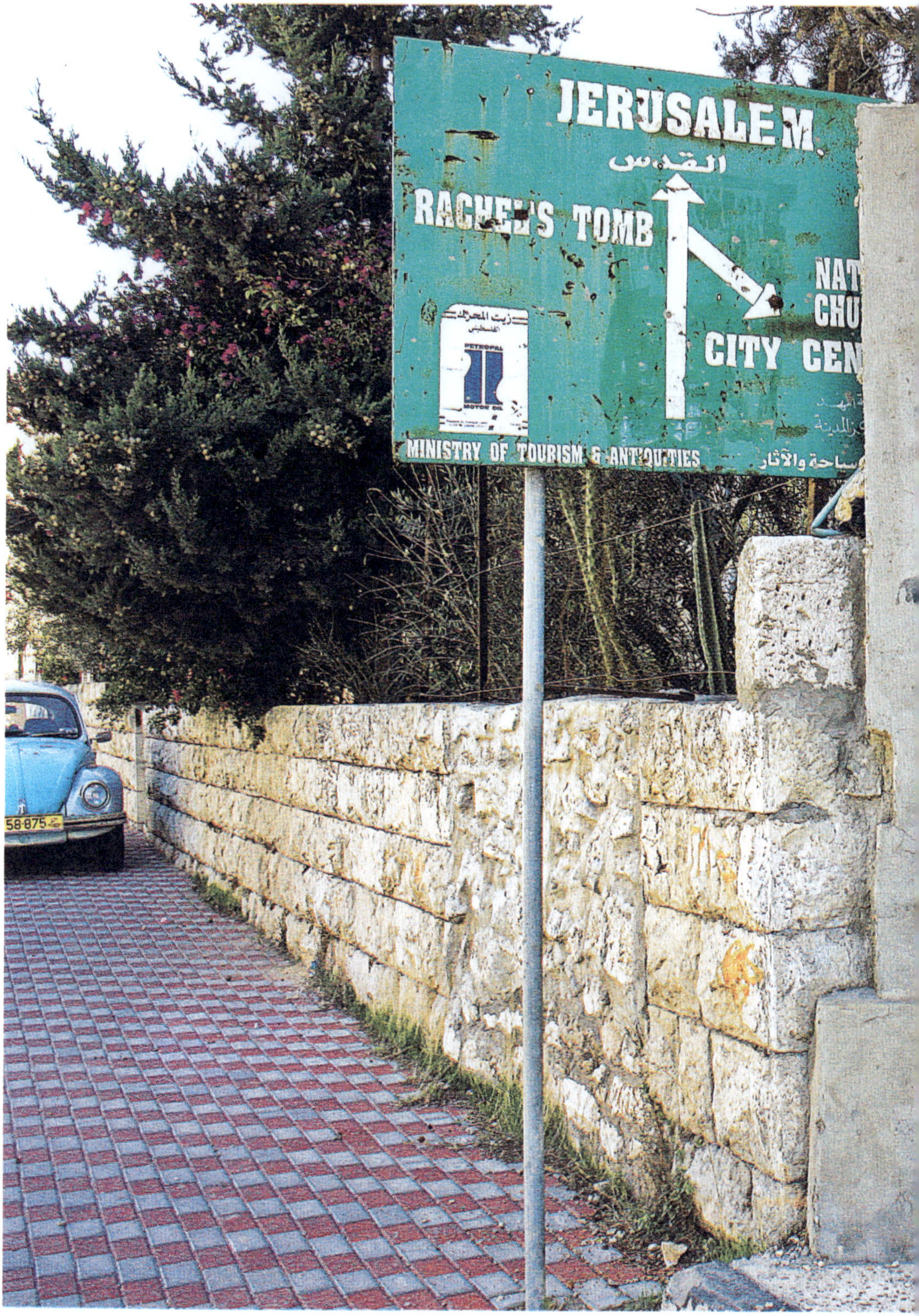

BANKSY, Bethlehem. Photo © Liam Shove

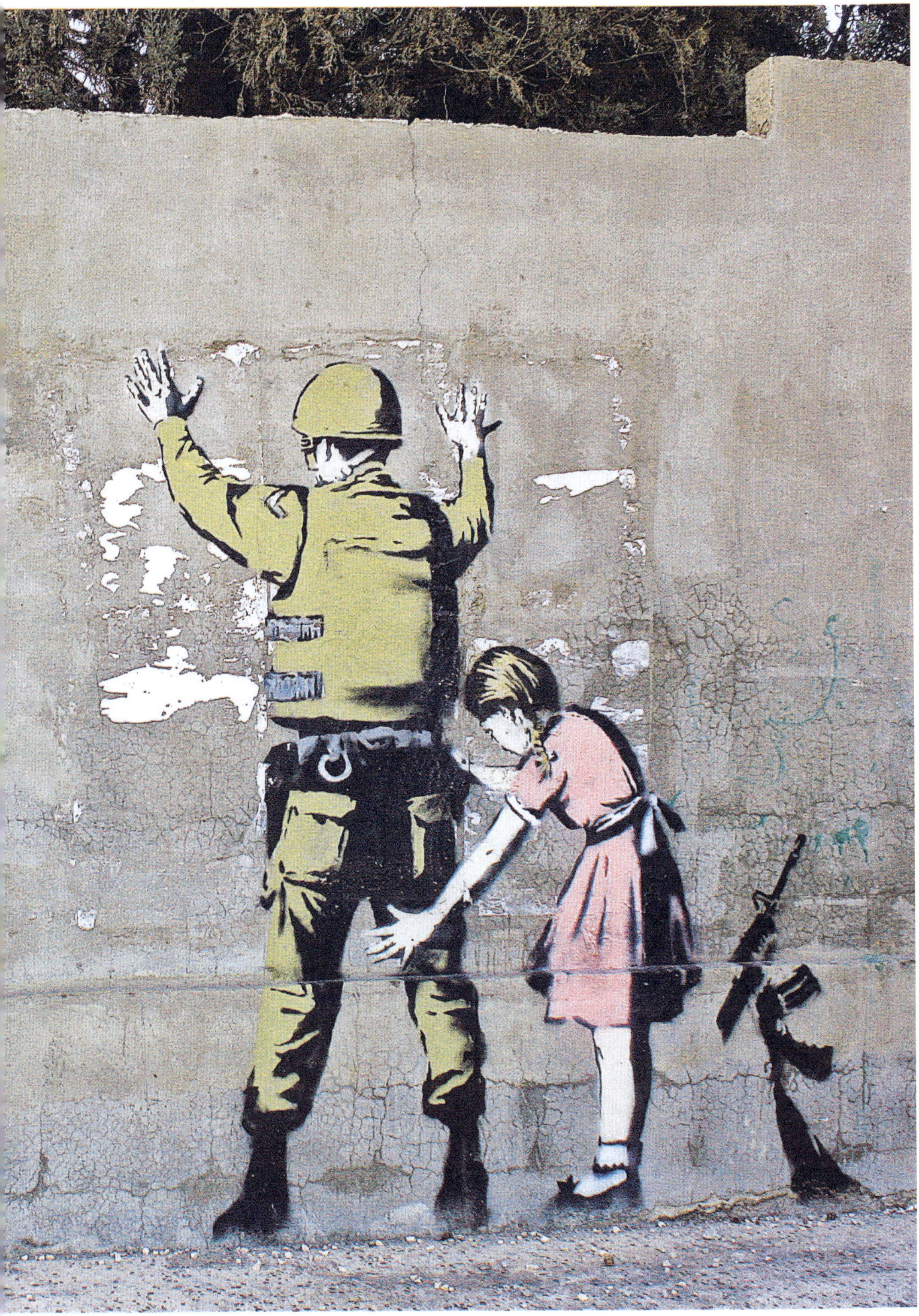

this well. The less information he gives about his identity and his mysterious signature, the more the public attempts to unmask him and follows his work. What is appealing is that the artist is everywhere and nowhere at the same time. This is something that New Yorkers, who in December 2013 discovered new works by him every day in different locations in the city, will verify. There is something fun about this giant treasure hunt.

Through this approach, BANKSY actively queries the value of the artist. Only associating this figure who has no physical incarnation with a name leads to a questioning of the relationship between the art and the brand. Could the artist have become a trademark—a simple, recognizable signature that functions like a logo? Anonymity thus raises many questions. Beyond the curiosity that it arouses, it questions the validity of the signature and the artist's real role. Which is more important: the work produced or the person who produces it? The art market and its speculative escapades can lead us to think that sometimes the creator can become more important than his or her creation. The performance (one could even call it a sociological experiment) staged by the artist in New York in 2013 seems to validate this analysis: original works were on sale on an anonymous street stall in Central Park, for the derisory price of $60. In the end, while BANKSY's name was enough to panic the auction rooms, only seven paintings were sold to three buyers.

Whatever the case may be, by keeping his identity secret, this English agitator raises another question related to the artist's status: Is this a normal man, a fictional character, or even an out-of-the-ordinary individual? At the end of an article on him, the *Guardian* concluded: "The question isn't who is Banksy. The question is who cares?" BANKSY—a person who seeks only one thing: to reach the greatest number of people—would no doubt agree with this conclusion.

Anonymity as a means of action has now combined with another phenomenon. Thanks to the instant sharing of information through the rise of social networks—Facebook was founded in 2004 and Instagram in 2010—street art has gained the ability to be pervasive.

An environment can be called pervasive when all the elements that comprise it can be recognized and located and can interact with one another. For this to happen, objects have to be connected through electronic means. However, within the movement, the artists themselves are connected as much with each other as they are with the whole of society. Their art is ubiquitous and accessible to all, and it provokes a reaction, whether desired or not.

Pervasive art uses all formats that it deems appropriate for its existence. These could be street furniture and the immediate environment of daily life, or conversely galleries, museums and institutions. Everything can be a means of dissemination and is worth considering as such. Upsetting

the hierarchies established between contemporary art and folk art, street art queries the usual art authorities. In parallel, an inexorable march and an invasion are under way, and the fan base of these urban practices is growing.
Although the creator of the term "pervasive art," Gary Baseman, is not part of the street art movement, he boils it down to this motivation: "I believe art is how we share our lives, hopes, dreams, fears, and thoughts with others, either old friends or others in different cultures. If I had to use one sentence to describe my art it would be: to celebrate the beauty of the bittersweetness of life."

Pervasive art is not just about being present everywhere. Its peculiarity is that it makes itself visible through all possible channels. In addition to the previously mentioned forums of the street and exhibitions, social networks (Instagram in particular), the audiovisual industry (cinema and television), publishing (books) and other channels are also used. All means for becoming known are valued.

When he printed fake 10 pound notes featuring Princess Diana in 2004 or when he released his film *Exit Through the Gift Shop*, which was nominated for an Oscar in 2011, BANKSY joined the group of artists who constantly "embed" themselves everywhere. *Exit Through the Gift Shop* tells the story of the artist Thierry Guetta (born 1966), who is better known as Mr BRAINWASH. Mr BRAINWASH unabashedly floods the market with his works made of icons and universal messages, which mix graffiti and pop art. This funny and satirical yet serious film launched his career and made him a global star.

MR BRAINWASH, *Hitchcock*, stencil, collage and acrylic on wall, Les Bains © A.R.R.

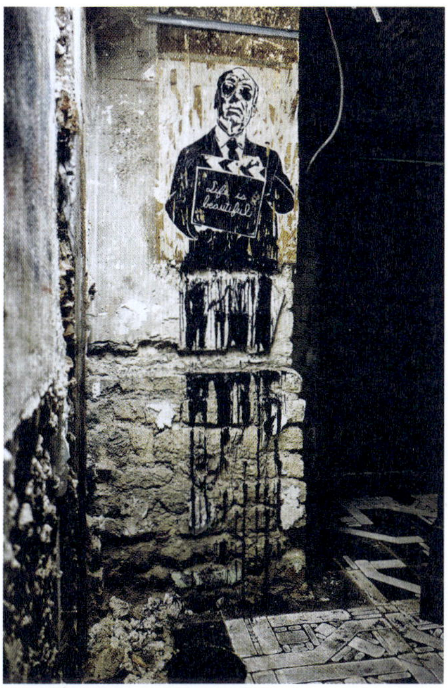

JR, whose artistic practice is pervasive in more than one respect, adopts a similar approach. This omnipresent figure with more than 600,000 followers on Instagram makes collages that feature in his films (*Women are Heroes was* presented at Cannes in 2011, and *Les Bosquets* was released in 2015 and presented at the Tribeca Film Festival) and in his many publications. From the slums of Manila to the townships of Liberia, his monumental collages, which are intended to reach the largest number of people possible, never fail to provoke a reaction.

JR was born in the Paris suburbs in 1983. Like other street artists, he maintains a relative anonymity. He started doing graffiti as a teenager, but his art quickly became more invasive. Legend has it that he started in photography by accident, after finding a camera on the metro. "I got into street art through graffiti and a bit by default. But graffiti in itself was not enough for me, and I did not really excel in it. Led along by some friends, I went up and down the tunnels, and while

MR BRAINWASH, *Kate Moss*, stencil, collage and acrylic on wall, Les Bains

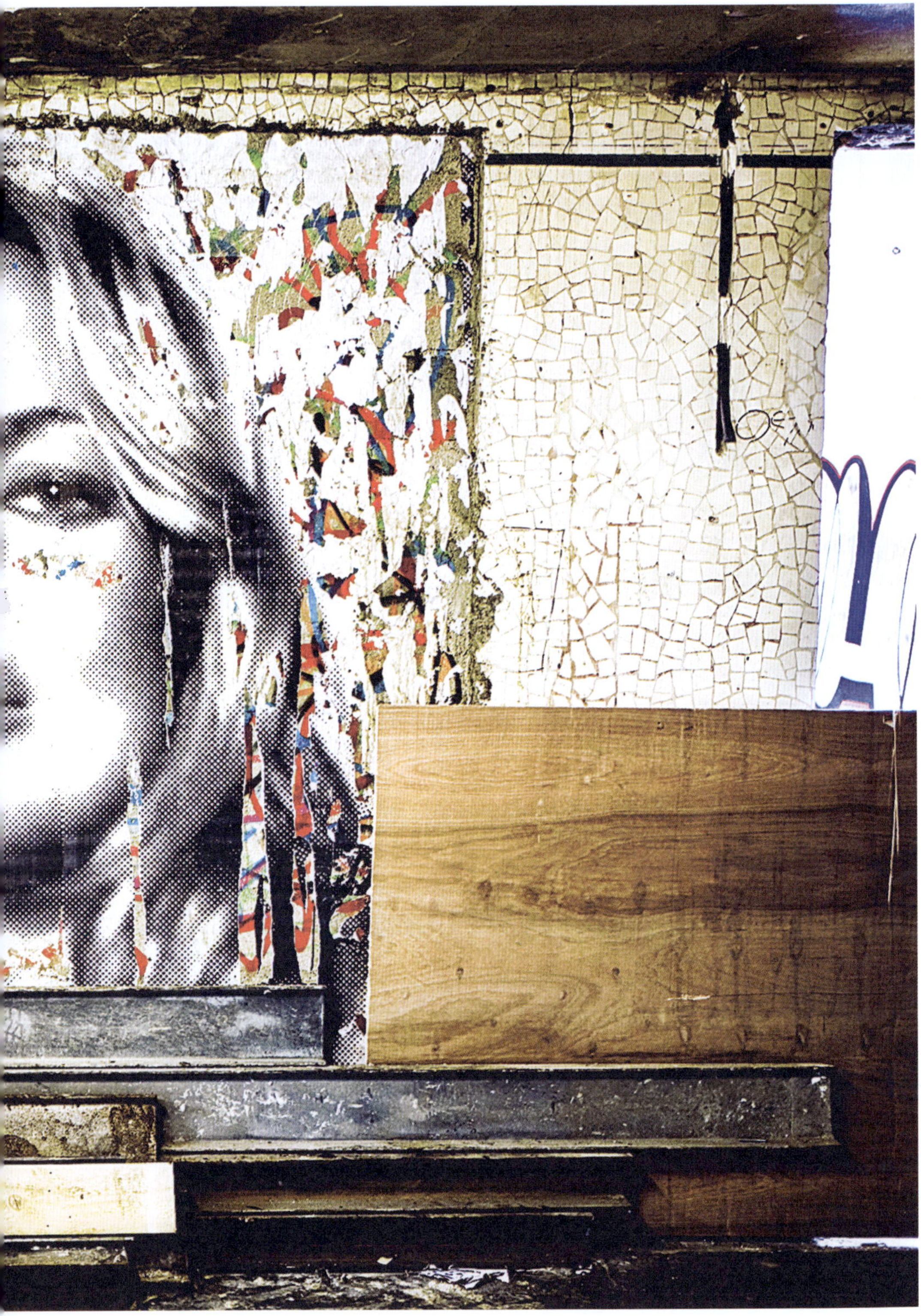

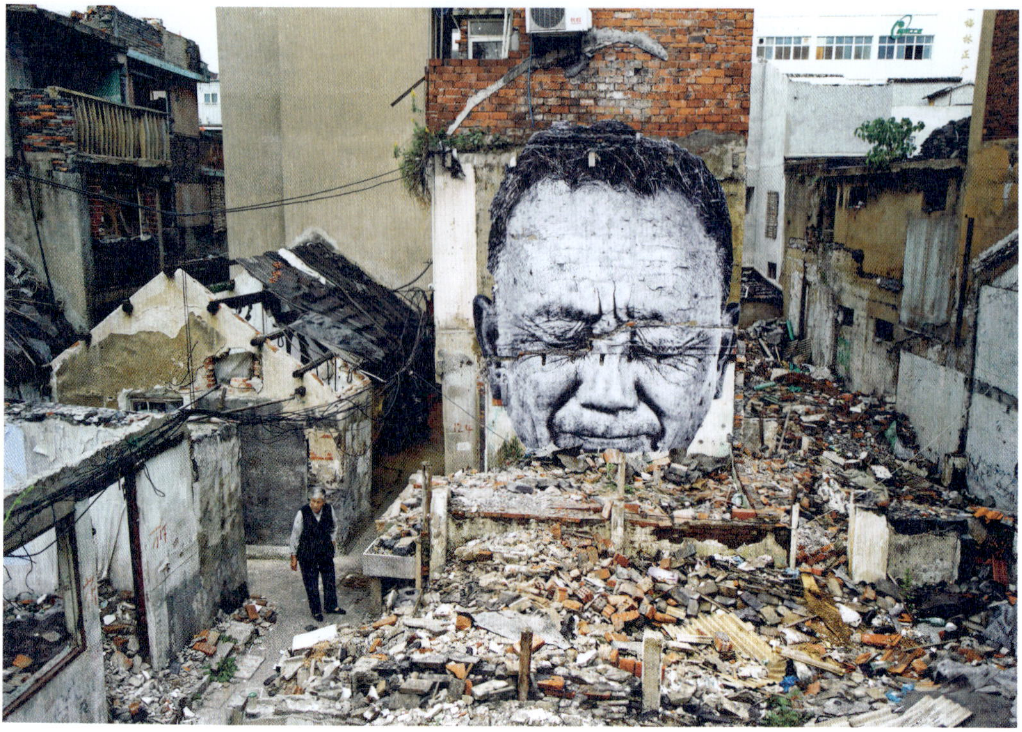

JR, *The Wrinkles of the city*, Shanghai, Zhai Zhixin, China, 2010, Courtesy JR

they were trying to paint, I wanted to keep track and document the moment and the action." In 2001, JR produced his first series of medium-size photographs, which he stuck on walls in the city. He would draw around his first collages with spray-painted lines and write the words "Expo 2 Rue". This frame around the work recalled the tagging aesthetic. JR has described these first acts as "portraits of taggers that had themselves been stuck on walls and then retagged." This is how his use of mise en abyme came about, and it would subsequently prove to be dear to the artist in a number of his series.

Already drawn to methods of spreading his name that were off the beaten track after his first informal exhibition, a collaboration with Ladj Ly, an actor and director from the Kourtrajmé collective, in 2004 JR displayed a series of monumental portraits of the inhabitants of the Cité des Bosquets in Montfermeil on the estate's walls. Ironically, the artist's career took a new turn in October 2005 during the riots that took place in the suburb of Clichy-Montfermeil. In a sort of amalgam of artistic project and current events, images of the riots on television showed JR's photos. The power of street art went beyond even its own limitations in the respect that it was completely reinterpreted by television.

He continued his approach with the *Face 2 Face* project, which was produced in 2007 in the Middle East. JR posed the following question: "Why can't Palestinians and Israelis simply live together?" He made portraits

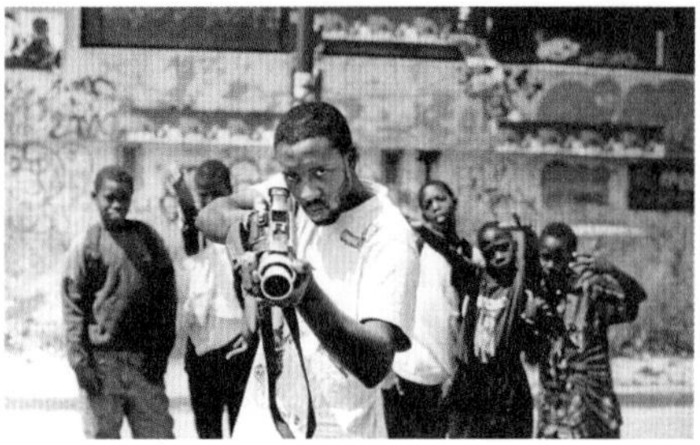

JR, *Portrait d'une generation*, Ladj Ly, 2011
Courtesy JR

of people from the two communities who work in the same jobs within their own countries, and he placed huge versions of them facing one another in places that people have to pass through, such as the Palestinian and Israeli sides of the dividing wall. In so doing, he masterfully highlighted how small the difference between these men and women who have been in conflict for many years is.

In 2008, his *Women are Heroes* project was developed in the same way. Its stated objective was to stress the central role of women in Kenya, Sudan, Sierra Leone and Liberia and to show their dignity and their beauty through gigantic portraits placed on these regions' trains, walls and hills. He then developed the project in the favelas of Rio de Janeiro in Brazil, shedding light on their simple but outstanding women. *Women are Heroes* was the subject of a book and a film, which gave the project even greater exposure.
Yet although he is often presented as a photographer and invited as one to professional festivals—including the prestigious *Rencontres D'Arles* in 2007—or as a filmmaker at Cannes, JR remains deeply linked to the street, its culture and its energy.

In keeping with this tendency of not being confined to a single field of activity, JR stands at the intersection of different questions related to the representation and presentation of photography. Like many artists who work on the decontextualization of photography, from Éric Poitevin to Édouard Levé, JR questions the relationship to this art. He interrogates photography through its own presentation. When enlarged and affixed on exterior walls, his works fit into unusual exhibition spaces where their artistic device is to interact with everything that surrounds them, such as the architecture, the city and bystanders.

JR also invites reflection on the impact of the image, whether it comes from the media or from a prestigious photographic collection. And he does not only use shots that he has taken himself for his collages. For his *Unframed* series, which began in 2010, he has used photos by Man Ray, Giacomelli and Salgado. He touches here on what the historian Nicolas Offenstadt calls "functioning through icons more than through contexts." Offenstadt warns against the potentially pernicious use of certain images, using as an example those taken in the trenches of World War One that are published without adequate captions in school textbooks. By positioning Capa's[5] shots of the D-Day landings on the banks of Lake Geneva,[6] JR has also contributed to awareness of this point.

In 2010, his *Wrinkles of the City* project took him to Shanghai, where he sought to highlight a city's nooks and crannies of history and the twists and turns of its memory through the portraits of its oldest inhabitants.

[5] Robert Capa's photography of American troop landings, Omaha Beach, Normandy Coast, 6 June 1944.

[6] During the Festival images in Vevey in 2010.

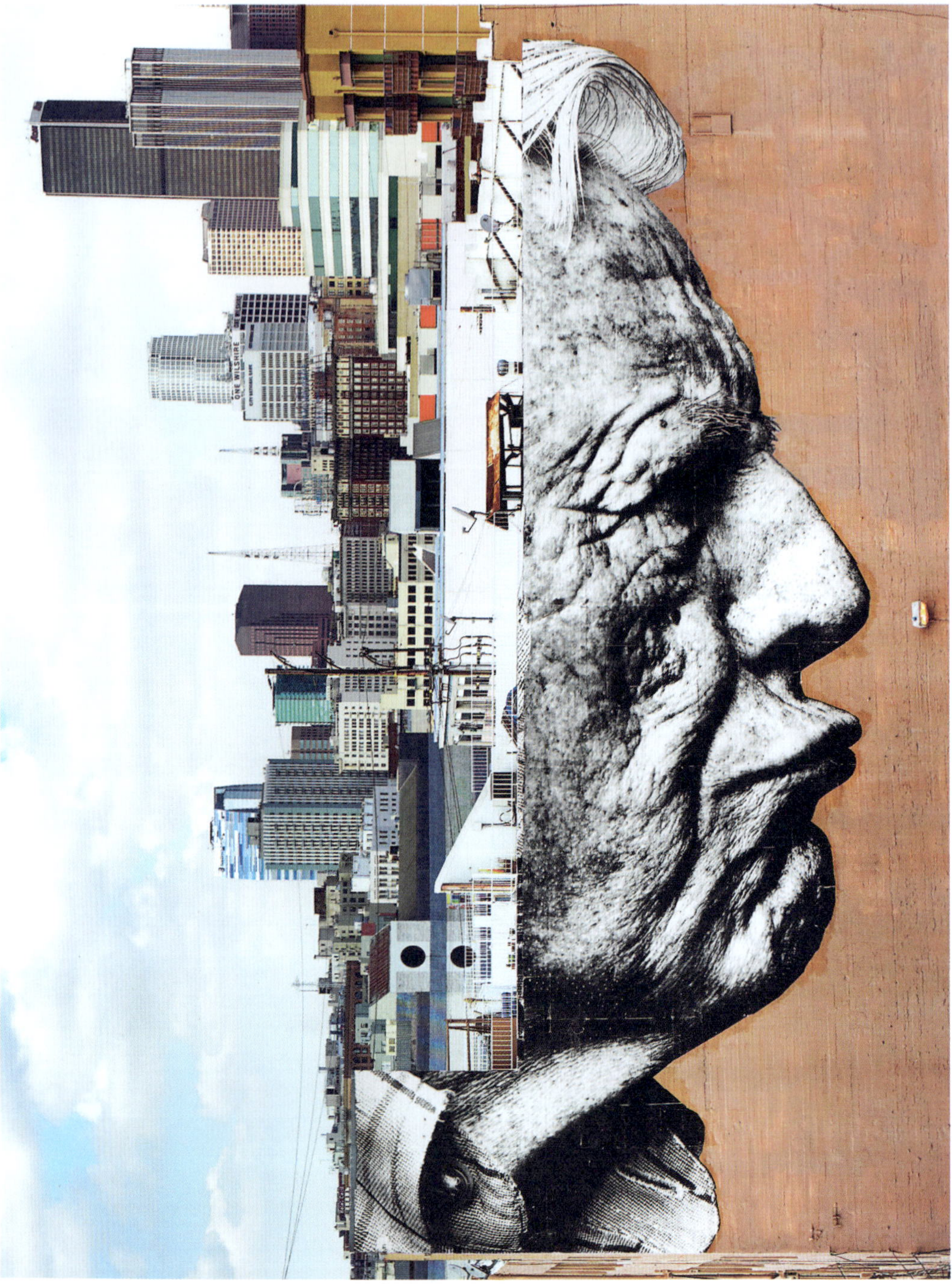

JR, *The Wrinkles of the City*, Los Angeles, 2011, Courtesy JR

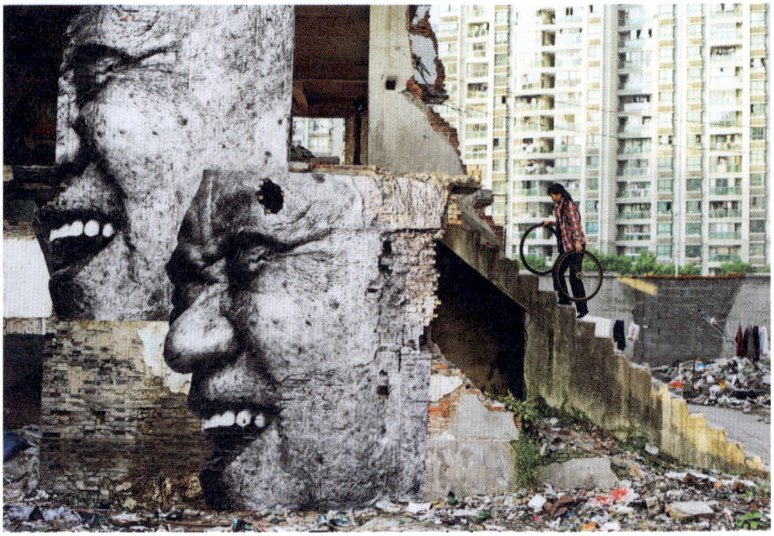

JR, *The Wrinkles of the City*, Shanghai, Li Xuanhua, 2010, Courtesy JR

JR, *Inside Out Project*, Haiti, 2012, Courtesy JR

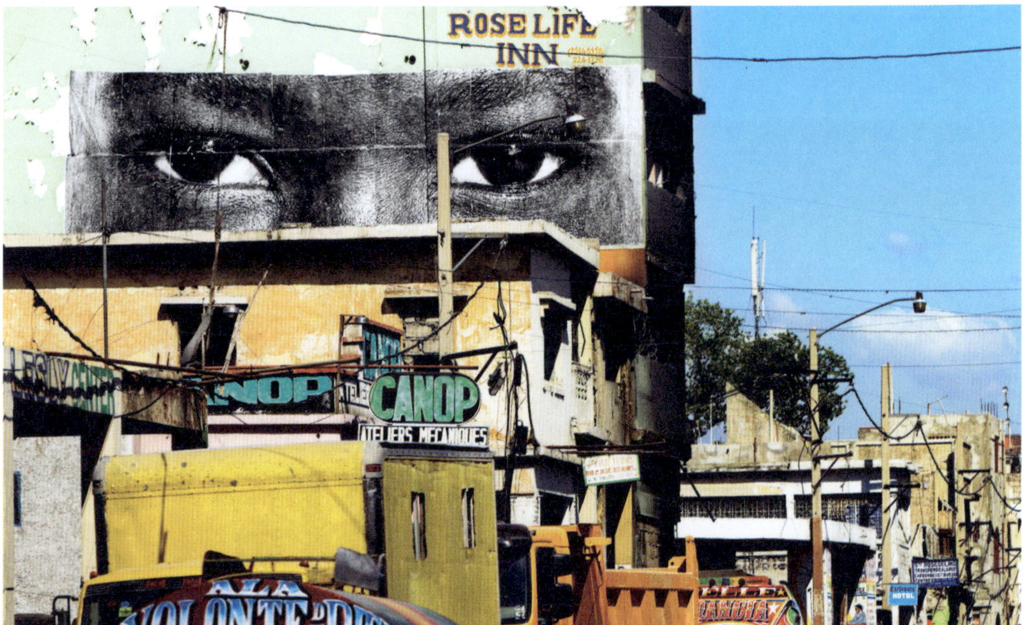

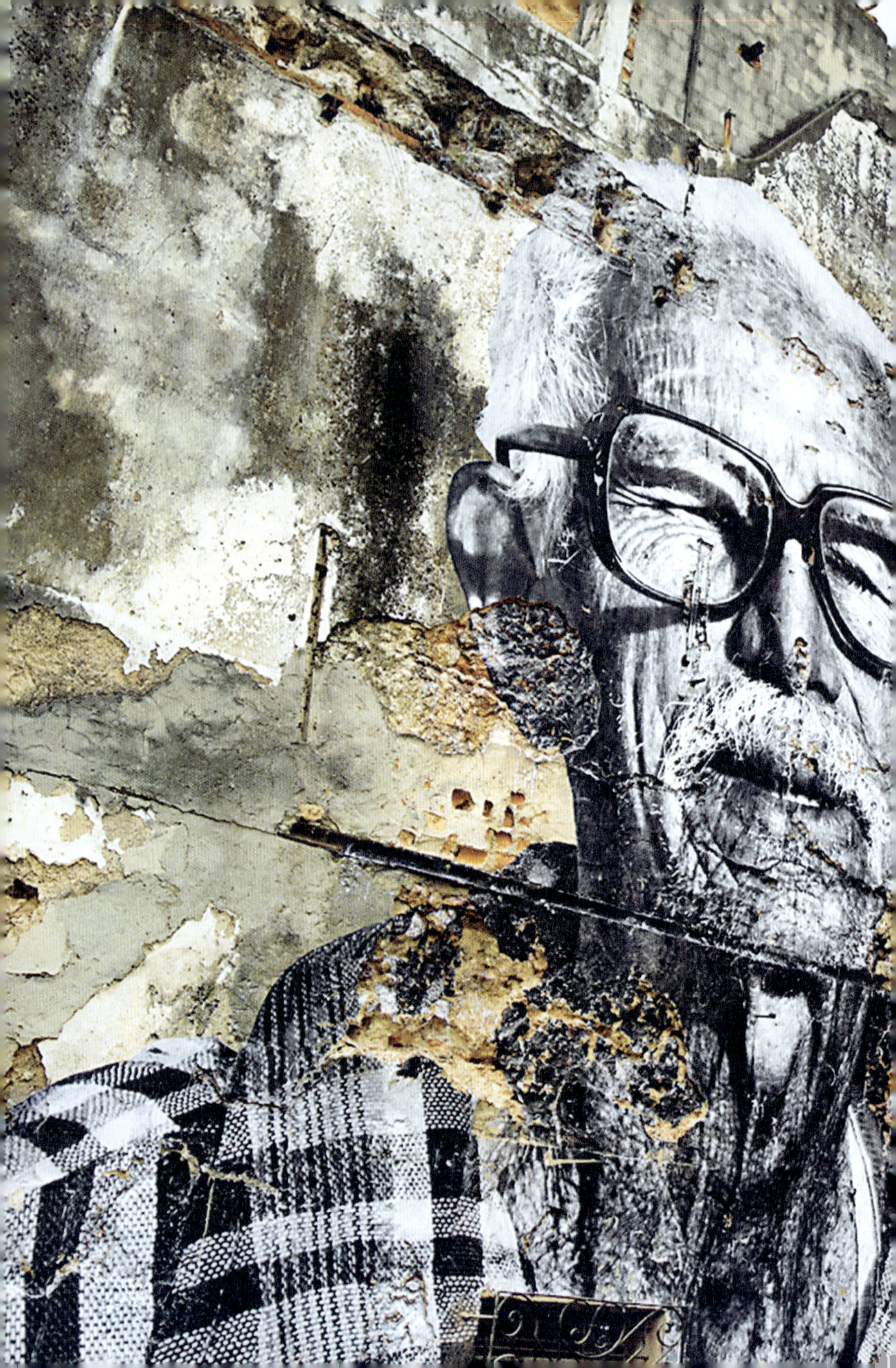

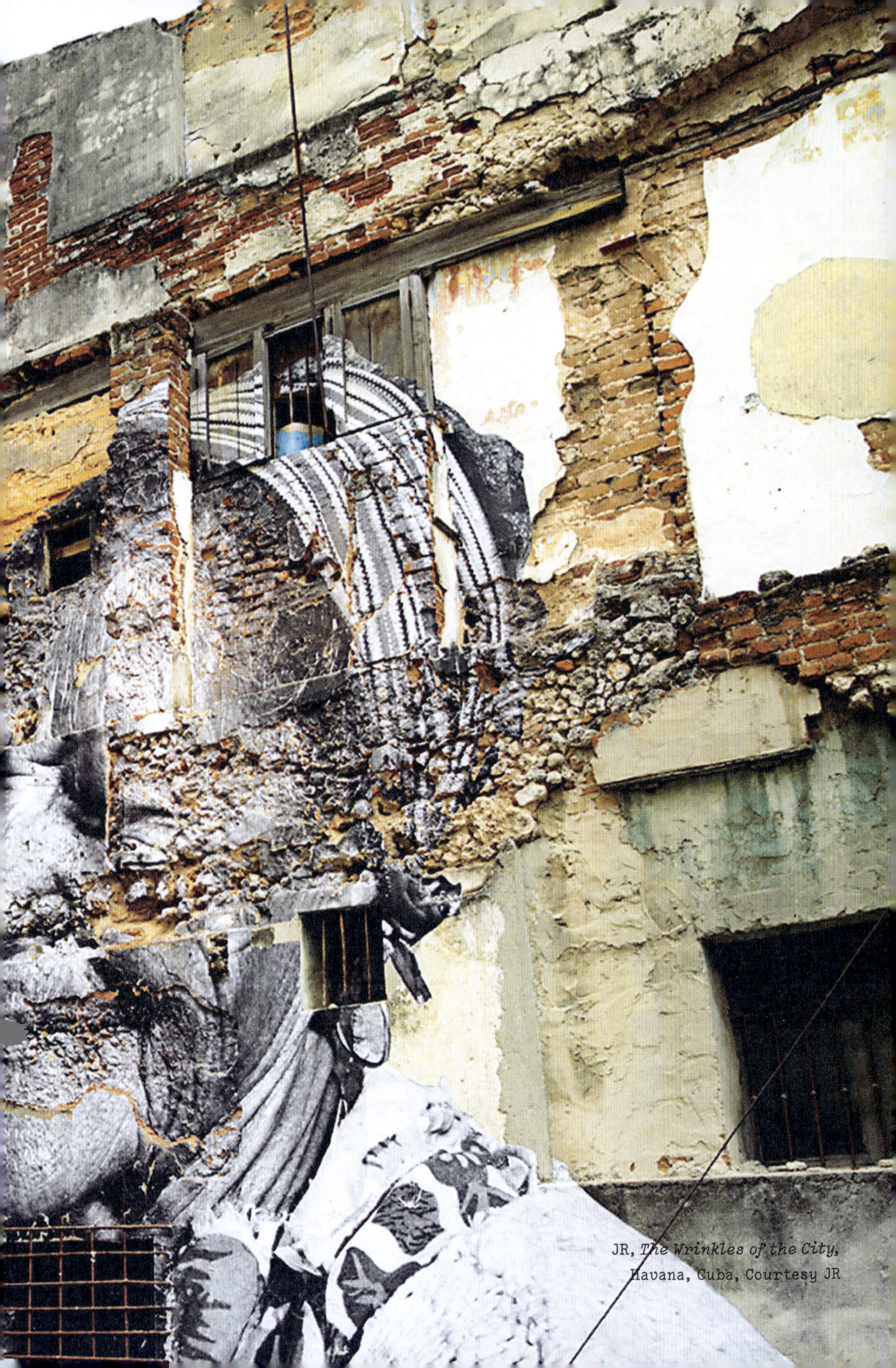

JR, *The Wrinkles of the City*, Havana, Cuba, Courtesy JR

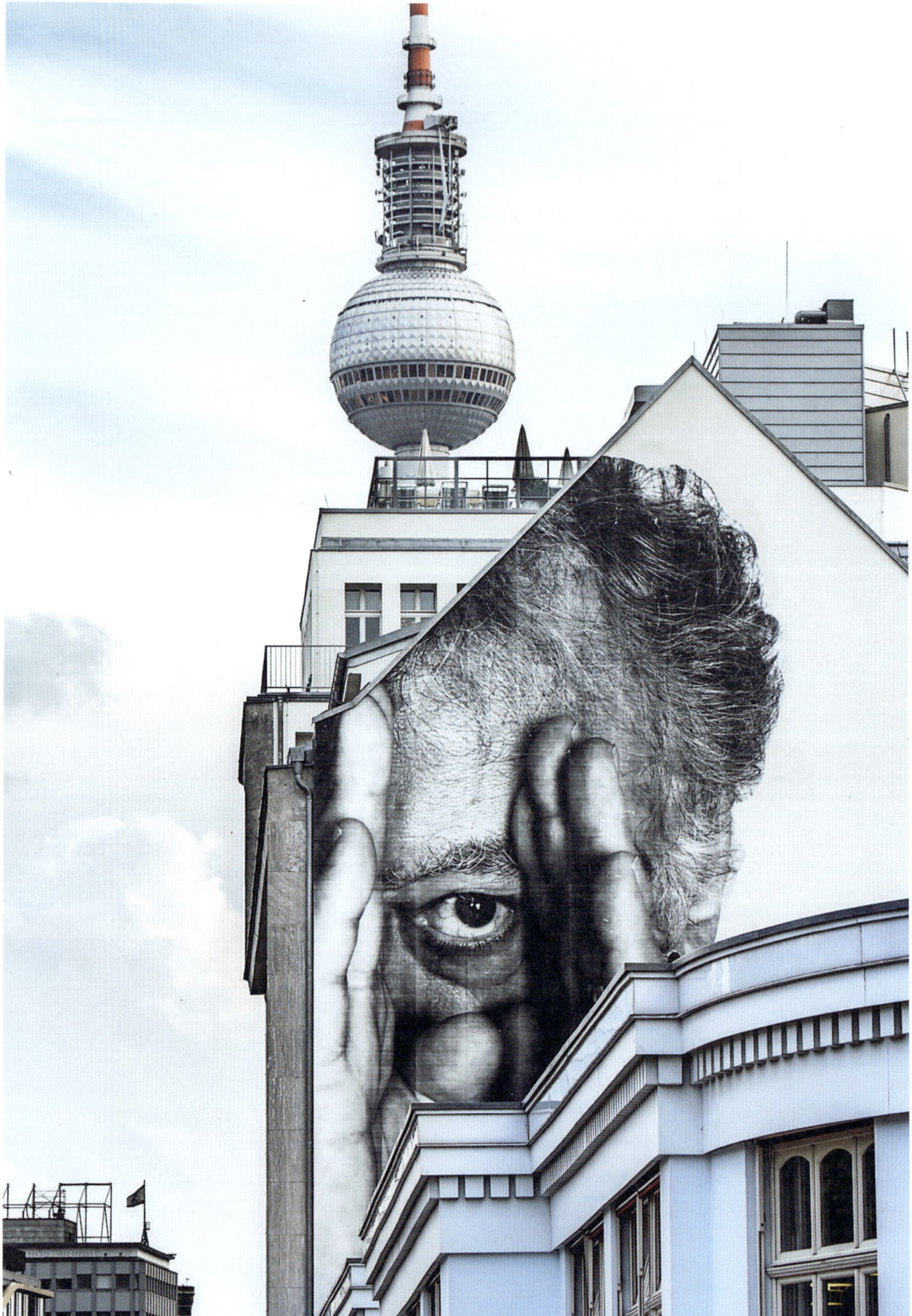

JR, *The Wrinkles of the City*, Berlin, 2013, Courtesy JR

The city is therefore, once more and in its urban and historical entirety, a subject of inspiration. The streets are like the wrinkles of the subjects whom he photographs and attaches to the walls of this megacity. "Memories fail. They have their traps and their paths, which vary as life flows along. But wrinkles rarely lie. Everything is there, burrowed in like a sculptor's chiselling or the engraving lines that depict a historic scene. The acid of life has attacked the models' faces. Life has often not granted them any favours, but they are there and pose with dignity. It has nothing to do with pride or ego. It is about moments of sharing in which the subject gives over and lays bare his life's body,"[7] JR says.

[7] Preface of the catalogue JR: *The Wrinkles of the City Shanghai.*

On 2 March 2011, JR won the TED Prize in Long Beach, California. As part of the occasion, he launched a participatory, comprehensive and highly pervasive art project with the goal of "changing the world." The project is called *Inside Out*. Inspired by the large-format collages that JR produces in the street, *Inside Out* gives each of us the opportunity to share our portrait and to convey a message that we care about. JR intends this activity to serve as a global platform that enables everyone to share their story and to transform a personal message into a public artwork. Each *Inside Out* group activity around the world is documented, archived and published on the Internet. The project has travelled through New York, Paris, Ecuador, Shanghai, Nepal, Mexico, Israel and Palestine, where it has inspired group activities on many topics such as hope, diversity, social violence and climate change. The pervasive has also become participatory; there were nearly 300,000 portraits in 112 countries in 2015. This large-scale project transforms strictly personal identities into a more global artistic work that invades all media and types of places. From the Panthéon to Times Square, JR's art is everywhere.

Turning the street into the world's biggest gallery

JR likes to call the street "the world's biggest gallery." It is not only the space where he places his works to be seen by all, but also a source of inspiration where he often meets those whose portraits he creates. The Portuguese artist VHILS has the same relationship with the street.

Alexandre Farto, aka VHILS, was born in 1987, the period when Portugal had just joined the European Union. He began by producing traditional graffiti in the streets of his neighbourhood at the end of the 1990s, but he soon turned to stencil. "I started to do graffiti when I was ten years old, but I only became serious about it when I was thirteen. In the beginning, it was just an activity between friends. It was better than staying cooped up at home." He then continued by working on trains, and he became active in the Portuguese graffiti scene.

In parallel with this activity, he became increasingly interested in his country's mural tradition. After the revolution of 1974, the streets came under assault and were covered with politically focused murals. It was a quite unique and popular pictorial movement. VHILS also became aware that his generation had completely forgotten this tradition, and that walls had subsequently become covered in advertising. And so he decided to work directly with these two materials: walls and advertising posters. These are not media for self-expression but rather the very material that this artist works with, transforms and uses.

For VHILS, the idea is to "dig through these layers of history. I never know what I'll find. I tear the billboards in the streets of Lisbon... There is a striking contrast between the utopian revolutionary frescoes and all the advertisements for consumer goods that are found everywhere now."

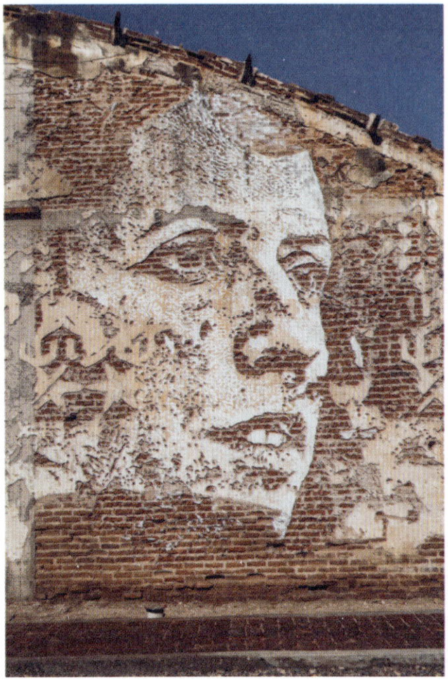

VHILS, *Hermosillo*, Mexico, 2019.
Photo © Jose Pando Lucas

He then developed a technique of his own that came about through experimenting with multiple formats, including walls, posters, doors and metal sheets. "My work is based on the search for materials in situ and converts vandalism into a form of art." He advocates destruction as an act of creation.

A precocious talent, VHILS was quickly spotted in the scene. In 2008, he was invited by BANKSY to participate in the Cans Festival in London, where his series *Scratching the Surface* was exhibited to and praised by a sizeable audience. He was only twenty-one years old at the time.

VHILS principally uses recycled materials that he often finds in situ—scraps of posters, for example. He then tears them, revealing the form and substance as he does so. He works on walls with a pneumatic drill, digging into the different strata in search of the essence and soul of the structure. He works on metal plates with acid to reveal an image within the rust. On paper, he uses ink and bleach in a curious mixture that brings out layers of meaning: faces mix with architectural, graphical or even plant elements. In 2010 and 2011 respectively, the museums of contemporary art in San Diego, California, and in Elvas, Portugal, exhibited his work.

He therefore seeks to explore and expose the ephemeral nature of things—the contrast that comes from the opposition between old layers and new ones, and between the "faded" and the glamorous. This approach is cast in the mould of the history of his country, where the old was engulfed under a process of rapid urbanization.

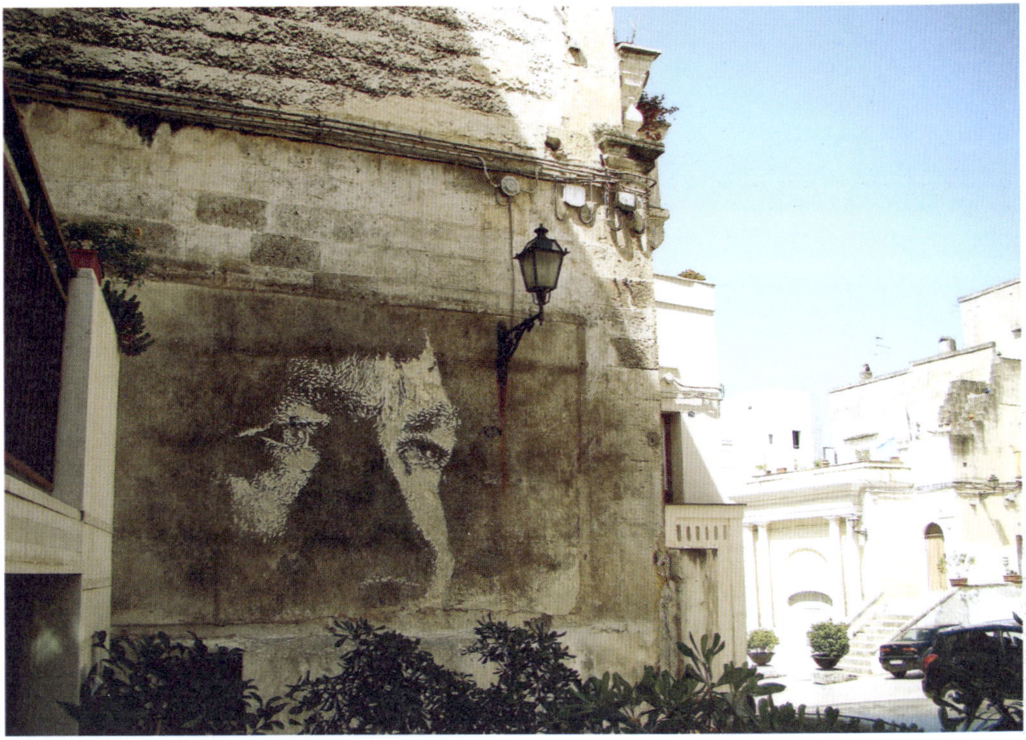

VHILS, Grottaglie, Italy, 2009. Photo © Vhils Studio

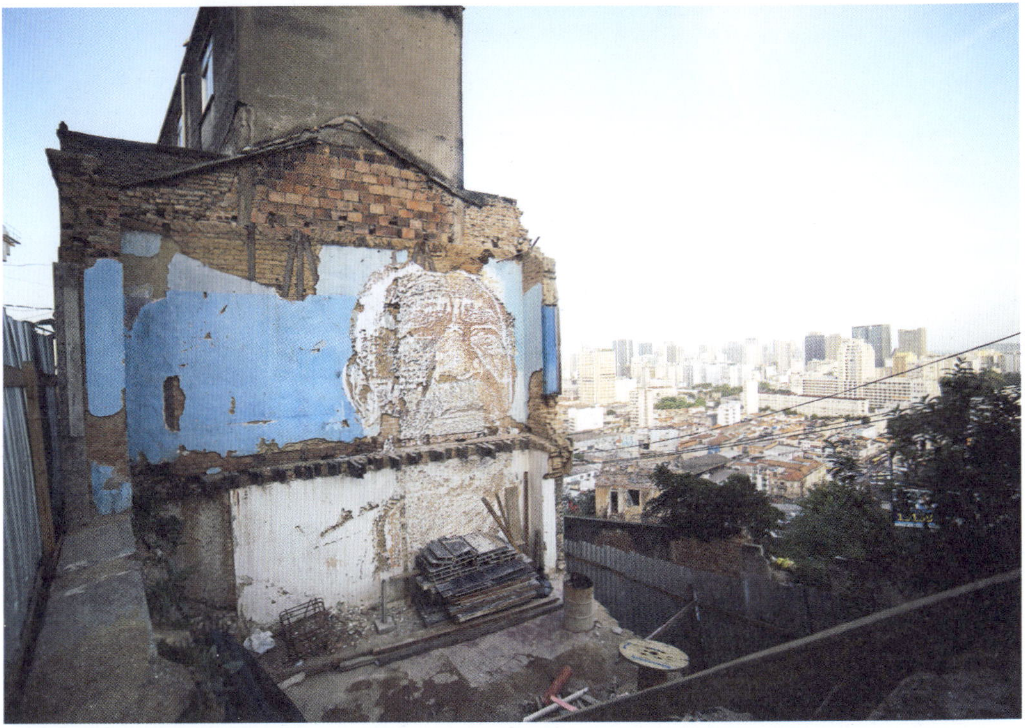

VHILS, Portrait of Edson da Silva Oliveira, wall sculpture,
Morro da Providencia, Rio de Janeiro, Brazil, October 2012. Photo © João Pedro Moreira

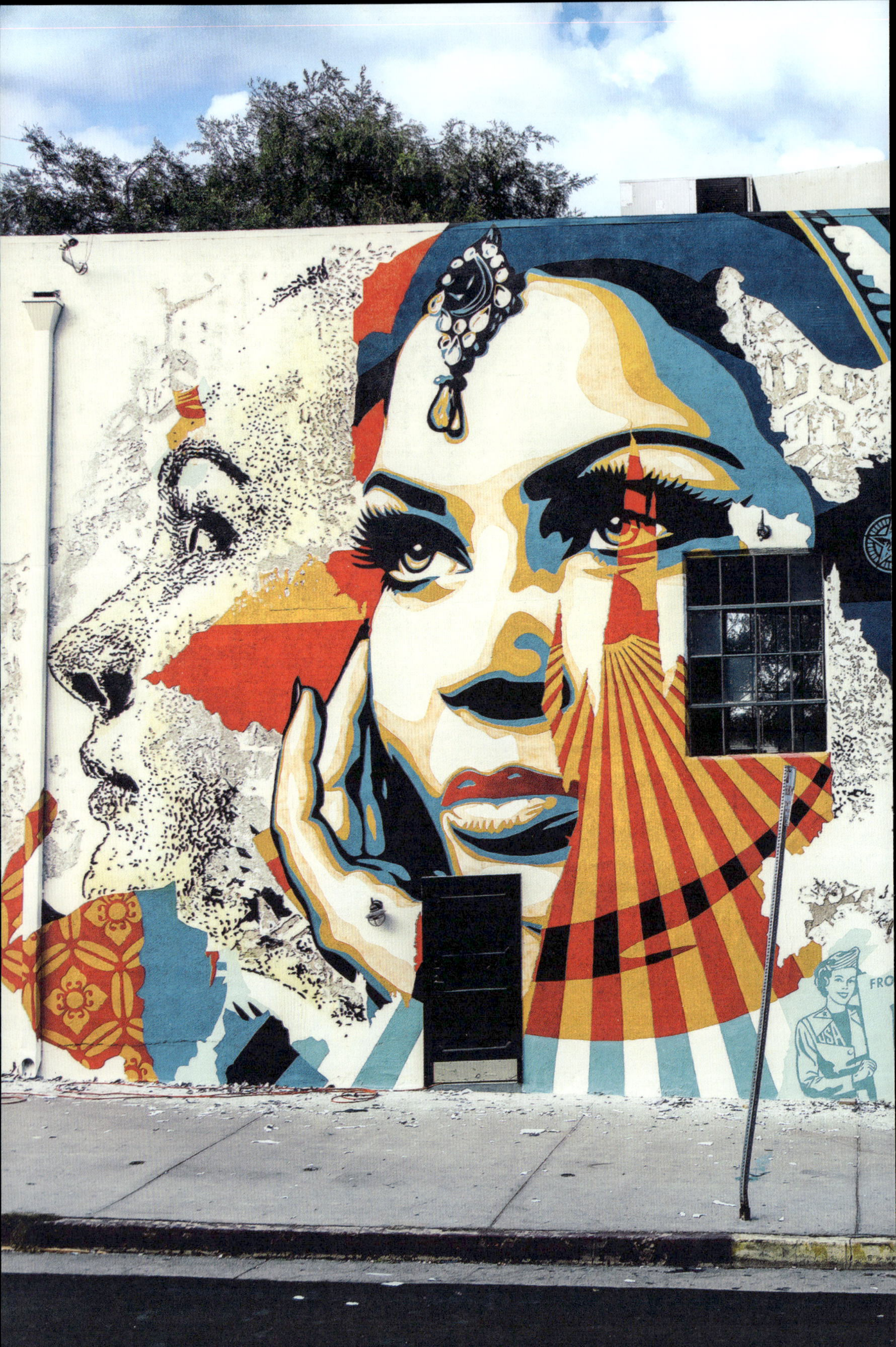

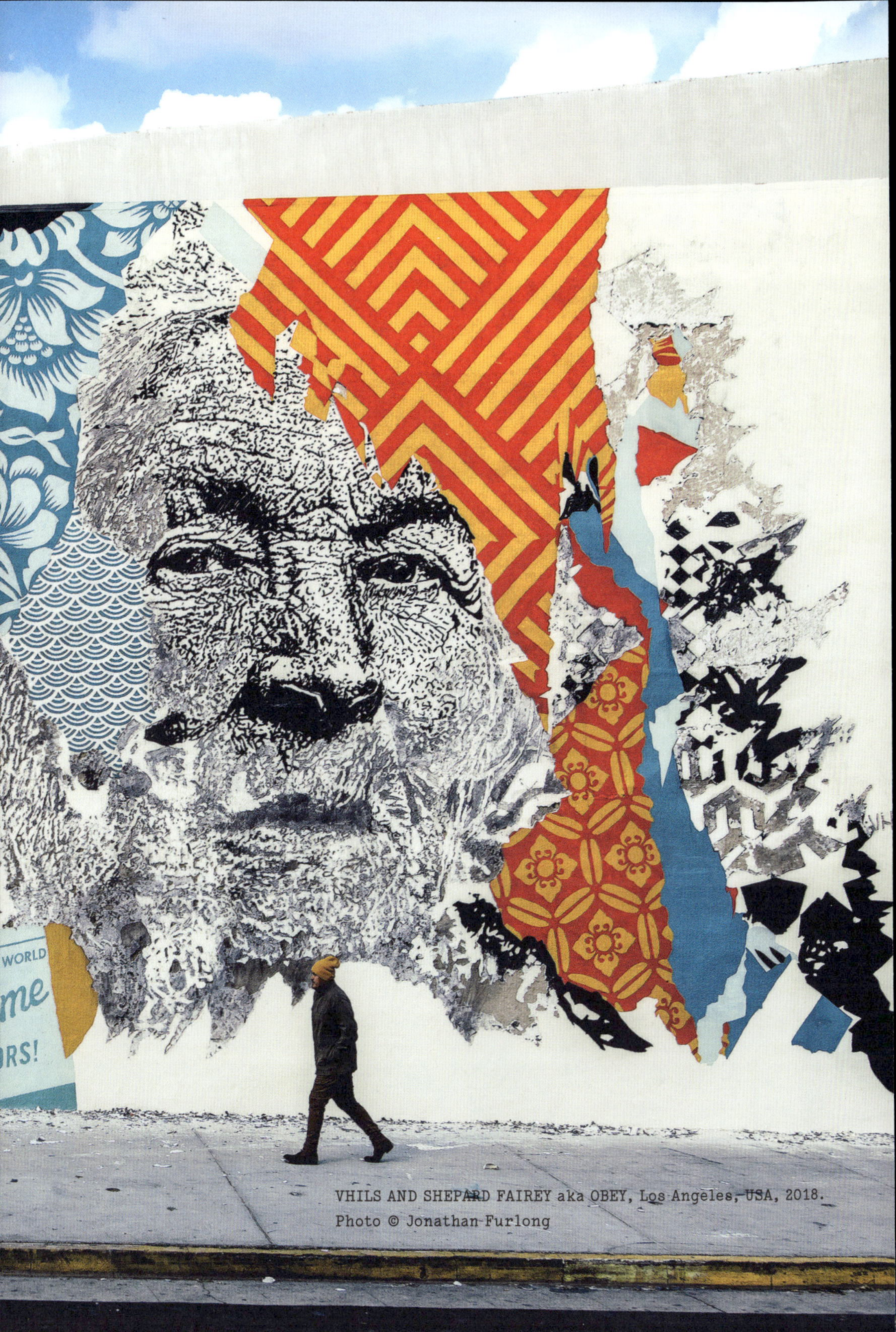

VHILS AND SHEPARD FAIREY aka OBEY, Los Angeles, USA, 2018.
Photo © Jonathan Furlong

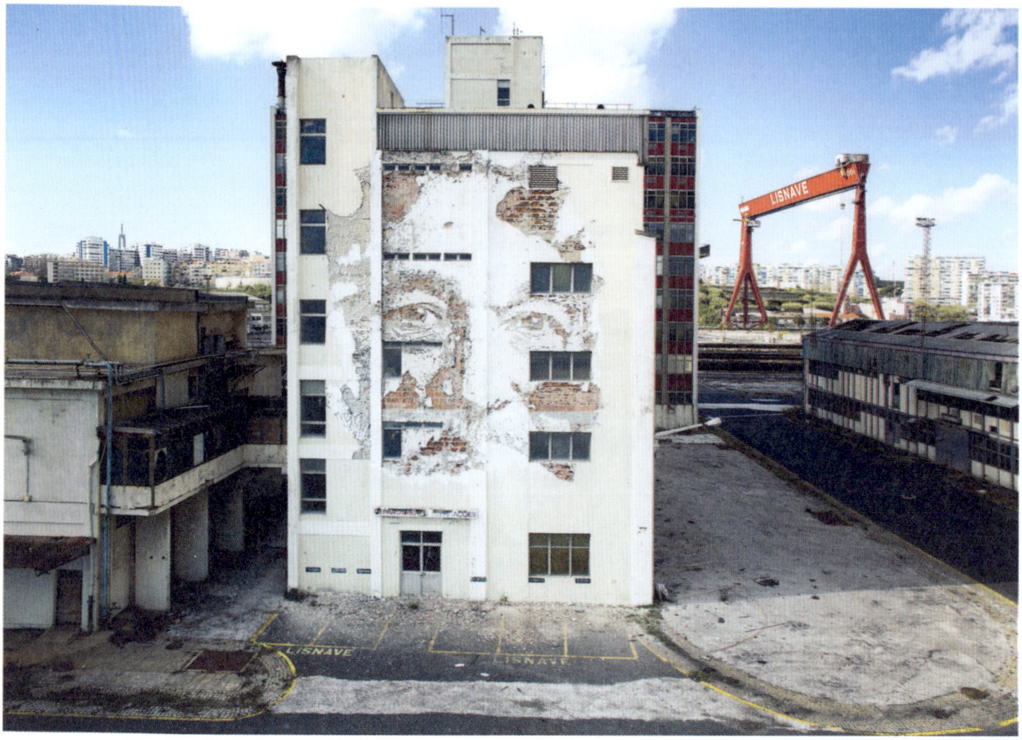

VHILS, Lisbon, 2014 © Alexander Silva

VHILS, *Scratching the Surface Project*, Lisbon, Portugal, 2014. Photo © Alexander Silva

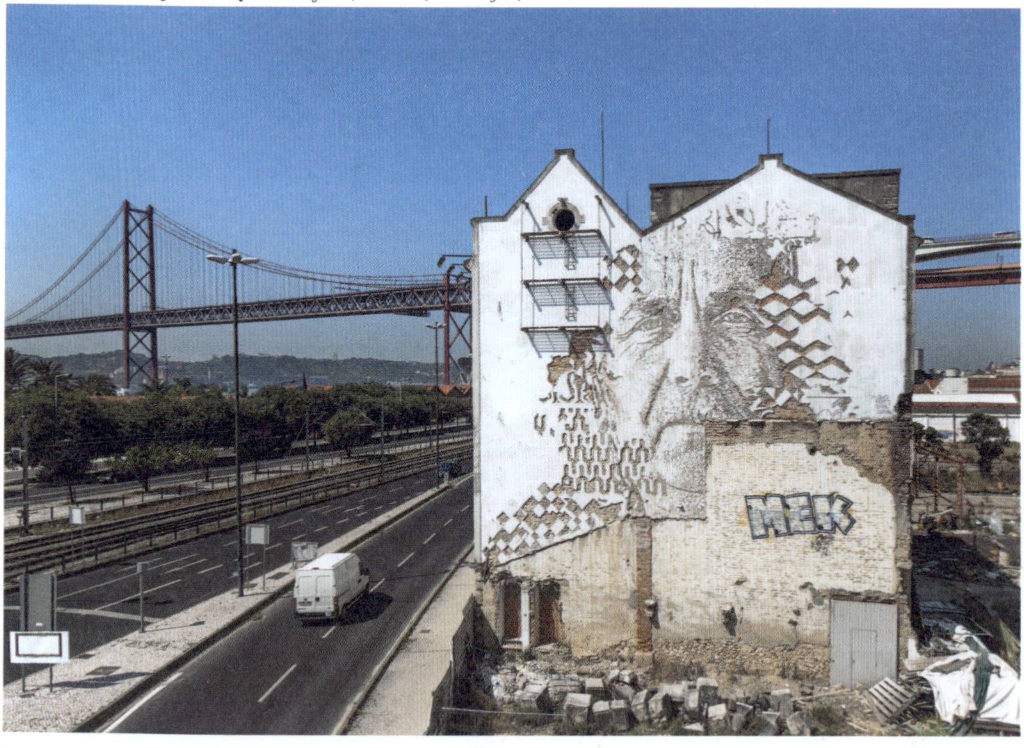

VHILS's works are both complex and poetic, and they act as visual metaphors. Although he reflects on the challenges of our society, he does so without claiming to have solutions to all its problems. In fact, his art simply aims to give economic, social and political systems a resonance in materials such as walls, wood and metal and in processes such as "scratching the surface" and removing layers of paint and digging into the material. He creates frictions between different areas and thus brings individuals face to face with their realities and their environment. This is an active critical process that is shaped by the environment that it is reflecting upon. As an example, in 2011 at the *Fame Festival* in Grottaglie, Apulia, through his work he shed light on the issues facing a town in the far South of Italy. Traditionally, Apulia has been a region that has suffered from the very pronounced socioeconomic dualism between the North and the South of the country. Thus, while in some regions like Emilia-Romagna almost full employment prevails, there is an unemployment rate of 16% in Apulia's working population. Joining the world of work late is one of the main causes of this southern scourge. Despite a recent willingness to develop the region from an economic point of view, the standard of living in the South contrasts starkly with that of the North.

VHILS remains faithful to his roots: "Everything is the result of my earliest work involving pure graffiti, which I still appreciate." His rise to the top, the crowning achievement of which came in 2014 with an impressive personal exhibition at the museum of the EDP Foundation in Lisbon, owes much to his personal and prolific style. He has a clear preference for portraits and focuses on closely framed faces. "I remember reaching a point where I started thinking more and more about what I was doing. I started to rationalize things, attracted by the opportunity to reach a wider audience, to be able to communicate with more and more people. So I focus on trying to push the limits of communication with others. I speak to anonymous individuals with portraits of people who are like them. Why can't each of us be an icon?"

Secret exploration and Urbex

In contrast to those who express themselves loudly and clearly, a number of street artists prefer to play the secrecy card, choosing to speak in urban locations that are often inaccessible to people. This new trend has a name: Urbex (urban exploration).

It involves exploring built structures, ruins that have preferably been abandoned and elements that are rarely in the foreground in the everyday environment. For its practitioners —who are akin to urban speleologists— the idea is to infiltrate places to which access has often been banned and possibly to leave a mark in them that is known only (or almost) to the person who made it. In this respect, these artists have close links to the tradition of the first graffiti writers who descended into subway tunnels. This urban exploration of abandoned structures, ruined warehouses and buildings that are being overhauled explores a new relationship with creativity and exhibition. The artists' inspiration is also linked to the context, the soul of the place and its walls.

More broadly, many photographers who are involved in urbex speak of the feelings they have in response to the disintegration of these unoccupied spaces. Creation emerges from destruction, and they admire the "beautiful decay" that is so dear to many of the movement's artists. Similarly, inspired by spaces like underground passageways, certain artists both from within and from outside of street art explore every nook and cranny of such places.

As is the case in street art, urbex aficionados have only the documentation that they produce themselves as a memory of their visits. The Mausolée project of 2010 can still be seen today through an online time lapse video.[8] When LEK and SOWAT discovered an abandoned supermarket in the North of Paris, they had the idea of surrounding it in the greatest secrecy and turning it into an unauthorized artistic residence. For a year, nearly forty artists took turns painting frescoes in this 40,000 m² space. Together they built a mausoleum—a shrine dedicated to their underground urban culture.[9]

[8] A video that presents in a short time frame a series of photographs taken at different times or at regular time intervals.

[9] The project gave rise to a video on YouTube entitled Mausolée, and also to a book: *Mausolée, Résidence artistique sauvage*, Sowat and Lek, éd. Alternatives, 2012.

[10] *Les Bains, Résidence d'Artistes*, photos by Stéphane Bisseuil and Jérôme Cotton, éd. DRAGO, 2012.

Since then, many projects have emerged that raise the question of the ephemeral once more. Works made through these projects are in most cases doomed to swift destruction.

For example, in 2012, the Les Bains and Tour 13 projects aimed to take over two buildings, one of which was earmarked for renovation and the other of which was due to be totally demolished. These temporary exhibitions also focused debate on the idea of work in progress and the notion that the making of a creation mattered as much as the final result. For example, the Les Bains artist residence brought together fifty artists (from Jacques Villeglé to VHILS and legends like FUTURA and SPACE INVADER, as well as figures from the Parisian graffiti scene such as ASH, SKKI, JAY and PSY) in a mythical, nonaccessible and ephemeral place, the only trace of which is a book.[10] Street art survives in publications, which can be the only evidence of the masterpieces that have been produced.

A writing of the illegible

As we have seen, the history of street art has become considerably richer as time has gone by. The artists who are active today claim a part of this collective culture, or at least common beginnings within it that opened the doors of artistic expression for them.

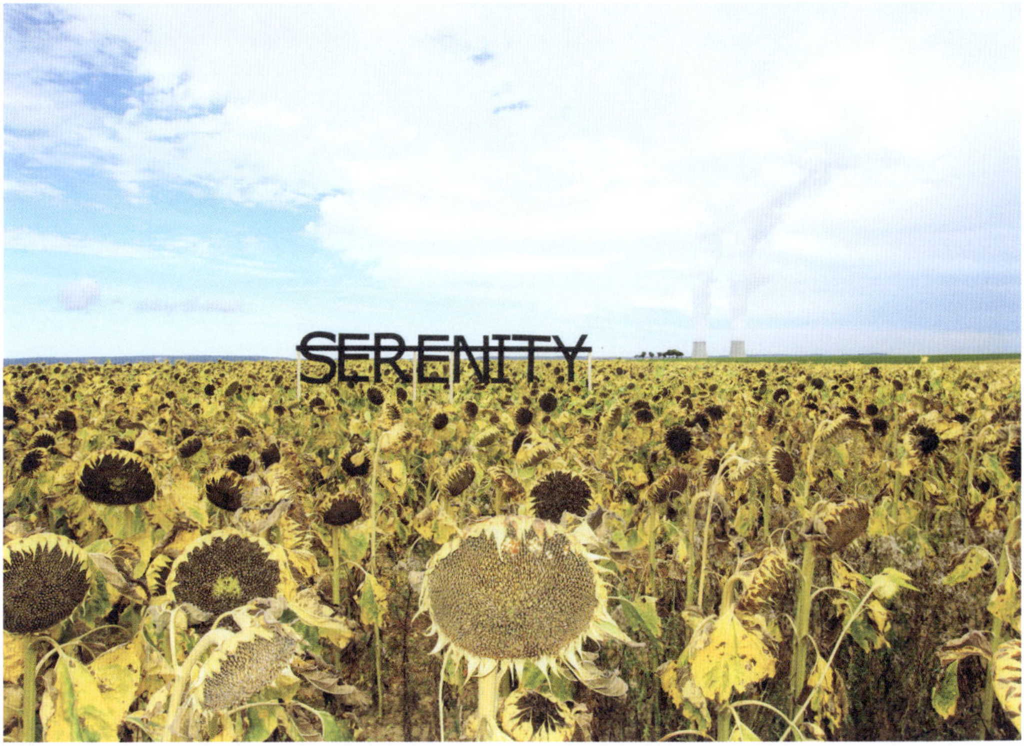

RERO, Untitled (SERENITY), Nogent sur Seine, France, 2013 © A.R.R.

Within the movement's many branches, the street appears to be one of the common denominators. It is treated as a space of visibility that allows artists to be heard, seen and recognized. Yet it should be noted that two schools have come into being as street art has evolved: illegibility and the hypervisibility.

Artists who focus on the illegible are committed to writing from their first steps into the scene, and yet they do all they can to make that writing difficult to decipher. This deliberate desire can be explained first of all by the intention of many artists to develop a personal and original style that is often complex, and second of all by a decidedly cryptic approach. Indeed, they assert illegibility as a system and as a set of values that must be penetrated and therefore deciphered. Paradoxically here, "image making" goes through a complete deconstruction of the image itself.

Next double page spread: RERO, Untitled (DECADENCE...), Lana paper, France, 2012 © A.R.R.

In his artistic practice, the Frenchman RERO, who was born in 1983, stands out by playing on the boundary between the legible and the illegible. He paints messages in imposing letters that he then strikes out. Their meaning initially seems obvious, but in fact it raises more questions than it answers. In a more general sense, enriched by street art culture, RERO questions the boundary between inside/outside and the environment. Other artists play with optical effects.

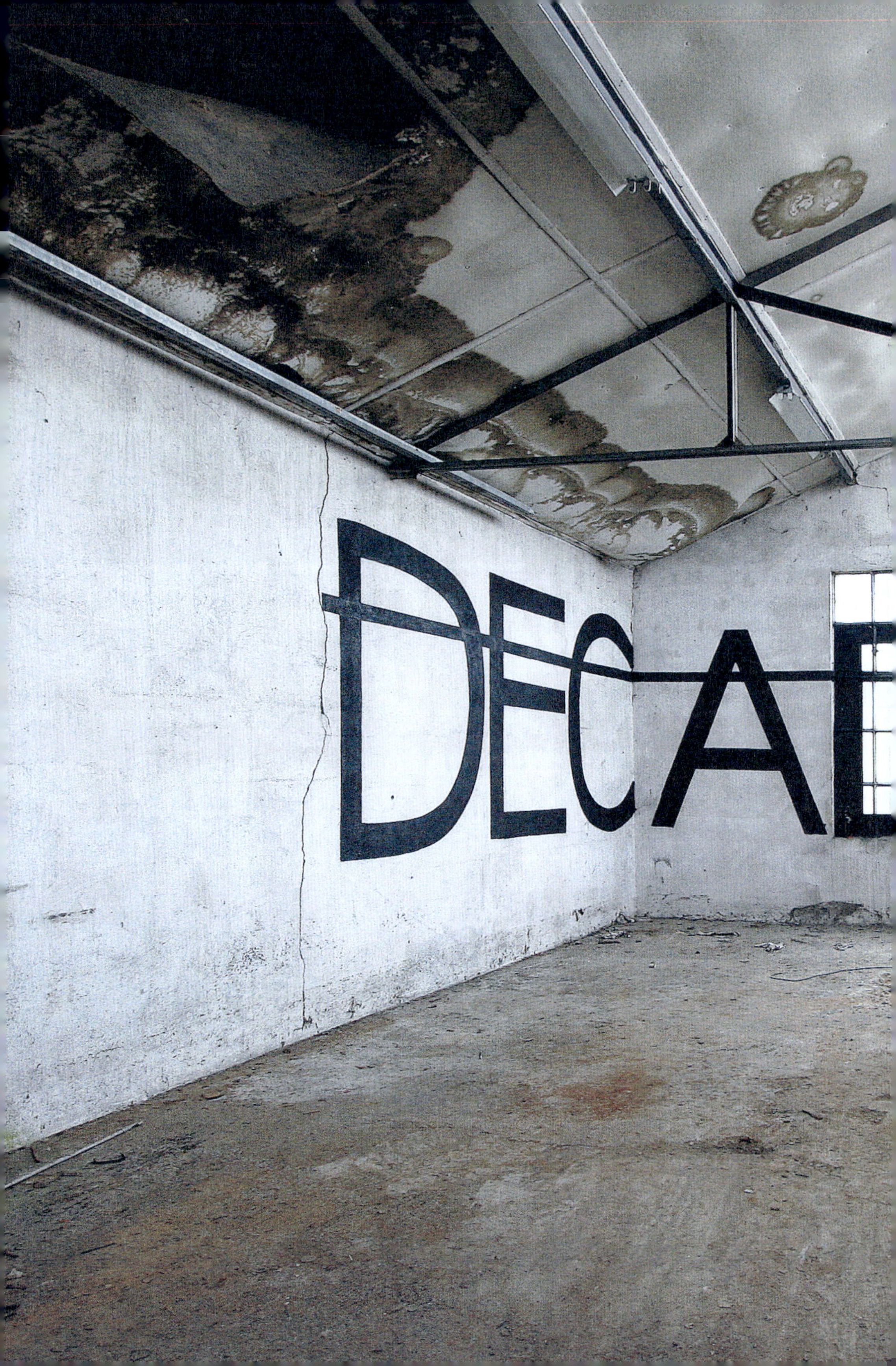
DECA

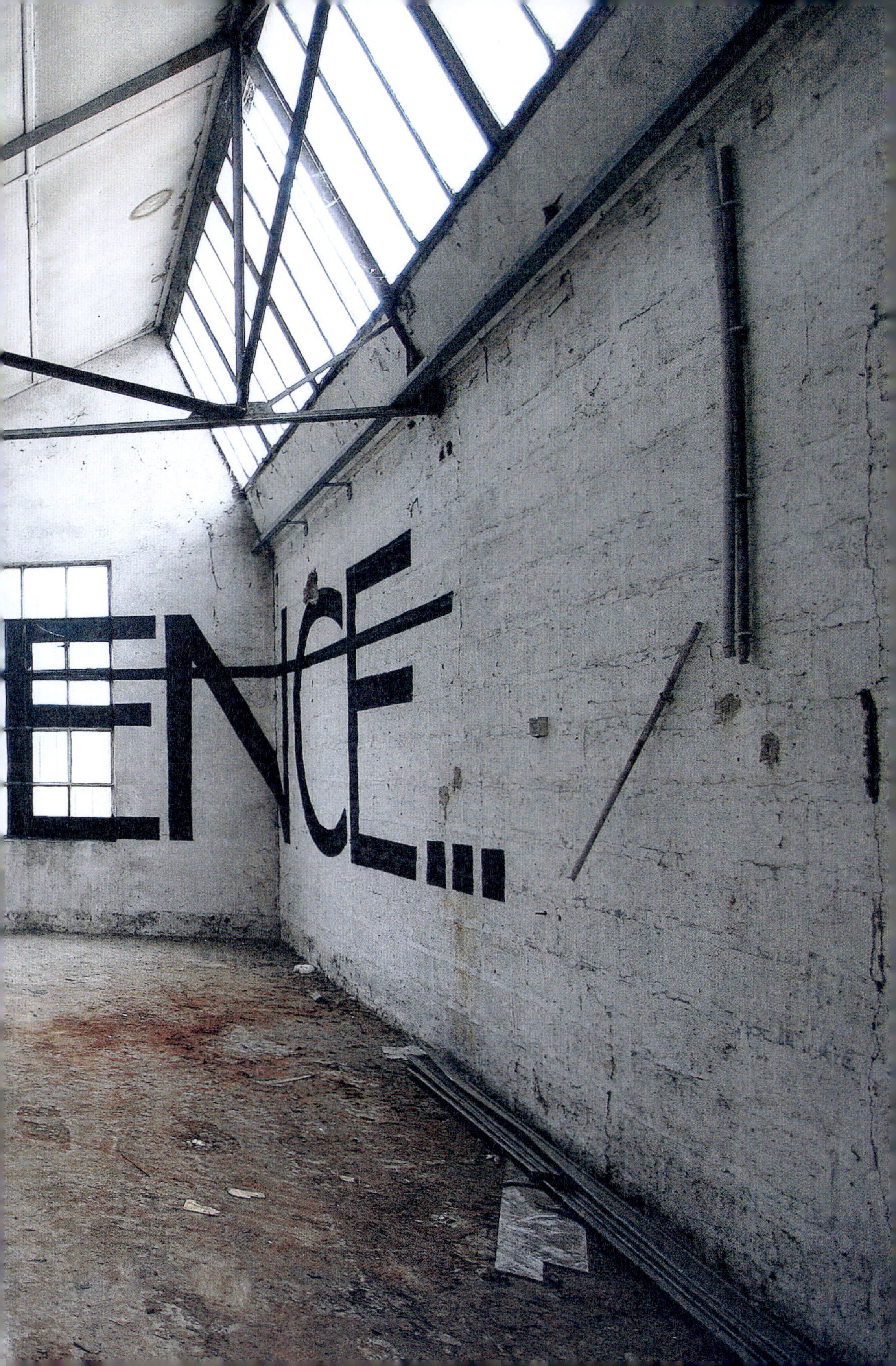
ENCE...

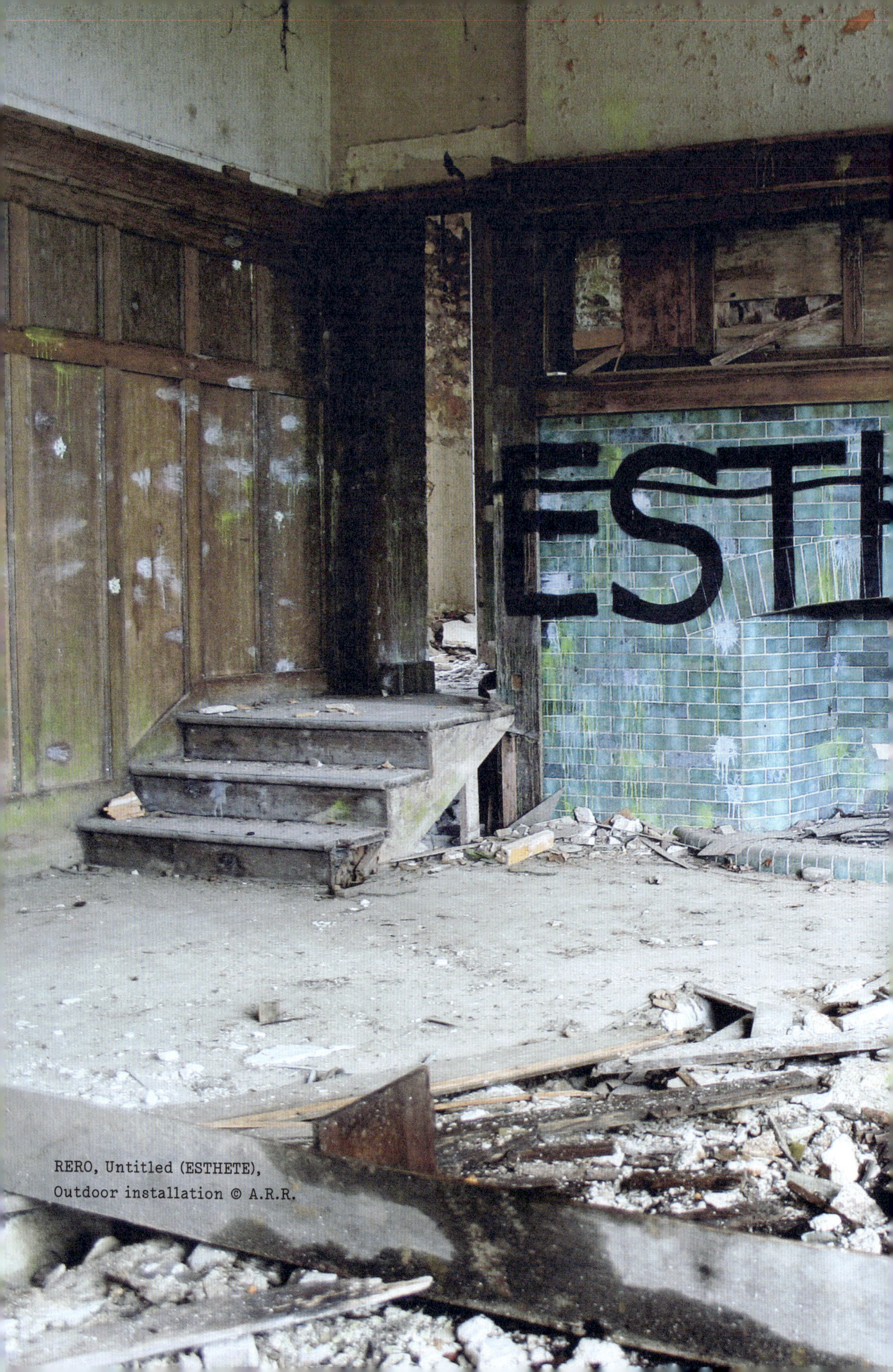

RERO, Untitled (ESTHETE),
Outdoor installation © A.R.R.

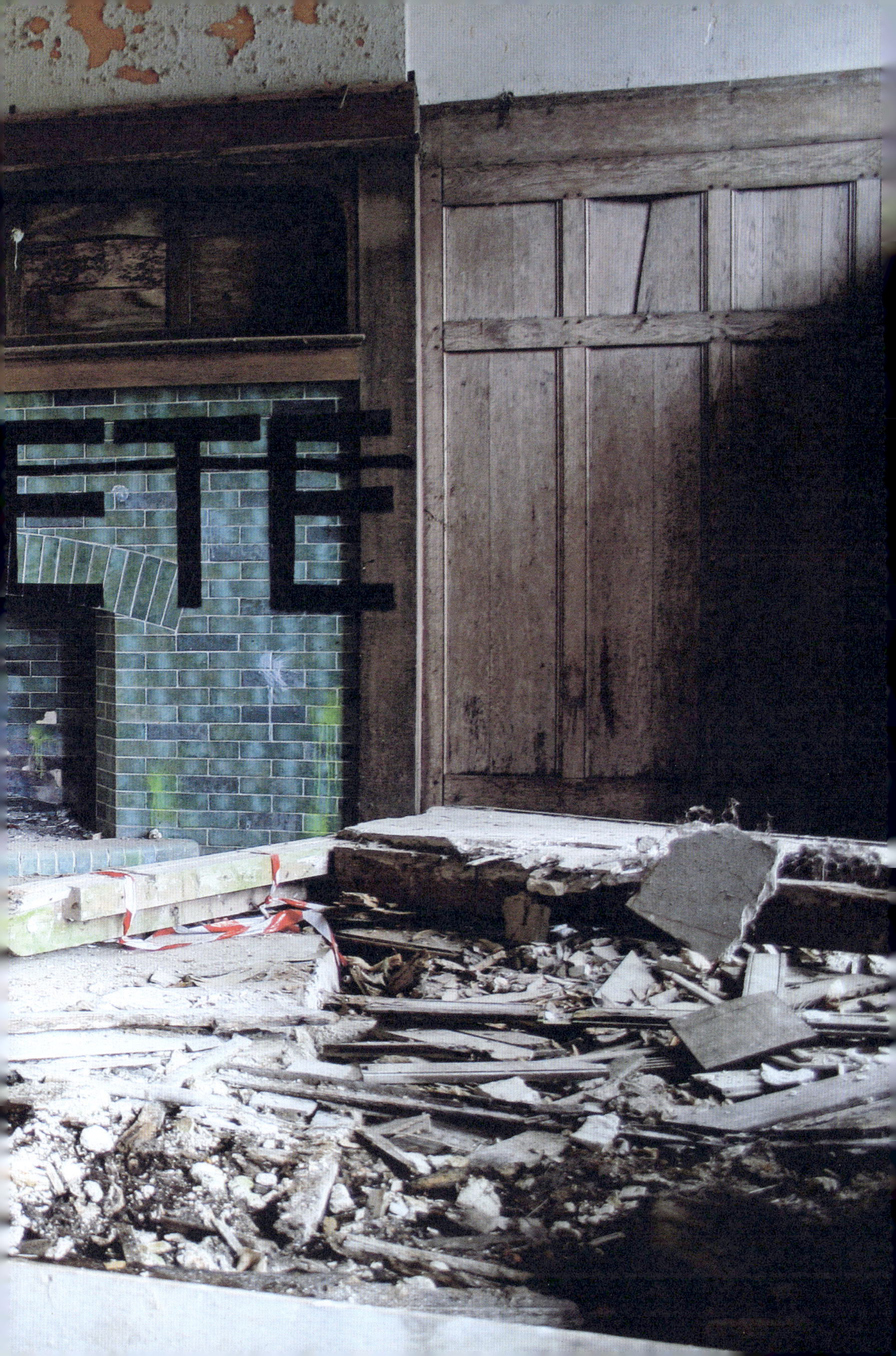

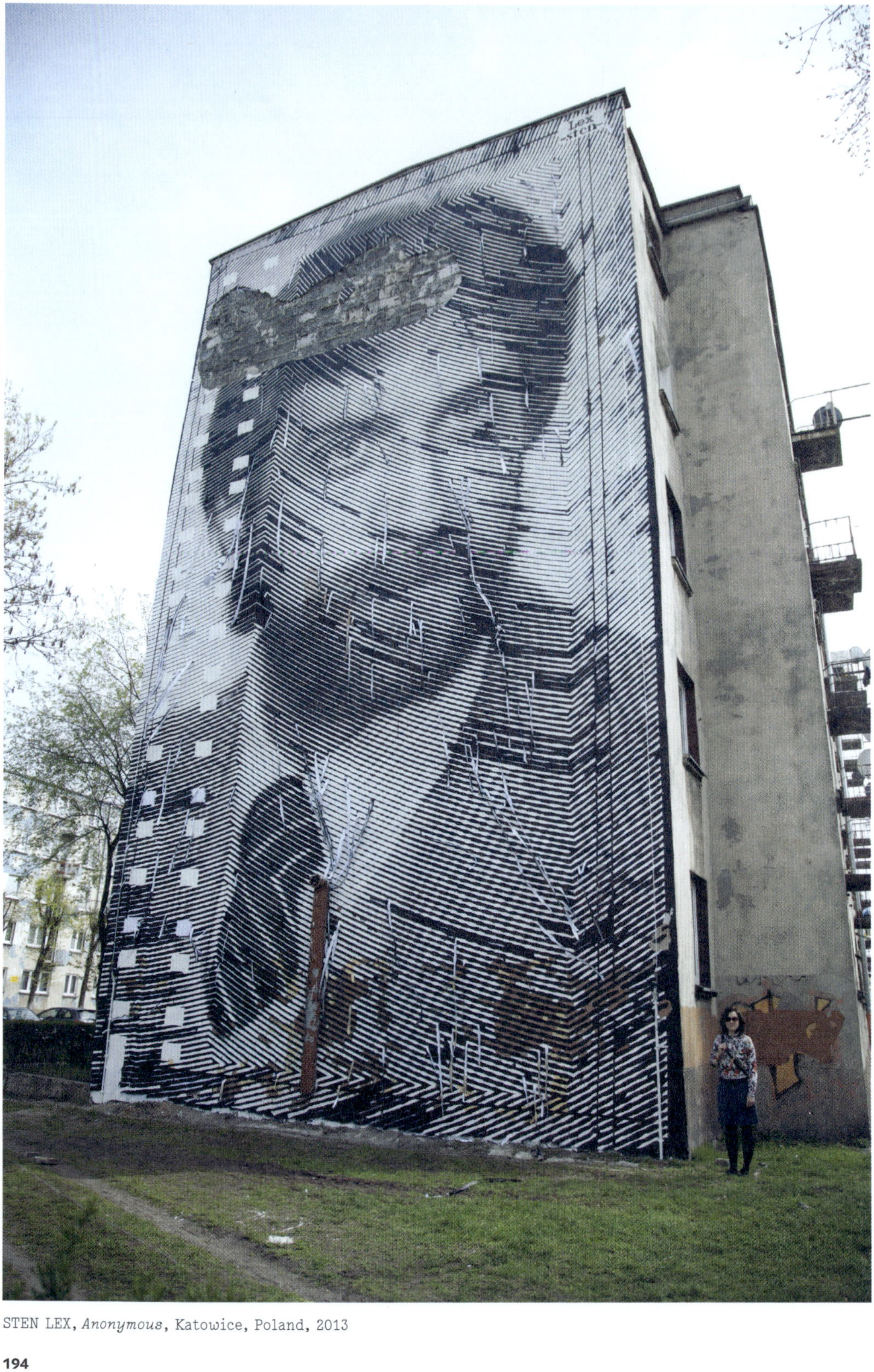

STEN LEX, *Anonymous*, Katowice, Poland, 2013

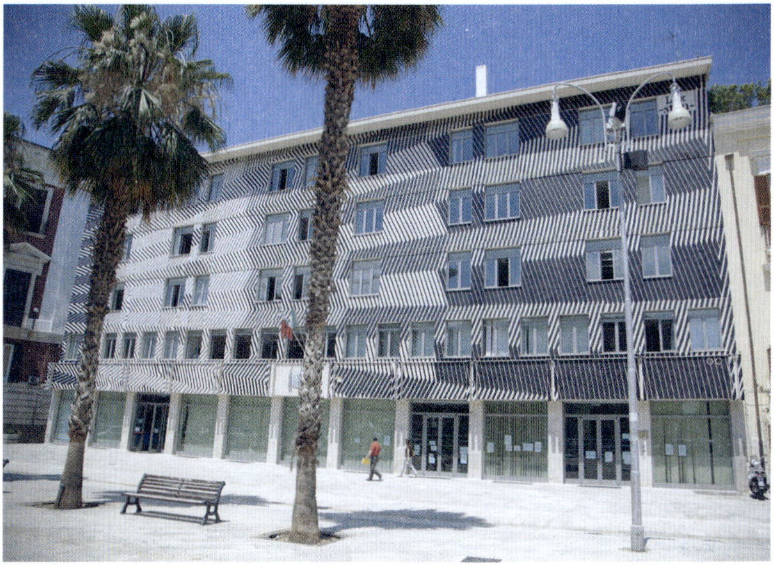

STEN LEX, *Raggio*, Bari, Italy, 2013

The Italian pairing of **STEN LEX** stand out through their mixture of street art, stencilling, photography and optical art. Through patient and painstaking work, the duo create monumental cut-outs. They superimpose two stencils that they then cut out directly on the wall, creating an optical effect where the outline is more visible than the subject of the work. Only by stepping back does the painted motif appear. Technically, their template is integrated into the work itself and cut into shreds. The remnants stay glued to the wall, and unlike in classic stencilling, the initial design cannot be reproduced. It is a poetic experiment that rejects the reproducible nature of the stencil. This atypical use of the technique is actually a reflection on street art itself. STEN LEX question the reproducibility of the signature or of the stencil and preach unique in situ work instead. Rather than endlessly reproducing their signature or their "images," they make their technique their hallmark and the thing that makes them identifiable to everyone. This interplay between visible and illegible has become the pair's signature and teaches us once more to seek out the meaning hidden behind the appearance.

Entirely in line with this exploration of the illegible, the Frenchman TANC, who was born in 1979, indulges in automatic writing (using spray paint), while L'ATLAS, who was born in 1978, is particularly interested in the Kufic style of Arabic calligraphy. He transposes its geometric forms and codes to the Latin alphabet, allowing him to create his own typography. He has developed a pictorial world where any letter is regarded as a form, and any form as a letter. Often compared to Arte Povera, the Italian protest movement of the late 1960s, he attaches great importance to his process, and more specifically to the creative act. His work on logos and calligraphy has led him to other forms of street creativity.

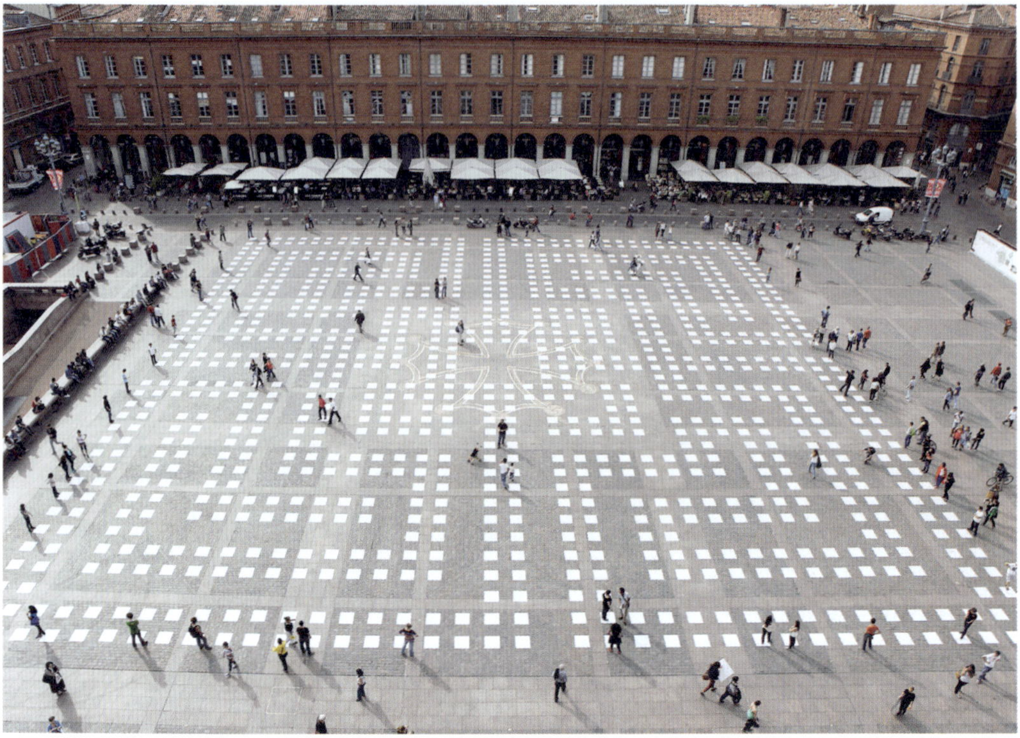

L'ATLAS, *Monade*, installation at Place du Capitole, 2012 © A.R.R.

L'ATLAS, installation on the square by the Pompidou Centre, 2009 © A.R.R.

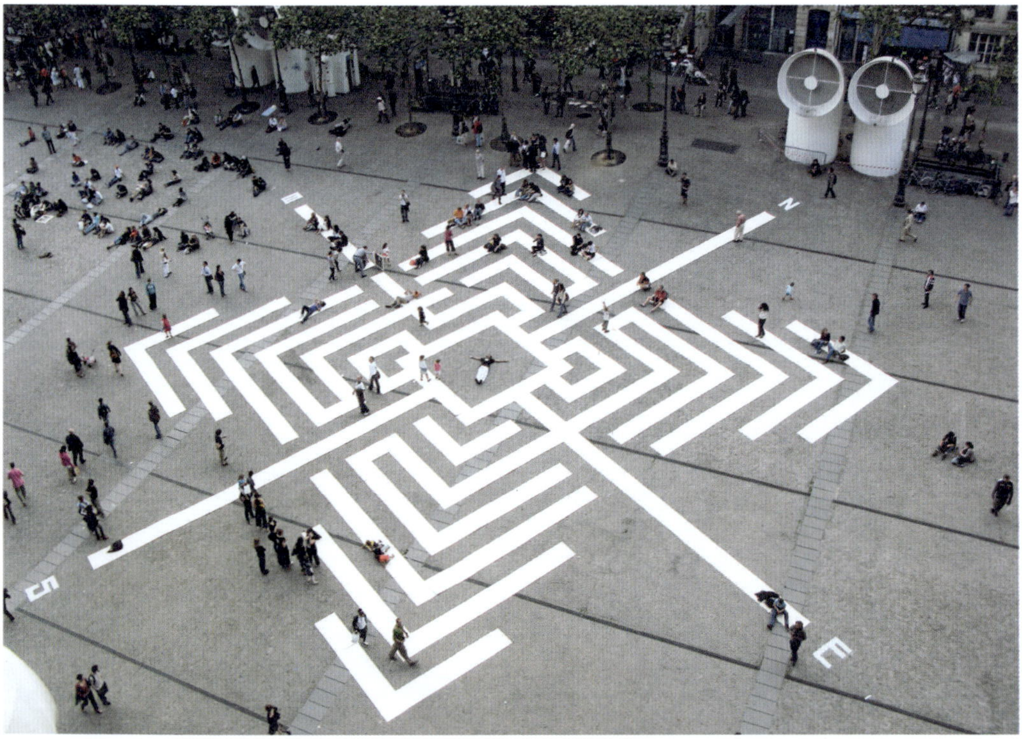

Alongside ZEVS, he has become a figure of the postgraffiti current, and he has created a series of outdoor projects such as outlines of urban compasses—including one in front of the Pompidou Centre—that are sometimes made using gaffer tape, one of his tools of choice. Although it appears cryptic in many people's eyes, L'ATLAS's work is about conciliation between the city and man and between outside and inside.

While the essence of graffiti is to be found in repeated writing, a connection between graffiti and Middle Eastern calligraphy emerged relatively late on in the history of street art. Although some artists like SHOE (from his real name, Niels Shoe Meulman) have been exploring this graphical relationship for a long time, the term "calligraffiti" only appeared in 2007. SHOE recalls having originally started exploring traditional calligraphy to stand out from conventional graffiti: "Ancient painted Japanese characters, Arabic writing, illuminated medieval books: all this is part of calligraphy. The somewhat new art of graffiti and its rigid rules require us to look a little more back into the history of writing."

SHOE was born in 1967 and began doing graffiti in the Netherlands, where he quickly gained great recognition. In the 1980s, he met some of the legendary artists, including DONDI, RAMMELLZEE and KEITH HARING, and he gained an initiation into Paris's street art from BANDO and MODE 2. A star of the early days of European graffiti, he experienced the turn of the 1990s as a need for renewal. He hit upon calligraffiti in 2007, which he describes as a mixture of abstract expressionism with a calligraphic origin.

The events of the Arab Spring in 2010 resulted in an increased appetite for creativity and freedom of expression in public places. Giving a more current echo to writing has opened up new possibilities for expression. There has therefore been a renewal in the way in which calligraphy is understood. The artist and publisher DON KARL notes that "until recently, Arabic calligraphy was considered a dead art. During the Arab Spring, there was an explosion of graffiti in all countries that experienced the rumblings of revolution."[11] Many artists have emerged from this context, such as EL SEED.

[11] In *Le Graffiti arabe* by Pascal Zoghbi and Don Karl, 2012.

As DON KARL notes, "More and more young people have grasped this art that was born in the seventh century and initially reserved for the sacred scriptures of the Quran, in which writing is a source of beauty, and in which the letters can be appreciated without the need to understand the meaning of the words. The artist EL SEED has said that he refuses to translate his works."

Born in France to Tunisian parents, EL SEED travels the world to produce his calligraffiti. He explains that his wish is to "open dialogue between two worlds through the meeting between calligraphy, traditional Arabic art and more modern and Western graffiti. It is an invitation for tolerance and exchange." EL SEED uses Arabic calligraphy to express his exploration of his French-Tunisian identity. He paints entire

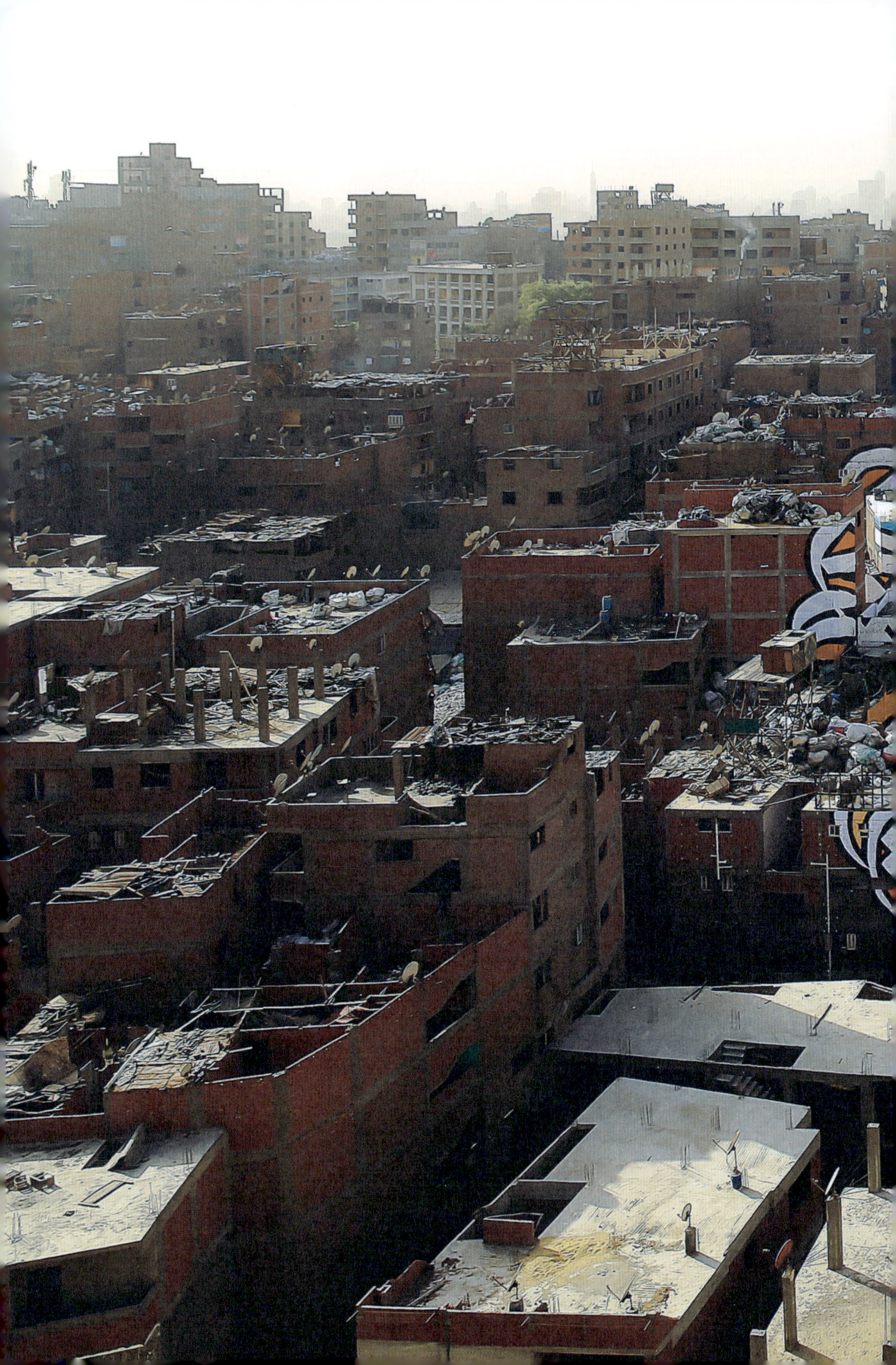

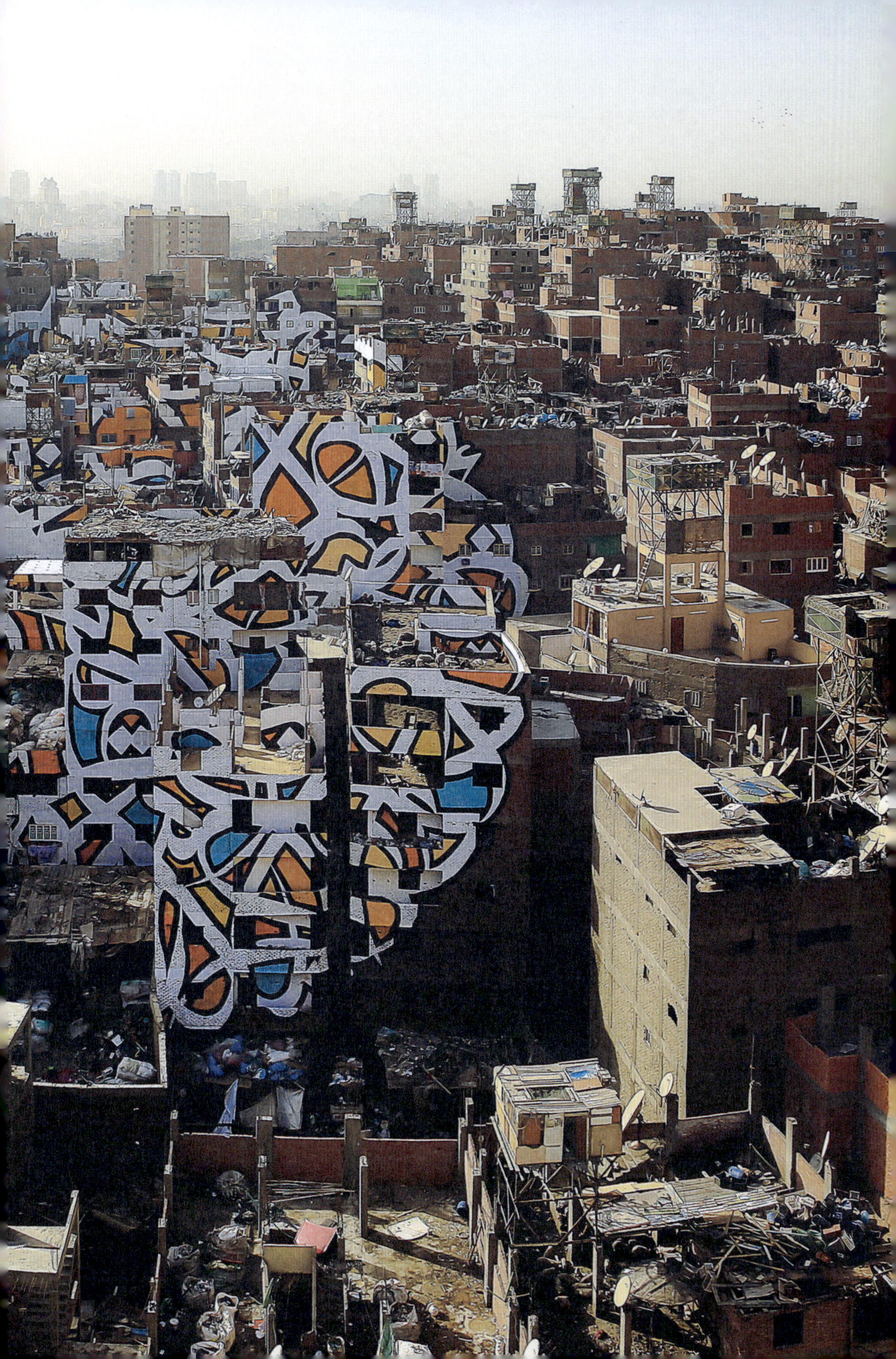

verses on the façades of buildings. His monumental and quasi-abstract works are a whirlwind of calligraffiti. Through his messages on the walls of cities, he creates bridges between the East and the West.

Like L'ATLAS and EL SEED, the French-Lebanese artist TAREK BENAOUM also explores the calligraphy aesthetic. At the same time as writing long sentences in the Roman alphabet, often in a spiral arrangement, he also draws on the peculiarities of Kufic script, which is characterized by its angularity.

The vitality of street art, especially since 2010, is also a product of the abstract explorations of some of its new figures. The San Francisco-base-dAmerican street artist POESIA combines such approaches in the term "graffuturism," which has now gained acceptance from those who practise it. After more than twenty years of practising graffiti, POESIA explains that it is a term that is "both poetic and lacking a dictionary definition, suggesting something inexplicable." Yet beyond currents, schools and (often reductive) labels, the term encompasses a reality, an aesthetic and a "common thread that brings us as graffiti artists and painters together."
Formally recognized since 2010, graffuturism brings together artists from around the world. Their background is in graffiti, but they have moved away from its traditional practice. This trend reflects changes in practices, with simple lettering and the old characters finding other, often more abstract forms. In its own time, the work of the visionary FUTURA had already ushered in this practice of deconstructed abstraction.

Since then, those who have swelled the ranks of this current have often come from art, graphic design or architecture schools. They are visual artists who have developed a body of work that ranges from geometric abstraction to a deconstructed figuration. Frequently, these types of works, which are carried out in the street and also in the studio, question visual resonances, are based on vanishing point lines, or attempt, in the same way as the Italian Futurists, to depict as fully as possible the movement and speed inherent in our society. These artists blend many influences and have spanned the gaps between official and popular art, legitimizing increasingly urban practices in a contemporary artistic form.

The hypervisible and its context

In contrast to this illegible writing, some artists promote the logic of hypervisibility. Here, figuration often bears a message, engagement or a life philosophy. SHEPARD FAIREY attempts to convey political messages, or at least to awaken consciences. VHILS invites us through his faces etched into walls in cities across the world to think about the shallowness of our society and focus on what lies below the surface.

Previous double page spread: EL SEED, *Perception*, Cairo, Egypt, 2016

Since 2010, hypervisibility has taken on a figurative form. The urban artists who engage in it seek to describe the world that surrounds them and to educate passers-by on the subjects that matter to them. They assert an engagement anchored in the present. Their works are inspired by the ups and downs of recent history.

For example, SWOON (whose real name is Caledonia Curry), an artist who was born in 1978 in Connecticut and who moved to New York at the age of 19, began her career by producing collages in the streets of her adopted city. After graduating from the Pratt Institute in 2002, she mastered printmaking techniques. However, refusing to conform to the classical art-student curriculum, she quickly moved into the urban space. New York became her playground, and in this incredible city she was finally able to free herself from art's established circles. SWOON's work is a reflection of the city. She found inspiration in traditional graffiti and in other artists who have used the city as creative inspiration, such as Gordon Matta-Clark and Jean-Michel Basquiat. Her work is based on the complex relationship that she has built with an urban environment perceived as an entity. "I had to be in New York because it is the largest, the strongest, the most intense city that we have." Her works that are a cross between collages and installations portray figures such as relatives or total strangers, women from the four corners of the world or disadvantaged children. Having become involved in street art and collective projects very early on, she offers a humanistic and engaged vision of the world. In addition to representing her universe through portraits of the people whom she meets and the cities she has visited during her many trips, she is also influenced by German expressionist prints such as those of Egon Schiele, Gustav Klimt and Alphonse Mucha. She etches portraits on linoleum and then prints them on recycled or tracing paper, before then either bonding them with pieces of recovered wood or enhancing them with acrylic colours.

However, SWOON's work cannot be reduced to her technique alone. Its content and its engagement with society are essential. Inexorably attracted to the immediate and the ephemeral in her artistic activity, her idea is a simple one: create a fragile, vulnerable work that will not outlive its own necessity. This necessity is echoed in the humanitarian projects that have led her to travel, through which she has met people who have then become her models. This inveterate humanist continually travels the world with the desire to convey a message of peace. In the aftermath of the devastating hurricane that hit Haiti in 2010, SWOON actively contributed to the Konbit Shelter Project and its work on reconstructing a village. She became very involved in the island, where she developed projects and then brought them to the walls of Western cities and prestigious museums such as the MOCA in Los Angeles, the Tate Modern in London, the Brooklyn Museum and the MoMA in New York.

SWOON also fights for ecological causes, once more putting her art to work for her beliefs. At the 2009 Venice Biennale, she developed the project *Swimming Cities of Serenissima*. For it, she created vessels composed of recycled elements from the land or the bottom of the seas (for example, dilapidated furniture and the carcasses of cars). Her work crossed Europe, drifting along the rivers and canals of Slovenia up to the Adriatic Sea, before reaching Venice. SWOON viewed this experience as a personal commitment and an artistic project. "I have been working on the issue for many years, and my way of understanding the subject evolved. For me the most important thing now is to work where people live and to encounter people who don't necessarily visit places dedicated to art. If they don't like my work, they get rid of it. The mere existence of such a democratic space, in which everyone is able to express themselves legally or otherwise, is essential for me. It gives me another type of freedom, one that can only be found out in the world of the street."

She began the *Braddock Tiles* project in Pennsylvania by redeveloping an abandoned church in an economically stricken area into a ceramic workshop and community cultural centre. In New Orleans, she has used her art to build a "music house" that combines original architecture with a community cultural centre in a project that she has named *Dithyrambalina*.[12] For SWOON, building a better society is the basis of her artistic thinking, which she spreads around the world through her works. The faces that she paints are full of hopes and seem to believe in a better world and future.

12 "Dithyramb": an ancient song from the cult of Dionysus, which, for the artist SWOON, symbolises respect for all types of music that can come together in one place.

Street artists increasingly seize their environment and loudly proclaim this appropriation. For some artists, their observation of their surroundings is linked to their relationship with history. Drawing inspiration from the past in the present is also a form of contextualization of the work and the artist's reflections.

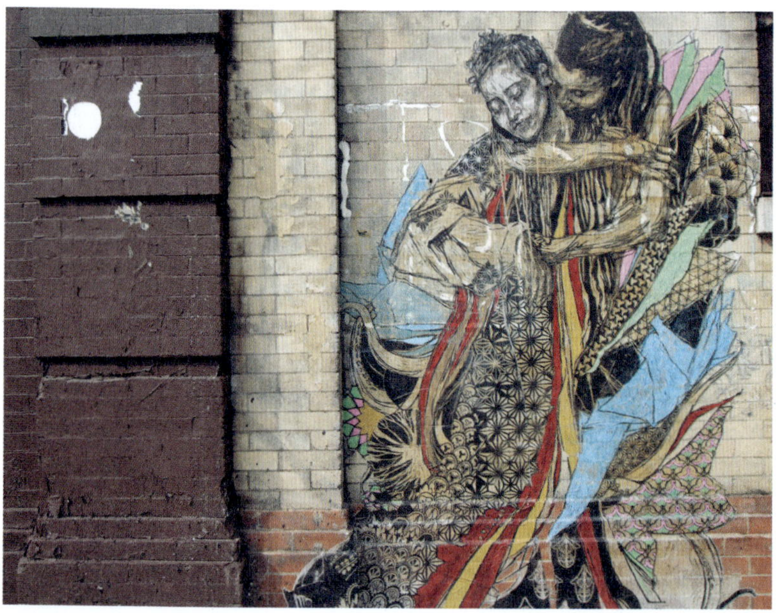

SWOON, *Alixa and Naima*, New York, 2008

YZ, pronounced "eyes," was born in France in 1975. She became better known in 2003 through the *Open your eyes* series, her first major urban project. In it, she created giant stencil works of enigmatic black and white faces. YZ calls on us to open our eyes and to go beyond what we see, just as artists such as SHEPARD FAIREY do. YZ started out as an artist by focusing on video and documentary. From the beginning, portraits were what interested her. Over time, her approach has become clearer as her technique has developed through experimentation. Her work has become more substantial and deeper, and it has also gone beyond its mere graphic appearances. Inspired by history and literature, YZ has found a personal style that involves the use of inks and washes. Because of her pieces' complexity, each of her street projects also routinely involves systematic work in the studio. She thoroughly prepares her subjects on paper, before then affixing them outdoors. YZ's work has expanded over time. She explores our relationship with history (in particular through nineteenth-century literature), as well as her own family history. "When I read the story of the women of the last century, I am always full of admiration. They inspire me," she says. In her Woman from Another Century project, she uses images of old nudes and recontextualizes them in the present day. "I love mixing classicism with very urban techniques. I really like Ernest Pignon Ernest's approach. For him, place is very important. Poetry and the very strong emotion of Giacometti's characters have also had a big effect on me. What I like is immersing myself in a place."

Through this aesthetic, YZ seeks to make walls speak in a way that transcends time. "And so I pitched into my great lake of melancholy": these words that Virginia Woolf recorded in her diary in 1929 are echoed in YZ's painted works. In keeping with the English author's words, YZ's visual works allow viewers to immerse themselves in the waters of memory, nostalgia and other eras. With their falsely aged and antiquated look that is present regardless of whether they have been made on the wall or on canvas or video, her works share this sense of nostalgia.
On the surface of these memories, where the waves of a sometimes too current present break, all that is left is a comforting, even protective sensuality that gives the subjects of YZ's works their psychological substance.

YZ focuses less on a formal description of her subjects than she does on the emotions that they provoke. Her exploration goes beyond the surface. She provides a bigger portrait: one of an era. Thousands of details that are invisible from view develop out of the subconscious mind. She strives to capture these in her subjects and in their attitudes. Her art is in this regard both piercing and detached. It embraces the world, flying over souls and penetrating the tiny stirrings that it encounters. Neither really photography nor painting, but clearly a work of art, her pieces play on the disquiet that the artist's subtle technique produces. Recycling memories and images from another time, YZ inevitably plunges us into a striking melancholy.

Among the other "sensitive" subjects that could be described as "figurative" and that inspire street artists from the hypervisible current is the evolution of society and its contradictions, and the development of a world where nature is under attack and technology has run wild. This subject is addressed by LUDO, an artist who was born in Paris in 1976, and who started out by tagging his home city's walls. In 2007, he made the transition to collage, which is now his trademark. His favourite colours are black, white and the iconic fluorescent green that he uses to paint his vegetable-robotic, half-natural, half-technological creatures. Often referred to as the new "French Warhol" because his inspirations come from mass culture, which he likes to turn into a provocative vehicle for his message, LUDO has developed a singular and recognizable aesthetic. With skill and attention to detail, it combines mechanical and plant elements, morphing them into hybrid creatures that are entirely his own. Fascinated by the energy of the street that inspires and stimulates him, he draws his material from daily life. Thus, a documentary, a reflection, a trip or a particular work become sources of reflection that lead to the creation of new pieces.

An engaged artist, LUDO's denunciations are made in a playful and aesthetic way. Although his works do not carry an overbearing mark of ecological or anticapitalist arguments, his personal reflections on the world that surrounds him run through them. These often have dimensions that are not seen at first glance, and they invite the viewer to reflect on pervasive and accepted violence, the consumption of GMOs or technology's dominance over nature. Green —the quintessential colour of nature— is used in a unique way that reestablishes plant life where it has been excluded. Accordingly, concrete walls, galleries and museums are all invaded by a modern forest.

His 2015 project *Shanghai Dust*, which came about following the revealing experience of his first visit to Shanghai and was produced in situ in the heart of the city, is an example of this approach. Strongly influenced by the visual shock that he experienced during the trip, he immediately decided to return to China to put to work his effervescent and unshakeable inspiration.
The series is designed as a living opera. It is a ballet of futuristic buzzing bees that he arranged in a postapocalyptic —or rather, in his words, a "salvational"— choreography. For his idea here was not to make an idle denunciation of the frantic pace of industrial growth, but rather to pay tribute to the special energy of Shanghai as an urban entity.

Far from placing an emphasis on things coming to an end, here LUDO is evoking China's renewal. To the sound of laughter from the people whom he encountered while there, LUDO was able to capture the poetry of a city that wakes up every day in a unique type of frenzy. A saving breath, like a second life, and angel wings are what give LUDO's unusual insects —recurring figures in his artworks— their desire to buzz around. He offers us a dose of the characteristic dynamism of early twenty-first-century China.

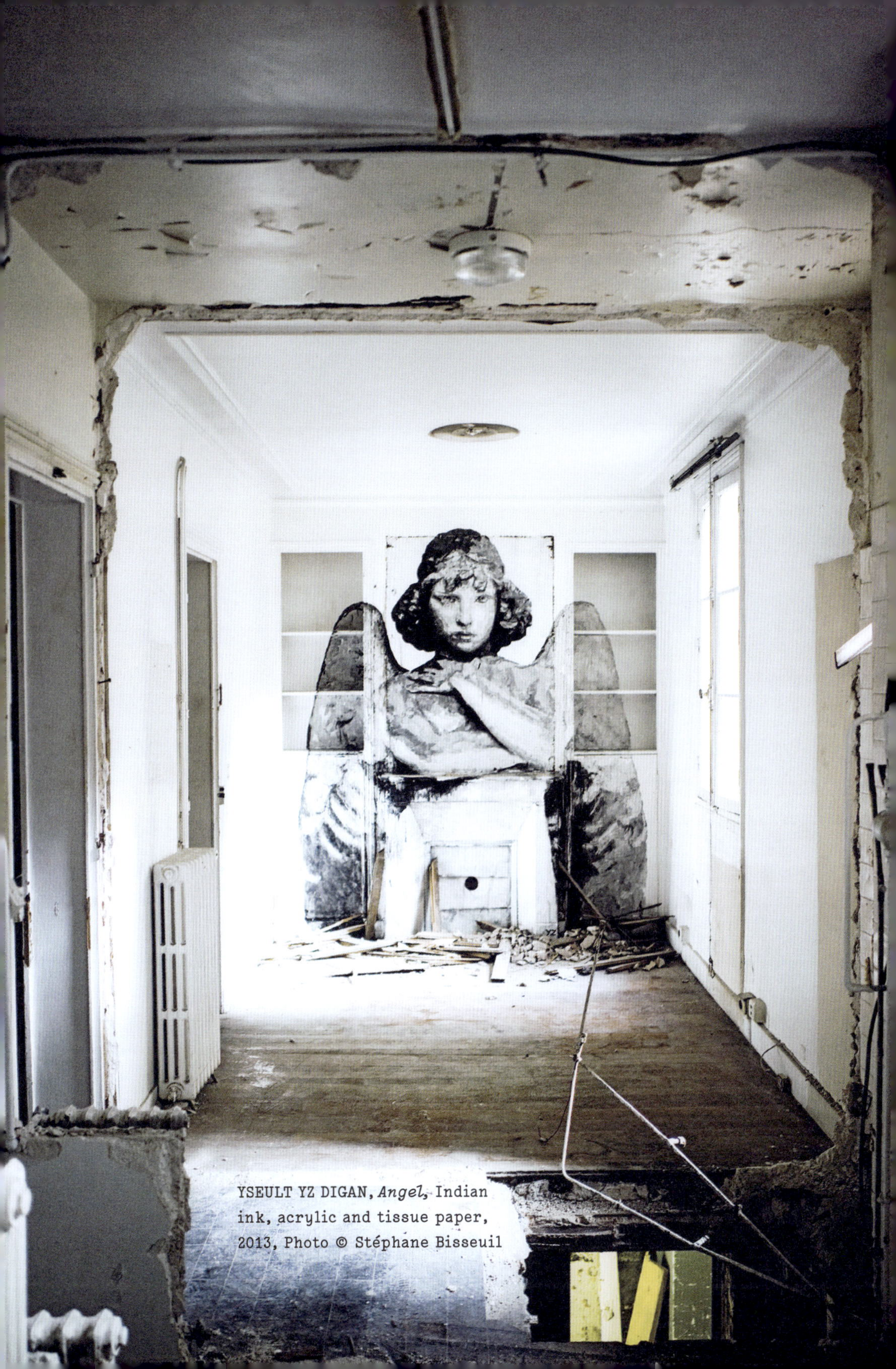

YSEULT YZ DIGAN, *Angel*, Indian ink, acrylic and tissue paper, 2013, Photo © Stéphane Bisseuil

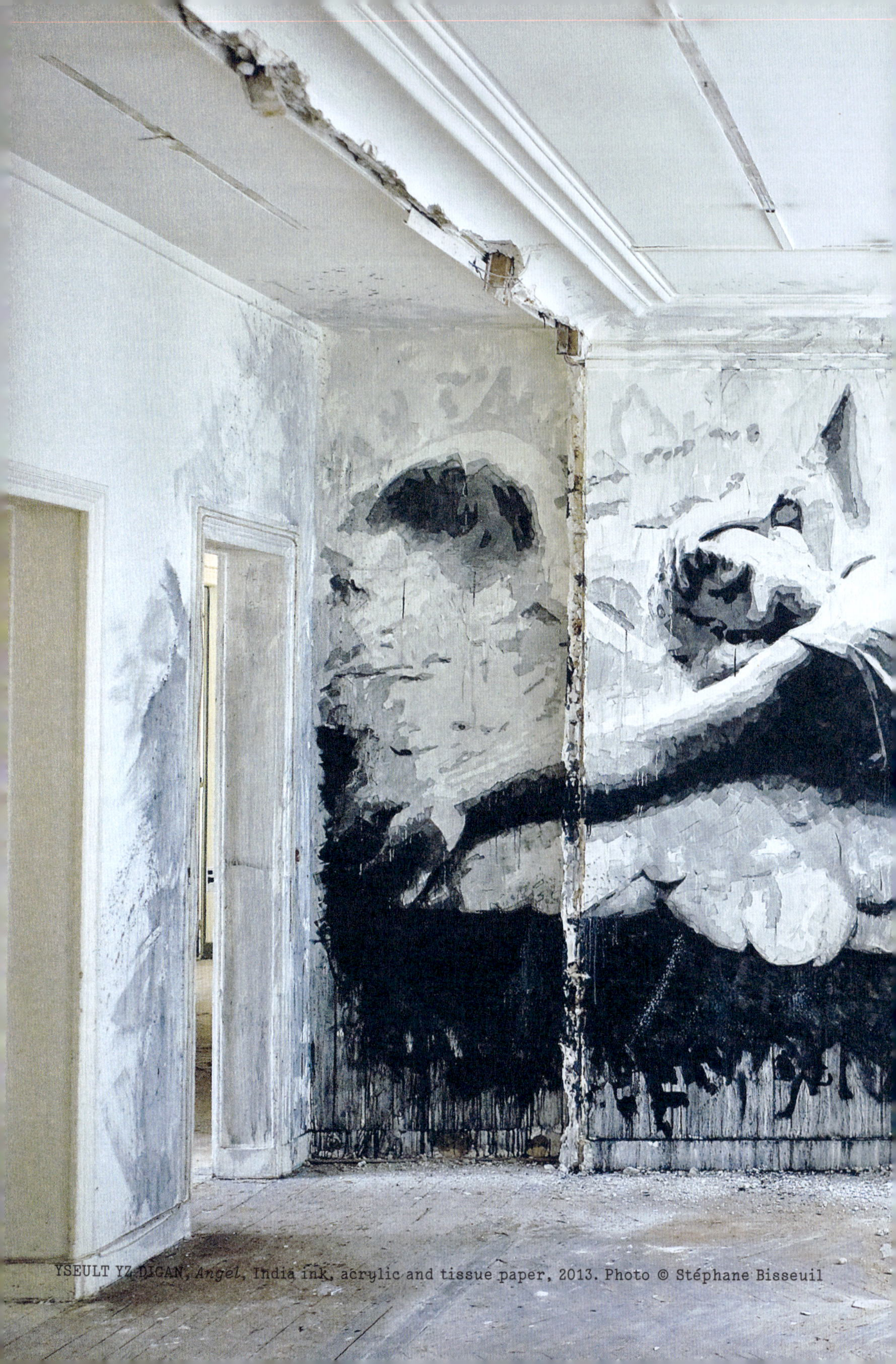

YSEULT YZ DIGAN, *Angel*, India ink, acrylic and tissue paper, 2013. Photo © Stéphane Bisseuil

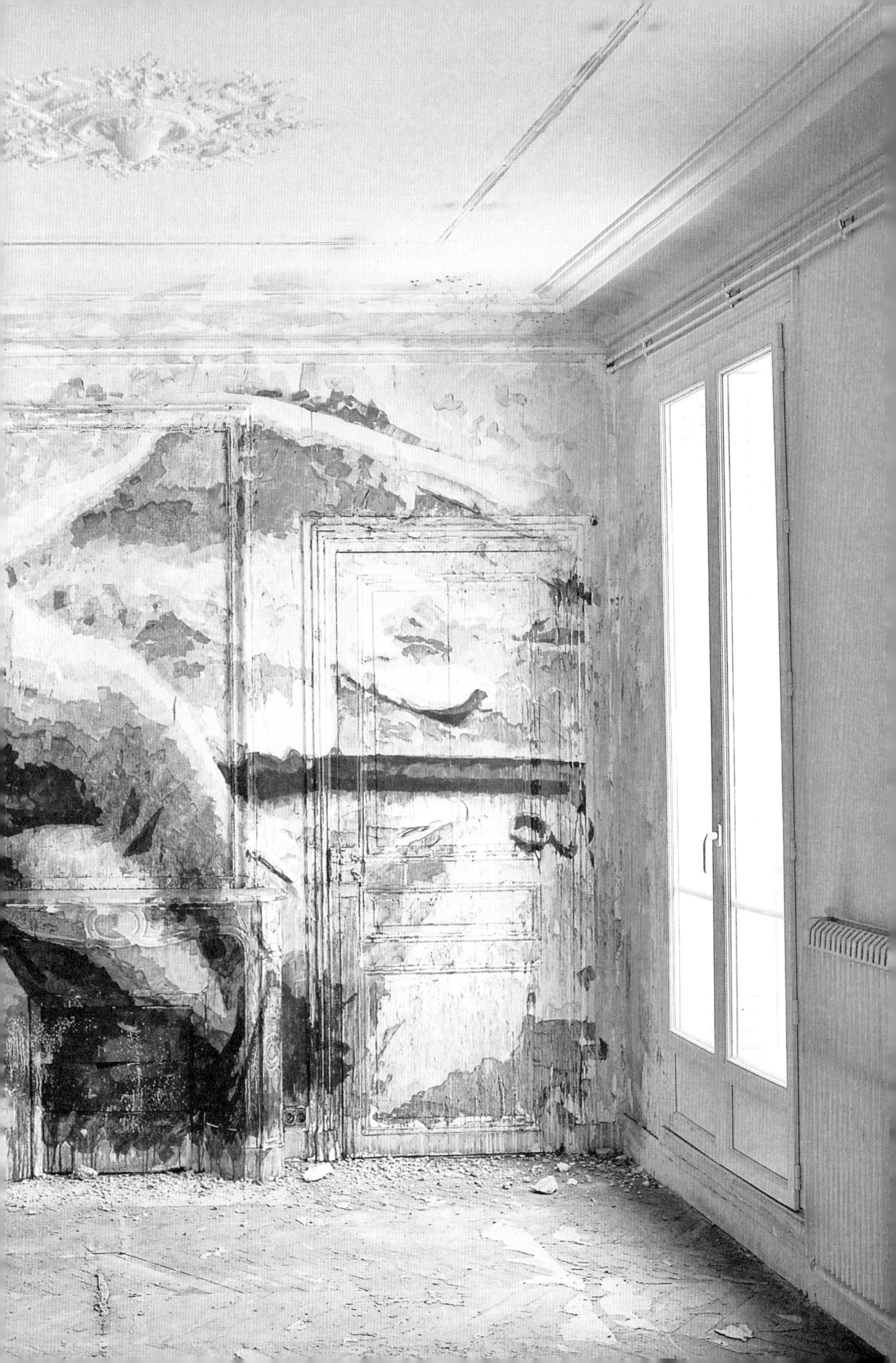

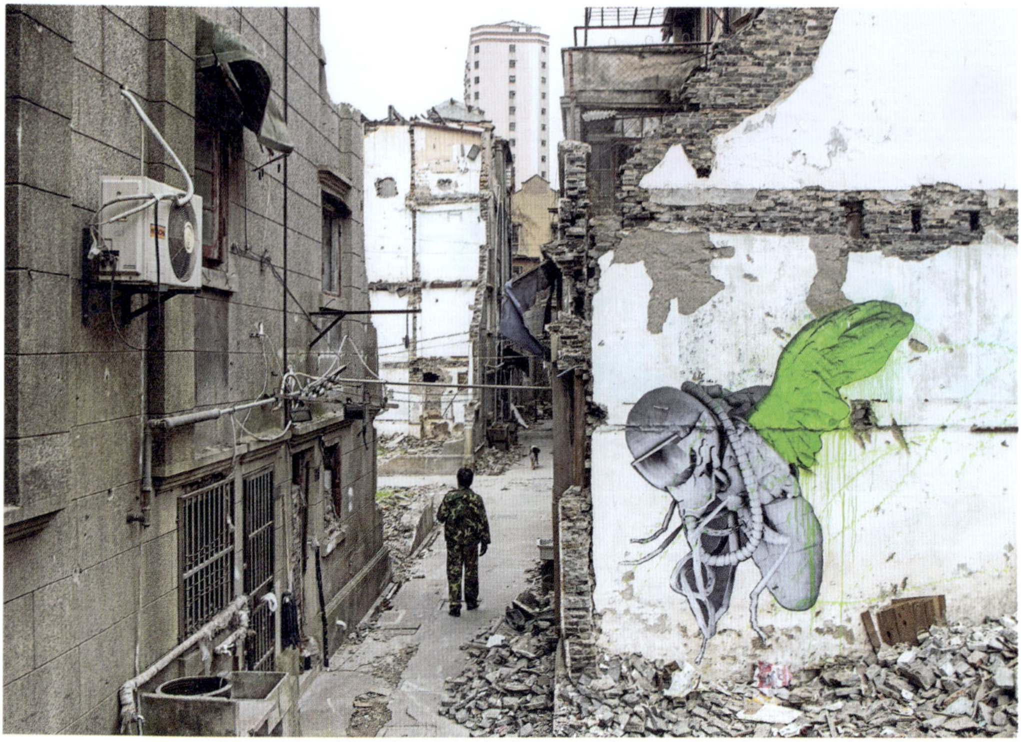

LUDO, *Shanghai Dust*, Shanghái, october 2015 © A.R.R.

LUDO, *Modern Tulipa*, Paris, 2013 © A.R.R.

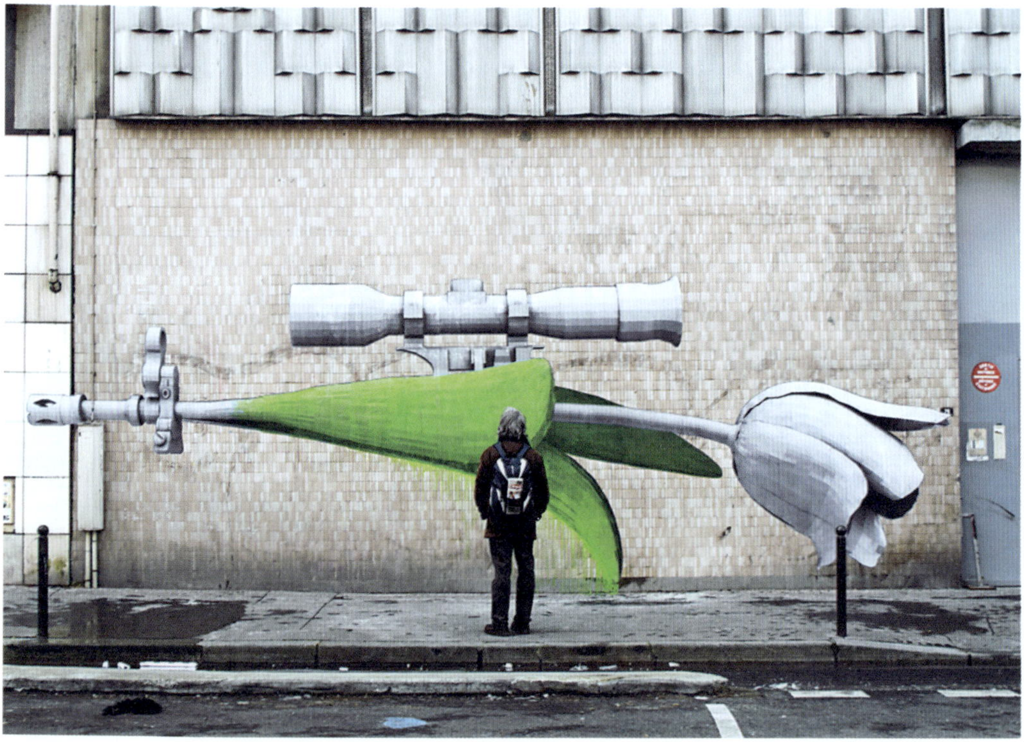

The bee decked out in its oxygen mask could on the surface seem to refer to the image of a city battling its demons. Yet with his creative urgency, the artist is focusing more on the amazing adaptability of individuals to daily life in motion. This insect that is said to be endangered seems in this case to in fact be able to adapt and find a way to survive without too much trouble. The abundance of elements is a metaphor for the plethora of resources that are put to use. Similarly, his highlighting of his works with "fluorescent green" (or is it "LUDO green"?) perfectly conveys their intrinsic —and explosive— energy.

STREET ART IN THE SPOTLIGHT

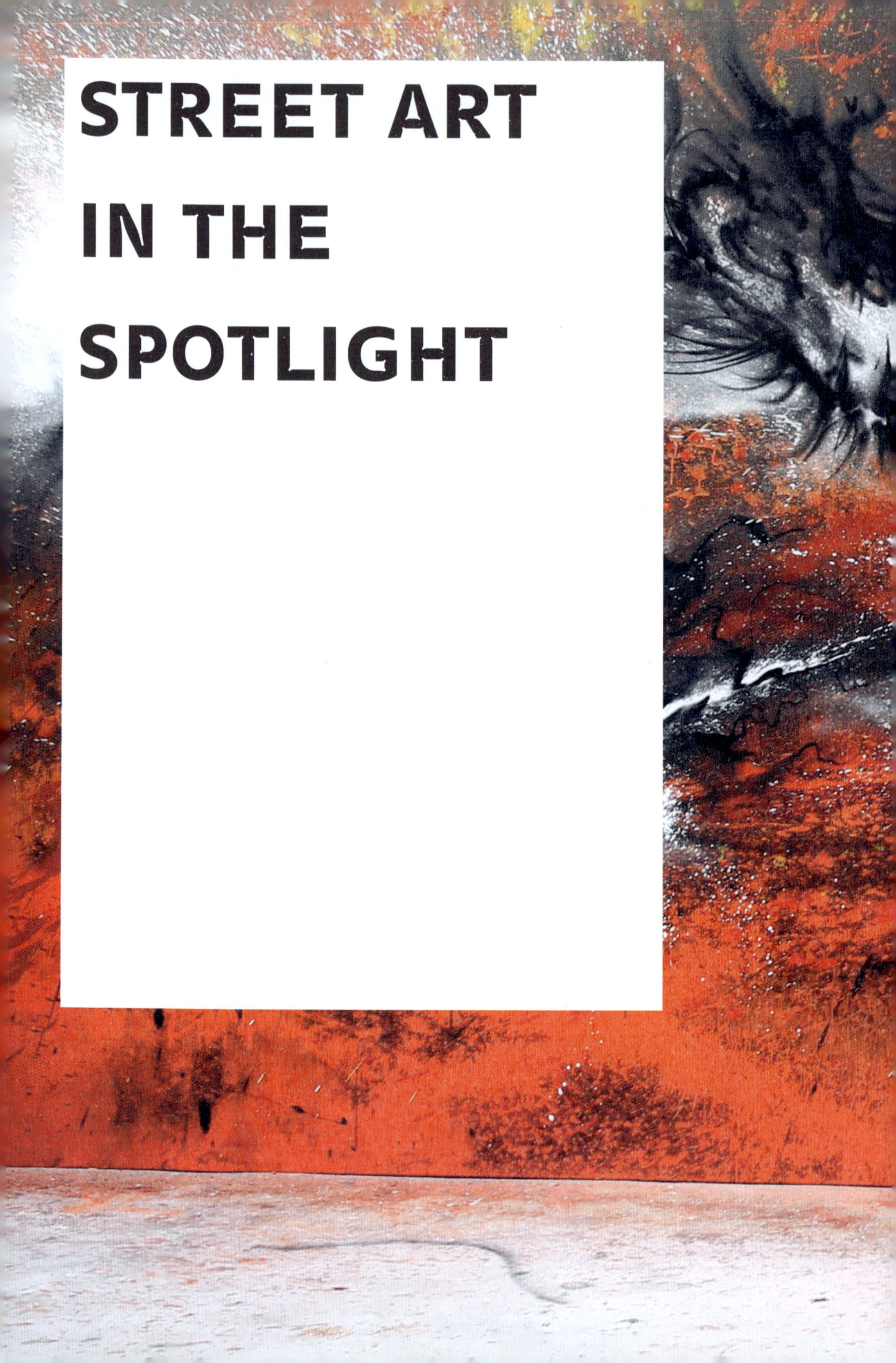

EXPOSURE AS A MEANS OF LEGITIMATION 213

How to exhibit Urban Art 213

Taking a different approach to museums 214

Institutional exhibitions on movement 216

Individual exhibitions 221

The city, an open-air museum 224

A PRACTICE INSCRIBED INTO THE HISTORY OF ART 229

Returning to art's roots 229

Resuming the thread of 20th century history 236

ARTISTS' SOCIAL ENGAGEMENT AND IMPACT ON SOCIETY 247

The beginnings of a socially-conscious urban art form 247

Image theft 248

Weaving the social fabric 249

Addressing the world's crises 252

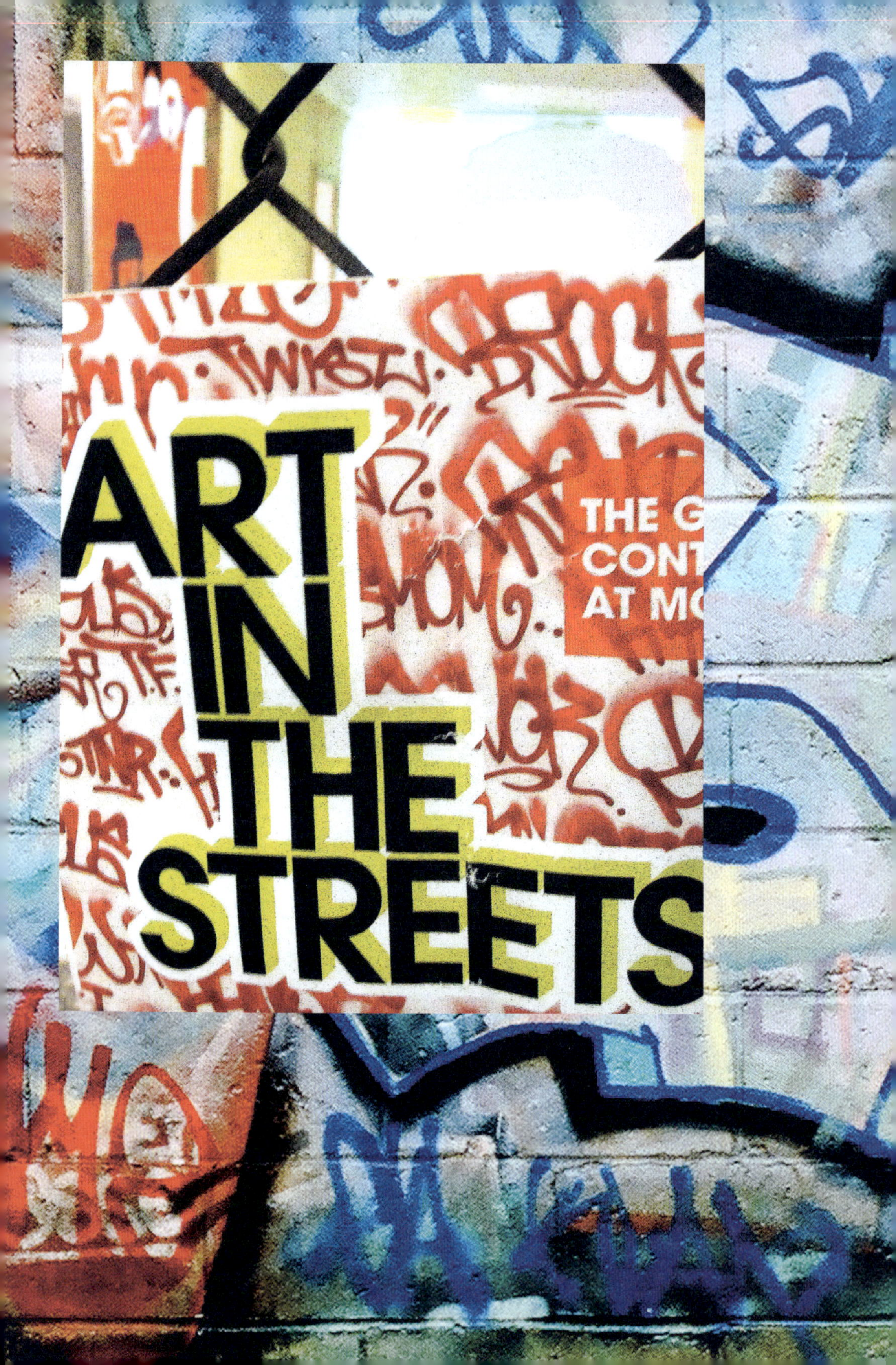
ART IN THE STREETS
THE G
CONT
AT MO

EXPOSTURE AS MEANS OF LEGITIMATION

How to exhibit Urban Art

In spite of its increasing popularity and exposure as well as its wealth of new forms, urban art struggled in the first decade of the twenty-first century to gain recognition from the cultural authorities. Exhibitions in museums were not forthcoming. Nevertheless, debate on the exhibition of urban art did take place. But is it possible to exhibit works that were originally intended to be outdoors? This is a question that does not take into account the fact that the artists concerned also produce their art indoors. For example, from his first days as an artist, DONDI also worked in a studio. And then there are all the graffiti artists with their blackbooks filled with drawings and sketches. Works produced inside do not have the same purpose as ones executed outside. Creating indoors entails working in a more precise way and perhaps over a longer period of time, allowing the development of a more accomplished work. Exterior and interior work are therefore two complementary facets of the artist's work. Was Michelangelo ever asked if it was contradictory of him to paint the Sistine Chapel and to produce *The Holy Family* in 1507? Each medium and format has its own justification. If, as ICOM (the International Council of Museums) has it, a museum can be defined as "a non-profit, permanent institution in the service of society and its development, open to the public, which acquires, conserves, researches, communicates and exhibits the tangible and intangible heritage of humanity and its environment for the purposes of education, study and enjoyment," more than ever street art needs people to conserve it in order for the history of the movement to be preserved and shared, for its developments and its evolution to be studied, and for new projects to be implemented.

Art in the Streets, exhibition at the MOCA, Los Angeles, 2011 © A.R.R.

Behind: graffiti in New York.Photo © Stéphane Bisseuil

Little by little, it appeared more clearly in the first decade of the twenty-first century that street artists' talent lies in their ability to explore their environment and its context, and also to transcribe these thoughts through other media. And some of these artists like to bring different environments face to face. Accordingly, an exhibition space can be just as

interesting as an outdoor surface. The context as such is what the artist grasps. As a set of circumstances in which an event or an action occurs and from which it gains its meaning, this context is multifaceted.
Coherence between the work and what surrounds it is essential to understand street art's scope. Just as was the case with the carriages on which the first graffiti artists decided to make top to bottoms that would pass through one district of the city to another, producing a work on a wall depends on what there is around that wall. Similar to the way in which photographers prepare their framing, street artists have an instinctive eye for the whole. They can be just as inspired by the texture of a wall as they can by its location "saying something." The wall, its context and the piece produced form a whole, like a complete installation and not just an element affixed to a white wall or a place that is too obvious. With works produced indoors, the idea is not to ape the outdoor approach, but to transmit its energy in a different way. Like in an outdoor work, the subject is chosen in advance, and it is then a question of working with the materials and form that communicate the same message. Artists often use collages and installations to support their indoor work. This allows the outside approach to be supplemented.
Nevertheless, holding museum exhibitions raises the question of the mode of displaying this type of relatively atypical art. All the artists in the movement have stressed from their earliest days that their main exhibition gallery is in the open of the street. Whether exhibiting outdoors is not better than indoors was raised, among other questions, by BANKSY in 2013, when he spent a month producing works on the streets of New York. He called this project *Better Out Than In*. The artist authenticates each new piece on his newsfeed, and includes a free telephone number where callers can hear an audio guide like those available in museums. The highlight of his "exhibition" was his anonymous selling of works for $60 (at least a thousand times less than their market value at the time).
Laurent Le Bon, President of the Centre Pompidou in Paris, emphasises the importance of the institution for these artists, but also raises the fundamental issue of appropriate display. "...perhaps what stands in the way of Street Art entering the museum space is that an appropriate form of exhibition has not yet been invented... The story of art in museums is often one of relocation, regardless of the piece itself. Originally, masterpieces were not necessarily intended for museums, but for other types of buildings, such as cathedrals. The same philosophical and ethical questions are raised now."

Taking a different approach to museums

As they await institutional recognition, urban artists often find their way into the world's major museums by the back door. The beginning of the 21st century saw a proliferation of projects by art centres or museums specialising in ad hoc Street Art. From Amsterdam to Berlin, via

Miami, it is the artists themselves —or passionate collectors— who set about creating the structures they deem necessary to showcase the movement. Similarly, some renowned curators, tired of waiting for museums to call, organise ambitious travelling exhibitions. Roger Gastman's *Beyond the Street*, for example, is held alternately in a warehouse in Los Angeles and on two empty floors of a Brooklyn office block.

While urban art often fails to attract the attention and interest of official bodies in terms of exhibitions or purchases, it often finds its way into institutions via the public or outreach channels. Far from the legitimising gaze of museum curators, the aim is to open up the institution —albeit in a roundabout way— to other forms of artistic expression and to widen access to new audiences, even if this kind of exhibition often has to take place outside the spaces usually dedicated to this purpose.

THE WORKSHOPS OF THE CENTRE POMPIDOU

Since 2007, the Centre Pompidou's young audiences team has invited the French collective known as 9ème Concept to take part in workshops there. This group of artists from the Urban Art scene has come up with an original proposal. In a space on the ground floor of the Centre, they paint on site every day, revealing their creative process to the general public. In 2013, the same management team repeated the experiment, inviting seven urban artists. MARK JENKINS, JONONE, LUDO, OX, RERO, VHILS and YZ participated in an "artistic experience" called Ex-Situ, made up of participatory workshops and ephemeral installations in the

RERO, *Do Not Cross the Line*, Centre Pompidou, Paris, 2013

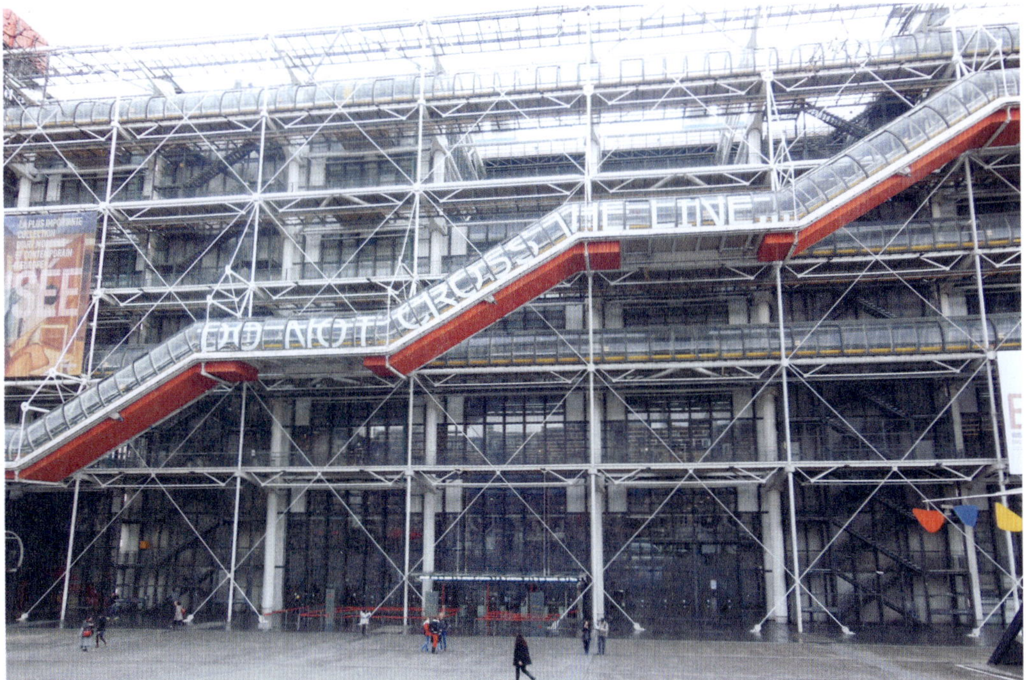

common areas of the building and in its immediate surroundings. Having already taken over the Public Forum in 2011 with his collages on the interior lifts, artist JR was invited to create an "exhibition-workshop" for young audiences in the "children's gallery" in 2016.

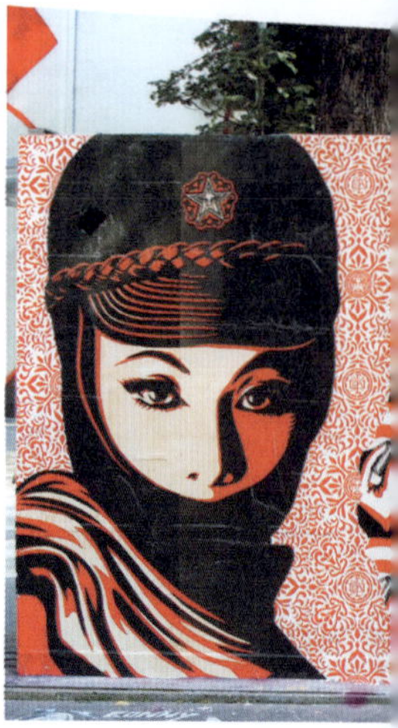

SHEPARD FAIREY aka OBEY, Fondation Cartier palisade during the Born on the Street exhibition, Paris, 2009. Photo © Lionel Belluteau / un œil qui traîne.

STREET ART AT THE TATE MODERN

In 2008, an exhibition at London's Tate Modern presented the work of six urban artists: the Italian BLU, the FAILE collective from New York, France's JR, the Brazilians NUNCA and OS GÊMEOS, and Barcelona's SIXEART. In place of a classic exhibition, the artists were invited to produce monumental works that were more than 50 metres high on the Tate Modern's imposing façade.

The exhibition was complemented by a Street Art Walking Tour, an urban itinerary of works created throughout the city for the occasion by five. Madrid-based artists, as well as a night-time performance by the GRAFFITI RESEARCH LAB, whose work is always produced using light. The idea behind this outdoor approach to exhibition was to probe the methods of displaying a movement that is so prolific that the classic exhibition does not seem to be sufficient. But why always keep these artists out even when many of them have equally legitimate indoor modes of expression? As one of the project's artists pointed out in this respect: "I do not consider myself to be only a street artist. The street is just another method of or place for self-expression. The only difference is that a significant number of people see you and so you have a quick return."

JR AT THE LOUVRE

The Louvre, the "largest museum in the world", was also interested in the artists of this movement. In 2016, JR proposed a project based on one of its symbols: the Louvre pyramid. The project consisted of making the museum disappear by means of a rather curious anamorphosis, a process whereby the public has to stand at a specific point in order to see the complete piece correctly. In 2019, with the help of 400 volunteers, he created a collaborative piece on the site again, but this time on the scale of the entire courtyard, where the Pyramid is located. Three years after making it disappear, he would reveal it in a new light by means of an ephemeral collage of almost 15,000 square metres of paper in a monumental trompe-l'œil. Under the effects of the sun, the paper peeled away, prompting the onlooker to reflect on presence and absence, reality and memory, and the nature of transience.

Institutional exhibitions on movement

The recognition to which all these artists aspire also involves exhibiting and sharing their creations with the public. Despite the success of open-air exhibitions, they refuse to be systematically relegated to the backwaters of the art world and its museums. The 1980s saw a significant number of international events bearing witness to the emergence

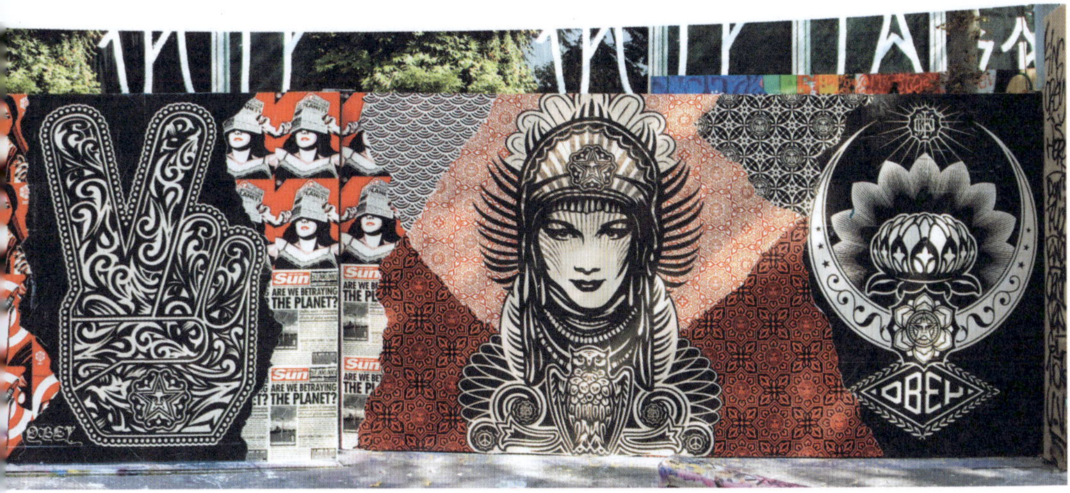

of graffiti. Nevertheless, despite the endorsement of the media —and existing for almost four decades now— major qualitative exhibitions providing a comprehensive and critical look at the practice and the movement are still too rare...

NÉ DANS LA RUE AT THE FONDATION CARTIER

In 2009, the Fondation Cartier pour l'art contemporain in Paris opened its *Né dans la rue* (*Born in the streets*) exhibition. Built in two separate parts, it invited the visitor first of all to discover a comprehensive historical section that combined artworks, blackbooks and memorabilia from the early era of graffiti. The artist SOWAT recalls, "The first part of the exhibition, by far the richest and most moving, led the visitor into the basement. Walls painted black, subdued light, a muted and unsettling soundtrack, a big archival collection: everything was made to transport the viewer to the beginnings of graffiti and the New York of the 1970s and its idle kids who were just fifteen and were having fun with shaking up the history of art, and perhaps of painting... An impressive set of original documents showed the creative impulse of the time. Nothing was left out in understanding what could jolt a gang of self-taught kids towards the idea of going to paint their names on a subway over and over again, thus creating the most beautiful and clumsiest of rolling museums." The exhibition then led on to the artists' large in situ works. These included pieces by that most Parisian of Americans, JONONE, the Dutchman DELTA and the Brazilian VITCHE.

With this journey, the Fondation Cartier provided the opportunity to discover the graffiti world from its birth to its entry into cultural institutions. The exhibition was simultaneously thematic, chronological and geographical, plunging visitors into the New York hood and the Brazilian favela. The exhibition also extended to the façade and the garden of the building, thus highlighting the extraordinary vitality of this movement that quickly became a global phenomenon. By providing a reading of its origins and a panorama of the plurality of contemporary writings

that coexist within it, *Né dans la rue* offered a renewed take on both street art and the city.
Nevertheless, the exhibition did raise some controversy. One visitor commented, "I felt that something bothered me. Graffiti is essentially an act of rebellion. There was something absurd about seeing it exhibited in the middle of admiring bobos in a museum founded by a brand of jewellery." Fortunately, in her view, "The graffiti of the twenty-first century seems more promising than that of the previous one." The exhibition was hotly debated, but it was also a success; and it was extended to a total run of more than seven months.

ARTS IN THE STREETS AT MOCA, LOS ANGELES

It would take two years for another major museum exhibition to take place. In April 2011, the Museum of Contemporary Art, Los Angeles (MOCA), under the directorship of Jeffrey Deitch, opened its doors for the exhibition *Arts in the Streets*.
Having organized numerous exhibitions that caused a sensation at the time —such as those with OS GÊMEOS, STEPHEN POWERS and BARRY MCGEE— in his three New York galleries that comprised the Deitch Project, on 1 June 2010 Deitch was entrusted with directing the MOCA. Suffice to say, Jeffrey Deitch knows plenty about the subject of street art. For this exhibition, he chose two exceptional curators to give visitors a sense of the history and philosophy of street art: the author and artist graffiti Roger Gastman and the director and curator Aaron Rose, who gained fame through his *Beautiful Losers* project.

This exhibition was the largest to date on the history of graffiti and street art. It traced the evolution of the movement from the 1970s until the present, at the same time as highlighting the connections between these two types of production and other subcultures such as hip-hop in the Bronx and skateboarding in California.
The programme featured paintings, sculptures, photographs, videos and interactive installations by fifty of the most dynamic and representative artists from the scene, including FUTURA, BANKSY, SHEPARD FAIREY, OS GÊMEOS, BARRY McGEE, SWOON, MISS VAN, ANDRÉ, SPACE INVADER and JR. There was also a particular focus on the photographs and films of big names like Martha Cooper, Henry Chalfant, James Prigoff, Steve Grody, Gusmano Cesaretti, Estevan Oriol, Ed Templeton, Larry Clark, Terry Richardson and Spike Jonze, which provide an essential record of a bygone era. This rich yet current exhibition did not skip over historical context. For example, the Fun Gallery was reproduced as part of it. Seldom-seen works by the artist and theorist RAMMELLZEE were also presented. The historical perspective was complemented by blackbooks from the 1980s —the sketchbooks so dear to all graffiti artists— from the Martin Wong Collection (which were donated during his time at the Museum of the City of New York).
The most current orientation took the form of the presence of a skateboard ramp, which emphasized the link between the two cultures, as well as a significant set of outdoor walls.

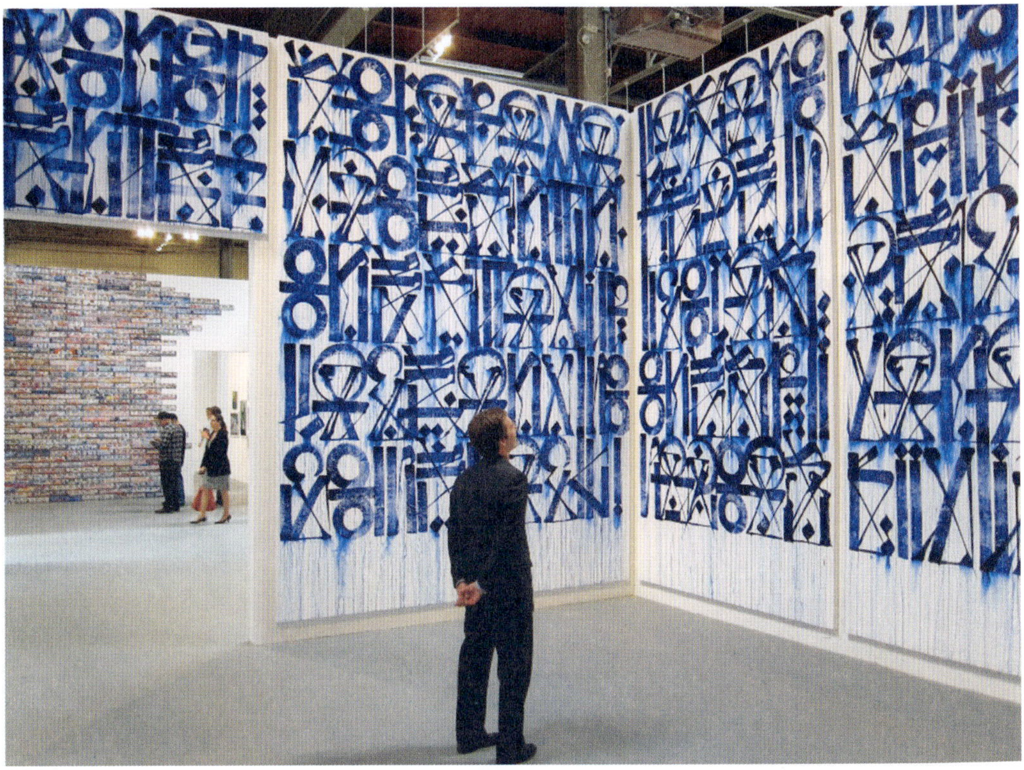

RETNA, *Los espiritus de la calle van a sobrevivir*, Los Angeles (MOCA), 2011, acrylic on canvas

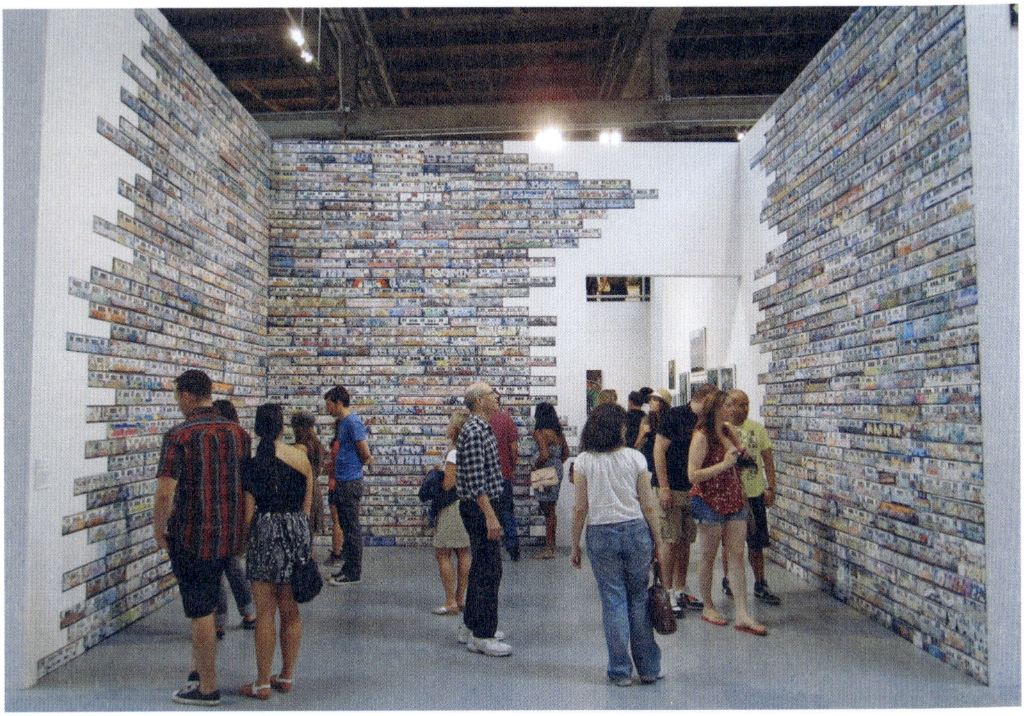

HENRY CHALFANT, *We Drenched the City With Our Names*, Los Angeles (MOCA), 2011, ink on adhesive paper

Art in the Streets proved to be a great success in terms of museum attendance. With a little more than 201,000 visitors, the exhibition edged out a 2002 Andy Warhol retrospective and a Takashi Murakami one (which had 195,000 and 149,000 visitors respectively). These impressive figures should not, however, overshadow the controversy surrounding the outdoor fresco commissioned from the artist, BLU. Depicting coffins covered in dollar bills, it was censored by the MoCA, illustrating the delicate collaboration between institutions and an art form that remains contentious.

CITY AS CANVAS AT THE MUSEUM OF THE CITY OF NEW YORK

In 2014, the Museum of the City of New York organized the exhibition *City as Canvas: Graffiti Art*, which was based on its own collections. Since 1994, the museum has been in possession of Martin Wong's significant collection, which contains many works related to graffiti. Wong, an artist who died of AIDS in 1999, had for a long period collected major works from the early New York scene.

City as Canvas: Graffiti Art began when curator Sean Corcoran came across the many photos and blackbooks bequeathed by Martin Wong. In total, there were fifty-five books of sketches and more than three hundred paintings on canvas, cardboard, paper or plywood. The fruit of the early intuitions of this enlightened collector, the works he amassed perfectly reveal the movement's stylistic transformations during its early stages.

The exhibition led into a presentation of photographs of graffiti on trains and buildings. The photographs featured were intended to trace a context that may be hard to imagine for those who never experienced this period.

It also included around a hundred works by legendary artists and writers such as, among others, DAZE, DONDI, FUTURA, KEITH HARING, LADY PINK, LEE and SHARP, alongside historic photos by Charlie Ahearn, Henry Chalfant, Martha Cooper, Jon Naar and Jack Stewart. It accurately recounted the joyous vitality of this scene and the fact that graffiti has democratized artistic creation. And it also reflected the abundant contributions of the era. Yet this anarchy had its rules. Although only an insider can easily decrypt tags and understand their hierarchy, the exhibition made it easier for visitors to step into this world. It showed off an impressive set of artefacts collected by Martin Wong through friendships, bartering and persuasion.

Despite the absence of large-sized pieces, these having disappeared because at the time they were produced in the street, Wong endeavoured to keep traces of what had been done outdoors. The exhibition additionally showed the changes that had taken place in a city that, since the 1990s, has experienced disproportionate levels of real-estate growth and gentrification, pushing graffiti away from New York's walls.

IN THE BOWELS OF THE PALAIS DE TOKYO

In 2012, the Palais de Tokyo embarked on an innovative project. The Lasco Project would take place in the bowels of the building: underground interstitial spaces such as corridors, stairs or passages, and usually located underneath the classic exhibition rooms. The quality of the numerous artists invited to take part reveals both Hugo Vitrani's tenacity as curator, and a rigorous approach that has fuelled ideas and debates on how to present this art form within the institution. Held over a number of successive years, the *Lasco Project* has provided an opportunity to see the most important artists in the movement paraded within the walls of the Palais de Tokyo, from founding fathers such as FUTURA to more emerging or cutting-edge talents. To mark the tenth anniversary of the *Lasco Project*, the Palais de Tokyo has invited Jay Ramier, aka JAYONE —a pioneer of hip-hop in France who has also developed a significant body of work in the studio— to express himself with a solo installation in the institution's museum spaces.

FROM BEIJING TO SINGAPORE

In Asia, interest in Urban Art is growing. Paradoxically, it is worth noting that institutional exhibitions are taking place in Asian countries - a part of the world where the movement was not born out of graffiti as illegal vandalism. In 2016, the management of the CAFA Art Museum in Beijing decided to produce an exhibition entitled Street Art: A Global View, which draws from the premise that this movement is part of a great muralist tradition found in both South America and Asia. In 2018, Singapore would host the Art From the Streets exhibition in the 2,500 square metre ArtScience Museum, with more than fifty artists —from FAB 5 FREDDY, DONDI, A-ONE and FUTURA to VHILS, FELIPE PANTONE and Indonesia's EKO NUGRORHO— all presenting their work for the first time in Southeast Asia from within a historical perspective that brings together old and new talent. Yesterday's pioneers are today's accomplished artists, inspiring new generations who in turn push the boundaries of the movement even further, inventing and renewing the craft.

WRITING THE FUTURE: BASQUIAT AND THE HIP-HOP GENERATION

In 2020, the Museum of Fine Art in Boston organised a group exhibition entitled *Writing the Future: Basquiat and the Hip-Hop Generation*, where BASQUIAT's works were displayed alongside those of A-ONE, ERO, FAB 5 FREDDY, FUTURA, KEITH HARING, KOOL KOOR, LA2, LADY PINK, LEE QUIÑONES, RAMMELLZEE and TOXIC. By highlighting BASQUIAT's various links to these artists, the exhibition establishes the idea of a coherent movement that has its rightful place in the history of art.

Individual exhibitions

Recognition is also established through individual exhibitions. While they do not provide a comprehensive overview of the movement, they do allow the artists' careers to become part of a museum discourse, thereby taking them out of the "urban ghetto" to which they are sometimes confined and placing them within the realm of contemporary art. As Jeffrey Deitch, American curator and director of The Advent of a Contextual Art 225 at MOCA Los Angeles from 2010 to 2013 reminds us: "No

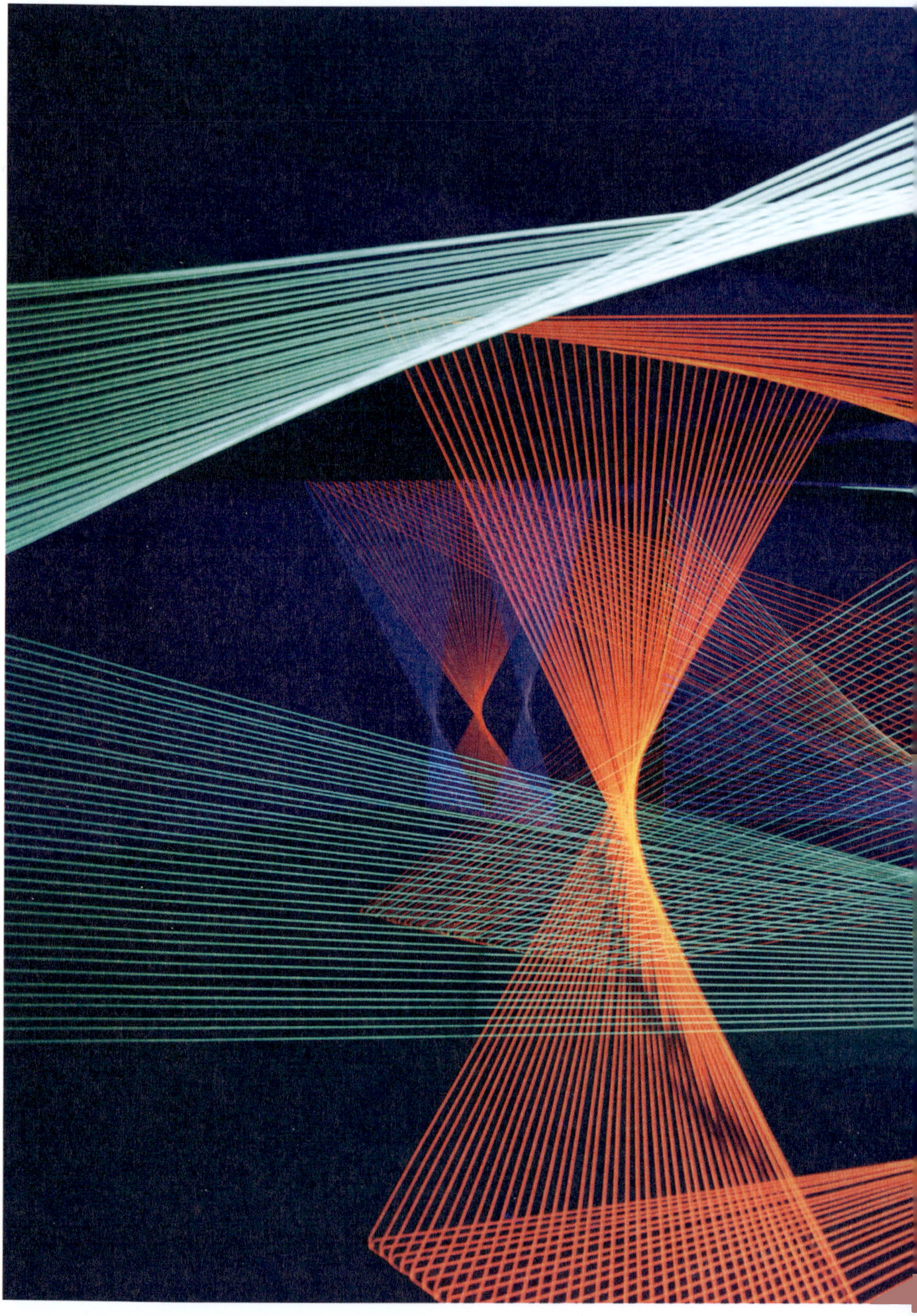

SÉBASTIEN PRESCHOUX, *Lasco Project #1*, Palais de Tokyo, Paris, 2012. Photo © Aurélie Cenno

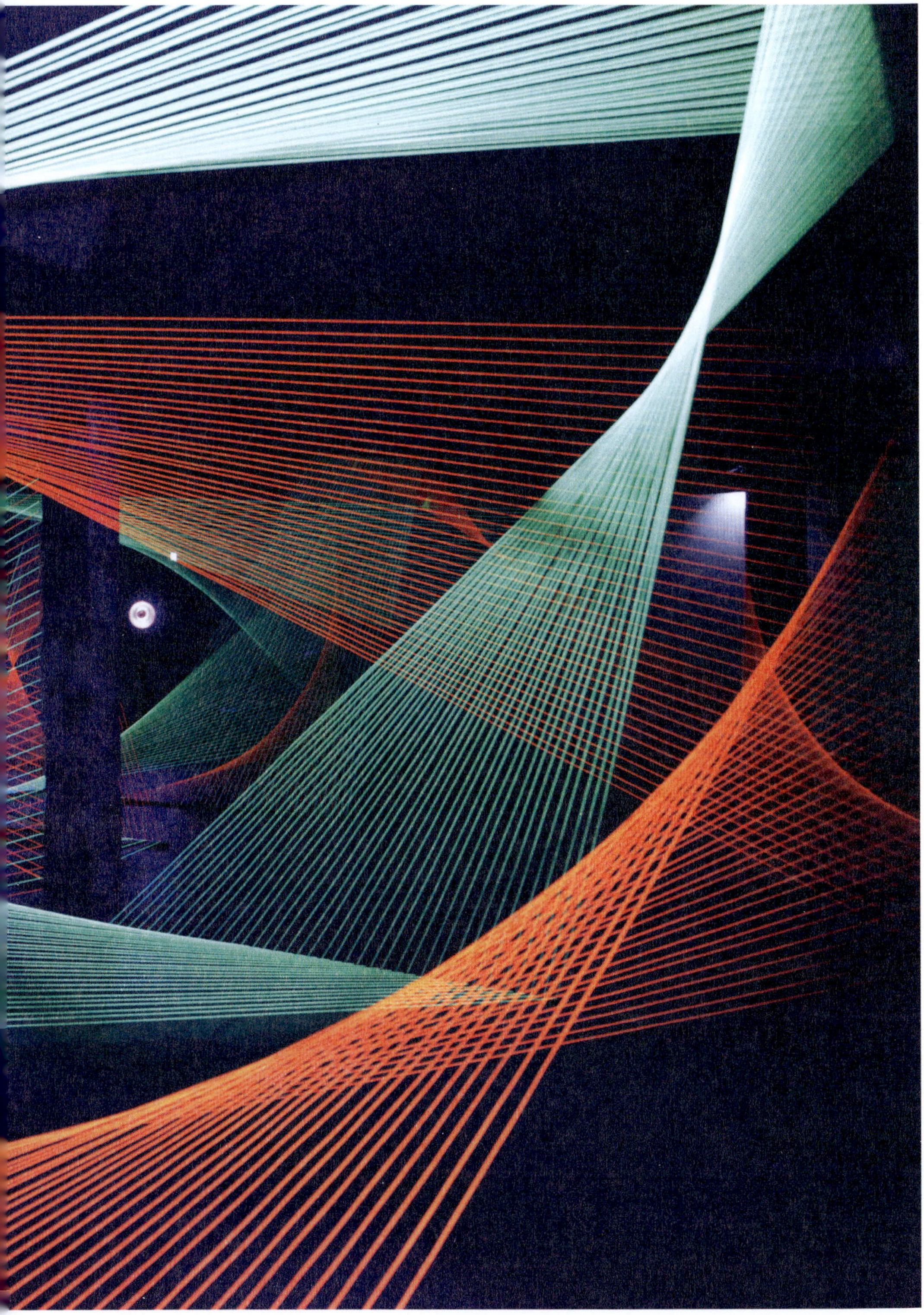

matter how serious the artist, whether their work is Street Art or not, all they want is to be recognised as such, as a veritable artist. None of them want to end up in a subcategory. Being labelled a 'street artist' is quite annoying and artists don't tend to like it. But that being said, we need the term 'Street Art' from a critical and historical point of view. In order to take a look at this whole movement and reflect on it, we need to give it a name".

In 2009, the Institute of Contemporary Art in Boston presented the first exhibition of work by SHEPARD FAIREY, who was described as "one of the most influential urban artists of our time". In 2013, as part of its *Hammer Projects* series, the Hammer Museum of Los Angeles commissioned MAYA HAYUK to create several monumental frescoes for various spaces in the building. That same year, the Dallas Contemporary hosted the *Where Wild Won't Break* exhibition by artist duo, FAILE. The following year, it was Brooklyn Museum's turn, presenting SWOON's work in the form of a monumental installation. In 2019, the Brooklyn Museum once again chose to honour an urban artist by presenting a comprehensive exhibition on JR's career. In 2020, VHILS presented his first retrospective on US soil at the Contemporary Arts Center in Cincinnati, where he demonstrated his ability to work in a wide variety of techniques that underpin his research into different forms of urban exploration.

Unfortunately, however, these examples are still exceptions to the rule: compared with other contemporary artists, those from the urban art scene find it hard to carve out a place for themselves in the institutional world – proof, if any were needed, of the milieu's reticence towards them.

The city, an open-air museum

In Italy between 2008 and 2014, the *Fame Festival* turned the small town of Grottaglie into a museum of street art. In 2010, the *Crono Festival* in Lisbon was a massive success and saw the Portuguese capital transformed by the work of major artists such as OS GÊMEOS, BLU and VHILS. In France in October 2014, the highlight of the 13th edition of *Nuit Blanche* was an open-air museum of contemporary street art in Paris's 13th *arrondissement*. It featured offerings by young artists in the field of contemporary or digital art, and a large number of works by artists like SWOON, JEF AEROSOL, YZ and THOMAS CANTO.

José Manuel Gonçalvès, the director of *Nuit Blanche*, envisaged this event as the start of a museum that, in its own way, ought to become sustainable through the combined activities of the movement's participants and promoters. The challenge to pick up the ball and continue the initiative in terms of quality was laid down. The Ville de Paris's culture officials asserted that "The idea is not to start a half-hearted project. The fact that it is labelled street art does not mean that it should not be of a high quality."

During the Nuit Blanche, the director makes no concessions on this point – in his view, it is vital if Street Art is to be recognised as a quality artistic movement, and it must now be showcased to the general public in satisfactory conditions. This context of institutionalisation —of the street-as-museum— exists in many cities around the world, either at the instigation of the public authorities or on the initiative of various associations.

MUSEUM COLLECTIONS

With the exception of museums that specialise in this area, most of which are privately owned, institutions have very few works of Urban Art in their permanent collections. In the two emblematic museums, MoMA in the United States and the Centre Pompidou in France, the facts are clear. Keywords such as "graffiti" or "Street Art" tend to produce search results that lump together artists whose work has nothing in common, such as Philip Guston, Cy Twombly or Antoni Tàpies. The only ones to stand out in a more legitimate way are BASQUIAT, KEITH HARING, BARRY MCGEE and VILLEGLÉ – a notable exception in the Centre Pompidou's collections and acquired for reasons other than his status as a tutelary figure of the movement.

For President of the Centre Pompidou Laurent Le Bon, "The scope of museum heritage has expanded enormously. But certain blinkers and categories remain. Unfortunately, some people still have the mistaken idea that this is street art in the most basic sense, and therefore has no place in a museum. But the institution is important for these artists, because it can provide a historical perspective".

Next double page spread:
SWOON, Masséna station, 2014, *Nuit Blanche* 2014, City of Paris © Martin Argyro

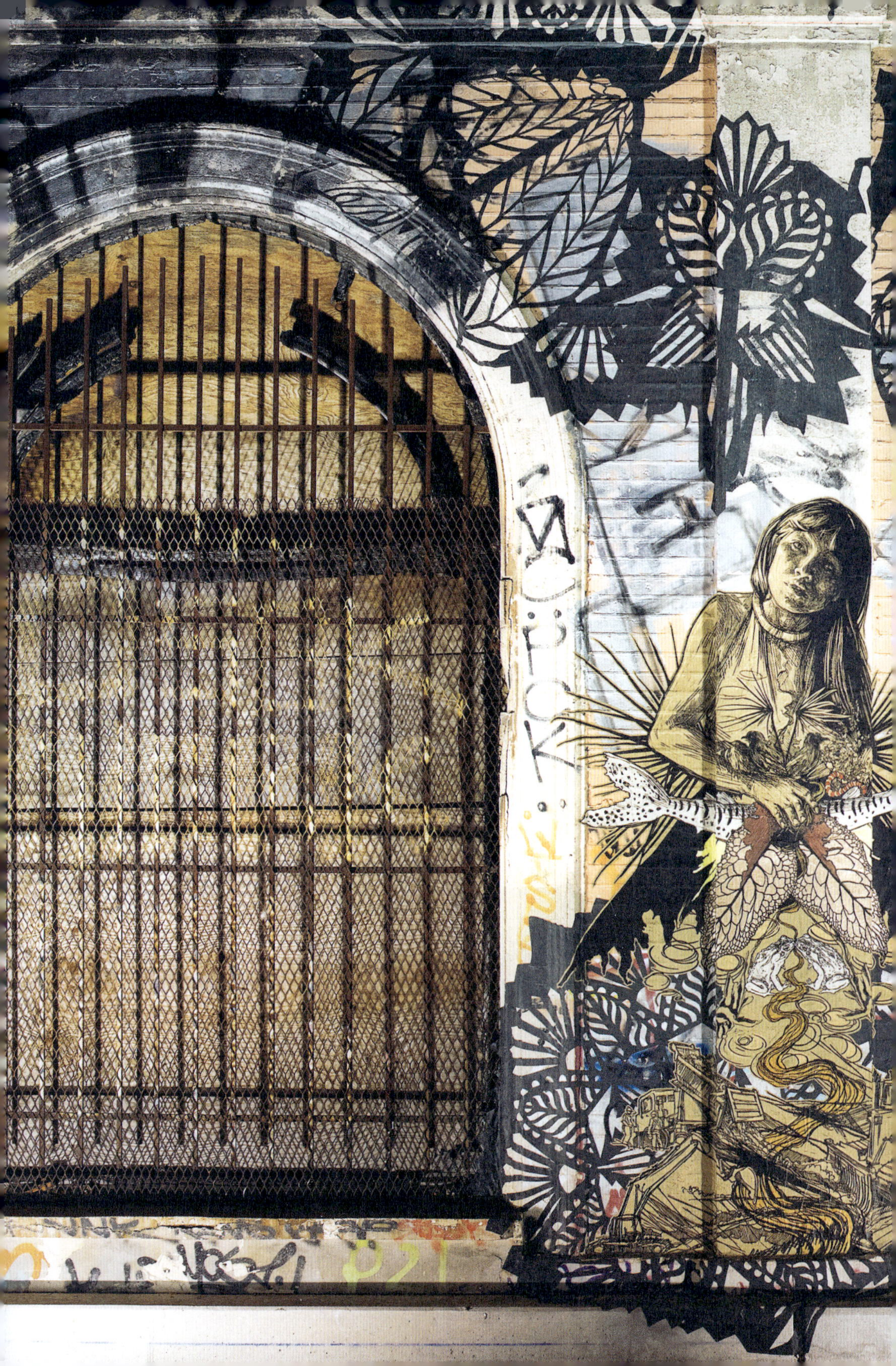

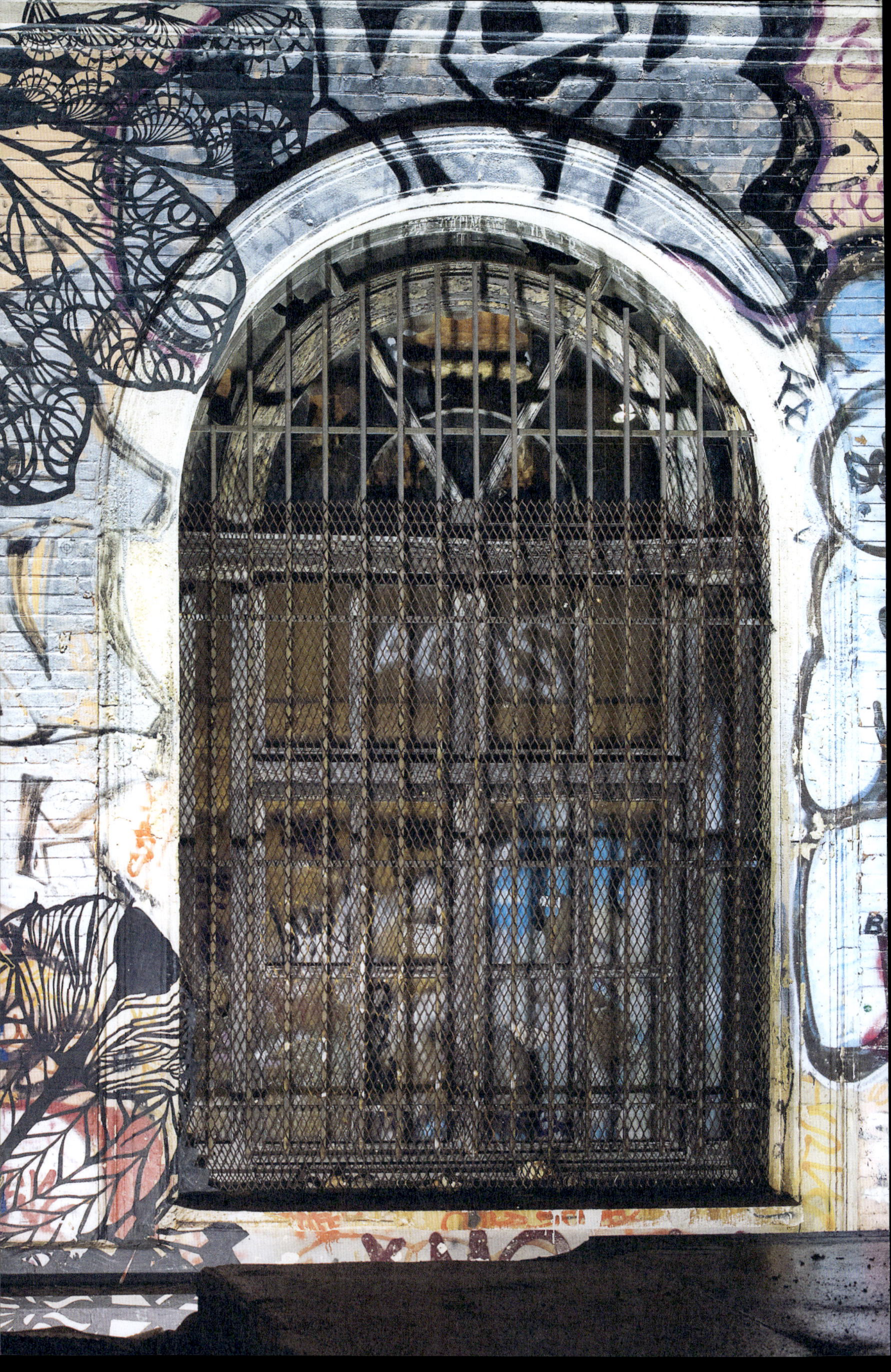

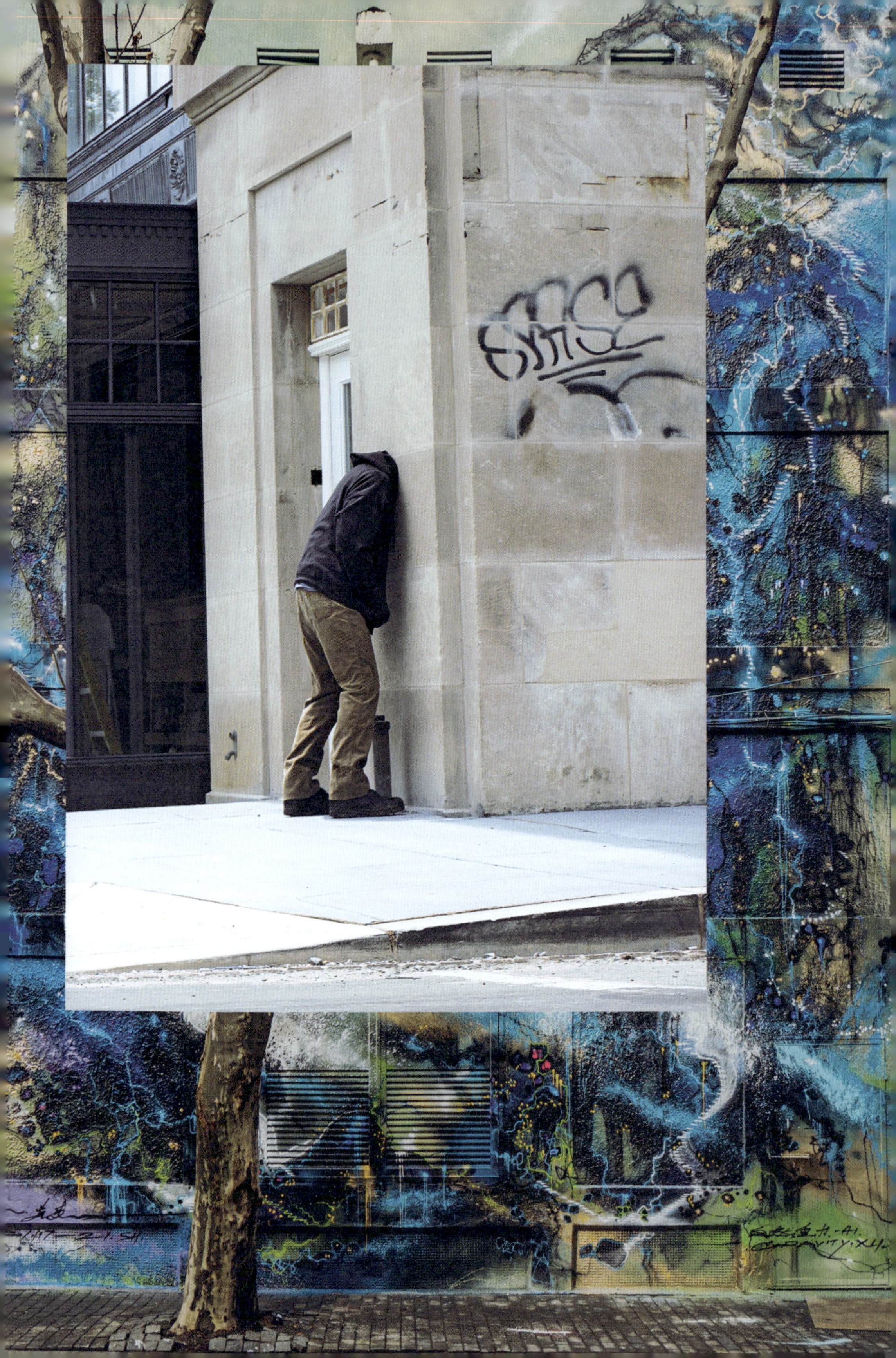

A PRACTICE INSCRIBED INTO THE HISTORY OF ART

Astonishing, the industry was still debating the question of whether or not Street Art belongs to contemporary art at the turn of the 2000s. Aside from the inevitable —and all too often unique— references to KEITH HARING and JEAN-MICHEL BASQUIAT (the guarantors of a recognised artistic lineage), a critical and more in-depth look at how the movement has evolved shows that its roots in the history of art lie much deeper.

Returning to art's roots

This reference to the history of art as we've come to expect it is perceptible in the work of many street artists, who often draw their inspiration from classical sources, not only in terms of subject matter, but even more frequently in terms of renewing old techniques. By way of example, INVADER's small ceramic tiles that are dotted all over cities echo the golden age of Roman mosaics, which were used extensively to decorate the floors and thresholds of patrician dwelling places.

For instance, Pompeii's House of the Tragic Poet greets visitors with a mosaic to the left of the entrance that depicts a huge tethered dog, with the inscription, "Cave canem" (Beware of the dog). The mosaic at the entrance of the Masons' House depicts a skull suspended from a *set square by a plumb line (masons' traditional tools) and bears the inscription* "Memento mori". With its skull and symbols of a beggar and a king, it is surprisingly contemporary, and perfectly in line with INVADER's favourite figures: Pac Man, Mario Bros...

MARK JENKINS, Washington DC, USA, 2006

Background image: CHEN YINGJIE, see p. 232

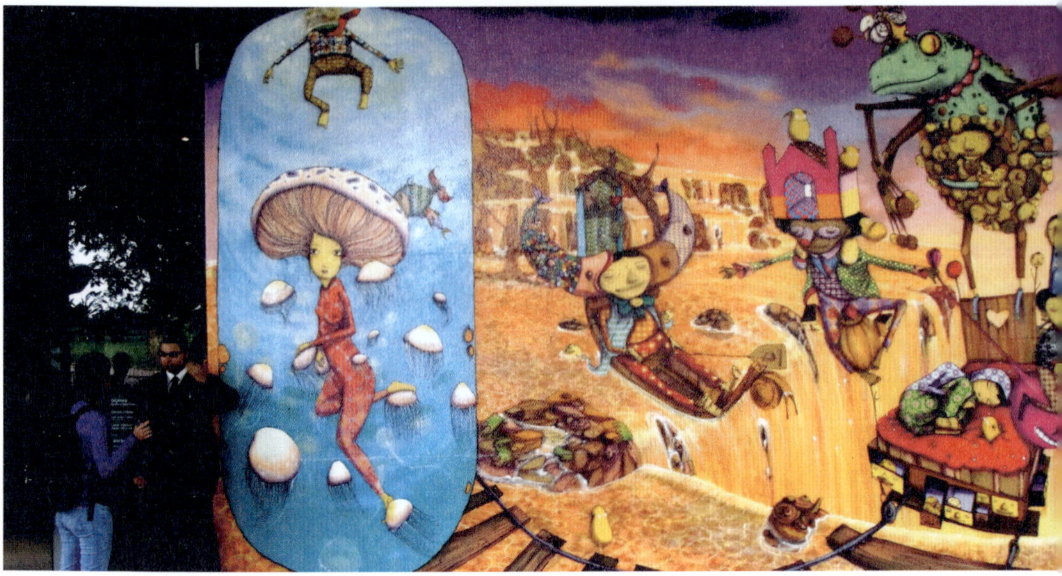

OS GÊMEOS, São Polo, Brazil, 2015

The *Tablinum* mosaic also offers an astonishing parallel between past and present. It portrays a complete scene. The bald Chorège, with his white beard and unfurled manuscript, gathers the actors together and has them rehearse for the theatre play. Similarly, in 2003, in his more complex, stage-sized works that replicate video game screens, INVADER also bears witness to the leisure activities of his time. By updating this decorative technique for today's tastes, he has given his work a historical perspective. The context here is no longer that of the palace or the noble residence, but that of the street: an essential living space for many passers-by.

The same relationship with art history can also be seen in the work of OS GÊMEOS, whose work is particularly reminiscent of that of Hieronymus Bosch: the same interwoven scenes, the same attention to detail, the same apocalyptic vision of the world where all kinds of misfortune accumulate and collide. In an aesthetic of chaos, this 15th century Flemish painter distinguishes himself as much by his immediately identifiable style as by the cynicism of his message. He abandons traditional iconography to paint humanity as corrupt, caught in the clutches of its own demons. Once devoid of this religious aspect, the works of the OS GÊMEOS, whose first solo exhibition took place in 2003, also appear to be based on a profusion of scenes and the questioning of an established order. Just like in Hieronymus Bosch's work, we find caricatured characters from an imaginary world. The phantasmagorical worlds of Bosch and Os Gêmeos serve as a scathing critique of society in their respective times. Several centuries apart, we can see the recurring expression of the same preoccupations: good, evil, vice, pain, suffering. All of these artists question humanity's responsibilities here on earth, and the practice of painting (in the case of Bosch) and mural frescoes (in the case of OS GÊMEOS) has undergone a definite revival.

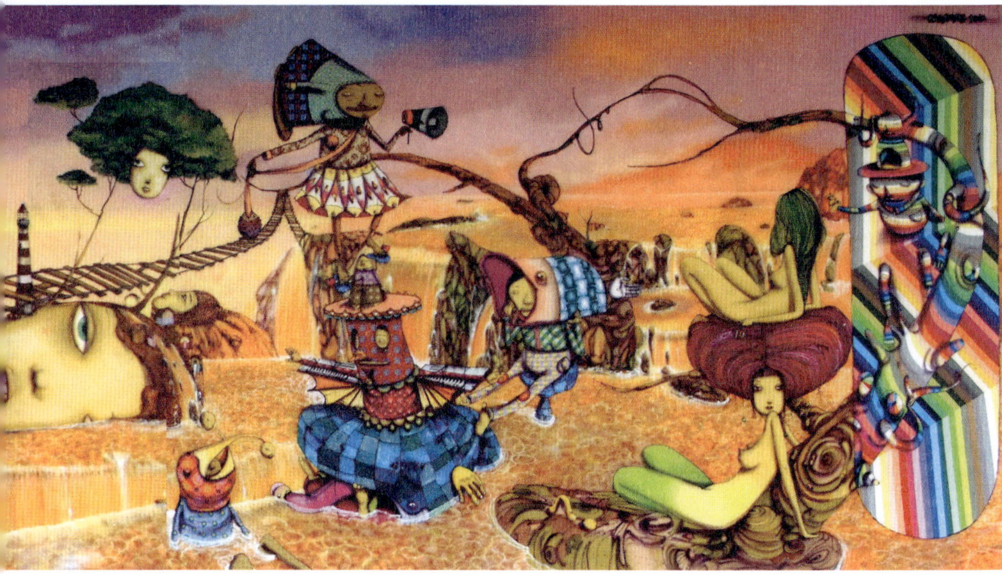

Through the symbolism and language they use, the two brothers are determined to speak out against the excesses of humanity. So much for staying in the background! The form is certainly not immune to comparisons. The art of Hieronymus Bosch is representative of a Gothic style that OS GÊMEOS strive to revive through the use of light tones, distinctive shapes, extremely delicate brushstrokes and specific use of materials. Moreover, the fact that Bosch was recognised as a "master" by the 20th century Surrealists also affiliates OS GÊMEOS, as if by ricochet, to this artistic movement.

The undeniable link that some street artists have with classical art is also found in the work of the best-known among them, BANKSY, even if it is to denounce its institutions. In 2005, the celebrated Briton managed to

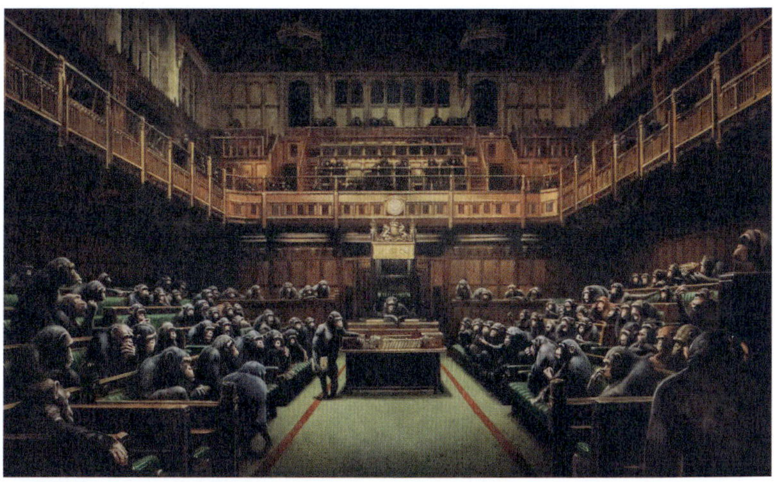

BANKSY, *Devolved Parliament* (or *Question Time*), 2009

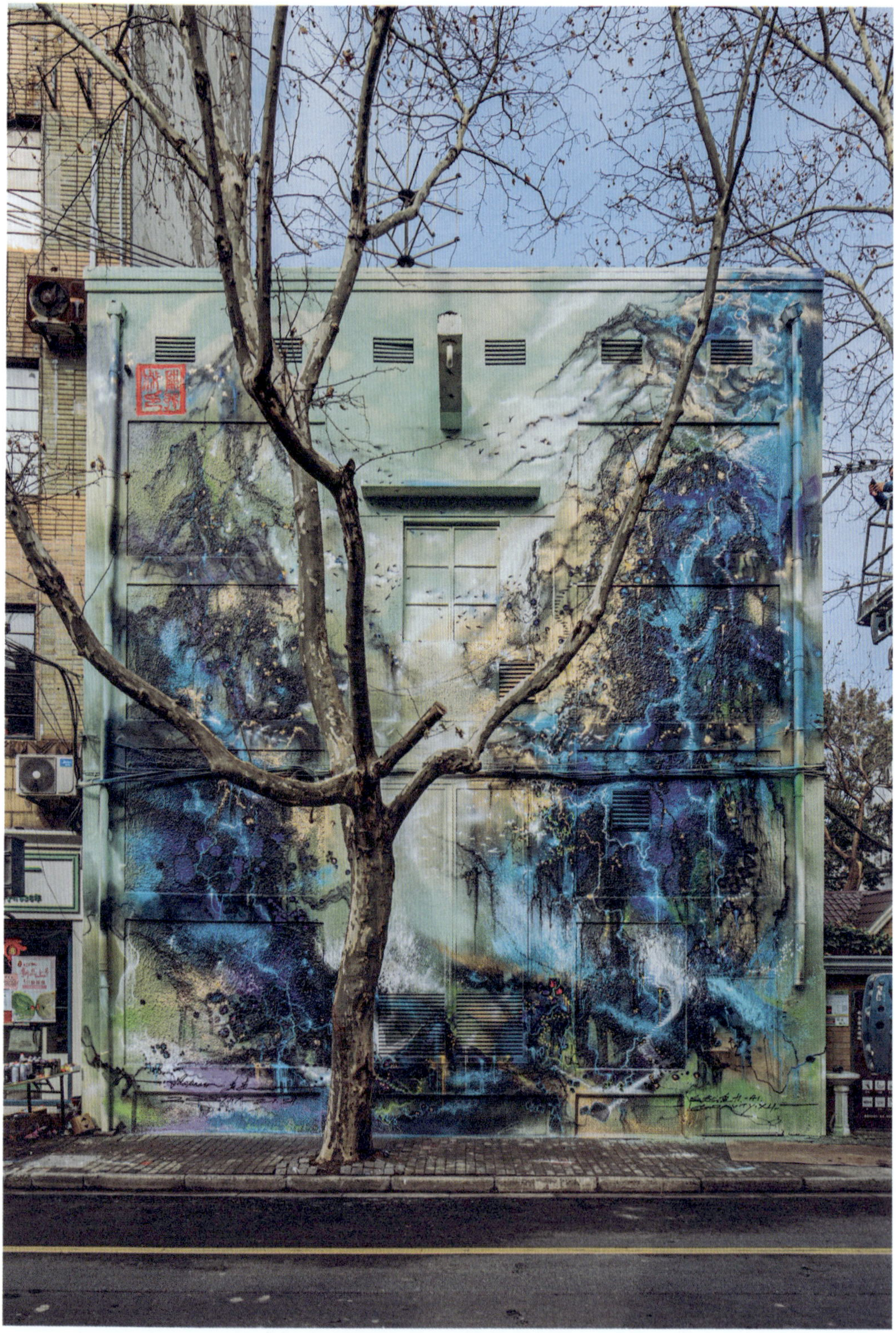

CHEN YINGJIE, *Gravity XLI*, *Nanchang Road Mural*, 10×9 m, Shanghai, 2021

gain access to some of the world's greatest museums —MoMa, Tate Gallery and the Louvre— to display his own works, which were adaptations of existing paintings, alongside the works of the great masters. And in 2009, he did it again in his home town: for the major exhibition of his work at the Bristol Museum, he created canvases that looked like classical oil paintings, but with distorted versions of the subject matter (apes in the Houses of Parliament, car wreckages in landscapes, and so on). For BANKSY, institutional picture rails are as good as urban façades when it comes to getting a message across.
This attitude towards classical art can also be seen in Asia. It is this very bridge that allows some Asian street artists to go further than simply reproducing old school New York graffiti. CHEN YINGJIE, aka Hua Tunan, born in 1991 in Foshan, China, is working to reconcile classical Chinese painting with contemporary practices. Being part of a referential tradition is not unknown to Asian artists, for whom art must avoid ruptures and respect the gradual evolution of practices - unlike the history of Western art, perhaps, which is marked by clear-cut revolutions. With this in mind, CHEN YINGJIE constantly seeks to preserve the precepts of classical painting while infusing them with urban energy and inspiration. The artist picks up his cans and sprays the paint onto the canvas in a choreography worthy of the greatest action painters[2]. Using jets of paint, aerosol sprays and subtle dabs, he progresses gradually from a composition that appears to be abstract to creating a classical Chinese landscape, for example, around which, as the artist himself shares, "you may feel like a dynamic and invisible breath of air is flowing (...). Then, you will also be able to perceive the breath of life, the power of nature, the battle of life, and also the gravely unbalanced relationship that humanity has with nature today".

[2] Action painting: an abstract painting technique that emphasises the gestures and expressions of the painter's impulses.

For CHEN YINGJIE, graffiti is an artistic performance that combines sensations, power and speed. After a lengthy experimentation phase, during which the artist practised and measured the impact of his gestures, he came to achieve a perfect mastery of this spray-painting technique. In addition to combining traditional Chinese ink practice with contemporary Western graffiti art, he also works in oil on canvas and mural painting. The diversity of the materials and places that CHEN YINGJIE chooses for his work means that he is constantly exploring the fruitful relationship that he patiently builds up between two artistic practices that would otherwise be difficult to reconcile. He created a unique style of Chinese graffiti and, because of this, was named one of the "25 Contemporary Chinese Artists You Need to Know" by American Complex magazine.

CHEN YINGJIE at work in his studio.
Courtesy of Chen Yingjie.

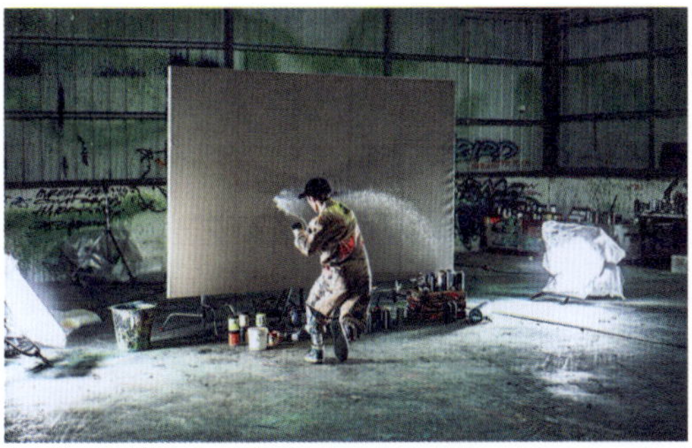

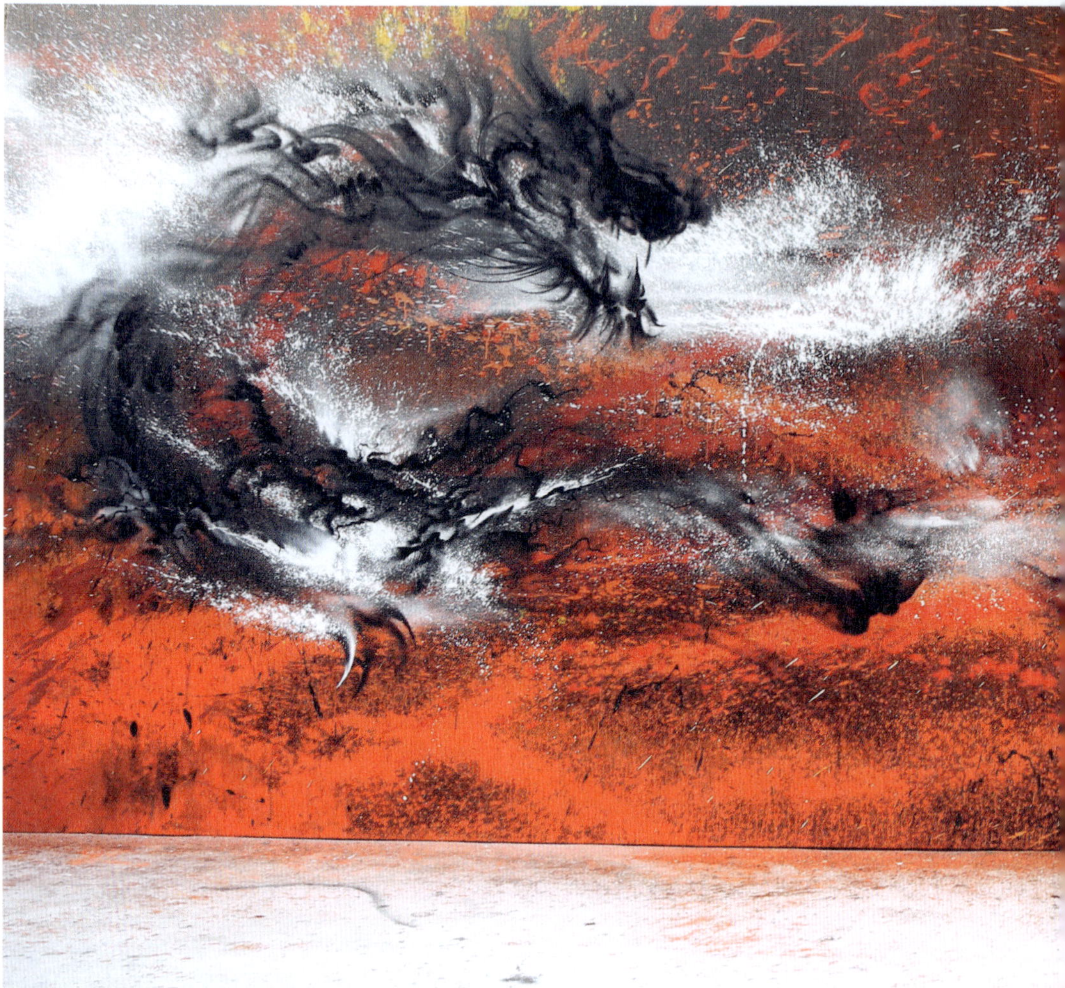

CHEN YINGJIE, *Red Dragon Traveling*, 3×8 m, 2014

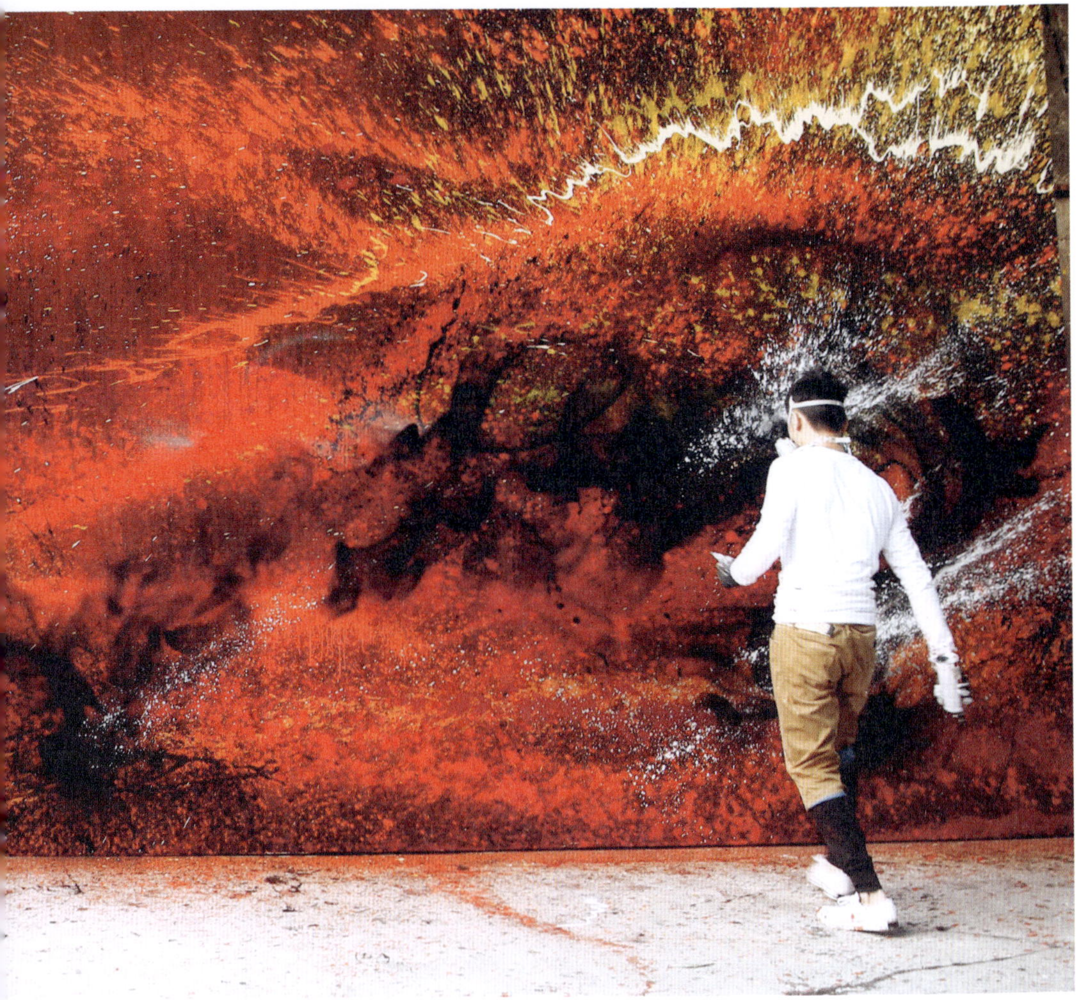

Resuming the thread of 20th century history

Conceptual Art, Land Art, Folk Art, Pop Art and Op Art are all movements that have defined the modernity of the 20th century. At the beginning of the 21st century, some of the most renowned specialists wondered what would rekindle the embers of the last century's myriad creative revolutions. How can we still speak of avant-garde or innovation today? How can we succumb to wonder, amazement and disconcertment when it comes to new artistic forms?

The more the practice of urban art grows, the more the connections with the various trends in the history of art are felt – not in order to plagiarise them, but to try to take up the thread of recognised practices and bring them into a new era, with today's techniques and audiences. From sculpture to Land Art and the revival of Optical Art, a number of Urban Art proponents are pursuing an intergenerational cultural dialogue.

While the innovative nature of most of the movements that swept through the 20th century is undeniable, it is nevertheless true that some of them have been frozen in their original era, as if, despite the passing of generations, the torch had not been carried on with any vigour. At a time when everything is speeding up, styles —as much in fashion as in art— seem to come and go without leaving any lasting trace.

Influenced not only by the great names in the history of art, but also by their own history and the environment in which they live, the new generations of urban artists are reinvesting a "classic" artistic heritage with unbridled creativity – in particular, by tackling new media. American artist MARK JENKINS (b. 1970), for example, is as much a conceptual sculptor as he is an urban artist. While he follows the long tradition of realist sculpture, he also pursues what he describes as a quasi-sociological approach by mounting his works in the street. From the realist tradition, which aims to unsettle and awaken the viewer, JENKINS cites inspirations such as Balthus (1908-2001) and Hans Bellmer (1902-1975). The way their work addresses the body takes different forms, but all of these share a disturbing incongruity that forces the passer-by to reflect upon the notion of the physical body in the context of the social body. There is something surreal about JENKINS' artwork. His faceless bodies in the city echo the figures and masks painted by Giorgio De Chirico (1888-1978). "Looking like a fool never killed anyone" is a phrase that suits some of the poses that the artist has his figures adopt. Behind each of them, the underlying critique of society is indeed profound, and in turn gives us food for thought about our relationship with the Other, the suicide rate in our societies, the impact of cultural standardisation and climate issues.

When asked why his figures are faceless, JENKINS invariably replies that it corresponds to the need to make his characters anonymous and therefore universal. References to the cultural lore of the faceless man can

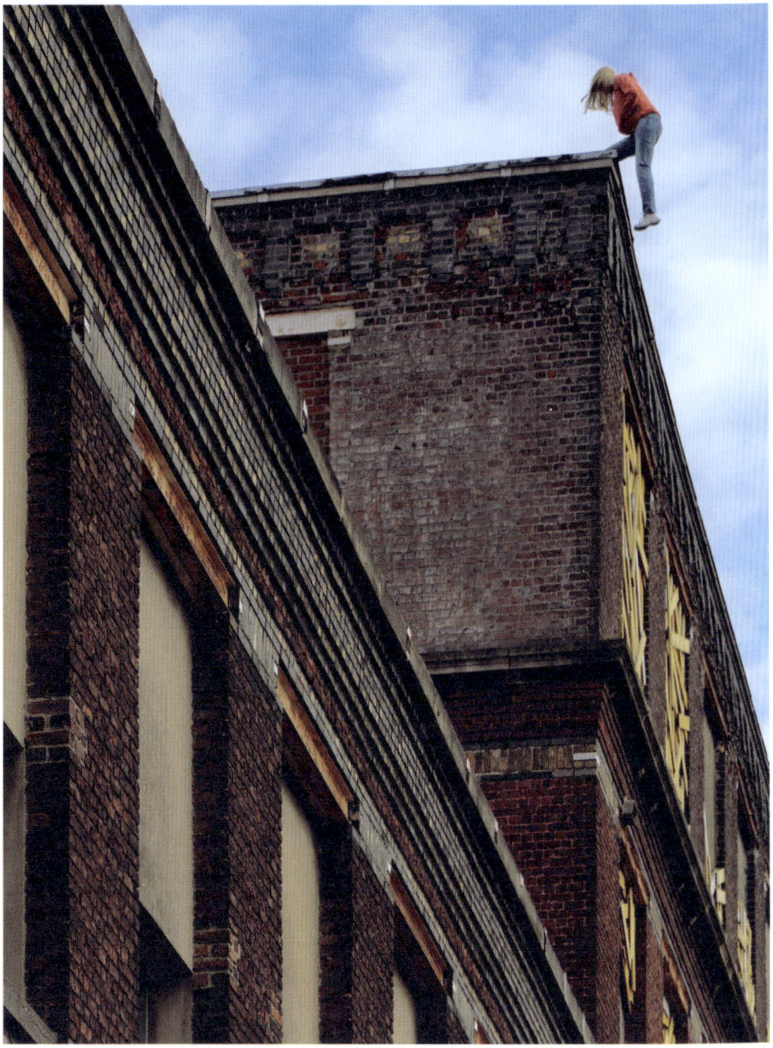

MARK JENKINS & SANDRA FERNANDEZ, *Step Up*, Roubaix 2022.
Photo © Maxime Dufour photographies

also be found in his work. Moreover, the question of doubt and disorder is key here. The spectator is invited to consider what the "anonymised" figure might signify. His art echoes a recurring preoccupation with contemporary culture, be it cinematic, with films such as The *Phantom of the Opera*, or more recently with *Daft Punk's* music: he wants to make people think, to provoke them rather than just describe what is going on.

"When confronted with a work by JENKINS, the urban stroller becomes aware of the need to interpret both the work itself and its place in a shared social environment. Indeed, the surprised pedestrian doesn't just think about the artist's work or what other passers-by might think. More deeply, they become aware of the need for a shared interpretation. They become aware of the interpretation itself in relation to Umberto Eco's idea of "open work" or Barthes' concept of "scriptable work"[3]. Like many of his predecessors with a penchant for this mode of expression, MARK JENKINS' realism is disturbing, as well as socially and artistically unique. Incongruity is nothing new. In the mid-1990s, Paul McCarthy (American sculptor and performer, born in 1945) and his Tomato Head explored the relationship between consumerism, contemporary culture and a certain form of innocence. "Certain aspects of Mark Jenkins' approach are reminiscent of the work of Maurizio Cattelan or Ron Mueck. But unlike Robert Gober, Cattelan and Mueck, Jenkins is less known for his museum pieces and more for his surprising and facetious interventions, which he situates in urban settings".[4] Through his work, JENKINS therefore seeks to disrupt the routine of the passerby while being sensitive to the effect it has on them. The artist stands back and observes the reactions, police involvement and consequences that the simple act of leaving a work of art in the street can bring about.

3-4 Ronald Shusterman: "Singularities in the Streets: Bodies, Incongruity and the Metaethical Effect" in *The Journal of Somaesthetics* Volume 4, Issue 1 (2018)

Among the artists working on the borderline between urban art and other modern art practices, French artist SAYPE also stands out. Born in 1989, SAYPE began his career in graffiti, under this pseudonym formed by the contraction of "Say" and "Peace". He now combines Street Art and Land Art, creating large-scale installations on the ground outside (grass, earth, sand, and so on). Just as MARK JENKINS uses the codes of conceptual sculpture, SAYPE revives the tradition of Land Art, an artistic movement that emerged in the 1960s and was driven by artists who wanted to get art out of the galleries and museums.

As part of a new generation of urban artists seeking a more innovative, visible and socially conscious approach, he specialises in eco-friendly urban art that reveals its full potential from the sky. SAYPE has invented a biodegradable paint that he applies to thousands of square metres of grass and other natural spaces in France and around the world, in places such as Le Champ-de-Mars in Paris and Venice's canals. His works are exposed to the elements until they erode naturally, something that adds a significant poetic layer to his practice. This ephemeral aspect is a common feature of many works of urban art, which by their very nature are inevitably destined to disappear.

The rekindling of 20th century artistic trends can be seen as a continuation of a creative dialogue that carries with it a wide range of possibilities. As such, urban artists propose taking a new approach to the modern and contemporary chapters of art, in order to give them renewed vitality. Trends such as Pop Art have also been given fresh momentum. American duo FAILE, made up of Patrick McNeil (born in 1975) and Patrick Miller (born in 1976), have a similar approach to Pop Art and Folk Art. Deconstructing the popular imagery that surrounds them, they rebuild it piece by piece like collages reminiscent of those by Kurt Schwitters (1887-1948), heir to Bauhaus, or the American folk patchwork quilt.

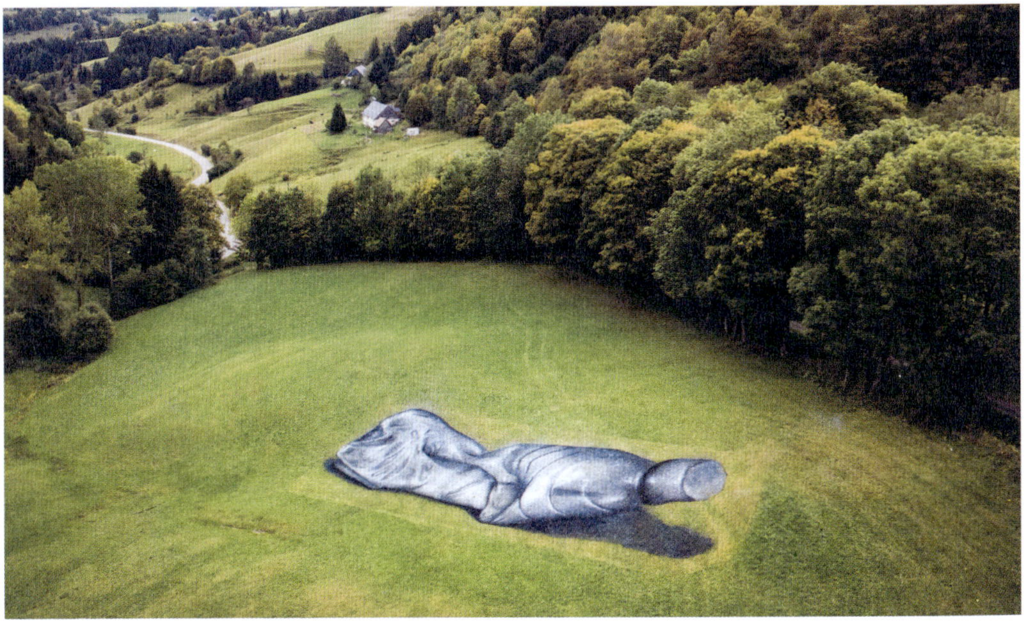

SAYPE, *Trash*, 2019, biodegradable paint on grass, 1,000m², Les Bagenelles, France

Both artists draw inspiration from the visual world of their youth, which was dominated by 80s comics, Hollywood films, cowboy movies, children's stories, advertising imagery and events in recent US history. The duo cut up and manipulate fragments of this vast iconography, transforming and combining them in a thousand different ways. As though playing with a modular construction game, they arrange, diffract and recompose images, text and patterns, boldly experimenting with temporal and contextual telescoping. This approach is reminiscent of collage art, to which both artists ascribe; through their use of contrasts, they present a distorted reflection of American pop culture and shed light on the mechanisms, archetypes and structures at work in our popular representations.

FAILE pays close attention to how the elements overlap. The material itself matters little. Their pieces, which are often monumental and sometimes created in urban spaces, can be painted, use a mixture of fabrics and copper plating, or be made of wood or ceramic tiles. Their creations are colour-saturated iconographic representations of everyday life, in a similar vein to Andy Warhol's works.

In 2008, FAILE was included in the selection of artists exhibited on the façade of the Tate Modern (along with JR, SIXEART, BLU, NUNCA and OS GÊMEOS) for the Street Art exhibition. Taking the form of a collage of torn paper, their monumental work depicts a native American surrounded by objects that are meant to represent him. These observations are part of FAILE's reflections on the nature of objects, and physicality in both digital and physical space. As the artists themselves have said: "This perspective transforms the way we look at artworks. We see a greater physical dimension beyond a single image or a tapestry of images on the same plane. Our work blurs the lines between the worlds of 2D and 3D.

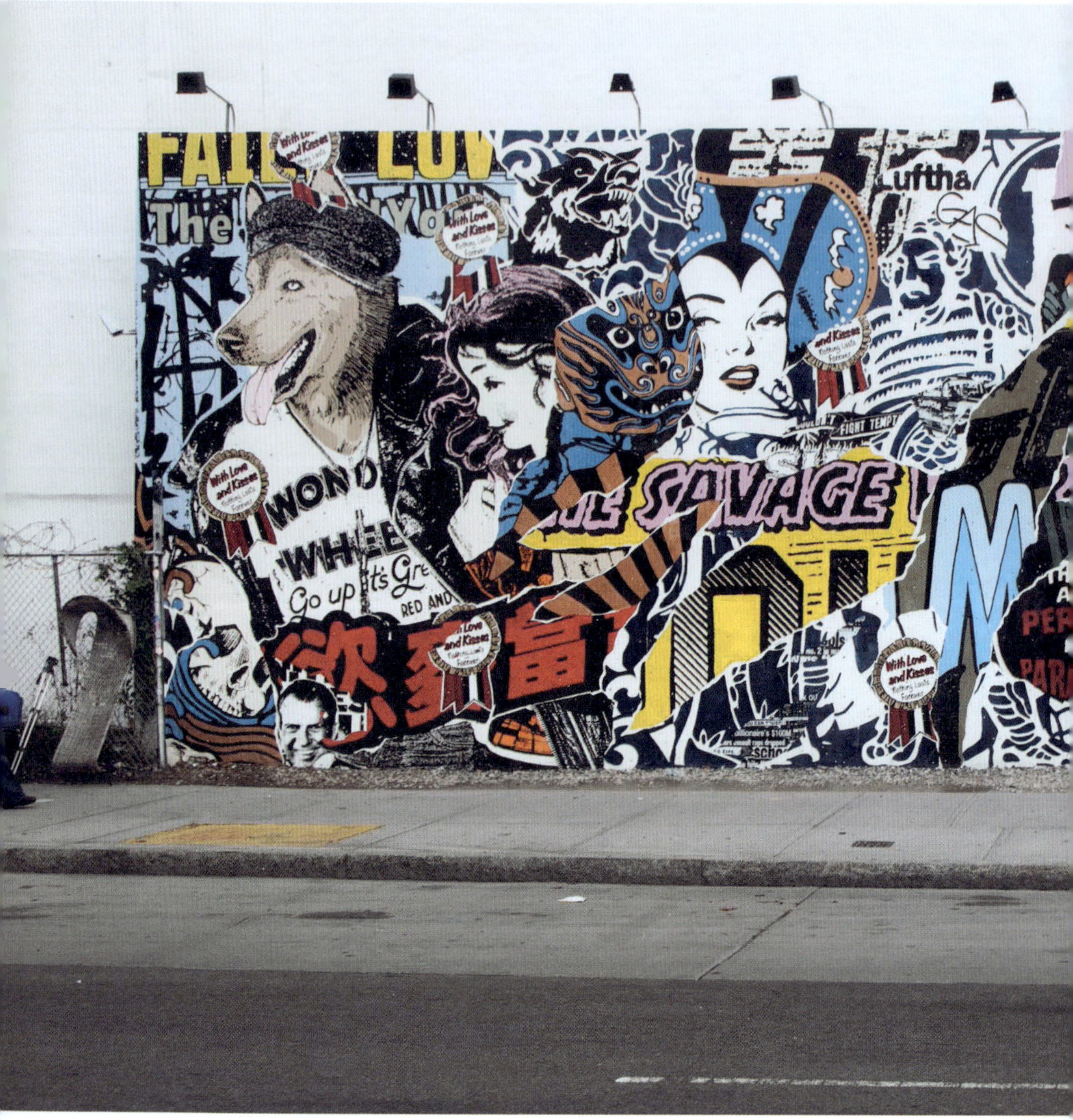

FAILE, *Houston & Bowery*, New York, 2011

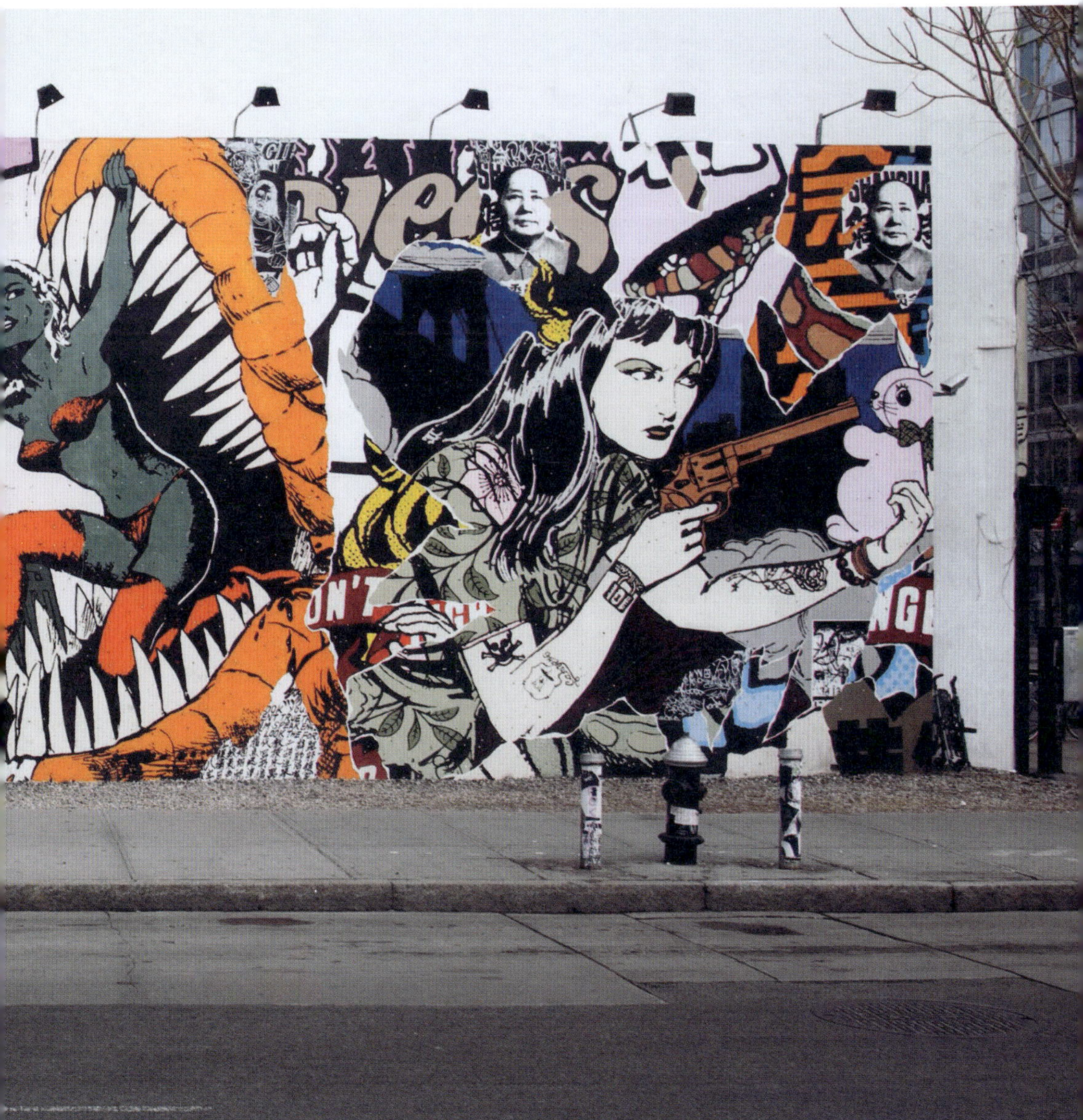

It's about reconsidering our perspective as both creator and spectator, and appreciating the physical space captured in the frame, as opposed to the space experienced in each moment." This piece is made up of contrasting superimposed images, and sits somewhere between harshness and gentleness. Characters from graphic novels collide with colours and textures in an undulating mix of form and abstraction.

In the vein of Pop Art, Brian Donnelly (alias KAWS, born 1974 in Jersey City) also defends popular art by producing icons that are accessible to all, and evoking —as does FAILE— emblematic characters from television culture. In his early days (the 1990s) KAWS was particularly inspired by graffiti culture and skateboarding. He started off tagging the letters of his pseudonym in colour on bus shelter posters. Then, a distinctive style began to take shape with the appearance of his iconic Skully: a pirate's skull, with crossbones protruding like ears and crosses for eyes. He often hijacks major brands. Advertising posters selling beauty and wealth are embellished with the artist's skull, allowing him to reveal the falsity and illusion of these campaigns. Gradually, this emblem has grown in size and length. The painted figure coils like a snake between the limbs of the models in the posters.
KAWS' work makes a clear reference to consumer society. Everyday objects are transformed into veritable works of art, making his work easily accessible. Fascinated by Japanese culture and art, he headed out to Tokyo. From this journey came a series of paintings called Package Paintings, featuring cartoon figures wrapped in plastic film. In keeping with the idea of art rooted in everyday life, KAWS also explores other artistic media. His universe is developing everywhere we look. He has set up a shop, a kind of pop-up store like Warhol in his time, ironically named *Original Fake*. The Chum, Skully, and Companion are reproduced in an infinite number of ways, with the only constraint being the artist's imagination. These characters and designs can be found on T-shirts, trainers, sweatshirts, scarves and even keyrings and bath mats. Through merchandising, KAWS directly mixes art with consumer goods; he is no longer just an artist or an image creator, but a creator of everyday objects.
Exploring all existing territories, urban artists leave no chapter of their work uncharted. After Pop Art, it is research into Optical Art, or Op'Art (which began in the 1960s), that is now being revived. Making use of optical illusions, vibratory ripples, and strong chromatic contrasts, this artistic movement offers new visual experiences. One of its most prominent protagonists, Victor Vasarely (1906-1997), often spoke of his desire to make his art as accessible and visible as possible to people in all spheres of society, from the world of fashion, all the way through to advertising and architecture.
Spanish artist FELIPE PANTONE (born in 1986) is a worthy heir of this artistic movement. He prides himself on accuracy and rationality, and makes use of recurring forms that are like a nomenclature, a periodic table, or even the building bricks of a code that can be combined ad infinitum, in an evolutionary movement where the artist introduces breaks, disruptions, or changes in scale – something he calls "jumps in space".

Patone's work consists of controlled chaos that serves as a representation of the world in the digital age. In doing so, he invents a pictorial language that strives to capture the dynamism and versatility of this digital reality that has become all of ours. Quite literally, one could say that PANTONE paints the internet.
Claiming to be a descendant of Carlos Cruz-Diez (1923-2019), a champion of kinetic art, he has made numerous projects in the public space as part of his drive to reach as many people as possible, and has also applied his studio work to a wide variety of substrates: building façades, shopping centres, walls, sports cars, motorbikes, barges, and so on.

Art critic Juan Bautista Peiró writes: "The 20th century is no longer our century, and even less so that of the younger generations of artists born in its slipstream (...) We must look at the kinetic excesses of Víctor Vasarely, Jesús Rafael Soto, Carlos Cruz Díez and Eusebio Sempere, which Pantone has radically transformed in an original, two-fold way, by revisiting their aesthetic roots and giving them their own unique and unmistakable personality. It is paradigmatic that Pantone should appropriate and update one of the most characteristic structures of modernity. From this point of view, prefixes (ultra, plus...) that insist on going beyond that which is established, known and accepted are especially consistent with this."
By creating monumental works of optical art on the façades of buildings all over the world, FELIPE PANTONE is undeniably renewing the language of urban art through the use of complex grids. In dialogue with subjects such as the speed of communication, the internet and digital creation, the artist offers visual experiences in giant format.

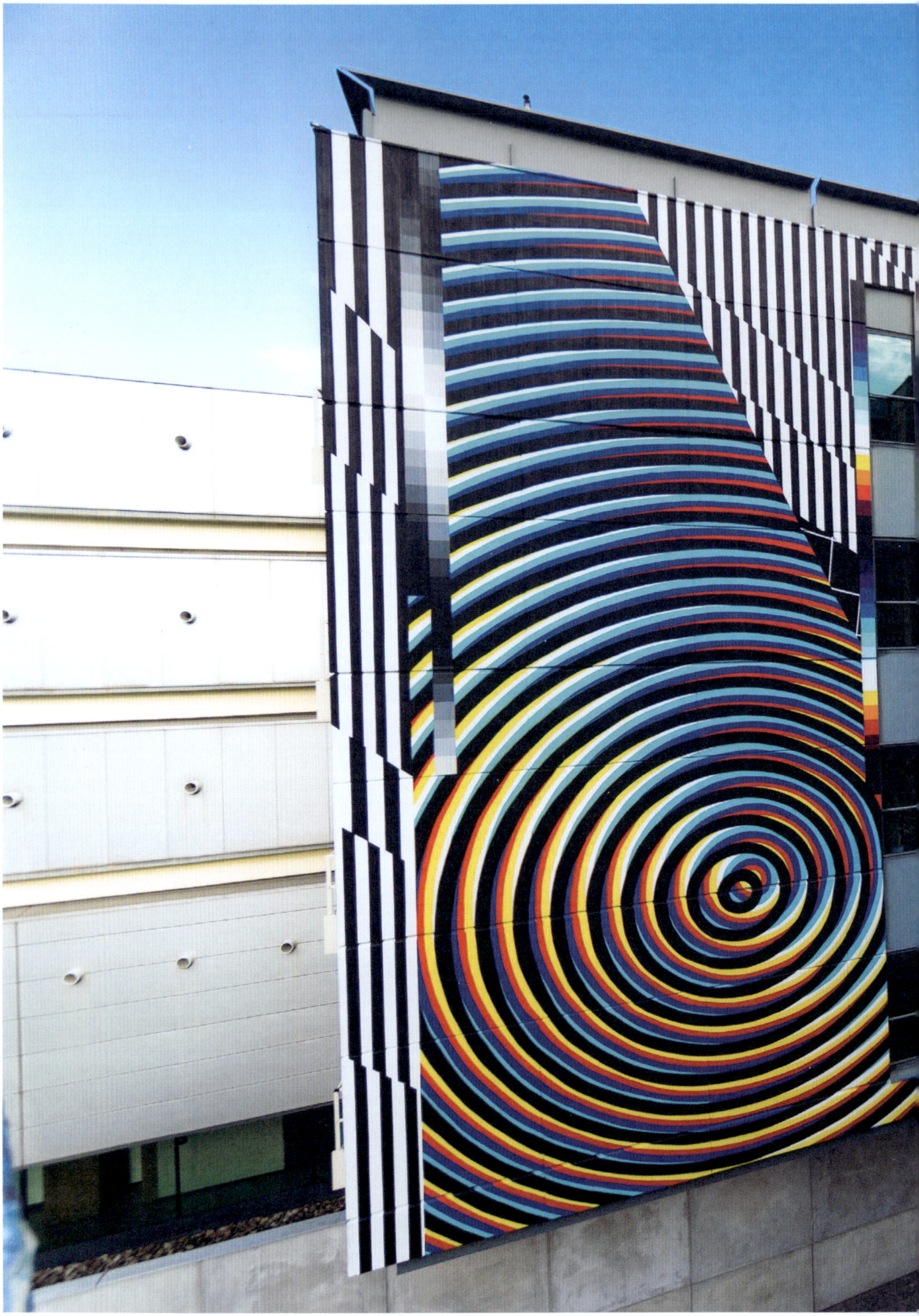

FELIPE PANTONE, *Optichromie FNLBRD*, Fuenlabrada, Madrid, 2019. Photo © FPSTUDIO

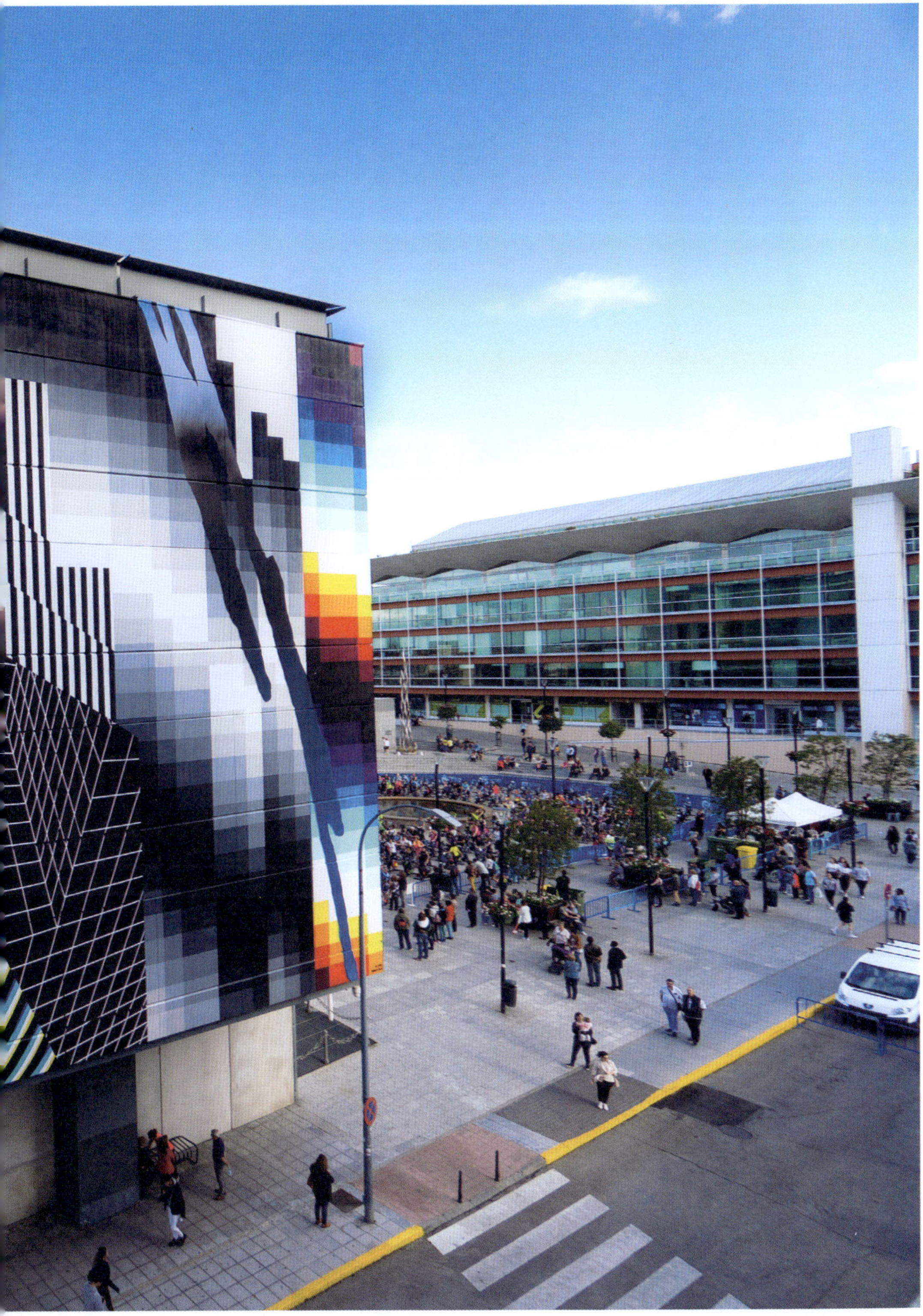

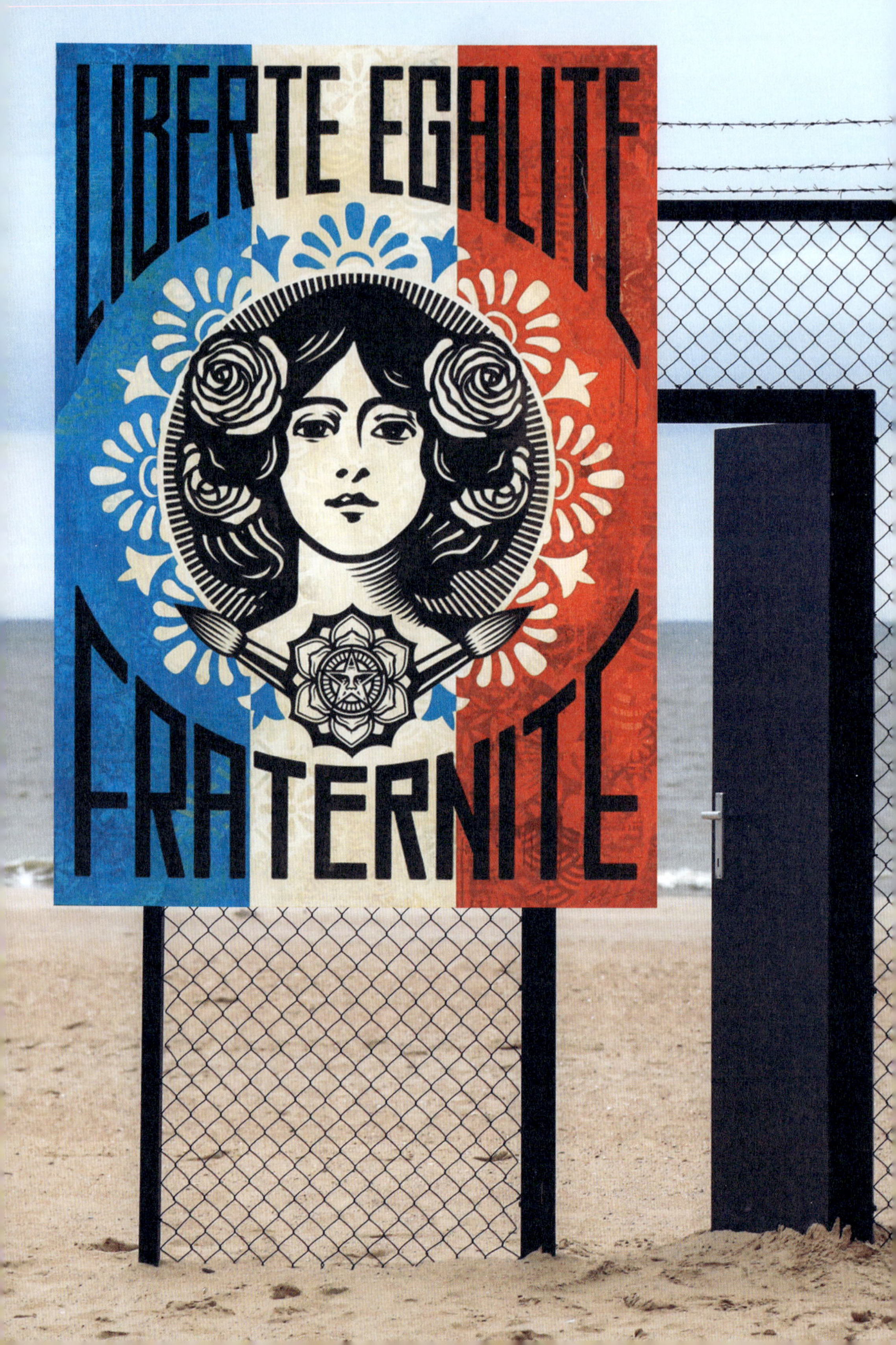
LIBERTE EGALITE
FRATERNITE

ARTISTS' SOCIAL ENGAGEMENT AND IMPACT ON SOCIETY

Seen from a historical perspective, graffiti and Street Art underwent a fundamental revolution with the advent of messaging in the 1990s. Since then, the movement has increasingly taken on a socially conscious stance, and its urban presence has inevitably made it political.
In the broader sense of civilisation or *politikos*, it relates to the organisation or management of the city (Greek: *polis*, Latin: *civitas*). The movement can therefore play an important role in people's lives if it is seen as a "political" art form, something that addresses subjects that concern us all and initiates a form of reflection, if not dialogue.
Sensitive to the world around them, every artist responds in their own way to the major debates that run through our societies. Their own commitments (multiple, in some cases) lead them to take sides on fundamental issues such as ecology, migration, diversity and emancipation, with their work as a means of expression.

The beginnings of a socially-concious art form

SHEPARD FAIREY aka OBEY, *Liberté, Égalité, Fraternité*, stencil, spray paint and collage, 183×132 cm, 2018, private collection

Background image: *Icy&Sot*, Open Door, 2019

Although, strictly speaking, they are not part of the urban art movement, activists GUERRILLA GIRLS are known for their subversive poster art. Hijacking the codes of advertising to call for the "visual disobedience" advocated by SHEPARD FAIREY is one way of speaking the visual language of the time.

Founded in 1985 in New York, the GUERRILLA GIRLS collective was born out of a reaction to conservative America in the Reagan years (1981-1989). One approach the group uses is the technique of hijacking advertising space. Their first project, in 1989, was a poster campaign that highlighted the fact that "less than 5% of the artists in the Modern Art sections [at the Metropolitan Museum] are women, but 85% of the nudes are female". Over time, their denunciation of inequalities in the representation of women in museums broadened to include other fields, such as the film industry. Fifteen years after their first action, the collective updated the stats on their poster, noting that no significant change had been achieved.

At the same time, BARBARA KRUGER, an icon of conceptual art in the second half of the 20th century, would also hijack advertising images to combat social stereotypes. These would be large-format works that combined black and white press photographs with shock slogans, written in white print on a red background.

These so-called "political" artists have paved the way for urban artists. Since the latter work in public spaces, nothing is more natural to them than to co-opt the advertising spaces dotted around the city, and to challenge their messages and legitimacy.

Image theft

At the dawn of the 2000s, urban artists drew undeniable strength from the assertion of their convictions. Heir to the visual warfare waged by the GUERRILLA GIRLS, SHEPARD FAIREY began theorising his approach in 1990 with his manifesto, which was described as a "social and psychological explanation". By developing his practice of poster collage, he asserts his desire to raise public consciousness. Hijacking the visual elements of propaganda to assert "Make Art, Not War", he then turns the spotlight towards

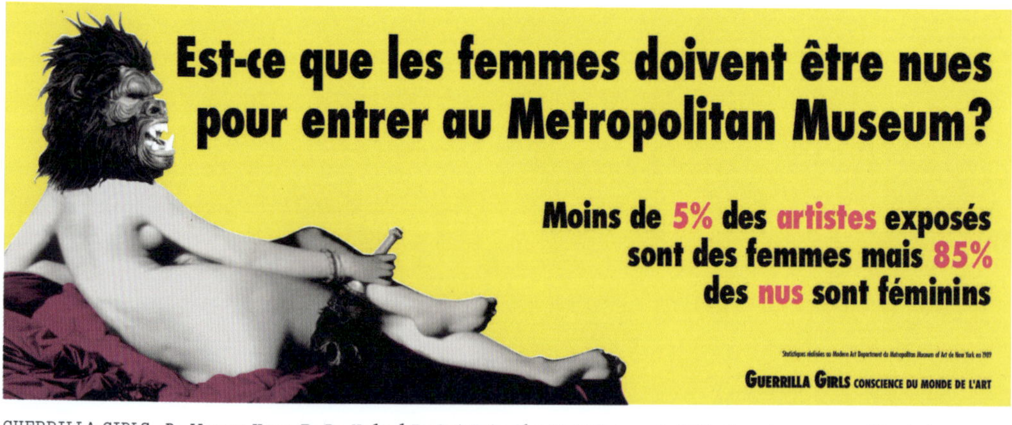

GUERRILLA GIRLS, *Do Women Have To Be Naked To Get Into The Met Museum?*, 1989. Courtesy guerrillagirls.com

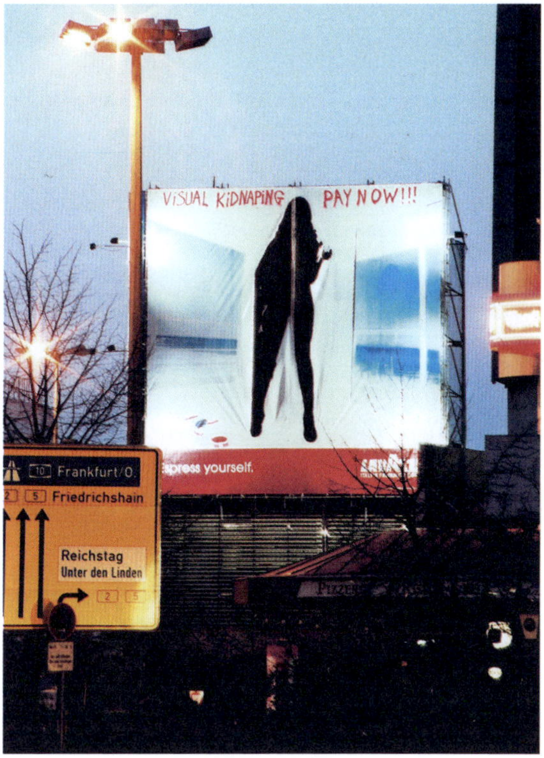

ZEVS, *Visual kidnapping*, Berlin, 2002

revolutionary women before openly attacking the bellicose policies of US President George W. Bush. His posters would carry slogans such as "Obey Bush Hug Bombs", 2004 or depict people in gas masks to symbolise "The New World Odor", 2004 in reaction to the Second Gulf War being motivated by issues related to oil exploitation. Over time, the artist has become increasingly engaged in specific causes, publishing new screen prints every year in support of issues such as migrants' rights, women's rights, the importance of voting or, more broadly, the climate emergency. In 2015, he was invited by COP21 to produce an emblematic piece in the shape of a terrestrial globe suspended from the Eiffel Tower in Paris.

The omnipresence of advertising images in our cities, and more specifically, the way in which advertising appropriates women's bodies, turning them into accessories in the service of product sales, is also a source of concern for artist ZEVS. One night in 2002, he cut out the model posing for the Lavazza coffee promotion from a huge advertising tarpaulin in Berlin. Above the gaping hole in the poster, he writes, "Visual Kidnapping – Pay Now!", challenging the stereotypical way in which women are viewed and used. Following this project, ZEVS began a new series in 2006. He paints logos and lets the excess paint drip down onto the wall, prompting a reflection on the omnipresence of brands. Later, in the context of climate change, the artist would continue this series by "liquidating" the brand names of oil companies such as Total, Exxon, Shell, and others.

Weaving the social fabric

The social engagement of these artists is gradually becoming part of a broader approach that touches on all aspects of society. Many of them raise questions about the social contract in a more general sense. In 2011, on winning the TED[5] Prize and in response to the question "Can art change the world?", JR launched his participatory project Inside Out. The platform helps campaigners to defend their cause by carrying out poster drives. Each group is invited to put up posters in a public space that bear the portrait of all the people defending the same cause. JR provides printed portraits to anyone who has a cause to defend, on request. To date, nearly 450,000 portraits have been displayed in 138 countries.

5 The TED Prize is awarded in the United States every year from 2005 to 2018. It originated in the TED conferences, which are broadcast around the world and focus on innovative ways of looking to the future. Each winner is asked to share an inspiring, impact-driven idea that could change the world. Past winners have included the likes of Bono from U2 (2005), Bill Clinton (2008) and artist JR (2011).

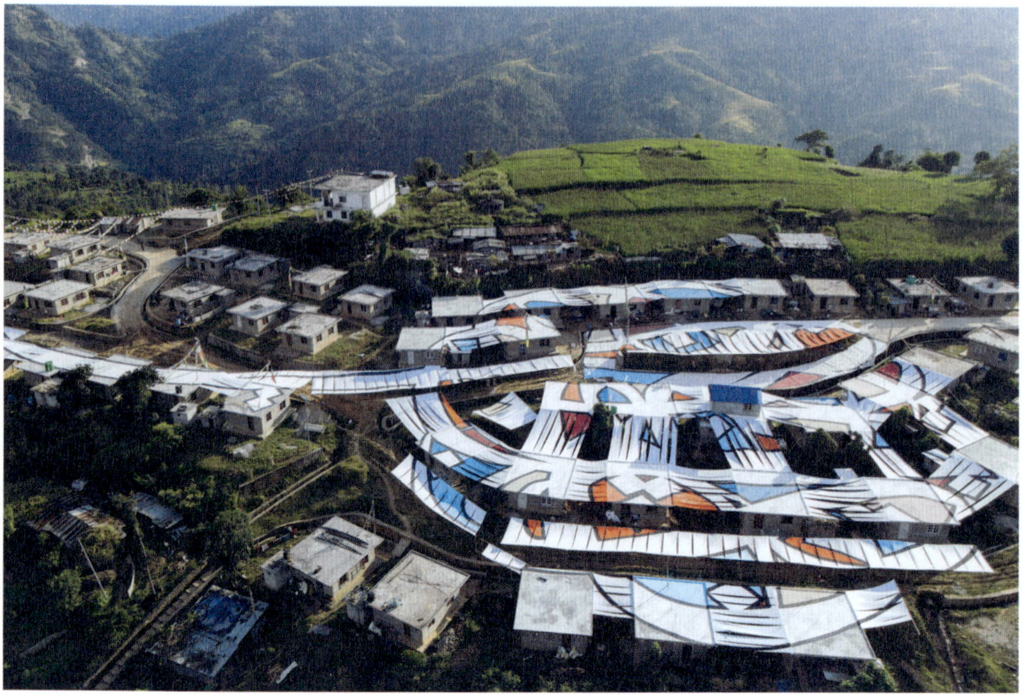

EL SEED, *Like Her*, Népal, 2021

JR's approach is based on a desire to draw attention to issues that resonate around the world. In 2017, for example, after three months of preparation, he installed an ephemeral work of art in Tecate, on the Mexican side of the border between Mexico and the United States. The piece depicts a Mexican child, Kikito, looking over the wall that separates the two countries. For the artist, "it's about getting people to talk, to think. I don't have the answer, what I want is to hear what people have to say about the artwork". Ever sensitive to the plight of those who are often overlooked, in 2019 JR convinced the American prison authorities to allow him to carry out a project in a prison environment. He would spend several weeks in the Tehachapi maximum-security prison in California, creating a participatory work of art that included recordings of the prisoners, allowing their stories to transcend the walls and raise questions about the subject of rehabilitation.

Concern for the world's forgotten occupies the minds of many urban artists. With a desire to build bridges around the world, Franco-Tunisian artist EL SEED strives to give a voice to the various communities in which he works. He uses Arabic calligraphy and his own style of graffiti featuring elaborate typography. In 2016, he would pay an enormous tribute to the 65,000-strong Coptic community that collects and recycles the Egyptian capital's litter by hand. His collaborative work Perception is displayed on almost fifty buildings in the derelict Manshiyat Nasser district in east Cairo, and uses a clever anamorphosis to reveal a reference to the wisdom of Athanasius of Alexandria: "Anyone who wants to see the sunlight clearly must first wipe their eyes." In this way, the artist "shines a light" on this community of "litter pickers" who are all too often forgotten, discredited, and even ostracised.

In 2019, EL SEED would unveil a new project in the small Nepalese village of Giranchaur, three hours from Kathmandu, which was devastated by the 2015 earthquake. Having been trained in construction work or the production of earthquake-resistant bricks, a number of local women played a key role in rebuilding a society that had suffered so much damage. As a tribute to their efforts, EL SEED went on site to create a collaborative work with twelve women from the village. Linking each house together, his giant artwork connects the stories of each protagonist and explores the theme of their empowerment. "The idea behind 'Like Her' is to celebrate the women of this remote community that has been devastated by the earthquake, and to shed light on the issues they face —as women all over the world do— while sharing their beautiful stories of wisdom, strength and resilience", says EL SEED.

Humanitarian activism is probably as important to the American street artist SWOON than her artistic practice, if not more so. In each of her creations, we can see her concern for others: passing down stories, extending a helping hand, and organising mutual aid are at the heart of her work. Her activism has also led her to use her creations to tell the stories of men and women who, like her, have faced hardship in their lives. Archetypal characters are classic features in SWOON's work. *Dawn and Gemma* symbolises both motherhood and the artist's complex relationship with her own mother. Alison, meanwhile, is a nod to Vermeer's *The Lacemaker*, and pays tribute to weavers and the guardians of our stories. These two pieces have been the subject of monumental murals in Berlin and New Haven in the United States.

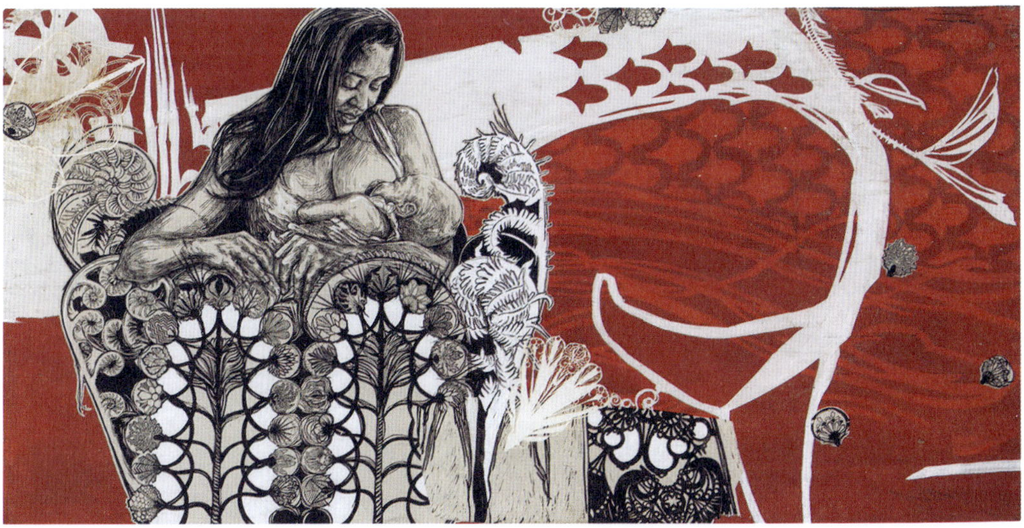

SWOON, *Dawn and Gemma*, 2014

Numerous artists shed much-needed light on those who are left behind in our societies, those who nonetheless carry within them the answers to the many challenges we face today and will face in the future. It's not so much the art or the artist that changes the world here, but the people who are depicted: these souls who, through their values, resilience and determination, can inspire others and contribute to improving our societies.

Addressing the world's crises

Artists working in public spaces are, by necessity, in direct contact with the physical environment in which they work: it is something they must always contend or even play with. By its very nature, therefore, Urban Art is eminently contextual. Today, however, this context is no longer just an aesthetic backdrop, a simple substrate; rather, it is understood in the broadest sense and also relates to the political and societal realities of the time. Each work of art that is displayed in a particular place interacts with its environment, says something about the issues of the time, and prompts us to ask questions.

Born in 1970, American artist MARK JENKINS has been developing a technique since 2003 that involves moulding shapes out of adhesive tape (usually bodies), which he then adorns with clothes and wigs, and installs them in various public spaces. He was joined two years later by SANDRA FERNANDEZ, with whom he now works as a duo. Since then, their works have been exhibited around the world. "For me, a work of art must first and foremost be a question," says MARK JENKINS. It's a question that the two artists like to address to the general populace by installing their sculptures in the public arena. For them, the street is never just a place to exhibit art, rather, it is a space where events can be staged. Their work is a combination of sculpture, installation, performance and social experimentation. MARK JENKINS and SANDRA FERNANDEZ have come to realise that no matter how artistic a sculpture may be, it is never just an inert object. Rather, it is an object that can modify the space around it and interact with its onlookers. To this end, this artist duo have created some strikingly realistic humanoid sculptures. For instance, in 2018, his mannequins were installed on the streets of London as a way to draw attention to suicide prevention. Disturbing, often arousing indignation or fear, these urban sculptures rarely leave anyone indifferent.

Drawing on their own life experiences, some artists take advantage of the wide exposure they get on the street to raise awareness of issues such as migration. For example, two Iranian brothers, Saman and Sasan Oskouei, alias ICY & SOT, born in 1985 and 1991 respectively, began to make a name for themselves in the streets of the northern Iranian town of Tabriz in the early 2000s. Since the stencils of their early years, the message —often a political one— has been central to their work. ICY &

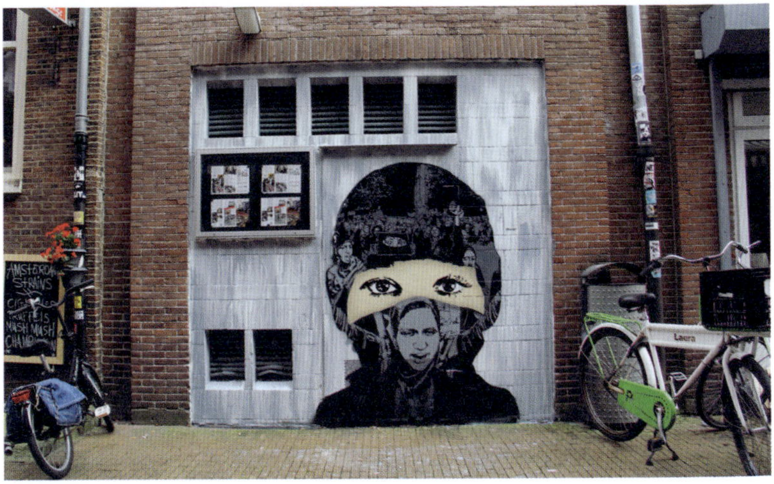

ICY & SOT, *Rebelian*, Amsterdam, 2015

SOT produce literal art in the noblest sense: art that seeks out and finds the fastest way to communicate. Due to the socially-conscious subject matter of their work, they are forced to flee their country. Their stencils raise questions about child labour, women's rights and, more generally, freedom of expression in society – all sensitive subjects that some people don't like being addressed. Today, they are well-established figures on the international Urban Art scene, having emigrated to the United States, where they have found a home that allows them to express themselves and bring their artistic practice to maturity. They have continued to build on the tradition of politically engaged art, bringing universal attention to the obstacles, difficulties and tragedies encountered by migrants. In their efforts to address the issues affecting the world today, these two artists also tackle ecological issues.

Founded in 2008, Madrid-based artistic duo LUZINTERRUPTUS also speaks up on climate-related topics. Using light as a medium, the city as a space for their work, and the night as a backdrop, they create a number of ephemeral, participatory artistic projects, often with underlying social, civic, ecological or, more simply put, political considerations. The visual impact of these installations is particularly effective in engaging the general public. In 2014, for example, the duo set up a labyrinth in Katowice, Poland, composed of 6,000 plastic bottles grouped together in plastic bags, all of which were illuminated by LEDs. The goal was to point out our excessive and devastating consumption of plastic. In 2021, as a guest at the *Essen Light Festival* in Germany, LUZINTERRUPTUS would present a piece entitled *The Plastic We Live With*, which had previously been on display in France, Bordeaux and Jelsa in Croatia. In Essen, the artists covered all of the windows of a historic building with plastic bags in various colours, giving the impression that the building was about to explode under the pressure of the plastic – a spectacular illustration of the excessive use of plastic in our everyday lives. The contrast between traditional architecture and the colourful appearance of the windows is both paradoxical

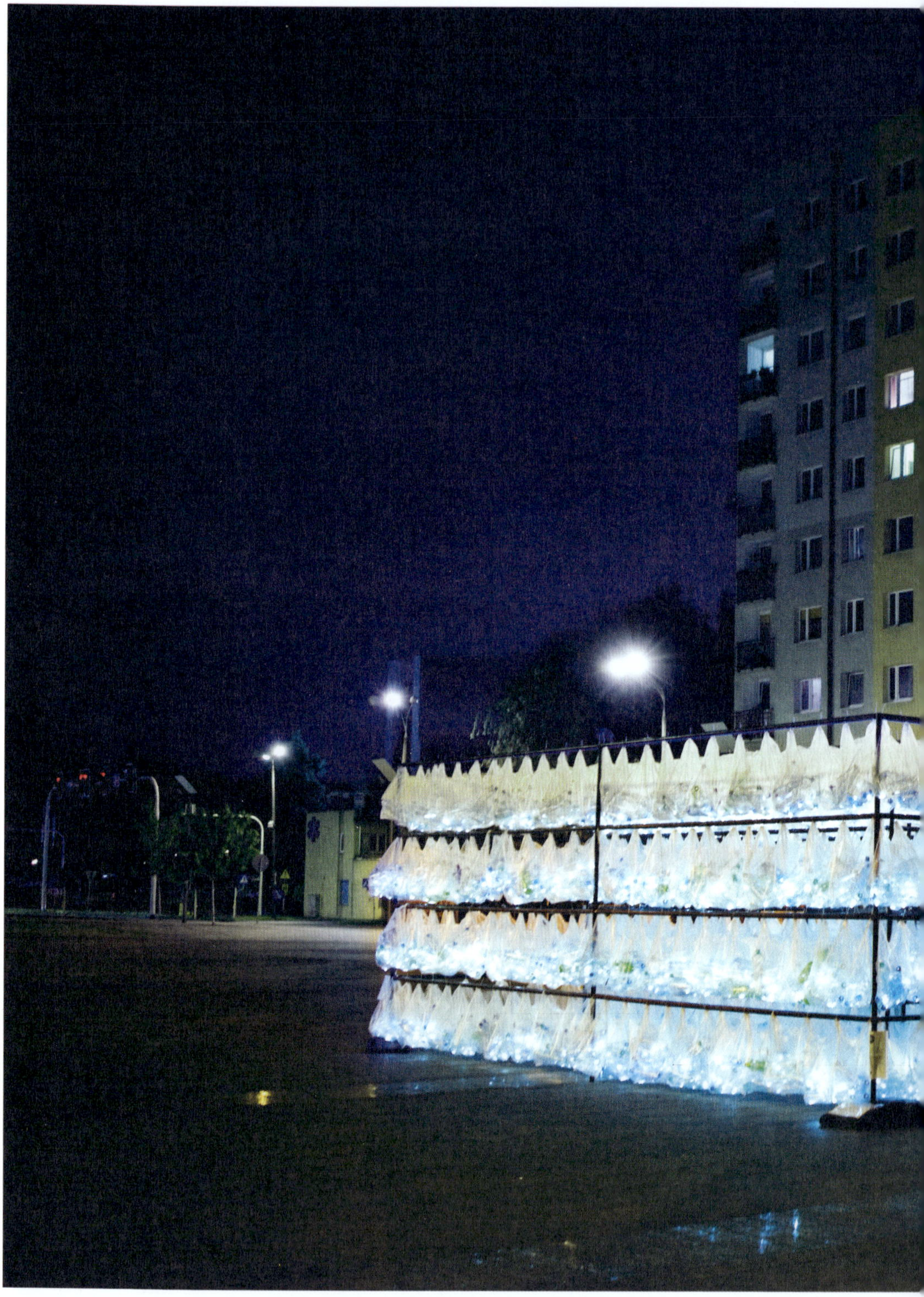

LUZINTERRUPTUS, *Laberinto de residuos plásticos*, Katowice, Poland, 2014.
Photo © Gustavo Sanabria

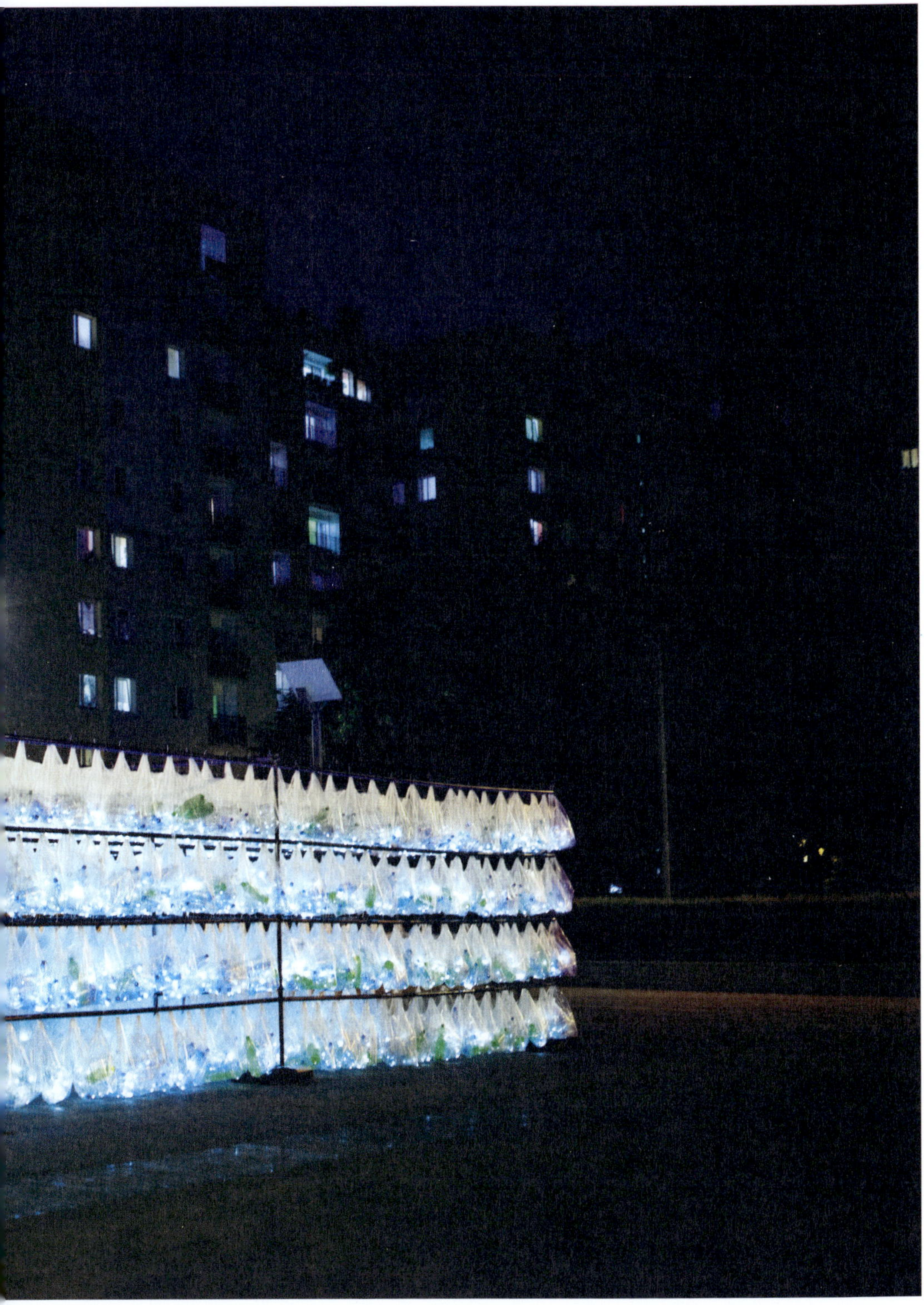

and aesthetic, reminiscent of the stained glass windows of a cathedral bathed in light.

At the beginning of 2020, the climate emergency was probably, but not exclusively, one of the topics that was most frequently addressed by urban artists wanting to make their views known. Such was the case for artist, SHEPARD FAIREY. While he created an official monumental work on the Eiffel Tower, he also incorporated this subject into his street work, printing numerous posters and collages to alert the general public. His favourite subjects range from climate issues to women's rights and the importance of voting. Illustrating his concerns, the titles of his works —whether murals, paintings or screen prints— continue what the artist defined as his manifesto back in 1989: *Eyes Open*, *Voting Rights are Human Rights*, *Workers' Rights*, *Two Americas*, and *Liberté, Égalité, Fraternité*.

On the other side of the world, in Egypt, artist AYA TAREK, born in 1989, is one of her generation's pioneers of Urban Art, a practice that constitutes a real challenge in this country. And yet, steeped in the transgressive nature of this movement, the artist has managed to make her voice heard. With a subtle approach to expression —which is specific to the context in which she lives— she tackles issues such as gender and the representation of women.
AYA TAREK started doing graffiti at the age of 18. She has gradually developed as an artist, revisiting her roots in the most classical forms and exploring new directions in response to current societal and technological issues. Playing on the codes of urban communication and the dynamics of public space, she combines controversy with a sense of humour. Despite being an outspoken critic with forthright opinions, her priority is to make art accessible to all. In 2010, against the backdrop of the revolution in her homeland, her work inspired many people to join the graffiti movement. As a character in the feature film *Microphone*, directed by Ahmed Abdalla, AYA TAREK embodies the art scene of the time, highlighting the fact that all works of art run the risk of being hijacked for political purposes. But today, she defines her work as going far beyond this context.

In Indonesia, artists like EKO NUGROHO are also challenging the world around them. Born in 1977, he is part of the generation that offered an artistic response to the tumultuous period following President Suharto's fall from power in 1998. As the artist himself says, he makes art for the people and makes the people his main source of inspiration. EKO NUGROHO's early experiences as an urban artist are evident in his frescoes, paintings, drawings, installations, animations and tapestries, which are populated by cartoon-like figures with masked faces, who hide, argue and struggle as much as the human beings they represent.

In his work, EKO NUGROHO also deals with women's rights in social and urban spaces. He does so in a skilful and engaged way, never hesitating to strongly and colourfully challenge the wearing of the veil, even though he lives in a Muslim-majority country. By referring to the anthro-

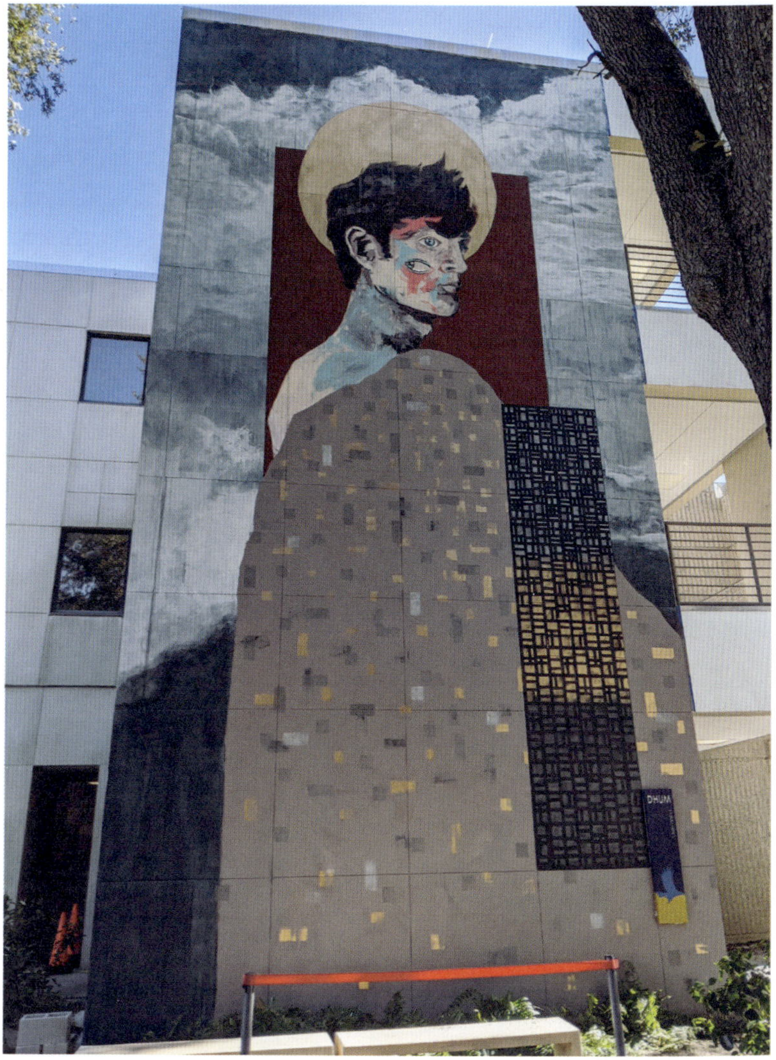

AYA TAREK, *Painting Ourselves Visible*, Tampa, USA, 2019

pological concept of totemism, he seems to want to point out, in a quasi-scientific and non-partisan way, the role of the veil as a mode of social and religious organisation. It is a "totem" object which, although it forms the basis of the community, is nonetheless shrouded in the ambiguity inherent in all totems: it is respected as much as it is feared.

The same feminist concerns are echoed by American artist MAYA HAYUK, who specifically questions the status of women in the art world. Although her work is abstract, with its large, colourful façades, she is no less socially engaged. Born in 1969 in Baltimore, MAYA HAYUK's prolific work draws on a vast repertoire of patterns, colours and media. Her style, which is both symbolic and political, spontaneous and meticulous, borrows as much from psychedelia and punk culture as it does from East European folk art. Often composed of wide, intersecting strips of col-

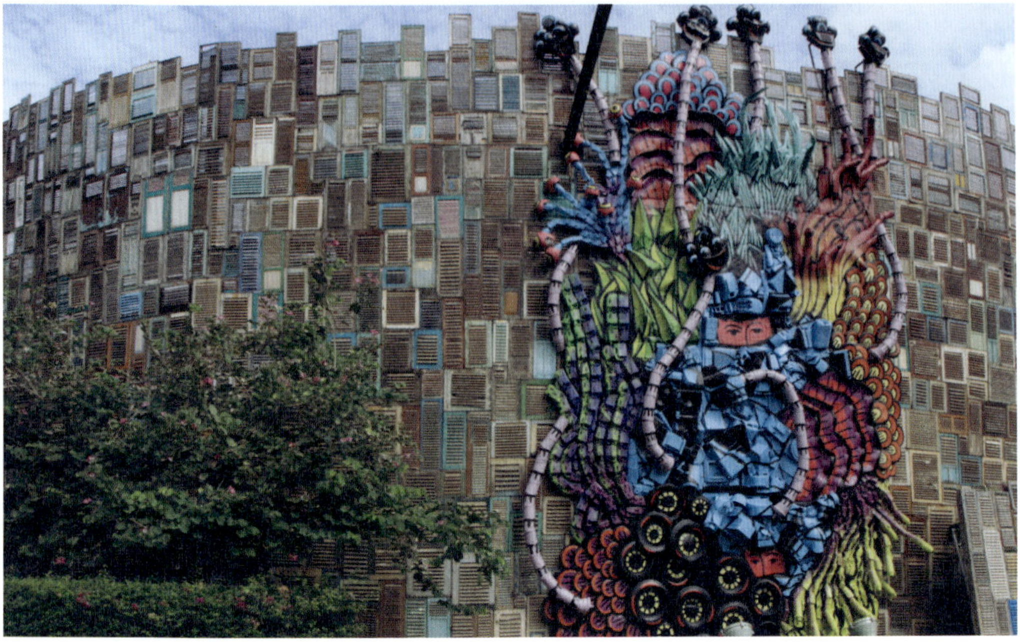

EKO NUGROHO, *Bouquet of Love*, Bali, 2017, courtesy Studio Eko Nugroho. Photo © Oki Permatasari

our, her works also sometimes incorporate rounded, more organic, flowing forms. For MAYA HAYUK, art is an organic process. Her works frequently contrast with the context in which they sit. The palette she uses is full of colour, reflecting the artist's obsession with symmetry or, more precisely, her obsession with seemingly symmetrical patterns that in fact contain imperfections that give them a certain beauty – something she refers to as "perfect imperfections". MAYA HAYUK is an American artist of Ukrainian origin, so she has been very visually expressive about her support for Ukraine regarding the country's military conflict with Russia since 2022.

Over time, female artists working in the field of Urban Art have developed approaches and practices that are as new as they are unexpected. Like MAYA HAYUK, some of these artists —in order to avoid becoming prisoners of stereotypical images— have adopted less direct but just as assertive approaches when it comes to the role that femininity plays in Urban Art. This is why MAGDA SAYEG chose knitting as a creative medium. In 2005, instantly attracted by the contrast between the warmth of wool and the coldness of metal, she used wool to adorn the door handle of her haberdashery in Houston. This simple, spontaneous gesture would be enough to write a new chapter in the Urban Art movement. She would then have fun with road signs, moving on to covering an entire bus, and even the monumental spider sculpture entitled *Maman* (Mother), by famous artist Louise Bourgeois. Her work soon becomes a global phenomenon known as yarn bombing, and spreads throughout the world, echoing vernacular practices generally reserved for the domestic environment. In an outrageously urbanised and digitally acceler-

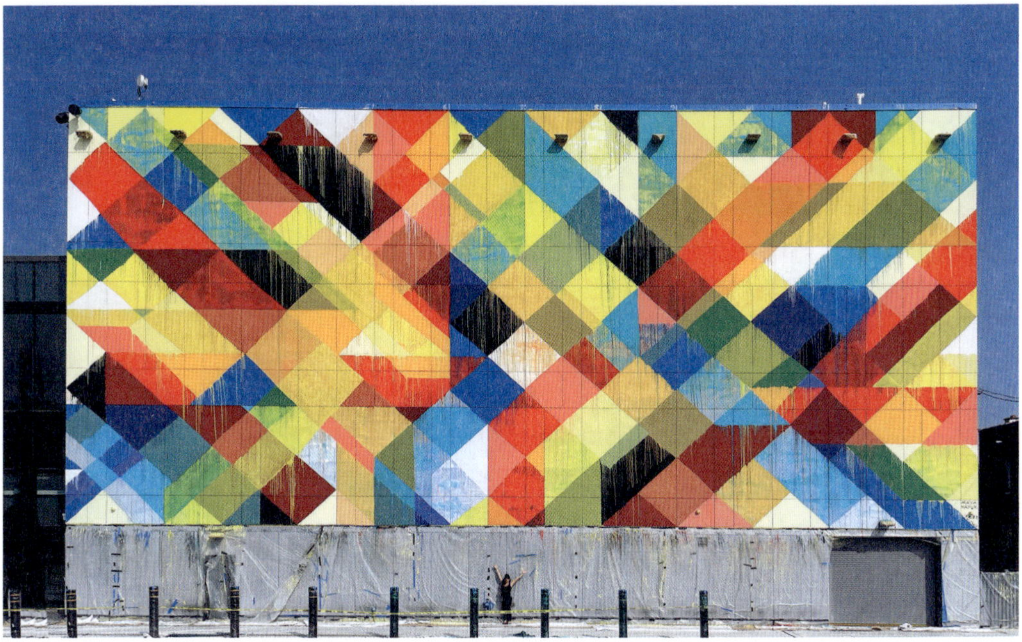

MAYA HAYUK, *Buffalo Soldier Wing Stance (The Tree of Y)*, Buffalo, USA, 2021

ated world, the artist sees her work as being motivated by experimentation and sharing. With wool as her material of choice, she exemplifies the diversity of artistic research. The way it transforms objects in space, it also speaks of harmony, interaction and identity.

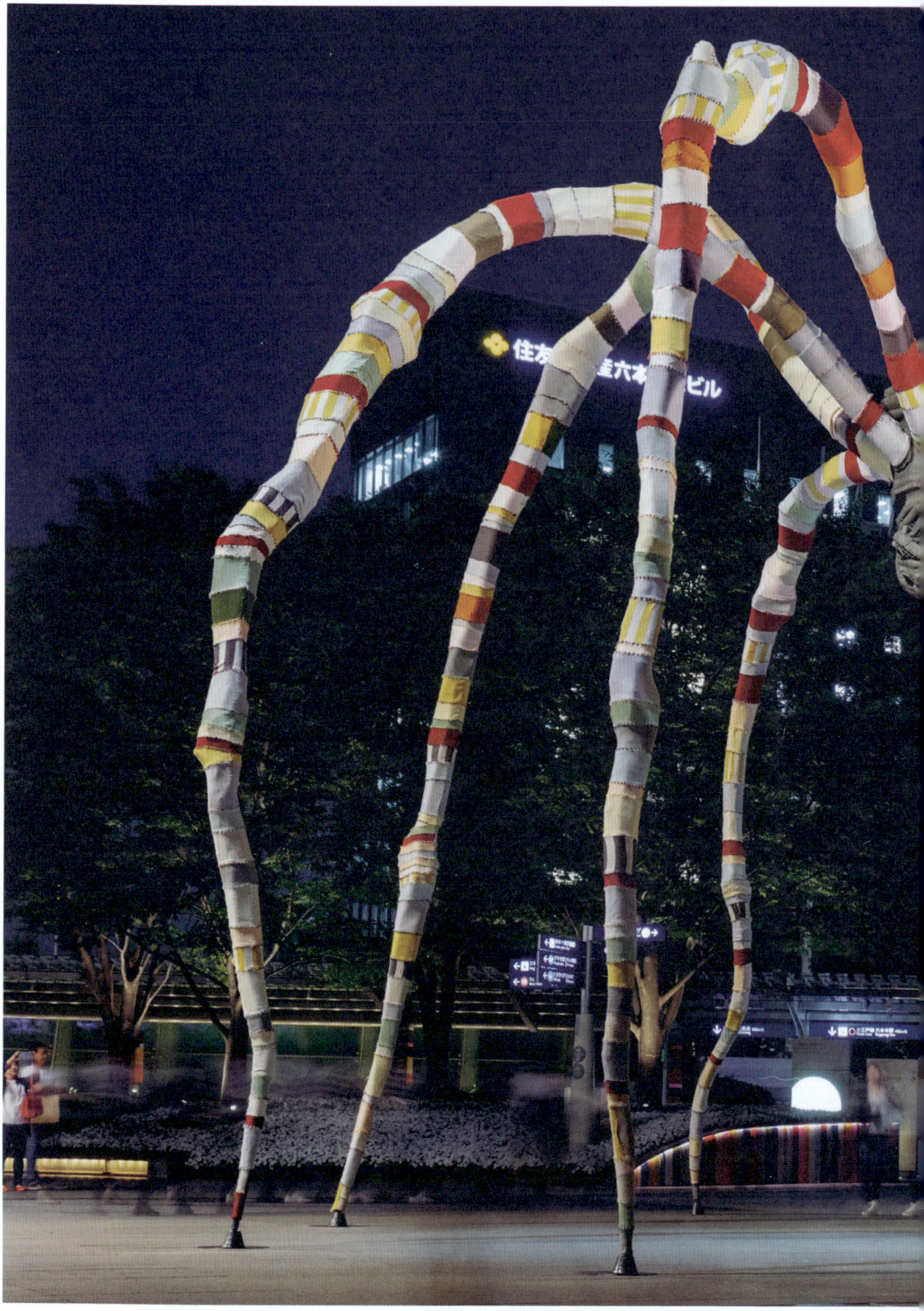

MAGDA SAYEG, transformation of the sculpture *Maman* by Louise Bourgeois, Mori Art Museum, Tokyo, 2018

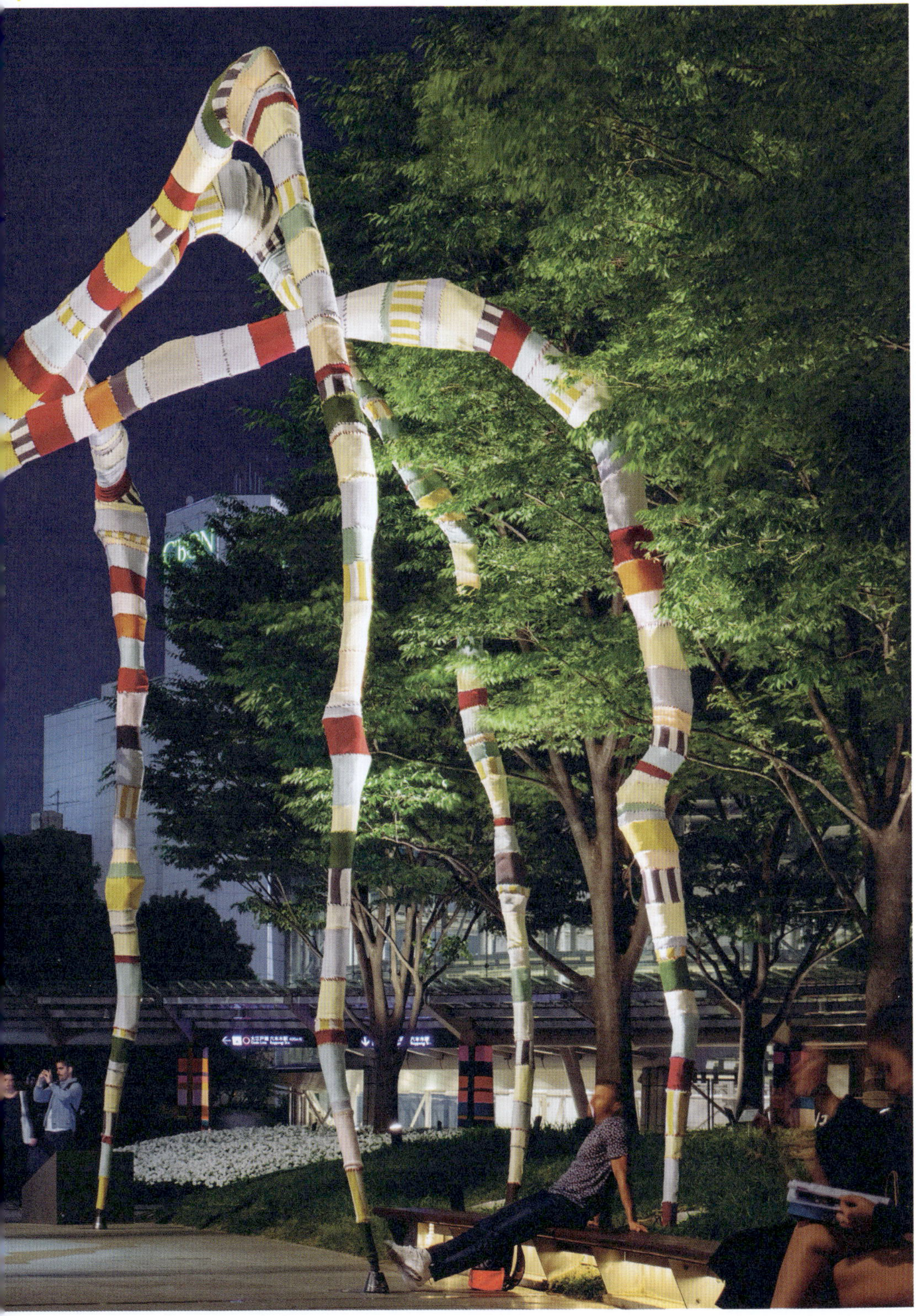

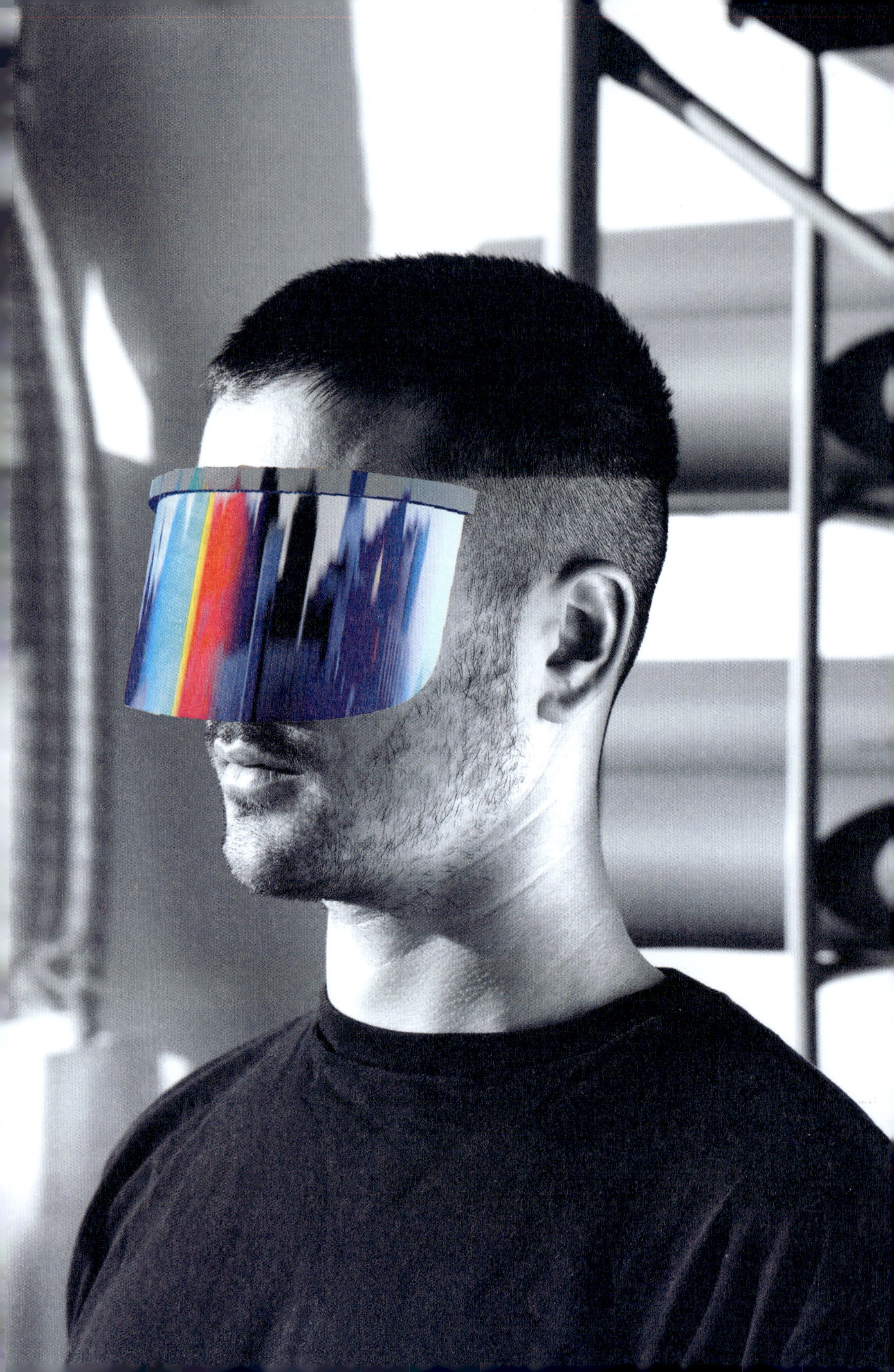

CONCLUSION

I discovered my first works of street art while on the way to school in the mid-1980s. I clicked with them instantly. Living in a family environment that was heavily influenced by my artist mother, I no doubt offered fertile ground for this discovery to blossom into a passion. I would have liked to report that very quickly, spray cans in hand, defying public authorities and family, I escaped at night to cover the dull walls of my neighbourhood with flamboyant fireworks. Alas, my drawing teachers would have confirmed for you that the young Magda Danysz clearly had no artistic talent and was best encouraged to follow another path. And I thank them for this, because it was while I was very young that I decided to live my artistic dreams by proxy. The profession of gallery owner struck me as the ideal way to achieve this aim. I was seventeen when I opened my first gallery. Today, two others have emerged, and I have the incredible privilege of going all over the world and accompanying artists who have offered me the chance to pursue this dream.

Each of them has given me an incredible energy, a desire to always move forward and a belief that even sometimes extends to the impossible. Jonone was the first to say to me, when I told him about my vague plan to one day open an exhibition space in Shanghai, that it was "crazy, great!" And he told me that he was "okay to do the first exhibition over there." I still didn't have a place, but I knew from that moment that Magda Danysz Gallery had just expanded. I also remember JR when he was producing the *Wrinkles of the City* project in Shanghai, and how every morning on the road leading to the gallery he would say to me: "Hey, Magda, you see the tank up there, in the middle of the demolished houses? I want to do a collage up there!" I would tell him that he wouldn't be able to access it and the gangway to get to it lay 30 metres below, but he would just keep on smiling and say, "But Magda, you know that nothing is impossible. We're artists, so we'll stick something up there!" A few days later, one of the most representative works of the project was produced on that inaccessible tank, despite a memorable police chase and some explanations to the local authorities. Three

FELIPE PANTONE, *Ultra-Filter*, 2019

FELIPE PANTONE would be the first contemporary artist to collaborate with Instagram in creating two filters for the social media platform.

years later, JR became the first foreign contemporary artist to be exhibited during his lifetime in a museum of contemporary art in Shanghai. I like to say to the journalists who ask me about JR's work that I would not be surprised if one day he announced to me that we was off to do a collage on the moon.

I also have memories of my first encounter with Vhils back when he was barely twenty-three. I was amazed by his truly out-of-the-ordinary artistic maturity. I still smile when thinking back to my reaction to his announcing to me barely three months before the opening of his solo exhibition at the EDP Foundation in Lisbon that he planned to cut up a real train to hang it vertically, piece by piece, in the middle of the showroom. Impracticable, impossible? Not with such talent and determination. I also remember JayOne and SKKI acting very early on as outstanding guides during my introduction to street art, as well as the 50 artists who agreed without hesitation to participate in the Bains Douches artists' residence. How can I share the emotion of seeing Jacques Villeglé, invited by Lek and Sowat to visit the place, grab the chalk offered to him and write the inscription "historic site"?

And what can I say about FUTURA, a veritable living encyclopedia of street art— that legend among legends, who encountered, worked with and collaborated with the movement's founding New York artists, and who also like many of them left us prematurely? One could recall his kindness and the simplicity with which he would share with you all the stories and anecdotes that contribute to the legend of the early years of street art. But first and foremost he needs to be remembered as an artist of precocious and probably unmatched artistic genius who underwent perpetual renewal.

The history of Street Art is above all an incredible human adventure that has been built up over the decades against all odds. And it wasn't always easy. INVADER's first vernissage, which took place at my Paris gallery in the early 1990s, culminated in the police coming to arrest the artist. It is interesting to see that today, the same authorities want to arrest those who try to rip down his street art. This shows the extent to which the perception and acceptance of this art form has changed in recent years.

But success has also led to growing criticism. Some people turn their noses up at art that is perceived as being too popular, and successful artists want to distance themselves from that infuriating term: "Street Art". Overly hasty labelling, reductive labelling, and conflation of the artistic and the financial make this term a subject of debate for connoisseurs and neophytes alike.

And that leaves the question of institutional legitimisation and how works are to be exhibited. With the 2015 summer opening of Dismaland, BANKSY's amusement park —or bemusement park as he prefers to call it—

where every attraction is a work of art, the artist responds in his typically provocative way, presenting an alternative perspective (an approach that has made him famous). Both cynical in its content (undermining our culture of fun) and highly participatory, the park denounces cultural institutions' approaches that seek to confine contemporary expressions of creativity. BANKSY couldn't care less who might validate his artistic expression. He would offer the residents of Weston-super-Mare (a coastal resort some thirty kilometres from his home town of Bristol) an exhibition featuring 58 artists (not necessarily street artists) taking part in an unusual project curated by himself.

So where are we? Is there room for an urban aesthetic within the four walls of a museum? Does Street Art deserve a place in art history? While this question might well have been asked thirty years ago, it is surprising that it still seems relevant today. Street art is one of the few artistic movements to have gained such a global presence, reaching such a wide audience, while also managing to gain legitimacy over the years with the approval of public authorities and certain cultural institutions. Although art history broadened its field of study to include new approaches (photography, illustrations, comics, outsider art...) throughout the 20th century, what was to blame for this relative disaffection? Or, to paraphrase Brassaï's thoughts on graffiti, "why is this visual language being overlooked?".

Like Warhol and Vasarely, many twentieth-century artists dreamt of art being more accessible and rooted in everyday life. With their long history of institutions and art history, gatekeepers of the temple of contemporary art have always been difficult to convince. Not waiting for the approval of cultural authorities, urban art has taken over the streets for all to see. For the first time in the history of art, artists are voluntarily presenting everyone something to marvel at, to wonder at and even to be inspired by. From the American continent to Oceania and Africa, most people around the world have a mental image of what "Street Art" is. The cultural tidal wave is in full effect, every corner of society is awash with urban art, thereby putting an end to an elitist and reductive conception of what "contemporary creativity" means.

Despite this notoriety, the world of research and museums should not be prevented from embracing it, but rather, they should embark on a journey towards greater recognition and address the issue of conserving and promoting this heritage that serves as a testament to its time. History is unfolding before our eyes; it's time to immortalise it and make it a veritable object of study.

Among the many difficulties facing the movement, the issue of image theft is central. Even though the disdain of intellectual authorities has not yet been completely dispelled, the constant reappropriation of Urban Art by fashion and luxury brands (anxious to refresh their image) or by public authorities (often anxious to add an artistic dimension to urban planning projects) has led to fears that it would take the oomph out of the artistic creations on display. It is for this reason that the movement's recognition and legitimisation by institutions is now more relevant than ever. Only through rigorous scientific work, documentation, historicisation and conservation of these practices will they finally be able to obtain their true status and rightful place in the art world. Now more than ever, the challenge is to ensure the physical and intellectual mobility of these works of art. How can we keep a record of them and protect them, even when they are often part of the public space, which is itself in a state of constant flux? More than being urban in nature, this art is contextual, and is defined as much by the space as by the circumstances in which it is created. Urban artworks are exciting because, as President of the Centre Pompidou Laurent Le Bon points out: in addition to "their intrinsic qualities, (they can) play with a more general context".

Paradoxically, is this conservation work desirable, or even conceivable, and if so, what methodology should be used, at a time when artists are demonstrating boundless vitality and inventiveness? In other words, how can we channel something that, by its very nature, is that which it is not? Can exploration and research be locked up in a museum?

Fortunately, artists who have emerged from this movement still pursue their exploratory approaches, pushing back the boundaries to discover other creative territories and create artworks that raise questions about the world. The "adventurers" of the Urban Art scene are always on the lookout for combinations and energies that they can implement. As much concerned with historical references as with the future, they eagerly explore relationships with new technologies.

This relationship was initially structured around social media platforms, which enable images to be shared in real time and on a very large scale by bringing together communities of people who are passionate about the same subject. For the first time, it became possible for artists to talk about their creations as they saw fit and with disconcerting ease, requiring no other hardware investment than a smartphone. For the general public, there's no need to be in the right place at the right time to be able to follow the work of artists all over the world: people can simply discover the latest OS GÊMEOS fresco in São Paulo or INVADER's latest mosaic in South America on social media. By freeing themselves from the constraints of space (the world at our fingertips) and time (ephemeral works continue to be visible), digital communication tools have undeniably increased the visibility and exposure of artists and their work.

But widespread distribution often detracts from that which is the essence of Urban Art: the context. Just as a reproduction of a work of art in a museum cannot capture everything that engages with the beholder directly (the scale of the piece, the texture, the details, the possibility of moving closer or further away, and so on), a reproduction of a piece produced in situ can only partially evoke the dialogue that the artist

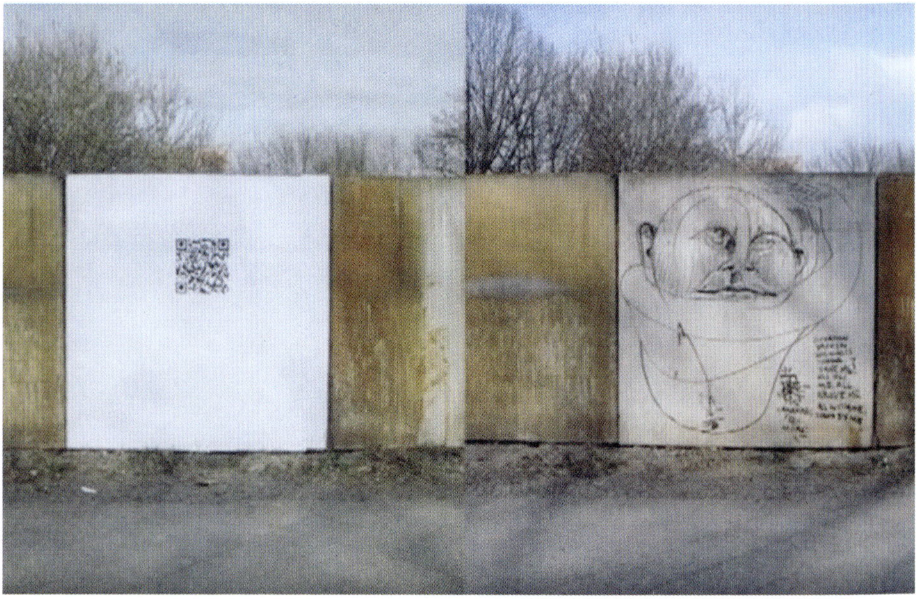

SWEZA, *Berlin*, 2015. © A.R.R.

sought to establish between their work and the environment in which they chose to set it. Without going so far as to talk about decontextualisation (several photographs or videos allow said context to be reconstituted in a fragmentary and partial way), this is nevertheless a case of using digital technology for purely communicative purposes.

This doesn't stop FELIPE PANTONE —whose work seems to be a metaphor for the all-digital age in which we live— from taking more creative advantage of the functionalities offered by social media. In 2019, he became the first contemporary artist to use Instagram's AR effects to create two face filters that use the iridescent and dynamic pixelation effects characteristic of his plastic art projects. But from globalised social networks to augmented reality, there's another creative step that some urban artists have taken.

In the early 2010s, German artist SWEZA incorporated QR codes into his street collages. Flashing these codes with a smartphone would give access to additional data (images and music), thereby creating a form of interactivity with passers-by. Affixing a QR code where graffiti has been removed gives anyone access to an image of the artwork before it was painted over.

In the same way, SAYPE —who uses plants as substrates for his ephemeral creations that disappear as the plants grow— plans to install QR codes on the sites where he worked. These QR codes provide access to enhanced content that bring the works back to life in the very environment where they were created. It's a way of going beyond the ephemeral nature of these creations and making them more permanent.

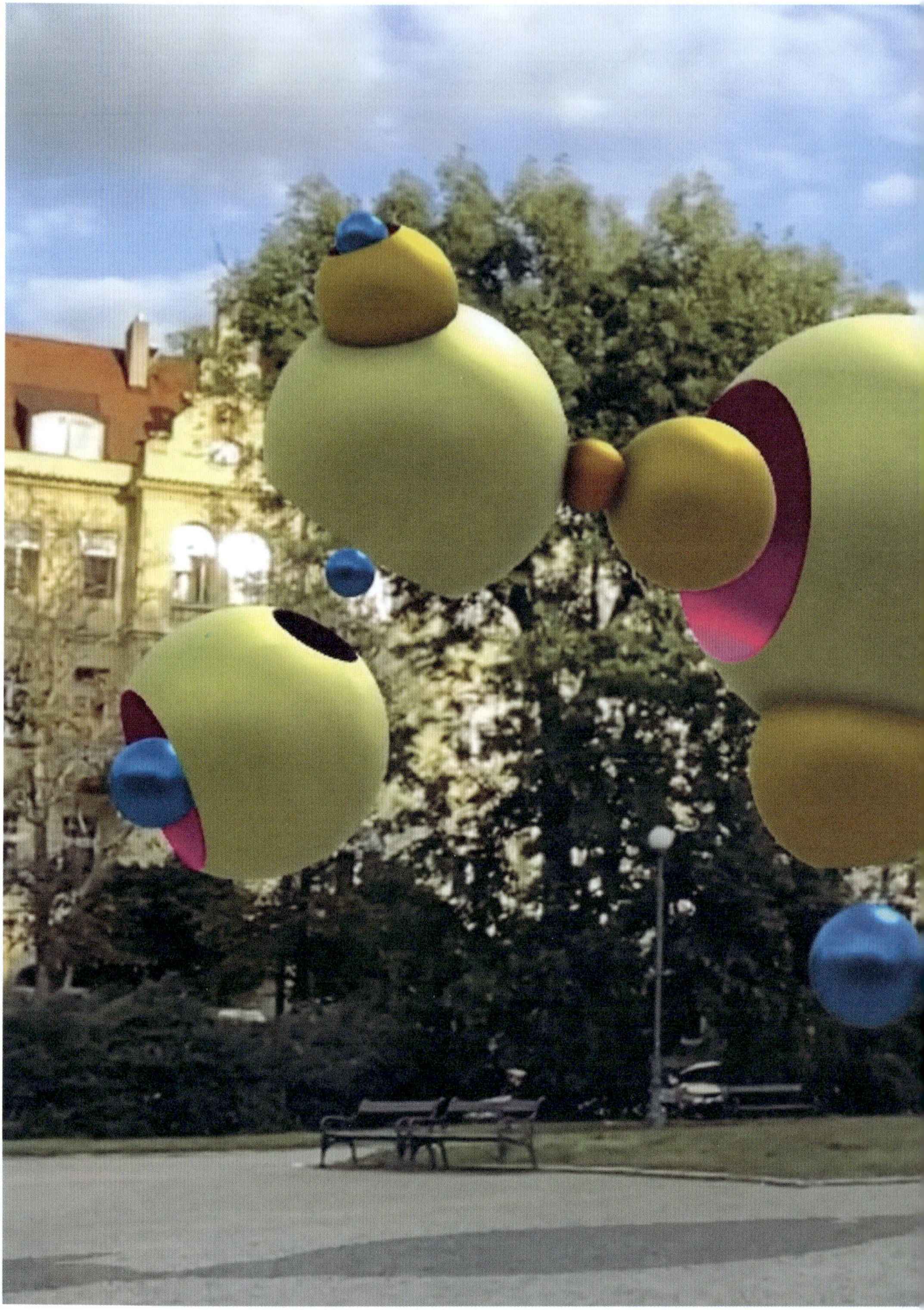

JAN KALAB, *Mechanic Galaxy*, 2021 © A.R.R.

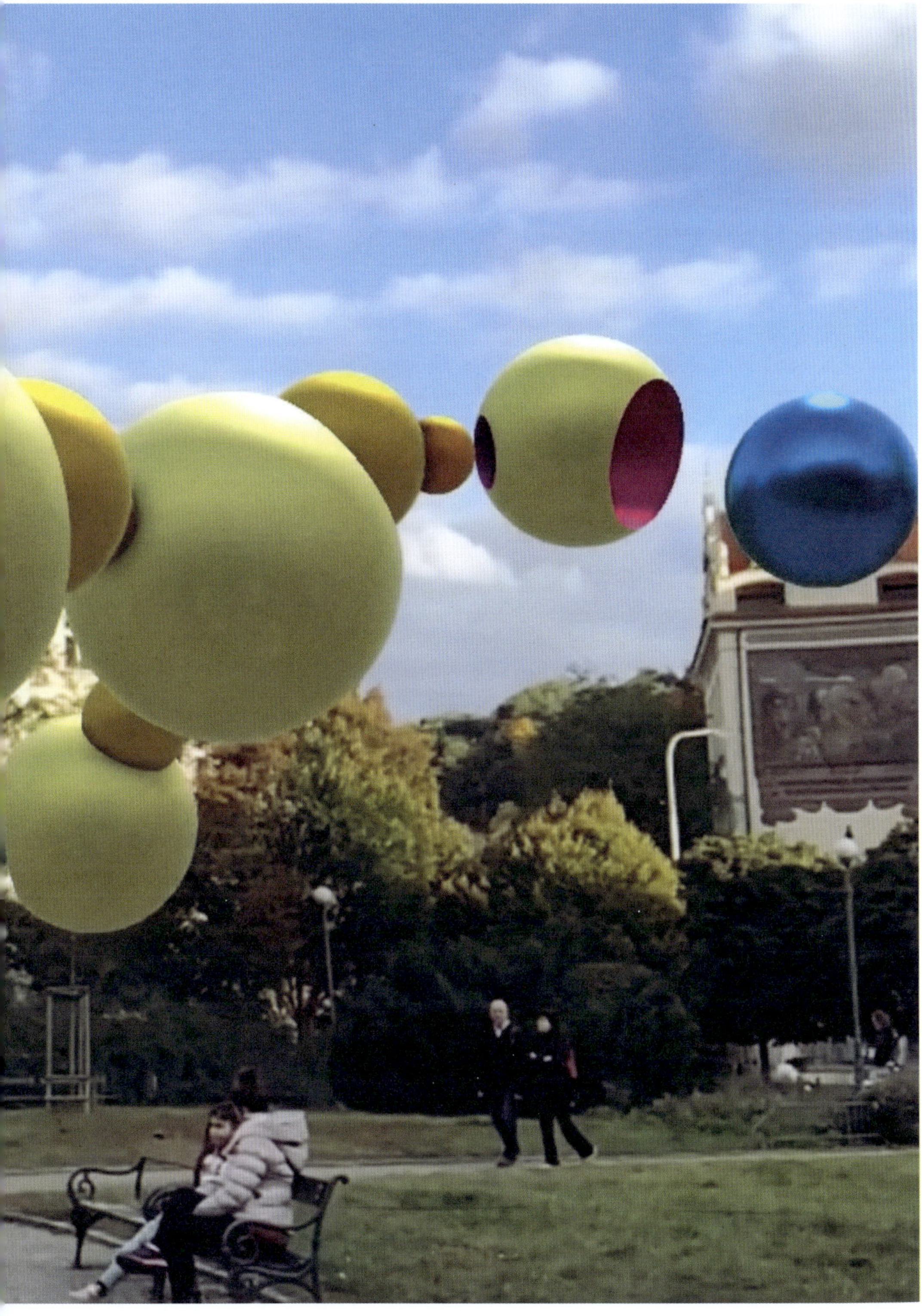

In 2014, INVADER launched FlashInvaders, an interactive app that engages a community of tens of thousands of "flashers", who become the protagonists of a global work of art. The app lets you flash Invaders mosaics that you spot in the street as you wander around. Images of them can then be archived, allowing you to build up a personal collection of Invaders that can be viewed at any time on the app. Anyone who wants to get in on the app's fun and competitive spirit can earn points for every Invader they flash, with all players then being ranked. A live gallery also gives immediate access —in a show that can sometimes be frenetic— to the many photos taken in situ around the world by the community of participants.

Some artists have pushed the interactivity and use of augmented reality even further. Their intention is not so much to use technology to allow us to see something that no longer exists, but to create works that are made specifically for the digital world - in some cases, these are only visible in situ through augmented reality.

In 2010, for example, British artist INSA created GIFs that animated his wall murals, and created a special app to view them with. By taking photos of different phases of an evolving fresco on the same wall, then editing them in the form of short stop-motion sequences, he was able to create animated frescoes that he calls "GIF-ITI" —a cross between GIF and graffiti— which survive long after their physical disappearance.

Meanwhile, in 2020, KAWS would launch a virtual exhibition entitled *Expanded Holiday*, in which he would show his iconic Companion character floating above twelve tourist locations around the world, from Times Square in New York to the Louvre Museum in Paris and London's Millennium Bridge. Thanks to a special app, users could browse the different places thanks to an interactive map. In addition, the app let users display a 45 cm version of the Companion appearing next to them, superimposed on their surroundings via their smartphone screen. It also offered the option of immortalising the image as a photo or video, all free of charge for 24 hours before the virtual work would be made available to lease or purchase.

In the same vein, but with a non-commercial approach, Czech artist JAN KALAB created a virtual sculpture in 2021 called Mechanic Galaxy, as part of Prague's Signal Festival of Lights. By flashing a QR code located on a terminal in one of the city's parks, visitors could see the work appear on their mobile phone: a monumental sculpture suspended above the ground, standing out against the park's real setting, which they were then able to walk around. Playing with the setting in this way, it provided an opportunity to bring art to the streets without being bound by questions of private property, thereby freeing itself from constraints of materiality, space, scale and even gravity.
Since NFT fever swept through the art market in 2021, there has also been a proliferation of initiatives in urban art, both by artists and specialist

platforms, with the promise of "capturing and collecting the ephemeral". Indeed, NFTs are often only digital images reproducing works in situ and bonus videos documenting their creation. The digital format is then used as an additional medium on which to display pre-existing physical works, rather than as a medium in its own right that enables specific creative work to be developed. Some artists, like VHILS, use this medium to create virtual objects in 3D, or to extend research they have been carrying out for years with video to the digital world. In 2022, VHILS collaborated on the creation of an NFT with Cai Guo-Qiang, a world-renowned Chinese contemporary artist.

There is no doubt that the doors of the metaverse —these networks of virtual and immersive environments in which large numbers of people can interact with digital objects and with each other via avatars— will also open up to forms of digital creation. Can we still talk about "urban" art in these pixelated spaces? Will they give rise to totally new types of spaces and interaction, or will they be content to be a playful, colourful and sanitised replica of the cities we know? Does the metaverse offer a place for the transgression and illegality that led to the emergence of graffiti and Street Art in the real world? Or, on the contrary, will the metaverse be a controlled, policed space? For fans of the movement, the future looks set to be just as rich in discoveries in the virtual world as in the real world.

APPENDICES

ACKNOWLEDGEMENTS 273

INDEX OF ARTISTS 274

SOURCES 276

THANK YOU...

To Stéphane Bisseuil for his unconditional support during the writing of this book. To Marie-Ange Bisseuil for her help. To Sabine Bledniak for her background work as an editor and to the whole team at Gallimard. To Line Celo for her eye. To Clémence Wolff for her invaluable work. To Léo Castelli, always present in spirit.

To my family in full: Mila, Romain, Baptiste, Théa, Bernard, Pierre, Albane, Blanche, Scarlette, Grazyna, Jan, Hanna, and to my extended family of Khalil Amry, Antoine Barrère, Hubert Barrère, Stéphanie Benzaquine, Cédric Dassas, Alexandra Dubourg, Aymar de Gunzburg, Virgile Hermann, Bounmy Phonesavanh, and Raphaëlle and Pierre Vergnes, friends who have always helped me to continue down this path.

To the team and extended family from the gallery: Cao Bin, Sophie, Stéphane, Louisa, Alexandrine Duhamel, Armelle Loeb, Camille Merklen, Clémence Ormières, Li Qiu Shi, Rae Yen-Jung Chen, Sophie Ying Xing and Zhenni Ying.

To these artists and their teams, whose confidence has not wavered and without whom this book would never have seen the day: Vhils; Duarte Cavalinhos and Pauline Foessel; Lenny McGurr (aka Futura) and his team Nikle and Sky; JR; Èmile Abinal; Marc Berrebi; Marc Azoulay; Shepard and Amanda Fairey; Dan Flores; Jef Aérosol; Jonone; and Maï Lucas. And to all the artists have inspired me over the years, including all of 9e concept (our best years), A-One (respect), André, Anne (.G), Ash (long time), Bando, Banksy and his team, Barry McGee, Blade, Blek Le Rat, Blu, Buf Monster, Steph Carricondo, Crash (France is fun and crazy), Daim, Dave Kinsey (peace from LA), David Ellis (keep the music going on), Daze, Delta, Dface, Dondi (R.I.P.), Doze Green, Faile, Force Alpha, Christian Guemy (C215), Jay (how quickly time has passed), Jerk, Lady Pink, L'Atlas, Lee, Lek, Lokiss, Ludo, M City, Mambo, Mare 139, Jérôme Mesnager, Miss Tic, Miss Van, Mode 2, Mr Brainwash, Nasty, Mark Newton, Ned, Nunca, Os Gemêos, José Parla, Phase 2, Ernest Pignon-Ernest, Poesia, Popay, Psy, Quik, Rammellzee (R.I.P.), Rero, Seen, Sharp, Skki, Sowat, Space Invader, Sten Lex, Swoon, Tanc, Tarek Benaoum, Jacques Villeglé, West, YZ, Zevs, Zhang Dali, Gérard Zlotykamien, and many others.

INDEX OF ARTISTS

139TH 59
A-ONE 59, 69, 70-71, 72, 73, 85, 116, 221
AK-47 158
ALI 59
ANDRÉ 83, 124, 218
ARYZ 132
ASH 77, 92, 103, 104, 109, 117, 188
AYA TAREK 256, 257
BAMA 23
BANDO 85, 88, 92, 104, 109, 116, 120, 124, 197
BANKSY 7, 132, 136, 165, 166-167, 168-169, 170, 171, 182, 214, 218, 231, 233, 264, 265
BARBARA KRUGER 248
BARRY MCGEE 136, 139, 218, 225
BASQUIAT, JEAN-MICHEL (ALIAS SAMO) 46, 55, 58, 59, 66, 69, 85, 93, 132, 201, 221, 225, 229
BBC 109, 120
BENAOUM, TAREK 200
BIL BLAST 93
BLADE 52, 54-55, 84, 93
BLEK LE RAT 99, 100, 101, 102, 109, 130, 136
BLITZ 116
BLU 132, 216, 220, 224, 239
BOXER 109, 124
BRASSAÏ 13, 124, 156, 157
BUG 170 19
C215 130, 132, 133, 134-135, 136
CAT 87 23
CHALFANT, HENRY 218, 219, 220
CLIFF 159 25
CLIFF COOL 120 19
COCO 144 23
COLT 23
CORNBREAD 14, 15, 18
CRASH 28, 55, 56-57, 59, 66, 85, 92, 121
DAN 23 132
DAZE 55, 66, 85, 220
DEGOTTEX 73
DEITCH, JEFFREY 59, 142, 218, 224
DELTA 217
DISCO 107 59
DISCO PCP 118-119
DON KARL 197
DONDI 38, 39, 40-41, 47, 59, 66, 92, 93, 120, 121, 197, 213, 220, 221
DOZE GREEN 116
EL MAC 132
EL SEED 197, 198-199, 200, 250, 251
EPSYLON POINT 130
ERO 221
FAB 5 FREDDY 52, 59, 66, 221
FABULOUS FIVE 28
FAILE 216, 224, 238, 239, 240-241, 242
FAIREY, SHEPARD (ALIAS OBEY) 7, 136, 142, 146, 147, 148-149, 150, 151, 153, 157, 160, 184-185, 200, 203, 216-217, 218, 224, 247, 248, 256
FERNANDEZ, SANDRA 237, 252
FLINT 707 18, 23
FORCE ALPHA 109, 116, 124
FRIENDLY FREDDIE 19
FUTURA 7, 29, 30-31, 42, 46, 48-49, 50-51, 52, 59, 66, 69, 85, 92, 116, 188, 200, 218, 220, 221, 264
GUERRILLA GIRLS 247, 248
HAINS, RAYMOND 93
HARING, KEITH 55, 58, 59, 66, 92, 197, 220, 221, 225, 229
HAYUK, MAYA 224, 257, 258, 259
HAZE 11
HICKS, LOGAN 136
HONDO 23
ICY & SOT 247, 253
INSA 270
INVADER 4, 7, 130, 136, 152, 153, 154, 155, 156, 160, 165, 188, 218, 229, 230, 264, 266, 270
JAY 109, 116, 188
JAYONE 88, 92, 105, 106-107, 109, 221, 264
JEC STAR 23
JEF AÉROSOL 130, 131, 132, 136, 224
JENKINS, MARK 7, 215, 229, 236, 237, 238, 252
JOE 136 19
JONONE 7, 85, 86-87, 89, 90-91, 109, 116, 215, 217
JR 165, 171, 174, 175, 176, 177, 178-179, 180, 181, 216, 218, 239, 249, 250, 263, 264
JULIO 204 18
KALAB, JAN 268-269, 270
KAWS 242, 270
KEL 59
KILL 3 25
KILROY 11,12
KING OF KOWLOON 157

KOOL EARL 14
KOOL KOOR 221
L'ATLAS 195, 196, 200
LA2 221
LADY PINK 20, 59, 66, 93, 220, 221
LAME 66
LASZLO 130
LEK 188, 264
LOKISS 109, 117
LUDO 204, 208, 209, 215
LUZINTERRUPTUS 253, 254-255
MATTA-CLARK, GORDON 13, 25, 201
MEO 116
MESNAGER, JÉRÔME 99, 102, 130, 136
MICO 23
MISS VAN 124, 125, 218
MISS.TIC 120, 121, 130, 136
MITCH 59
MIX MIX 130
MODE 2 104, 109, 197
MORLAY, HERVE 130
MOSKO 130
MR BRAINWASH 171, 172-173
NASTY 122, 123, 124
NEMO 130, 136
NO LIMIT 109
NOVA 25
NUGROHO, EKO 221, 256, 258
NUNCA 129, 142, 143, 144-145, 216, 239
OS GÊMEOS 7, 136, 137, 138, 139, 140-141, 216, 218, 224, 230-231, 239, 266
OX 215
PANTONE, FELIPE 221, 242, 243, 244-245, 263, 267
PAUL ETHERNO 130
PHASE 2 18, 19, 21, 22, 23, 25, 29, 33, 38
PIGNON-ERNEST, ERNEST 93, 98, 99, 132, 203
POESIA 200
POINT 1 23
PRESCHOUX, SÉBASTIEN 222-223
PSY 188
PSYCHOZE 109, 114-115
QUIK 13, 39, 42, 43, 44, 45, 59, 93
QUINONES, LEE (ALIAS LEE) 19, 26-27, 28, 29, 38, 52, 59, 66, 93, 116, 220, 221
RAC 7 116
RAMMELLZEE 46, 47, 59, 66, 73, 93, 197, 218, 221
REKAL 84
RERO 189, 190-191, 192-193, 215
RETNA 219
RIFF 170 23
ROUFFET, EDMOND-MARIE 130
SAHO 104, 109
SAYEG, MAGDA 258, 260-261
SAYPE 238, 239, 267
SCAM 104
SCHARF, KENNY 58, 59, 66, 116
SCOOTER 19
SEEN 17, 25, 29, 33, 34-35, 36-37, 38, 59, 66, 81, 84, 93, 121
SHARP 59, 116, 220
SHOE 104, 197
SIXEART 216, 239
SJK 171 23
SKKI 92, 108, 109, 110-111, 112, 113, 116, 117, 188, 264
SNAKE 1 23, 25
SOWAT 188, 217, 264
SPEEDY GRAFFITO 136
SPLIX 130
STAY HIGH 149 17, 18, 19, 20, 23, 25, 39
STEN LEX 194, 195
STEPHEN POWERS 218
SUPER KOOL 223 22, 23
SWEZA 267
SWOON 132, 201, 202, 218, 224, 226-227, 251
TAKI 183 18, 19
TANC 195
THOMAS CANTO 224
TKID 116
TOP CAT 126 14, 18
TOXIC 116, 221
TRACY 168 18, 19, 25
TWIST 136
UGA 23, 28
VANDALS 19
VEASONE 89
VHILS 181, 182, 183, 184-185, 186, 187, 188, 200, 215, 221, 224, 264, 271, 278
VILLEGLÉ, JACQUES 52, 53, 73, 93, 94, 95, 96, 97, 98, 157, 188, 264
VITCHE 217
WAP 23
WEST 14
WICKED 15
YINGJIE, CHEN 229, 232, 233, 234-235
YZ 203, 205, 206-207, 215, 224
ZÉPHYR 59, 92
ZEVS 136, 159, 161, 162, 163, 197, 249
ZHANG DALI 158, 159
ZLOTYKAMIEN, GÉRARD 93, 98, 99

SOURCES

BIBLIOGRAPHY

100 street art artists / under the direction of Paul Ardenne; texts by Marie Maertens – Paris, published by La Martinière, 2011.

Au-dela du street art: exhibition, Paris, Musee de la Poste, 28th November 2012 - 30th March 2013/catalogue by Celine Neveux, Magda Danysz, Valeriane Mondot, Paris: Musee de la Poste, Grenoble, published by Critères, 2012.

Crossboarding, Christian Omodeo with a contribution by Bruno Messina, 188 pages, Edition of 500, published by LO/A Edition & Le Grand Jeu.

Descente interdite, Karim Boukercha and Gautier Bischoff, co-edition L'œil d'Horus/ published by Editions Alternatives, Paris 2011.

Ernest Pignon-Ernest/collected remarks and afterword by Elisabeth Couturier, published by Herscher, Paris, 2003.

Extramuros, Chronicles of a Globe-Painter,

Julien Seth Malland, published by Editions Alternatives, Paris, 2012.

Graffiti: une histoire en images, Bernard Fontaine, published by Eyrolles, Paris, 2011.

Guerre et spray, Banksy, published by Editions Alternatives, Paris 2011.

In situ: un panorama de l'art urbain de 1975 à nos jours, Stephanie Lemoine and Julien Terral, published by Editions Alternatives, Paris, 2005.

Jean-Michel Basquiat, Musée d'Art Moderne de la Ville de Paris exhibition catalogue, 2010/2011.

L'art du graffiti: 40 ans de pressionnisme, Gallizia collection, texts by Henry Chalfant, Alain-Dominique Gallizia, Arnaud Viviant, published by Beaux-arts, Issy-les-Moulineaux, 2011.

L'art urbain : du graffiti au street art, Stephanie Lemoine, Decouvertes Gallimard, Paris, 2012.

Le Graffiti arabe, Pascal Zoghbi and Don Karl, translation by Charlotte Woillez, published by Eyrolles, Paris, 2012.

Le Graffiti dans les lieux abandonnes, Antonin Giverne, published by Pyramyd, Paris, 2012.

Le street art stencil book, les vingt artistes de la scene mondiale du pochoir, published by Editions Alternatives, Paris 2011.

Les Bains, residences d'artistes, text by Magda Danysz, photographs by Stephane Bisseuil and Jerome Cotton, published by Drago, 2013.

London street art, Alex MacNaughton, published by Prestel Editions, Munich, Berlin, London et al. 2010.

Ludo: Dualité, published by Editions Alternatives, Paris, 2015.

Mausolee, Sowat and Lek, published by Editions Alternatives, Paris, 2012.

Né dans la rue, graffiti: exhibition, Paris, Cartier Foundation for Contemporary Art, 7th July - 29th November 2009/ catalogue curated by Nerve Chandes, Cartier Foundation for Contemporary Art, Paris, 2009.

Paris : de la rue à la galerie /Nicolas Chenu and Samantha Longhi, published by Pyramyd, Paris, 2011.

Paris street art / Romuald Stivine, Vito Del Forte.-Munich; Berlin; London et al., published by Prestel Editions, 2008.

Planate graffiti : street art des cinq continents, Nicolas Ganz, under the direction of Tristan Manco, published by Pyramyd, Paris, 2011.

Rero: image negation, Samantha Longhi, Opus Délits collection, published by Critères, Grenoble, 2012.

Erreur dans le titre, Rero, published by Editions Alternatives, Paris, 2014.

Spraycan Art, Henry Chalfant and James Prigoff, Thames and Hudson, London, 1995.

Street Art and Graffiti, Anna Wacoawek, translated from English by Lydie Echasseriaud, Thames & Hudson, London, Paris, 2012.

Street fonts: alphabets de graffitis des quatre coins du globe, Claudia Walde, published by Pyramyd, Paris, 2011.

Stencil graffiti, Tristan Manco, Thames & Hudson, London, 2002.

Stencil History X, Samantha Longhi, Association C215, Paris, 2007.

The Art of rebellion 2: world of urban art activism, C100, Mainaschaff, Publikats Verlag, 2006.

The Birth of Graffiti, Jon Naar with an introduction by Sacha Jenkins, published by Prestel Editions, Munich, Berlin, London et al. 2007.

VIP – very important pochoirs, Jef Aerosol, published by Editions Alternatives, Paris, 2007.

Entropie, Vhils, published by Editions Alternatives, Paris, 2014.

VLP – Vive la peinture, Patrick Le Fur, Opus Délits collection, published by Critères, Grenoble, 2009.

Vous representez un niveau de menace acceptable, vous le sauriez si ce n'etait pas le cas, Banksy, translated from the English by Alexandra Maillard, published by Editions Alternatives, Paris, 2015.

YZ: open your eyes/textes Céline Malraux Opus Délits collection, published by Critères, Grenoble, 2012.

Zevs: l'execution d'une image, Toke Lykkeberg, published by Editions Alternatives, Paris, 2014.

FILMOGRAPHY

Writers: 20 ans de graffiti à Paris, 1983-2003, Marc-Aurele Vecchione, director, author, Vincent Cassel, voice; Jean Gillet, the Fitter, Soper... et al., music; Bando, Mode 2, Jay... et al., participants, released by Resistance Films, Paris, 2004.

Beautiful Losers, by Aaron Rose and Joshua Leonard, documentary about the lives and careers of the members of artist collective, Do-it-Yourself, V, 2008.

Style Wars, by Henry Chalfant and Tony Silver, documentary on the beginnings of hip-hop culture in New York, 1984.

Exit Through the Gift Shop, Banksy, documentary film, 2010.

Obey the Giant: the Shepard Fairey Story, Julian Marshall, biopic film, 2013.

Women are Heroes, JR, documentary, 2011.

Jean-Michel Basquiat: The Radiant Child, Tamra Davis, documentary film, 2010

Defense d'afficher, Jeanne Thibord, Sidonie Gamier and Francois Le Gall, web documentary, Liberation, 2012.

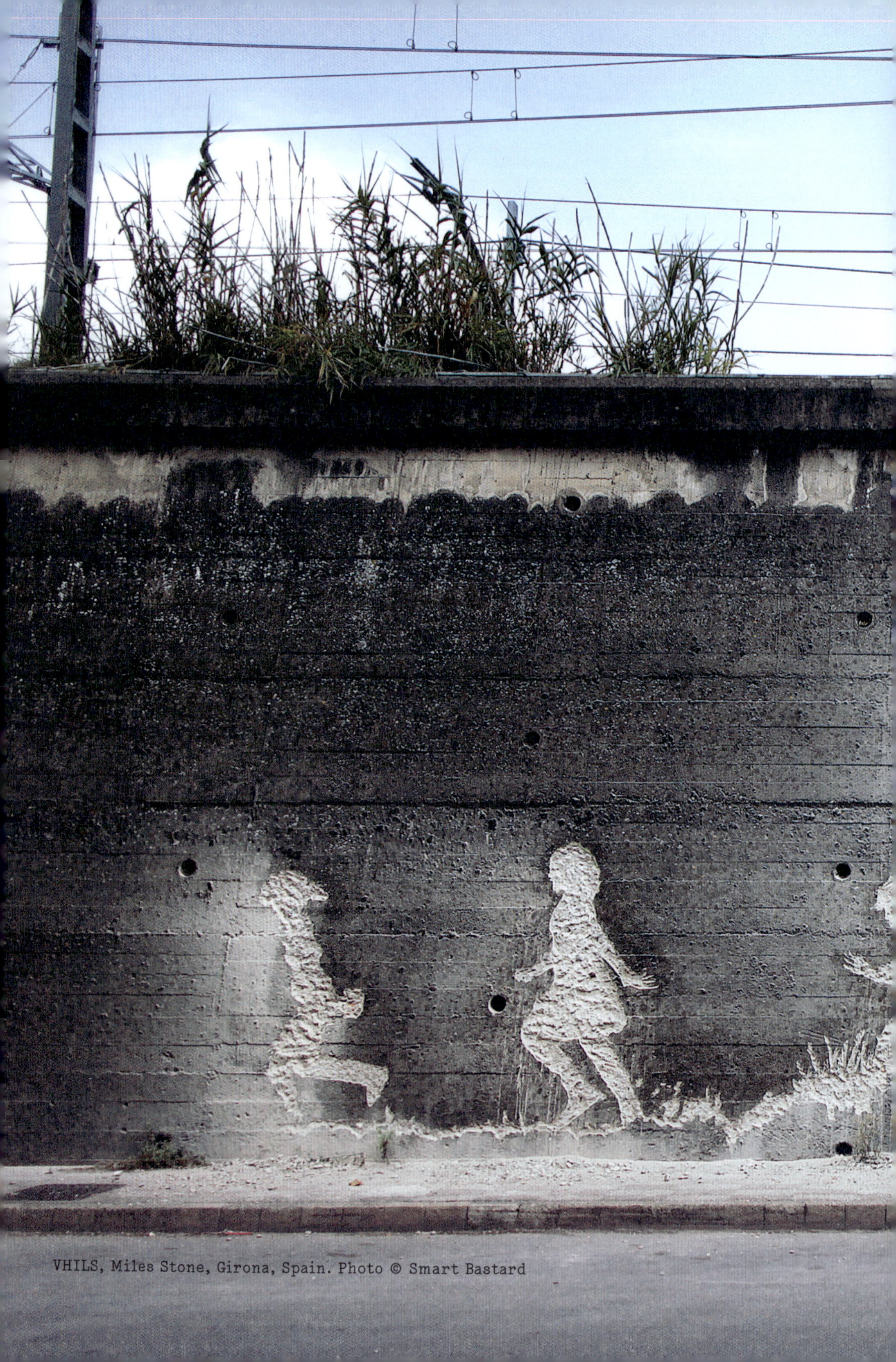

VHILS, Miles Stone, Girona, Spain. Photo © Smart Bastard

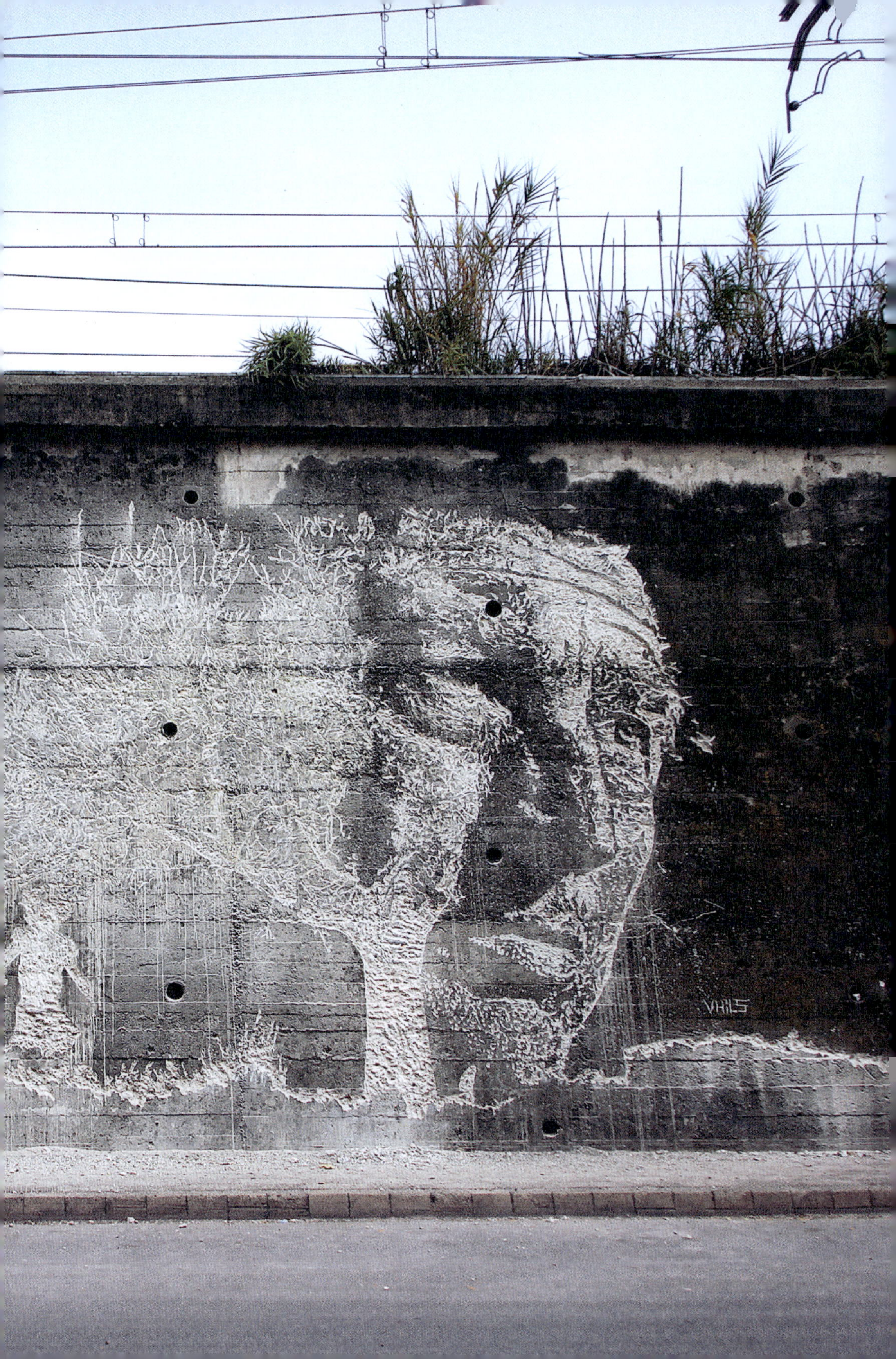
VHILS